A HIDDEN LANDSCAPE ONCE A WEEK

The Unruly Curiosity of the UK Music Press in the 1960s-80s… in the words of those who were there

A Hidden Landscape Once A Week, edited by Mark Sinker
Published by Strange Attractor Press 2018
ISBN: 978-1-907222-63-4

Cover image and illustrations by Savage Pencil

Layout by Keely MacCulloch

Strange Attractor PressBM SAP,
London, WC1N 3XX, UK
www.strangeattractor.co.uk

Distributed by The MIT Press, Cambridge, Massachusetts.
And London, England.

Printed and bound in the United Kingdom.

The Start of It All

In May 2015 I convened a conference at Birkbeck, University of London, in Bloomsbury. *Underground-Overground: the Changing Politics of UK Music-Writing 1968-85* brought together writers, editors and readers of the underground and trade music presses of the 1960s-80s with academics and other media commentators, to discuss the emergence and evolution of the countercultural voice in the UK, as inflected through the rock papers and music press in those decades. Funded by a successful Kickstarter in July 2016, this anthology includes edited select transcripts of some of the Birkbeck panels, plus essays and memoirs from and interviews with participants and others, to expand the story and dig further into some of the issues.

— *Mark Sinker, July 2018*

"I suppose I kept going to these movies because there on the screen was some news I was not getting from the *New York Times*."
— Joan Didion on biker movies in the late 60s; 'Notes Towards a Dreampolitik', collected in *The White Album* (1979).

INTRODUCTION: THE DOUBTS AIRED AS GAGS: THREE DECADES OF CROSS-CULTURAL UTOPIANISM IN UK MUSIC-WRITING

Late 1986, and I was frustrated. I'd given up my dayjob to dedicate myself full-time to writing, but I wasn't getting much work and what I did get was paying almost nothing. Only one title was giving me the space and freedom to find my voice — Richard Cook's still-small monthly *The Wire*, where he was building a team of new young writers — and it paid worst of all. Mostly I wrote about free improvised music and the more intransigent offshoots of post-punk (no surprise I wasn't getting enough paid work), but I'd also seen King Sunny Adé play at the Hammersmith Odeon in 1983, and fallen in love with West African pop, its dancing brightness and the strangeness of its vocal lines. Others were writing about it, no one very well. Or so I felt: I was young, and young often means arrogant. Two things had drawn me to the music-writing of that era, the weeklies in particular: its opinionated mischief-making humour, and the sense of young people travelling by touch, learning as they went — finding out about the wider world by throwing themselves out into that world. Master both, and there's your recipe for professional success, I thought. I had a headful of ideas about what music should and shouldn't be, and was intensely willing to argue about them.

The LP in front of me was *Coming Home*, debut release of a group of South African exiles under the collective name Kintone. Its quietly melodic afrojazz — with hints of Weather Report, but far less flashy — went right over my head that aggrieved autumn. I had come to hate jazz writing which damned musicians with bland praise, leaving readers swimming unconvinced in routinised tact. But re-listening now, 30 years on, I have to say I no longer hear what apparently so riled me then, when I scorned instrumental prowess and sneered at a cartoon idea of the meaning of fusion.

Talk about learning lessons in public. It was a ridiculous, self-regarding performance on my part. One of the group, guitarist Russell Herman, contacted me, hunting down my home phone number, to take me to task. Vehemently. My right to pronounce scathing judgment — an activity I entirely took for granted — could be the denial of oxygen itself to those surviving on the margins. Apartheid was still entirely in force in 1986 — however inadvertently, a snide record review could be a cruel erasure.

We discovered when we talked it through face-to-face that there was shared ground, and I wrote a friendly feature on them in a subsequent issue of *Wire*, but it's fair to say that many of my concerns — debates about rock and pop and modernism, experiment and noise and glamour — interested Kintone not at all. They had other matters on their minds in those times, and understandably so.

A Hidden Landscape, its Monuments and Spells, Shibboleths and Reversals

This is an embarrassing story for me now, but self-flagellation is less the point than the politics of the encounter. The story of the music press in the era that this anthology covers, the early 1960s to the late 80s, is one of gatekeeping and its discontents, a long, many-sided tussle over authority and access. What's good and who decides? Who ought to be deciding, and who selects the deciders? Which habits to challenge, which conventions to confront; when do gossip and spiteful fun turn bad? Who knows what, who's talking to who — who pays for it all and what's their cut? Should the critic channel the musician pushed to the margins by the industry, or the reader the industry is often bamboozling? What sells? What's interesting? Who gets to speak?

Land on the wrong page of almost any publication mentioned here and you're immersed in a welter of teenage obsession, confusion, ignorance and malice. Posturing, feuds, very bad writing about very bad music — except over the period examined, this was also a remarkable and an unlikely cultural pocket developing largely unnoticed by the wider media, in which could be found valuable engagement with any number of off-mainstream projects: besides music, obviously, you might discover films, fashion, street theatre, science fiction, poetry and vanguard art, radical politics and cultural theory — and hints, too, maybe, on how to access the sexual or pharmaceutical netherworlds.

This was a hidden landscape that changed from week to week: in every issue, or nearly every issue, there'd be something new and unexpected to explore. But there was something else here, too, which offered a thread of continuity even as the personnel changed. Some time in the early 70s, on a ground-soil of entertainment industry information, a loam of popcult ephemera, a handful of exiles fleeing the defeated 60s underground would establish a kind of settlement, a small counter-colonial outpost right in the decaying heart of the entertainment industry's empire-as-was. Here would be set up a shrine to the various dissident values that had sparked their ambitions and sense of possibility — and as a shrine it often rang with a ribald self-mockery, because this too was something of a countercultural tic. As early as 1970, Charles Shaar Murray (just 19 and arriving at *Oz*) was already cheekily reversing the polarities to clown the "hype, bullshit and hustling on the so-called progressive scene". Pop, he says, is "simple and honest: put it on the radio and people hear it and if they like it, they buy it. That's all, that's how they sold a million 'Love Grows' and five million of 'Sugar, Sugar'. The music is crap, but the people are honest. With us, half the music is good, but half the people are dishonest."

And if the shrine itself was less and less revered as the years passed, it nevertheless cast a spell for a surprisingly long time over this implausible secluded little space, literate in its own ideals and shibboleths, rich in arcane legends, quarrels and delusions.

Some of the quarrels and the legends went back almost to the dawn of jazz itself, of course. Founded in 1926 to cover the dance-band scene, *Melody Maker* (*MM*) was the oldest of the UK music weeklies. Arriving in 1952, *New Musical Express* (*NME*), rising from the ashes of *Accordion Times and Musical Express*, marking out its territory as the pioneer of the pop singles chart, was enthusiastic for the upsurge of rock'n'roll, which it covered largely as a novelty music. *Record Mirror* was founded in 1954 and in 1956 began carrying the official UK chart, the same year its prime rival *Disc* (later *Disc and Music Echo*) emerged. The early 60s saw a cheerful wave of teenybop titles, starting with 1959's *Boyfriend* — every week a new pop star thus identified, aimed at girls but focused on music — and continuing in various modes with *Mersey Beat* (1961), *Beat Monthly* (1963), *Big Beat, Music Echo, Rave* and *Fabulous*, later *Fabulous 208* (all 1964), along with many here-today-gone-next-month titles springing up purely to exploit a specific group or star.

So this was the popcult loam — and the writing about it was never entirely ephemeral. *MM* was respected and professional, if perhaps a little staid in the face of the 60s pop explosion (in 1964, newcomer Chris Welch would note that most of *MM*'s writers favoured jazz; for a long time its contributors had to be able to read sheet music). It described itself as a "musicians' paper" — its nether pages a forest of want ads for bands and (in later years) reviews of tech. Jazz and folk it covered admirably seriously, acknowledging the political issues pertinent to both. Shrewd, bereted and beloved, jazz writer Max Jones would be immortalised by Bob Dylan as the bamboozled Mr Jones: "*something is happening but you don't know what it is…*" In 1965, perhaps to discover what it was, *MM* hired Max's 16-year-old son Nick, in case he knew.

But in fact the jazz perspective was anything but fusty, and sometimes intensely alert to music's radical cultural roles in the US and the UK, as photographer and historian **Val Wilmer**'s contributions to this book demonstrate. These were very much a logical development of what already was, and yet a sign of something new as well: this young white woman from Streatham, and her care to document so rigorously and so sympathetically. In conversation with **Richard Williams** (pp.43-60), she explains how she became a conduit to *MM*'s readers for the voices of free jazz — which often embraced an openly revolutionary politics — while her essay (pp.61-66) sets out how she began, working for an underfelt of small black-run magazines.

Not all the important music being made at this time was so lovingly covered, though, as **Penny Reel** attests (pp.67-71). Despite Jamaica putting out "the third largest number of records after England and the United States", the UK music press seemed barely aware of the richness of ska, so it had to be hunted out by enthusiasts, disc by disc. And here was a young white working-class man, from one of the poorest parts of East London, far more drawn to these sounds than anything in his own background, and to the clubs and the dives they emerged from. This too felt new.

Closer to the emergent pop scene, the chart trade press and the teenybop glossies were quicker to catch trends and shifts — most trivial, some deeper and more unsettling. **Jon Savage,** chronicler of the roiling energies of the times, bright and dark, writes about 1966-67 (pp.72-85), that awkward season when Beatle Paul was advising us all to drop acid for wise enlightenment. How was the UK pop press (Savage focuses on *Disc and Music Echo*) handling its responsibilities towards its teenage readers at this time?

With the release of *Sergeant Pepper* in 1967, the Beatles would emerge as an implacable cross-cultural force, at once radical and middlebrow — and now the counterculture also broke through into the mainstream press. "Rock" was the new name of the music that was somehow both harbinger and social glue of many of the changes — and a story that required interpreting. Though he was mocked for it, William Mann, classical critic at the *Times*, wrote (correctly) of the Beatles'"pan-diatonic clusters". Geoffrey Cannon kept readers of the *Guardian*, the *Listener* and *New Society* informed. As well as columnist Nik Cohn, an early partisan of pop against the flattening threat of rock, the *Observer* hired a BBC film-maker, **Tony Palmer,** as their commentator. The Sunday colour supplements flirted with Carnaby Street tourist hipsterism, court illustrator to the Beatles Alan Aldridge kept busy at the *Sunday Times*, and so on. (Sharing a panel at the conference with chronicler of the underground **Jonathon**

Green and Rock's Backpages archivist **Mark Pringle, Palmer** discusses this collision of sensibilities on pp.97-117.)

But as the cultural turmoil accelerated after 1966, it was evident that the established broadsheet press, with its earnest duty to explain, adapt or denounce, simply had the wrong antennae for what was emerging, good and bad. Because London was at this time a ferment of sit-ins and lock-outs, arts labs, folk and blues clubs, happenings and demos. Psychedelia, with its collective trips and its lightshows, had a foothold in both clubland and art galleries. And at the heart of all, a Liverpool beat-group boyband, once beset by shrieking mobs, creating insouciant media copy just by being smarter than the hacks sent to confront them, now also made films and song cycles: *Pepper* was a concept album linking vaudeville and music hall at one end, Pop Art and fluxus-type pranks at the other, while 'All You Need Is Love' would debut as a live global broadcast link-up. Meanwhile Lennon was wooing Yoko Ono at the Indica Gallery, and would soon be chatting to Tariq Ali of radical underground magazine *Black Dwarf.*

Avidly if naïvely following events in the US and on the continent, the UK counterculture sought to remake politics from the ground up. And readers needed guidance through the chaos, this unprecedented worldwide collision of pop culture and radical protest, not to mention every kind of fad and pose and predatory put-on, turning to the underground press to sort the good from the bad. To *International Times* (*IT* or *It* or *it*, founded in 1966) or to *Oz* (founded in Australia in 1963, arriving in the UK in 1967) and its short-lived offshoot *ink*. Or to the offspring of an unsuccessful attempt to run a UK version of *Rolling Stone*, variously named *Friends of Rolling Stone*, *Friends* and finally *Frendz*. In 1968 Tony Elliott founded *Time Out*, a one-sheet listings magazine that would expand into a London institution, with sections devoted to racial equality, police brutality, housing, transport, agitprop, mysticism and more. An extract from **Jonathon Green**'s oral history *Days in the Life* (pp.89-96) sketches the early publishing story of *it*; **Mark Williams** explains how the underground press was funded (pp.118-122). And — bliss it was in that dawn! — **Mark Pringle** describes being young and reading it all (pp.161-164) while **Charles Shaar Murray** is interviewed about being young and a writer (pp.123-132).

This was a culture making it up as it went along, its primary glue being — as Murray notes — its music, a music considered by its fans to be nudging humanity towards a better future. Today, a half-century on, the original valence of the word "progressive" is largely dissipated. It's become a monosyllable in a thoughtless genre pigeonhole — prog rock or just prog — but it remains totemic in the lost language of this hidden landscape. Which is why it's worth trying to recover a sense of the future many hoped we were progressing towards. In 1970, a large contingent of the staff at the now-venerable *Melody Maker*, led by then-editor Jack Hutton, left to found a new rock weekly, which became *Sounds*. The territory covered wasn't very different, but it was centred less on jazz or chart-pop than on progressive rock.

In the mid-60s, when the charts had become the primary forum for imaginative exploration, the conversation had moved song by competing song, and *NME* had prospered. Now that longer discussions of LPs were the focus, *NME* was flailing and threatened with closure. In 1973, in desperation, it hired writers from the dwindling underground press: Murray from *Oz*, Mick Farren from *it*, Nick Kent from *Frendz*. The paper was revamped, with longer features, a quick-witted and irreverent fourth-wall-busting editorial stance and layout style, half *Private Eye*, half *Monty Python*, and (arguably the most important innovation sales-wise) the Gig Guide listings.

This turned the paper's fortunes round so sharply that it became market-leader and agenda-setter for nearly a decade, despite the churn among young writers. A kind of bundling was key, a bundling of roles and attitudes and topics. People bought music papers to answer basic questions which ran a wide arc, from amused consumer-convenience to something rather more anxiously, earnestly zeitgeisty: *When's the album? Is it any good? Where are they playing? Is it MY kind of thing? Does this music MATTER?* The pop dream beset by doubts, the doubts aired — as often as not — as gags.

Creole as Cosplay Power: an Imagined Double Identity

"Imagined communities", as the historian Benedict Anderson terms them, cluster not only round language but also round the technologies of the written word, particularly newspapers. As you bought and read these papers, you knew there were thousands of others like you, all with identical access and commitment to and self-taught recognition of facts and (tour)dates and names and values. Such shared written totems, argues Anderson, were how the early settler-led independence movements fashioned themselves into nationalisms, as colonies passionately fought to separate from the imperial metropole.

In the dynamic Anderson sketches, there'd typically be an unofficial use language that was a whirl of borrowings and street inventions and code-shifts, in all directions. In fact there'd be several, because a *pidgin* is not a *patois* is not a *creole*. A pidgin is a patchwork of words from two clashing tongues, its grammar often simplified for ease of communication. A patois is the adaptive form of the language of the colonised or the transplanted: as much a matter of concealment as communication (there's grammatically as much in Jamaican patois of Yoruba or Twi as there is of English). But what interests Anderson is the creole, the adaptive form the settlers developed, as amplified and accelerated by print technology. A speaking caught between cultures, a creole became respectable as new written form in the colony. And yet — just as participants in the Boston Tea Party, a revolt against imperial taxation, dressed as Native Americans — in its more fierce separatist forms, it often clothed itself in the forms and manners of the harder-pressed in the same locale.

The word is derived from *criollo*, a term for the settler community so intimately linked to the motherland, and yet disdained by it too. Those gathered into such a creole, this hard-to-unravel cross-ply of status and expression, were nearly always blocked from rising to their best level of achievement back home. As convinced of its talent as it was conflicted about its identity, such a community hungered for the cultural and intellectual validation of the metropole — and at the same time yearned for freedom from it.

Now a mild kind of imagined community can be fashioned round any publication, round escape into the micro-market passions of the cat-lover, the trainspotter, the self-trepanner. This book explores something more charged: an imagined creole, a semi-invisible counter-colony established at the post-colonial moment within the mother nation. Some were trying out full-on MC5-style cosplay: 'White Panthers' as the self-appointed bros-in-arms of their black precursors. Others seemed simply to wish they'd been born elsewhere. Creole means language as well as community, and this one emerged replete with its own blues-boy jargon, rich in words borrowed from the jazz argot of the early part of the century, such as *hip* or *cool*, or *man* as a mode of address. Courtesy the Beats and the New Journalism, it was more than somewhat American in rhythm and outlook, though later it would trend for a time quasi-Rastafarian, as reggae made itself felt. Much of the excitement of the mid-60s rock project came via what Charles Shaar Murray (on pp.124) calls "creative misunderstandings of the source material" — certainly among the misunderstandings was a fan-fiction resistance stance as cosplay, an idealistic insider-outsider code-shifting.

In *The Souls of Black Folk*, W. E. B. du Bois had identified a double consciousness in groups that society keeps marginal, and traumatised. No major black English-language intellectuals — C. L. R. James in Trinidad, say, or LeRoi Jones in the US — had direct presence in the UK music press in the 60s, but still there were white writers taking pains to ensure that the black originators weren't entirely edged out of this utopian commonality: Val Wilmer, Penny Reel, Richard Williams, Murray himself... As young people danced and drank and ate and smoked together, perhaps glimpsing a passage to something deeper (did I mention the fanfic?), here was the distant self-inflicted mirror of that double-consciousness, a conflicted white self-marginalisation, half intermittently acknowledged complicity, half radical hope.

And within the imagined creole that clustered round them were some of the most talented, naturally curious young writers in the English language (alongside — this bears repeating — some of the worst and least curious). Though only a handful would make it out to the wider world as anything but specialist reviewers: either those who bailed early, or (tellingly?) those who made their bones ferociously *rejecting* many countercultural values.

Still, the most seasoned warriors, hardbitten veterans of the 60s children's crusades, had landed at *NME* defending the values and the honour of the underground even as they acknowledged its demise. "We don't just write about the music," Murray recalls his *NME* colleague Tony Tyler saying: "We write about what the music's about." Which is partly how this paper — its tone as primary guardian caustic, hilarious, the opposite of earnest — ensured these dissident values remained at large within this secret playground for many years to come (such values as: free love, legalised drugs, racial harmony, an end to war, liberation from mechanised drudgery and suffocating routine).

As it reached out to a more working-class readership, *Sounds* had increasingly fashioned itself round street-bred rock, the scruffy denim-clad journeyman blues boogie many now saw as the deepest spirit of the counterculture. But it too covered a wide range of music, its loyalty to prog lasting deep into the 80s, by which time it was helping create a lasting media niche for metal. And it was also quickest to respond to punk, via **Jonh Ingham**, an Australian transplanted to London from first-hand encounter with the Californian scene in the late 60s. To someone with this trajectory, the Sex Pistols seemed a long-awaited, chaotic strike against the by-now bedded-in smugness and self-regard of the progressive ideal (for more on this, see Jonh's contributions to the panel found transcribed on pp.202-225).

The weekly that most successfully continued riding the chart-pop wave out of the 60s was *Record Mirror*. Swallowing its main surviving rival *Disc* in 1975, it remained the home of the official BBC charts — catnip to some — and the quality of its coverage of disco was far ahead of all rivals, thanks to the tireless inventiveness of James Hamilton finding ways to describe beats, as **Mike Atkinson** recalls (pp.273-276).

Countering the influx of New Journalistic practice elsewhere, stubbornly committed to the old-fashioned virtues of clarity and keeping yourself out of the story, *Melody Maker* was perhaps the least formally ambitious of the weeklies. But this was misleading. Its coverage of jazz and folk had linked it to political undercurrents long predating the underground, and it was still often the first to spot trends, from the Velvet Underground to reggae, as **Richard Williams** notes in a 2002 interview with Simon Warner (pp.151-160). Until 1980 it maintained the deepest coverage of the widest spread of musics, as avid reader **Marcello Carlin** recalls (pp.196-201). For more on the differences between *NME* and *MM*, and how each reacted to the arrival of the underground in the music trade press, see the transcription of the panel where **Murray** and **Williams** spar cheerfully with (no relation) **Mark Williams** (pp.135-150).

Rolling Stone, compromised US guardian of at least a strained version of the countercultural ethos, also continued to be an inspiration, though no lasting equivalent was ever established in the UK. Contenders in the early 70s included *Frendz*, Mark Williams' *Strange Days*, *Cream* (not to be confused with the US title *CREEM*) and *Let It Rock*. The closest, as **Idris Walters** argues (pp.190-195), was perhaps *Street Life*: as likely to put Spain's King Juan Carlos on the cover as Pete Townshend or Bryan Ferry, it was a source of long, deeply researched articles on all manner of topics (Juan Carlos had just saved Spanish democracy from a fascist coup). Enormously admired by the cognoscenti, *Street Life* was sadly short-lived, the plug pulled after just over a year.

(Possibly the least-examined benefit of this small world of half-forgotten titles is the backroom work it fostered: **Simon Frith**'s essay on pp.238-242, on the role of the editor, acknowledges how essential this was to the maintenance of intellectual quality in these years, correctly treating it as a collective rather than an individual characteristic.)

There'd long been small journals supplying information, impassioned expertise, knowledgeably researched detail, driven by the sense they were championing musics not adequately served by the weeklies: jazz, folk, country; blues and soul at *Blues & Soul*, which began publishing in 1967. Alert to overlooked histories, these were by no means necessarily backward-looking: championing the black music favoured in UK clubs in the 60s, the late Dave Godin — the gay fan-scholar who coined the term 'Northern Soul' — foresaw some of the dance-music dynamic of the 80s.

But in the 70s, three new things happened. First, rock itself began to exhibit the symptoms of being long-lived, complete with forgotten backwaters. Second, the appeal of some of the overlooked musics began to seem much more evidently political: if chart breakout was still sought — sales as the voice of the people! — its absence was often (in the same breath) considered a mark of credibility. Third, there was less sense than ever that these overlooked musics existed only on the margins.

Back in 1969, naming it for a Captain Beefheart song, Pete Frame had started *ZigZag*, as a kind of samizdat for the countercultural faithful, to cover figures he felt the music press were ignoring (such as Beefheart himself). Though the weeklies had picked up some of the slack, *ZigZag* continued intermittently in this corrective mode into the mid-80s. In 1973, as he explains on pp.165-172, *Melody Maker* writer **Alan Lewis** persuaded its owners IPC to set up *Black Music*, not least to provide a platform for the pioneering black British writer Carl Gayle. All kinds of musics — including soul, funk and disco — were now overtly, indeed eagerly political. Most strikingly, reggae now had its defiantly Rastafarian wing, prophetic, apocalyptic, minatory. *Pressure Drop* emerged in 1975, to focus entirely on reggae: there, and later at *NME*, Penny Reel was crafting a gorgeous written style which at its peak inflected the language of Rastafarianism through the lens of a Runyon-esque romance of gangsters, grifters, singers, players and producers...

Even classic 60s pop got its pushback, with Brian Hogg's *Bam Balam*, a harbinger of the punk fanzine explosion. I'll come to punk shortly — it's unavoidable, for good and evil — but arguably the most embattled counter-insurgency of the era came from the tiniest of all these magazines. Flyspeck-dogged over a four-year run, *MUSICS* magazine patched together projects and practices that sought to upend all process and form and tradition and habit in music, everything from free improvisation to interspecies music, plus music made by actual children. Longstanding among its many editors, **David Toop** — later one of the first UK writers to write with any authority about rap — tells this story and what came after for him in the 80s, mainly at *The Face* (pp.325-330).

A specialist magazine tends to cleave hard to the perceived narrowness of its readers' interests. But as inheritors (often despite themselves) of the legacy of the underground press, with its sense of mission to supply "alternative" information, these tiny challengers were different. Whatever the pretext, whatever the genre-hook, the entire world was potentially their subject.

Between Rock and an Art Space:
The Invisible Insurrection of a Million Minors

So the imagined community — this hidden counter-colonial micro-region — had its shared slant: but why had this turned out to be rock-faced, rather than any of these other musics? And what had turned its specialists into quasi-experts on everything, and its fans into readers impressed and excited by this assumed expertise? To understand this we have to return to its emergence as something distinct from its predecessors, and to what led up to this.

1966 — the year that rock began to coalesce as electric form and stance — had been a year of three-minute bursts of experiment and collage on all sides, the charts packed with battling ideas. It was the year that *it* first appeared, the year the students at Strasbourg published the pamphlet *On the Poverty of Student Life...* and the year the British Colonial Office finally closed its doors. The Empire, this centuries-long debauch of robbery with menaces and worse, was over.

From the late 40s, as India and the African nations seized their hard-fought independence, the UK had closed back in on itself, exhausted and diminished. Austerity was the watchword — and besides, many returning from war sought a haven of non-emergency. Yet many of the war-babies were hungry for ways beyond this stiflement. Paradoxically — and often at cost of being some kind of policeman — life in the pre-war colonies had offered escape and adventure to many Britons, not least some of its more ambitious working-class youngsters; after cramped slums or changeless fields, new sights, sounds, smells, tastes, the chance to unfurl your limbs and maybe make something unexpected of yourself.

The successor generation also wanted out. And a very different relationship with the rest of the world now seemed available: the 45rpm single came onto the market in 1949, bringing intimate and competing sounds and ideas and sensibilities from far-flung places, jazz, country, calypso, r&b, the voices of black and white working-class America and

Jamaica, into the reach of unpoliced teenage minds. Evocative or even nonsensical words, sometimes, but beneath these, the subtextual tales told by the phrasing, the growls, the shrieks, the clatter and heat of the beat, the sweetness, the unplanned-for weirdness. Folk and skiffle even showed you how to do it yourself. The blue note as the sound of liberation, universal friendship, sexual freedom, all somehow bound up in the forward march of Civil Rights.

All this had been the backdrop to 1966: this newly imaginable utopia of a post-segregation-world. The charts were become a syncretic playpen, reflecting everything attendant on the new possibilities, even anger and fear. Pop was fascinated by the ideals, yet tentative, confused and uneasy also: everything you most desired, everything you couldn't bear to dream. New studio technologies made it easy to drop all kinds of weird grabby noise into the mix — easy, and market-competitively smart — and musicians of every bent were picking up on this too.

If the word "progressive" increasingly named the assumed virtues of the emergent music, it's worth noting the form it largely took. *Progressive jazz* had been jazz quilted into classically composed structure. *Progressive folk* was folk that quit stroppy gnarled localism to explore global village klatches of multi-ethnic sonority. In the various bustling mid-60s London club scenes, jazz and folk and rock and roll promiscuously co-mingled as *progressive blues*. Purely musically, "progressive" was a kind of pidgin; politically it was insisting that progress meant allowing every different culture to share the same stage on equal footing. Decades before the internet, rock was the patchwork form the underground collectively listened to, and defined itself by: multiple tastes fashioned by technology into a smorgasbord of tiny helpings, its imagined all-inclusiveness a bewitching *fata morgana* for wider, self-sustaining readerships and their many squabbling fandoms.

The avatar of all-styles exploration was Jimi Hendrix: importing to a startled, receptive England fragments and voicings and traditions, some ancient, some modern, to slew across one another in a science fiction blues landscape of drift and grace and intense solos. The future was to be a welcoming pluralist hubbub — actively utopian, spiritually woke, loved-up: black, brown, white as equals, as free to meet and flirt as jazz and classical and blues and rock'n'roll. That was what rock promised. This was what it *was*.

Had Hendrix lived, the often somewhat self-serving hustle of this rhetoric might have encountered challenge sooner. Here was a musician of colour who'd quit the US scene, attracted by the new electric noise the white London lads were making, and who'd arrived in Britain to validate and to expand it. But with his new trio in 1970, the Band of Gypsies, he was back in dialogue with American black musicians. Miles Davis, sick of what he considered the backward-facing white-critic pedantry of the jazz world, had begun to be drawn towards a Hendrixian SF funk murk in his new music – and now Hendrix was moving towards Miles, and perhaps a sound far darker and more militant. But then his story had ended badly that same year, for him personally and for wherever he might have been headed. Perhaps wanting distraction from disenchantment, the counterculture mainly paid circus-stunt homage to his virtuosity. When the underground writers arrived in the rock press, this circus was part of what they were fleeing, and (self-critically) mocking.

The very first piece Charles Shaar Murray wrote for *NME* was a Q&A with David Bowie, with Lou Reed in sullen tow. Nick Kent would cover Iggy Pop, the New York Dolls, and the dark glamour gathering round the Stones. None of these figures were new to the music press — Richard Williams had covered the Velvets long years before at *MM*, Bowie had been an eclectic nuisance for years — but the approach was now very different. The sheer length of Murray's debut piece, published across two issues, was an index of a shift in sensibility, as was its seemingly unedited chattiness, its casual address of the sexual murk round Bowie and Reed and the Warhol people. Not to mention the revisionist ambivalence of Ziggy Stardust, Bowie's retelling of the Hendrixian enchantment: utopia as unilateral space-invasion, gorgeous alien celeb-royalty landed as despots among us. Thanks in part to Bowie's endless quotability, the pages of the rock weeklies became a kind of communal arts-lab brainstorm session, a patchwork whirl of intellectual fragments of wildly varied quality — Burroughs and Lovecraft, addiction and sexual perversity, post-apocalyptic social breakdown, nazi pyramids on the moon — thrown out before a readership largely starved of any such quizzical nutrition. Nothing like this had existed before in the UK.

The underground had always harboured naysayers. Dylan and Zappa weren't hippies; Pop Art notwithstanding, Warhol's Factory was as much about death as celebration. Via Hendrix and Stockhausen, Miles had dug into the stress and fear at the core of James Brown's beat, to unfurl vast interior headfuck dystopias. What glam's theatricality — half silly, half serious — now amplified was a question: *what if everything were a show, an act, a game?* Plus, with a gaudy retro-futurist shimmer to their dress-up, Roxy Music were crowbarring open rock's sense of its own history, re-importing the lounge-lizard croon alongside an imagined electronic future, all bleeps and swoops within the 40s and 50s revivalism. What if the entire counterculture were just another season's ephemeral fashion-phase?

Even a decade after its emergence, rock was after all still new, still evolving, not yet delimited. If it came from Chuck Berry and Little Richard and Elvis — from black meeting white in American teenage music — where was it headed? What else might it encompass? Already attitudes to its mid-60s promise included nostalgic melancholy and frustration at its various failures — but still there lingered in the music press a sense of gleefully destabilising undecidability, as if what was important was the continued refusal, even refutation, of all pre-existing divisions and categories. So was prog the visionary syncretic core — or a deviation for time-wasting show-offs? If rock included the Velvet Underground, did it include Miles or Funkadelic, or Beefheart or Annette Peacock? What about German groups like Can and Faust? Did it include ABBA?

Among the basic questions and the deeper ones being hashed in these publications: if folk music can be politics why can't pop be art? Are lyrics poetry? Everyone knows the recording industry is evil and bad for music — so how do we deal with the amazingness of some of the music that comes from it? Music made for fun or for money, music made for real: how to fashion an aesthetic that encompasses ambivalent political truculence and quickfire jokes? When and how is novelty a value (and when not)? What can't we do when trash is an index of value? And how — an urgent worry for any weekly — do we stop it all congealing into dead habits and tics and boredom?

For now at least the music papers still continued to circle a central idealised multicultural democracy, following what they saw as the ethos of the best of the music. The story the creole insurgency was still mostly telling itself was that *everyone belonged*. And so you arrived to find out Groundhogs tour dates in the early 70s, and left perhaps with your interest piqued by the Mahavishnu Orchestra or Bob Marley or Victor Jara or Wigwam; or directed towards Miriam Makeba's *Live in Conakry* or Manu Dibango's *Africadelic* or Nina Simone's *It is Finished...*

Here too was the primary media outlet for the youth perspective, the voice of the 60s children's crusade. But children don't stay children — and besides, few had ever actually been the unspoiled idyll-raised elves and angels of the Rousseau-hippie dream. As it evolved through the 70s and early 80s, the music press engineered its imagined community round a clash of different styles; a shared family quarrel, or perhaps a family of shared quarrels among the consumer pointers, with "rock" less one type of music among others than the agreed-on central platform on which all these quarrels took place.

By design volatile, perhaps inherently unstable, it was nevertheless a safe space of sorts: safe above all from intrusive mainstream supervision. Left for a season or three undisturbed by outside forces, a somewhat democratic clearing emerged in which the street-cred cat could spar with the rockstar king. But a reckoning was coming, an unmendable rip in the progressive continuum — a rip that would come to be seen as the permanent model of all future value. The problem with top-down quilting is who gets left out of the quilt.

Know-Nothing Authenticity and Other Vengeful Performances

Underpaid and exploited, required to deliver a phenomenal weekly word-rate, rock writing was a self-motivated discipline improvising a language to tackle these contradictory ideas, establishing for the reader practical canons of judgment out of this thrilling car-crash of the world's styles, from the Mississippi Delta via the Caribbean, Africa and the Indian subcontinent, to dreams of the robot future. Something new every week: the industry is built on planned obsolescence, and churn demands churn. The sub-generational turnover of contributors at these titles is as striking as it is unsentimental. All but the very strongest writers will burn out and move on after a couple of years, tying up the identities of the best-known papers in a competitive jangle of feuds and fashion-shifts. Continuity — meaning a recognisable look and sense and stance to allow readers to fashion a loyalty — is maintained at a less stellar level: the editors ensuring copy is structured, the researchers fashioning the chart pages, the photographers, of course — all of whom tending to stay with a paper far longer.

Awash with daddy's money, the counterculture had also always attracted the idea-hungry, change-hungry literate working class, into this bohemian sub-world where they began to have a control over their own creative lives that their parents had never even dreamed of. But the self-reinvention of a few was a mounting personality crisis for many, uncertain what they connected to, past and future, and who they were becoming. Reaction was inevitable.

Ian Hunter's *Diary of a Rock'n'Roll Star* details the let-down day-by-day, touring with mid-league midlands rockers Mott the Hoople, arriving in 1972 in his long-promised land America. He sees the unaccustomed thrill of trans-Atlantic flight devolve into stress and grind and disenchantment, plane-hops up and down the USA, and the uneasy realisation that the rewards here would only ever accrue to a few, however amazing the shows were. The dreamy progressive utopia was a delusion, perhaps even a trap, and music-writers increasingly knew their readers knew it. Once the USA had been the shining city on a hill; now a new quasi-religious metaphor took its place, borrowed from the Rastafarians — that we were all living in kidnapped exile in a grim Babylon, the hated invader-abductor that was also (for many) the birth-home.

For hippies, music been the universal language; for punks, musicianship would be suspect, all this cluttered information and the time required to process it — the sitars and harpsichords of the first rock decade's outward-turned explorations a class trick played on the excluded. Who even had the time to get good at all this stuff, let alone the opportunity? And you didn't need to chum around with world-weary rock-stars on Lear Jets to encounter fucked-up disillusion and trudge. Rock? If this is the people's music, shouldn't it be about ordinary people's lives? A gleeful know-nothing energy would became the bedrock of social authenticity, a rage of the particular and the local, demanding loudly assertive (and too-quickly generic) sketches of what it was to have nothing. A music reflecting damaged backgrounds, the experience of the left-behind: those realising that the places they had thought to escape they were very much still stuck in.

Between 1976-80, several related things happen, surprisingly quickly. First, of course, is punk; second, an unusually public sub-generational shift in name writers on the music weeklies; which led, third, to a greatly increased mainstream interest in the affairs of the same weeklies; fourth, the electric blue note began no longer to function as index of and glue for the music's universalism; fifth, the fight for women to be paid a different kind of notice began to take effect; sixth, the complex countercultural adoration-disdain for pop began once more to mutate; seventh, even as the affairs and attitudes in the imagined counter-colonial micro-community bled more and more up into the mainstream media, British music, somehow the source of the world's idea of universal teen revolt, began to pull its horns back in. In a world enjoying global broadcast link-up, the post-imperial British yen for "anywhere but here" was beginning to come to an end.

Race and the Xeroxed Real, or How Families Fall Apart

In July 1976, *NME* famously ran an ad (scripted by Charles Shaar Murray, himself only 25) for "hip young gunslingers", resulting in the arrival of Tony Parsons and Julie Burchill, the latter just 17. That same month, coked-up glam demigod David Bowie seemed to be flirting with fascism. In August, world-renowned white bluesman Eric Clapton aligned himself with glib Empire racist Enoch Powell. A demoralised and threatening turn for rock to be taking...

The National Front was mobilising; anti-fascist marches were meeting violent opposition. In this moment of high danger, the memory of what the music had been and could and should be flashed up before a group of readers, a letter appearing in *NME*, *Melody Maker*, *Sounds* and *Socialist Worker* robustly denouncing the trend and calling for a movement to fight for 'Rock Against Racism'. Semi-sponsored by the newly renamed Socialist Worker's Party, RAR organised festivals and published its own fanzine, *Temporary Hoarding*. As a home-made cut-and-paste collage of typed rants, hand-written captions and headlines, badly photocopied images, punk fanzines were now everywhere: *Temporary Hoarding* patched together an urgent, angry xerox refurb of 60s progressive belief — that "rock", as a people's music, was by definition implicitly and explicitly cross-cultural, rock and soul to reggae and beyond; and that urban working-class youth was naturally and vibrantly anti-racist in taste and sensibility. After all, this latter fact was why and how the counter-empire, the appeal of teen revolt all across the globe, had emerged at all — a fact that radical political magazines since the late 60s had often acknowledged, though not always with great insight.

(For Ruth Gregory's memoir of key RAR activist the late **David Widgery**, longtime music writer and East London GP, militant hippie and revolutionary marxist activist, see pp.184-189. And perhaps here's a place to note with much sorrow many other potential contributors to this anthology who passed on too soon, among them John 'Hoppy' Hopkins, Max Jones, Jack Hutton, Bob Houston, Penny Valentine, James Hamilton, Dave Godin, Felix Dennis, Mick Farren, Charlie Gillett, Ian MacDonald, Tony Tyler, Richard Neville, Steven Wells, Sue Steward, Roy Carr and my mentor Richard Cook.)

Whatever the SWP turned into since, this intervention was necessary, honourable, and above all effective. Fascism would find no useable foothold in 80s pop culture; the music press played its part holding that line. The SWP hotly courted the writers hired by the rock weeklies to respond to punk — to Burchill and Parsons adding Garry Bushell at *Sounds*, who'd already been writing for *Socialist Worker* since 1973. Self-taught and bright, ambitious and (as it turned out) politically flexible, all three were flaunted as *proletkult* pets in a political organisation that had lately tended to direct more of its appeal towards students. All three were also at war with the more comfortable habits of the countercultural gang they'd arrived in, and quickly came to the attention of the non-music media, Peter York at *Harpers and Queen* being particularly smitten. The music press in the 70s had operated almost unobserved, with newspapers and television more or less ignoring most of what was covered. Punk entirely changed this. The insurrection from below, in the form of hundreds of bands and dozens of xeroxed fanzines, in turn breached the protective ceiling. Sex Pistols manager Malcolm McLaren deliberately end-ran the rock press, to get the tabloids to do his promo work for him; following McLaren's example and advice a few years later, Adam Ant would repeat the trick. And the tabloids ran with it, and television and the broadsheets happily followed.

As for the guitar-based blues, perhaps tainted by Clapton's outburst it was falling out of fashion in the UK — at least as rock's assumed default model. Its strength had been its apparent universality: emotions recognisable to all, rich or poor; sound everywhere, especially in the form of the electric solo; easy to teach yourself a basic version; plus mass-produced guitars were cheap. But the way music was talked about was changing, and — index of a deeper crisis of authority — the blues, former unifier of rock's family of assumptions, was beginning to lose its salience.

Since the late 60s, the UK music press had valorised both the black voice and view and sexualised teenage enthusiasm for novelty — the irresistible combination that Chuck Berry hit on — as interpreted through a scrim neither black nor especially teenage; very straight and mostly male in fact. With so many now forcefully asking what rock should really be about, the question also arose who should best discuss it. Julie Burchill self-presented as a teenage working-class communist, a stroppy, mocking, bad-girl feminist, and (last and not least) a music fan who vehemently preferred black American pop made by women to sweaty and leering pub rock made by Englishmen several years her senior. In a series of impressive manipulative swerves, at least some of them rooted in reality, Burchill directed jets of scornful moralism into this question. In every direction, for the editors of rock papers as for socialist activists allegedly many years wilier than her, she set a maze of identity-politics bear-traps that she could negotiate and they mostly couldn't. *Why are only men writing, why only white men, why only middle-aged middle-class white men?*

While a solidarity with the Civil Rights movement had been implicit in the music these papers covered — and sometimes explicit — the feminist revolts of the 60s had taken longer to register. After punk, many more young women would step up as writers and musicians, eager to re-imagine the power-relations, practical and symbolic, that had become unpleasant routine in this community: to transform what girls were (or could be), and thus to change the meanings of their preferences, musical or otherwise. With this arrived a distinct reorganisation in the meaning, use, value and potential hierarchy of genre; of who loved what and how they used it.

A contrite Bowie would work his way back into post-punk favour fairly quickly; Clapton's apologies took a lot longer to arrive. The family of shared arguments was coming apart. With the protective ceiling breached, the dissolution travelled upwards also. A crisis of authority not unlike that afflicting 70s music-writing began spreading across mainstream media in the 80s, a crisis the hyper-capitalist forces of reaction found many ways to exploit. Now you could garner authority simply by mocking expertise, guilt-tripping liberals via your own version of the street-cred strut. Instant confident self-taught opinion about any topic under the sun became very saleable indeed, as Bushell, Burchill and Parsons all discovered — saleable, and fairly quickly no longer countercultural. Not many former music-writers have found well-paid opinion-forming careers in the world outside the music press, covering politics as a successor to pop — but these three all did.

Moods for Moderns: New Beats in Different Kitchens

In 1976, Mick Farren had written up an *NME* interview with ABBA, combining White Panther scorn for these irredeemable straighties with a baffled respect for the efficiency of the high-quality Swedish pop factory. And rock was never *not* pop, of course — its chart success was after all part of its implicit political claim. But very often it defined itself *against* pop.

Rock was this charged electric enclave within pop, voraciously proactive, all-devouring, reaching out, Hendrix-style, to embrace everything Western culture denied, while railing against the denial of the progressive dream, that all cultures could and would come together in a blues-inflected utopia. The pop around it, by contrast, was bland, silly, commercial, the amorphous compromised fleeting nothing that had swallowed up Elvis. But what if the past needs swallowing up?

Two schisms seemed to be emerging, related yet distinct. *Amateur versus professional* was the more venerable, a line once embraced by the Victorian upper middle classes now taking the form of critics enthused by primitive energy as it swept aside the hard-won skills of the technocrats. The second arrived with its two champions literally hand-in-hand, two conjoined faces of the same suspect coin. Burchill was the "poptimist", Parsons the "rockist" in today's too-slick shorthand: where she volubly favoured Motown over white-boy rock, Parsons's tear-soaked 1978 hymn to Bruce Springsteen enthroned him as a figure as passionately "real" emotionally as he was an accurate lens on the working-class condition. The year before, Parsons had interviewed the Clash: the exchange — offered by *NME* as a cover-freebie 45 — cast them in a role they never afterwards escaped in the UK, eliding all of their art-school elements to foreground their street-fighter credentials, the "thinking men's yobs" as the coverline yelled. Just months later, in *The Boy Looked at Johnny* (a book dedicated to Poly Styrene and Joan Jett and subtitled "*the obituary of rock'n'roll*"), the Burchill-Parsons tag-team were mocking Strummer as "a bit of posh" — unreal, in other words, as rocker *or* yob.

If not its actual death, punk's paradoxical gift to pop was rock's demotion: its unstitching as the centre at which anything of value had to jostle for attention and approval, and its remaking — for not keeping its promises — as just one music among many. With instant obsolescence recast as an avant-garde pop move, speed and flash and transformative unseriousness became an energy aspired to — every three months clear the decks to storm the charts, each new tribe jostling to replace rock as the lost moral-radical centre: mod, two-tone, New Romantic, psychobilly, Goth, industrial, New Country, as well as 57 varieties of indie, the spectre of the landfill sinkhole still decades away. Instead of rock as a debating chamber, imagine the whole of pop as the (much wider) marketplace space in which all conversation could now take place.

As **Liz Naylor** notes (pp.317-324), in her essay on the pioneering feminist monthly *Spare Rib*'s response to punk, where rock had been the podium allowing the likes of Patti Smith to re-invent performed womanhood, now young women were increasingly seceding towards other tribes to experiment with different ways to imagine gender and realise its possibilities. As onstage, so on-page: given her gunslinger origin myth and platform, Julie Burchill inspired imitators, until soon she too was just one among many. The entire entertainment industry (including the music press) was geared to the selling of the female body, to specific modes of performed sexualised labour (singing, dancing, etc): now the sheer thrill of asking who used pop how and why — including arguments about what girls liked and how this worked — encouraged performers and writers to throw off their shackles and put the crackle of uncertainty, which means possibility, back into conversation, and sometimes into the charts.

Parsons had established a "reality test" for music, Springsteen passing, the Clash not. But this only exacerbated rock's wider authority crisis. Aggressively (unwinnably) jockeying to be more real than itself, with self-conscious pop playacting bracketed off as a sin against social realism, this cockpit for the young, the male, the anxiously energetic, was setting out on its long retreat down from glam towards premature dad-rock. Such hold-outs as persisted — metal would turn out to be one — persisted because they recognised they'd been pushed back into the margin, and responded accordingly (which is to say entertainingly). With rock under attack and punk at sullen impasse, the issues of inheritor was initially hashed out between *NME* and *Sounds*. In late 1977, the latter had published two successive issues with the rubric 'New Musick', edited under Lewis's guiding eye by Jon Savage, Jane Suck and others, anticipating several possible futures, including guides to disco and dub, as well as features on Kraftwerk, Throbbing Gristle and (marking a key scission *within* punk) Siouxsie and the Banshees. Shortly after, the paper gave Pauline Murray of Penetration the headline 'The Future is Female'.

The 'New Musick' intervention was unpopular with other contributors, and Suck and Savage soon left the paper — but a genuine space had opened up, with rivals jumping in where *Sounds* lost its nerve. *NME* put a version of the idea at the centre of their Barney Bubbles redesign the following year, complete with Ari Up of The Slits on the dayglo cover and a construct-it-yourself pull-out manual, the *NME Book of Modern Music*. The swerve was now very evidently away from the word 'rock', towards a not-yet-named sound, a broader trickier spread of attitudes, an aesthetic often of audibly machine-like treatment (in voice or rhythm or distortion or effects), plus a commitment to exploration of the ugly world as it is, medically, psychologically, cybernetically: from artily strangled to quasi-emotionless, sometimes angry, unexpected, subtle; occasionally nihilist and depressive. Cabaret Voltaire, The Human League, Joy Division, The Fall, the Banshees and The Slits, a deepening fascination with the European sensibility of Kraftwerk, Can and Faust, and of course John Lydon's Public Image Ltd, whose groundbreaking *Metal Box* came out the following year, its review dominating *NME*'s cover. As reviewer Angus MacKinnon — who'd co-authored the *Modern Music* booklet's central essay with Charles Shaar Murray — wrote, the object to the PiL exercise was (as with Can before them) "simply to proceed with open ears, to somehow un-learn and then learn afresh... Nerves and tendons frayed and twisted... All this forward flow in 12 months — it's almost frightening. PiL are miles out and miles ahead. Follow with care."

(The driving force behind this booklet was likely *NME*'s Paul Morley, whose term for this genre was in fact 'New Pop', a genre that, for him, stretched from Buzzcocks to PiL, perhaps even to Faust — precisely because it was inclusive, as rock had been, and also, as Morley saw rock, at once avant-garde *and* popular: a disruption able to be heard and understood by all, like Hendrix or the Pistols. The current term of art is "post-punk", a name that obscures how many of these projects had begun in seclusion long before punk, and that perhaps erases its widest ambition, to be part of an argument actually *taking place in the charts*, even with a keen eye kept on anything not chartbound. By the early 80s, the term New Pop was largely reserved for styles of music able or willing to enter the charts.)

The Springsteen-Parsons exchange saw the no-bullshit working-class writer endorsing the anti-intellectual genuineness of the working-class rockstar. The rhetoric enjoined all honest readers to grasp this oneness of revolutionary purpose: as its audience made the world better, everyone should now revel in the only possible music worth our time. Sceptics saw only more self-mythologising cosplay here, and the flattering or sly bullying of audiences into missing the many ways class recognises itself. The New Music — if we extrapolate from the collision of its constituent elements — was suggesting other routes: less gullible, even pessimistic and untrusting, sometimes sexually ambivalent, often darkly playful. Identity was performance as much as reliable revealed fact, and much of the content explored the bleakness of the Ballardian terrain everyone faced. Two-Tone had its jolly side, of course, but Rhoda Dakar of The Bodysnatchers sang about rape; The Beat about mental illness. Here was a space in which women and younger non-white Britons, long battling to be heard and seen on their own terms, could for perhaps the first time redefine themselves against stereotype, and briefly seize the mic from those speaking on their behalf. London was even dethroned for a while as the space where music had first to make its mark. Many of the emerging subcultural tribes — even metal — allowed women bored with rock's more clueless sexism to find room for expression. And as the New Music mutated and divided, chasing pop's curiosity towards sound and style and imagination and noise, towards performance as a species of glamour, it not only recharged the energies of the charts themselves, but began to expand their potential.

As a glue, the electric guitar blue-note had suggested a music in everyone's reach, no matter how young they dropped out of school. But punk had punched open a newer, much broader confidence: if musical chops were a fraud anyway, anyone could surely do everything. Hence the New Music, this wave of self-taught intellectuals tinkering in a wide range of recondite subjects and techniques, often cultured in the pages of the music press, but by no means all musical. A pullulation of tiny political and quasi-political magazines and grubby local fanzines also contributed, drawing on a subterranean tradition stretching right back to the pamphlets of the 17th century dreamtime, a tradition now once again palpable, for a while at least, in every city and small town in the UK.

Many groups arrived with manifestos, and a grasp of sociology: "relevance" became a pest of a word, justification a knee-jerk. In the moment of the non-musician musician, people — they weren't all working-class, but plenty were — got pretty good at talking about meaning and its drawbacks. Suddenly there was a gleeful appropriation and repurposing of all manner of other material, including feminist theory and the far left polemic found in magazines out on the edges of this readership. Design was no longer something being left to large record companies: avant-garde gestures were imported from art-school. Everything previously shut away for niche specialists or the middle class was up for grabs — disco and funk and dub were hugely popular musics merely treated as niche, of course, but experimental electronic soundscapes or jazz, alongside movies, books, art, even philosophy, all this was considered part of the new playground, a dizzying cross-ply of voices, aesthetic and political, against category or branded platform.

Since the counterculture emerged in the mid-60s, it had been toying with an argument about the meaning and use of the word "intellectual": about what you needed to know about to earn such a title, how you needed to think, and how to express this thought. By virtue of its age and the diligence of its writers *Melody Maker* had earned the most serious reputation in the 60s and early 70s. But now its commitment to traditional journalistic practice worked against it; it was badly mauled by punk. *NME*'s residual undergrounder attitude and self-reflexive humour ensured a quicker response to seismic fashion shifts, to be bartered into both sales and heft. It had also — more than the other weeklies — absorbed the editorial talent of the various attempted UK *Rolling Stones*, *Street Life* and its precursors, with their commitment to exploring and explaining the whole of the alternative culture-style. It had become the spine of this still half-hidden world.

With the advent of the New Music, younger *NME* writers like Morley and Ian Penman were unleashed to revel in the task of informing themselves, travelling by touch under the skin of the many new fields opened, including film and TV, pre-rock and non-rock musics. French critical theory was far from pervasive even in academia at this date, but one of its vanguards — the film journal *Screen* — was supplying cinéastes with tools to unpick gender, sexuality, performance, how meaning is made and loyalty won, all the tricks played on the viewer-listener to construct attachment, orientation, perspective. The *hermeneutics of suspicion*, this unpicking came to be called elsewhere — and Penman in particular gambolled in it. Some readers found his autodidact urchin-play incomprehensible, even insufferable (decades on you'll still find him blamed for all of *NME*'s subsequent decline) but he was often also an extremely funny writer, and the sheer untrammelled exhilaration of difficulty caused at least a few — as Marcello Carlin, a committed *Melody Maker* reader through the 70s, hence no stranger to rebarbative music, once put it to me — to "feel inadequate *in the best way*." Decoding these messages was a challenge you set yourself — and as you did you learned, just a step behind your self-taught teachers. All the same, the editorial decision to be this demanding, week on week, and to put self-definedly daunting music with smallish audiences on the cover, came at a price. Some readers, not necessarily all averse to exploration and curiosity, felt shut out.

(For **Paul Morley**'s sense of a modernist Manchester imaginary at Oedipal war with — but always also in debt to — his immediate precursors, see his panel with **Jonh Ingham** and **Barney Hoskyns** on pp.202-225, which discusses the power of and the problems with any such dispensation to rewire your readers' worldview. For a sense of what it was like to be on the receiving end, see **Liz Naylor**'s panel on pp.298-316, where speaking alongside cartoonist and writer **Edwin Pouncey** and former editor and author **Nigel Fountain**, a historian of London's alternative press, she connects the loneliness and trauma of the outsider to the appeal of punk on one hand, and a deeper radical tradition of political journalism on the other.)

Regional Antennae, Dotty Eclecticism, Niche Pressures

The evident problem with editorial bundling is that it risks irritating any readers there for just one topic, especially now that every new sub-genre believed it had the punky right — and the tools — to seize the moment and the spotlight, and change the world. As a forensic device to take some deeper into how music or film or politics work socially, Penman's urchin hermeneutics had its followers, and still does. But a more populist glue was needed, to keep the many subjects from whirling away from one another.

After time in TV and as A&R for Island Records, Richard Williams had returned to *Melody Maker* as editor, and was putting together a strong editorial team to reestablish *MM* as the intellectually serious weekly, poaching writers from all over — among them Jon Savage — to cover everything the New Music threw up, but also to retrench the paper's 60s rep as the best for intelligent jazz and folk coverage. Sadly his plans were interrupted by a company-wide strike at IPC in 1980, over freelance payrates. When management demanded he publish a scab issue, Williams quit, as did his best writers. The pluralist project was shelved and the *MM* that emerged was feeble, confused and diminished: it ditched its jazz and folk sections entirely and wouldn't rediscover a convincing voice for several years.

Cannily led by Alan Lewis — who'd been headhunted by Jack Hutton from *Black Music* in 1975 — *Sounds* had already experimented with a kind of niche marketing, based round oi! With Garry Bushell its svengali, this was a noisy anti-music parody of a scene, skinheads as drunken cartoon idiots turning punk's visions of working-class self-representation into a degraded scribble. Oi! mocked ambition, idealism or intellect when it wasn't working towards nastier ends, and ultimately failed to thrive except as tabloid outrage fodder — the latter a vehicle for Bushell's later move onto those same tabloids. However, the weekly also pioneered two offshoots, *Noise!* and *Kerrang!* — the first fascinating but perhaps tellingly short-lived, the second busily active to this day.

As **Ian Ravendale** explains (pp.290–295), *Sounds* had long maintained the best regional antennae among the weeklies in the midlands and the north — and the north-east was the cradle of resurgent metal, as it began to make the best of its new niche status, unassumingly inheriting much of rock's "everyman" sensibility and prog's expansive will to experiment, and perhaps a little of the sense still of being the countercultural vanguard and the guarantor of its values. *Kerrang!* was a one-off supplement that became a long-running success, an unpretentious market-leader for the niche approach, at various times monthly, fortnightly and weekly.

By contrast, the other offshoot that *Sounds* had birthed was self-consciously, almost dottily eclectic. The cheerful pop-and-everything *Noise!* engagingly played its sense of clutter for a virtue, its covers a riotous multi-coloured list of artists and bands (37 on the first issue), everything from oi! to old-school prog, with Bow Wow Wow's Annabel Lwin grinning in tribal faceprint on the cover. **Beverley Glick** tells this story on pp.278-284, as well as the later travails of bringing a paper like *Record Mirror* together, with its various readerships that overlapped so little.

Noise! was somewhat following the lead set by Nick Logan's *Smash Hits*, which had started in 1978. Logan had been editor at *NME* during its insurgency as the counterculture-in-exile, when it had turned itself into a paper that put much of its brains into its gags. Battles with IPC management had made it an exhausting project to oversee, and in the late 70s he quit, to set up two more groundbreaking titles in succession. The first was *Smash Hits* — which by the early 80s was certainly proving the flirty silliness of pop could be the platform for a surprisingly wide range of musics, as **Bob Stanley** argues (pp.285-289). Here the glue of the bundling was flippancy, and it went on to be consistently the funniest music paper in the mid and late 80s, highly effective in appealing to newer, younger readers, many of whom would never afterwards make the jump to an inky. The second was *The Face*, in 1980, which along with *i-D* and later *Blitz* increasingly centred round clubs, fashion and what was coming to be called dance music. It also amplified the shift 80s magazines were making towards the look of the page — designer Neville Brody was inspired by the do-it-yourself freedoms of the fanzine to break and remake many of the old rules about the look of a magazine.

By now it was obvious the music weeklies were no longer the only place the widest conversation was happening. If it's wrong to say the centre of gravity shifted, that's because the challengers were offering a new centre — one of frivolity.

Everything in the Reader's Reach, and What Comes Of This

In the 1960s and early 70s, the rock-centred counter-culture presented itself more or less as a single conjoined terrain, in which every fashion spasm had its day at the top. Even in the late 70s, a multiplicity of titles — going far out beyond those just about music — existed in an argumentative post-underground space that seemed to share writers and readers; too strong, perhaps, to claim *everyone read everything*, but there was much crossover and intertitle movement. After punk, the time of the tribes: each insisting, as punk had, that it alone was the true inheritor — though of what exactly was no longer clear. If pluralism remained a value, the value of a single location for its expression did not. Choice began to mean choosing not to socialise: these fans like metal, those like funk, others enjoy jazz, trad or free, and all have their different magazines.

Nonetheless, *NME* weathered the IPC strike with editorial self-confidence undimmed, able now deftly to pick up some of the constituencies and contributors that *MM*'s management were stupidly casting away. Long strong on reggae, by 1981-82 it was expanding coverage of jazz and experimental noise. Tackling anything from Neubauten to Sinatra and Kid Creole to Cecil Taylor, it was becoming a meet-point where you could learn about Leo Baxendale or the Metaphysical Poets, Ghanaian highlife or Rainer Werner Fassbinder, Kathy Acker or Jacques Lacan or the Angry Brigade, as if they all existed somewhere on the same cultural plane, distinct but in mutual reach of one another — and (and this was key) *in reach of the reader.* It had an excellent film and television section, strong book reviews, effective political antennae, and some of the best photographers working. For exploration of what this felt like on the inside, the politics and the practicalities, see the essays by **Tony Stewart** (pp.229-237) and **Cynthia Rose** (pp.265-269), and the panel where both speak alongside **Beverley Glick** (pp.243-264). Certainly nothing else like this was available nationally, at this time or perhaps any other.

If *The Face* and *Smash Hits* (and *Noise!*) reflected the bright, instant pluralism of the charts — the energy of people thrown together in a club, dancing together now, tomorrow scattered — the *NME* continued to treat its pluralism as a kind of energised vanguard duty: a belief that everything should be placed in reach, pop and avant-garde, and everything wrong with either set out. But punk's success in getting impenetrable yammer to sweep all before it would not be repeated, and it was a risky time to commit to the experimental. After 1973, *NME* had dominated the 70s circulation wars; from around 1980 it was always fighting a rearguard action. It had reduced coverage of metal to occasional hostile jabs (in 1979 *Sounds* briefly overtook it sales-wise), and the strike allowed loyal readers a break in the weekly habit, the opportunity to shop around. A significant number never returned (Mark Williams teamed up with Felix Dennis, late of *Oz*, to bring out a paper for the duration of the strike, *New Music News*, to mop some of them up). *Smash Hits* was hitting its witty, glossy stride and younger readers in particular were now better targeted than ever by publishers, and siphoned away into different habits.

To the surprise of some in the 2015 conference audience who grew up as fans, there was no tremendous fondness for *Smash Hits* on the panels. There was a good deal less for its subsequent EMAP stablemate *Q*, which hove into view in 1986. Editors David Hepworth and Mark Ellen had grasped a looming problem sooner than many: can a music title even exist that speaks to 15 year olds and 35 year olds at the same time? As *Smash Hits* staffers, the two had chafed somewhat at the task of putting out a magazine aimed primarily at teenage girls. Why not fashion an approach that bluntly cuts off the young end of the scale? Fly-by-night pop will never vanish, and tweens will always be catered for — but what about those readers who'd started reading the rock press as teenagers but now had jobs and mortgages? The ligatures that had once unproblematically connected the young to 60s political values were now fraying with age. *Q* seized on the extensive past semi-buried in the archives, and began to dig it out, treasures on display in the cosiest of museums, intimations of deeper conflict or subterranean contradiction waved aside.

By contrast, in 1985, *NME* had run a feature across two issues boldly supporting the miners' strike, a provocative move only months after IPC saw a second strike, which the paper's freelancers and staff again honoured. And later that year, when Bob Geldof organised *Live Aid*, he more or less ignored the music press entirely, heading straight to television and the tabloids for attention and donation streams for his globe-spanning, money-raising, conscience-salving project. In the 70s Rock Against Racism had re-tooled the all-day rock festival to fashion a successful resistance coalition against the fascists, alongside a politics of active audience involvement. But by 1985, the music press lacked the heft to generate creative or critical responses to *Live Aid* — and besides, music press editorial was an increasingly professionalised affair, those with degrees in media shouldering aside those who'd worked their way up from glue-boy. Much of the earlier crackle of excitement had arisen from daily office banter and debate — between all ages, classes, races and genders, across a variety of titles in debate with one another. In the niche-structured world, this kind of encounter no longer happened so much; the many enclaves were no longer well able to interact with one another. There were probably more titles than ever — but far less sense that writers all read one another's work, or any longer came together as a larger argumentative family.

Though individual contributions inevitably blur this, at the conference and in this book, I've treated 1985 as the end-point of something. Not that the imagined creole ended there — its descendants exist even today, dispersed but tenacious across the internet. Nonetheless, round about the middle of the 80s, the community could no longer claim its primary topics and pretexts as purely its own, and how it went about its business was now very much policed by its marketing departments. The churn had obscured its sense of its own history. *NME* did pitch in behind the Red Wedge movement in support of Labour in 1986, and endorsed Neil Kinnock with a cover story in 1987. But there was something wan and forced about this; as if a break had been made with a deeper countercultural identity. Individuals would continue to bear their own highly politicised torches — none more rowdily than the late Steven Wells — but the battleground had evidently shifted elsewhere and the will to gaze outwards was diminished. Think of Morrissey complaining about music that "*says nothing to me about my life*", and how this — alongside hostile asides like "reggae is vile" — might in fact abut a growing indifference to anything outside a reactionary and parochial incuriosity.

Perhaps the best way to underscore what was vanishing is to take a quick look at the one title that continued — at least into the mid-90s —

to pursue intellectual pluralism as a virtue, as a project with radical verve (not to mention a continued affinity for jazz). It's also the magazine I edited for a short while: *The Wire*.

More importantly, it's the magazine Richard Cook edited for several years. The magazine had started in 1982 as a tiny scrappy quarterly to service the jazz fans that the *Melody Maker* had recently deserted; Cook had arrived from *NME* in 1985 to transform it into a stylish monthly piggybacking on a hipster-centred jazz mini-boom (a boom kiboshed by the 1987 market crash). In 1990 he put Michael Jackson on the cover and pushed towards an ultramontane full-spectrum broad-mindedness: a war on all niche instincts, perhaps especially those of the avant-garde. The paradox being that such pluralism was elsewhere becoming an entirely minority passion. *NME*'s pluralism in particular had been taking a more and more truculently moralising and worthy tone, until it was ditched in a 1988 turnabout, for a much narrower, deliberately and cheerily laddish line. And when I quit *NME* for *Melody Maker* that same year, I was told I couldn't write about Ronald Shannon Jackson ("We don't do jazz"): since its re-emergence in the mid-80s, a renewal achieved by writers I consider friends, even allies, *MM* hadn't been afraid to be intellectually demanding, and accordingly gave some black musics a limited coverage. But its understanding of them was rarely deep or complex, and its politics were often little more than a gleeful accelerationist nihilism.

In his first *Wire* editorial, in 1985, Cook had called for a conversation able to handle everything from Oscar Peterson to Einstürzende Neubauten: to handle the collision of life-won high technique *and* smash-it-all iconoclasm. Indeed "collision" was actually briefly a term, for a mini-trend in post-no wave proto-hiphop fusion. It was easy enough (for white British writers) to react to Public Enemy's 'Bring the Noise' as if it were purely chaotic self-realised futurist disruption, punker than punk — and to ignore the extent that hiphop was also very much (in Greg Tate's valuable phrase) "ancestor worship". The fact remains, just at the point the UK music weeklies had largely culled jazz from its pages, here it was returning, as traces and echoes in the soundscapes rap was building for itself — a new black music, at once in plain sight and underground, just like jazz and rock before it, exploratory engagement with its own history an inbuilt element, a layered, internally and half-consciously contradictory world-spanning shoutback against congealed or privileged versions of the universal. The UK rock press did in fact respond reasonably strongly to rap — but what it once knew, of the black music past especially, it had long cut itself off from. History is never just a museum, least of all a cosy one.

Pause and Reset: Doubts and Redoubled Clatter

In 1980 the Clash had released *Sandinista!*, an LP that began with one of the very earliest white raps, 'The Magnificent Seven', and moved through many other attempted musics, from country, folk and gospel to disco, jazz and dub. Even as a gesture it wasn't very convincing, but they'd always written songs about their fascination with black subcultures, reggae above all, and besides, this sprawling, shapeless and patchy triple album exactly reflected the wider countercultural confusion about where the expressive centre now was, or what even survived of the counterculture. If not rock or punk, was it going to be ska or soul, or synths and Europe-facing electronic experiment — or maybe Ant-music? This was after all the year that John Lydon's PiL played a New York show supported by James Blood Ulmer, new harmolodic star of the electric blues free-form fusion-funk pioneered some years before by Miles and Ornette (I like to think Richard Cook always had this double bill in mind when he was organising his review sections at *NME* and *The Wire*).

The Clash had encountered hiphop on tour in America, where the group were often now hailed as the greatest live rock band active, supplanting Zep, the Stones, the Who, perhaps even Springsteen. Given this, their approach in *Sandinista!* was a revelation for many American listeners, politically and culturally: this mix of military chic and leather-clad rebellion, globalist rebel rockers outing Uncle Sam as the oppressive hegemon (in the apparent cheeky belief that the Elvis Sun sides had been produced by Che Guevara rather than Sam Phillips). More self-regarding White Panther cosplay, others sourly felt.

In 1982, they recorded Topper Headon's 'Rock the Casbah', with its faux-muezzin wails, and its theme of, well, what, exactly? Rebel street youth casting down the local power structure? It's hard — as so often in Clashland — to extricate deliberate ambiguity from silly muddle: it really isn't the surprise it should be that, eight years later, this was the very first song played on US Armed Forces Radio during Operation Desert Storm, blasting out the sooncome triumph of the New World Order, the American tribal yell crushing its cultural-political enemies...

Which brings me back, in a roundabout way, to this project. It's been a bewildering time to be working on it. From a drive, however flawed, to find a space in which all the clatter of world can begin to speak to itself as equals at last, here was the circle turning back on itself: our entry (since the conference took place) into the era of Brexit and of Donald Trump. How bellicose and yet forlorn is Brexit's bid to establish British Empire 2.0, a global trade area policed by little Englanders imagining straddling all the world again, even as they sneer at it, fear it and hate it. At a time when climate disaster, war, hunger and the enforced global migrancy of millions confront all of us, what about the English turn back towards America, and not at all the America of Little Richard or Civil Rights or free jazz or even of *your huddled masses yearning to breathe free*? For those Britons allergic to the metropolitan crackle of city-based cross-cultural engagement, what seemingly beckons is the America of white supremacy, resegregation, predatory kleptocracy. The America of new-built walls...

Kintone's follow-up EP to *Coming Home*, I kept remembering, was called 'State of Emergency': this group, that favoured a recombinant afrojazz of a quizzical gentleness achieved in the face of state terror, here making reference to the topical specifics of South African politics with what was always already a metaphor, and very much remains one. As Walter Benjamin wrote in 1940, shortly before his suicide, in his *Theses on History*: "The tradition of the oppressed teaches us that the 'state of emergency' in which we live is *not the exception but the rule*" (my italics).

It's hardly the only road through the material, but I've tried to shape this essay with these words in mind, as a tale of counter-colonial curiosity after the end of empire. And by design, the anthology maps a baggy, sprawling tale involving many publications and many many people: not just a collection of the rock writers at the core of one strand of the tradition, now anyway fairly threadbare. It begins with Penny Reel, and with Val Wilmer in conversation with Richard Williams, and it ends with essays against the grain from David Toop and Liz Naylor and **Paul Gilroy** (pp.352-357). Jon Savage at the start and Bob Stanley towards the close ensure that the story of the teenage pop titles isn't merely sidelined for the sake of a "serious" history. And the final panel (pp.331-351) sees Simon Frith, Penny, Paul and Cynthia Rose asking *who gets to speak, how and where — and who do they speak with? Who maintains the space for engagement, and in whose interests? Who reads, who decides?*

These were some of the questions I began with. And since future histories are unlikely to be so structured by fond personal memory — valuable as that is to get down on the page — perhaps some others are worth outlining.

1). The New Journalism brought great freedoms — a thrilling new eloquence and brilliance of imagination to the page — but at what price? Sometimes, especially early on, it dug deep into the complexities of class or race or sex — but it was often also a weaponised narcissism that led you out the other side untouched, with prejudice affirmed. As adopted by tabloids and broadsheets, a version of punk helped this bellow of the atomised "I" evolve into a solipsistic top-down *faux* oafishness. In the 90s, a high-profile rock-writer-turned-political-columnist like John Harris could argue, for example, that reggae is of little consequence to him because personally he'd only even known public school lads listen to it…

(Peopling the conference panels in 2015, I decided at an early stage against involving some of the bigger beasts to have passed this way: *Oz's* Germaine Greer, say, or Julie Burchill or Danny Baker. "Standing the test of time" is anyway the least helpful phrase in pop thinking: I felt that high-platform success would overwhelm the conversation, given the subtly conflicted multiplicity I wanted to highlight.)

2). Younger writers and readers will likely be shocked at the anxious gender politics, complacent entitlement and cultural parochialism that was too often the norm in this story — and, for all the counter-colonial intent, at how long it apparently took to note this and fight back. It's very hard now to recall how culturally secluded the UK was back then. Yet even if Murray's "creative misunderstandings of the source material" were as much portal as erasure, can we be satisfied with that today? The flights of *Disraeli Gears* were irresistible because they did indeed bust open the cocoons of local heritage. But in just a few years they had flattened into white blues clichés, and faded marks of a vanished openness. Clickbait retro-simplifications of this story will find it hard to moderate their disdain for the performed creole at the heart of it, and the self-validated assumption that every twist still serves justice and equality. *A creole is not a patois*: some way away, the other end of the appropriative exchange continues to slip out of reach, as full of playful quicksilver curiosity as hurt or rage or refusal, rap and techno and dancehall and grime joining jazz or rock'n'roll or soul or reggae before them. There's ways to process all this, and ways not to: too narrow a set of minds and fingers, and the important contradictory detail gets shut down.

3). Though its emergence was no more planned than its demise, from the 60s to the early 80s at least, this squabbling family of publications was arguably the most-read place in the UK in which to encounter voices from beyond quite a narrow milieu, voices invited — on at least some guarded basis — to engage with the tenets and quarrels of pop culture. This sense of a forum for engagement (never a monolith, never monocultural, quite the opposite) was achieved by various means: by bundling as an editorial technology, by "agree to disagree" as both a virtue and a lure at a moment when world-wide broadcast outreach was first flourishing, in all directions. Blues virtuosity was followed as a shared value by disruptive noise, by 'theory', by frivolity, by unending anniversaries of everything — though none of these tactics were effective very long. And as noted, the structure — a contested space as a smorgasbord across rival fandoms — in some ways anticipated the internet. But in other ways the situation today is unrecognisably changed. With undreamt-of cascades of information from all across the globe smashing into one's awareness every minute, self-protection is supplanting curiosity. As the atomised oaf act flourishes, the will to process the hell-stream dwindles: *what if it's trolls all the way down now?*

4). As a young writer, a tail-end boomer battling on behalf of my own tastes, I enjoyed putting older writers on the spot by asking this: *if the past was so great, how did the present end up bad?* Over 40 years, in respect of these worries, in a time when the world's running emergency has at last impinged on us also, this has become a question my own mini-generation Brahminate should now also be asking itself more urgently: *are WE why we're here? Did we really eradicate the impulse to Empire in ourselves? What did we once know that's now needed more than ever?*

One such thing — for me, anyway — is this: the knowledge that cosplay never sleeps. Critical thinking can never *not* be a codeshifting dance across a double consciousness, however small-scale or intimate it may seem. Because it's always an act of translation: on one side the artist and what they want to say; on the other, what audiences believe they want to read or hear. The first needs a patient attention, not least to sift through all manner of showbiz swindle. The second can be a wild complex guesswork, peeling away complacency to reach the layers where fascination with others is found; where we yearn to set ourselves apart from the boredom of just ourselves...

And from the smallish lost world of the underground press to the never-sleeping panic-chatter of the internet right now, some things don't change. Dots are always going to have to be joined, between voices old and new, in vivid, clashing juxtaposition: between revenant old lags like Buckingham McVie or Milford Graves, for example, and Beyoncé or Belle and Sebastian. Between Stormzy or Stonebwoy, or Tryptykon or 2NE1; between Haim and Popcaan, Halo of Flies and (deeper magic from before the dawn of pop) Herbie Hancock. Nilüfer Yanya, TUNEyards, Migos, Zedd; LOOΠΔ or Dua Lipa or Lil Uzi Vert or Daphne and Celeste... Whether it's utopian self-mythologising fanfic or painstaking and self-abnegating exegesis, any guide today through the unprecedented worldwide machine-smash of pop and protest, meme and trend and grift, will only be a temporary surge in the chaos. In this book are some early maps of the achievements and the pitfalls of encounter as conflicted possibility, uncertainties of affinity in argumentative dance with one another, crackle and distortion not as erasure, but as trauma's response to complex mutual challenge. We learnt as we travelled; intermittently we hunted via the music for ways to pin down things that aren't music, in comic-books and fashion, in agitprop and in the avant garde. *Doubts aired as provocations*: I can't imagine all my contributors will agree with every thing I've written above, but that's to the good, because resurgent gleeful cacophony is much more the reality than nostalgia; a polyglot discourse rude *and* smart.

To return to the closing essay, Paul Gilroy argues that as we go forward, we must shift focus away from just these 70s/80s white-boy battles, from the "bromantic ethnography of the *NME* office," as he teasingly calls it in the panel, and from Paul Morley's "conceit". But then he turns this impatience back on itself a little, recognising that such arrogant reshapings and exclusions were also (sometimes) a summoning — a summoning of something, except "you don't know what it is."

— *Mark Sinker, June/February 2017-2018, Hackney*

SOME BEGINNINGS

"The offbeat was fantastic to dance to. I'm a big dancer"
— *Penny Reel*

Covering Lesser Known Musicians in the Mainstream Music Press

Val Wilmer in conversation with Richard Williams, about her career as jazz photographer and writer, and as historian of jazz and Black music in Britain

RW: Val was born, rather mysteriously, in Harrogate in 1941. I think of her as a South London person because that's where she grew up and began listening to jazz and the blues. I'll ask her about that in a moment, but when she was still a teenager she began writing for publications. The first, I think, was *Jazz Journal* and she wrote for many, many after that including, I think most obviously, the *Melody Maker* and *DownBeat*, various others. She wrote to begin with. She started taking photographs. She became as distinguished a photographer as she is a writer and in the years since she's published four important books. *Jazz People*, which is a collection of essays on musicians. *The Face of Black Music*, which is a showcase principally for her photography. *As Serious as Your Life*, which is a remarkable book, a classic study of jazz and the condition of the jazz musician. And *Mama Said There'd Be Days Like This*, which is an equally remarkable autobiography. And one hopes there will be others.

VW: One does.

RW: I know she's working on several others and perhaps we'll get to talk about that. But Val, what I'd like to start by asking you is how it was to be a teenage girl, interested in this music, and beginning to express that interest by writing about it? Before you wrote about it, were there any other women writers about jazz and the blues?

VW: That's a good question. In America there was Helen Oakley, who was Canadian. She produced records as well. There were one or two other people who wrote for *DownBeat* but when I first started out, I didn't think there was. I found out later there was somebody who'd written for *Melody Maker*, I think, at one stage. I can't remember her name, something like Betty Edwards. This is in the 30s, but it turned out that she was actually two people — one was the wife of one of the people who founded the Rhythm Clubs and somebody else who I think perhaps was Leonard Feather's secretary. So I think she was called Betty Edwards, but please don't quote me on that. So, in answer to your query, I don't remember any others. I'm sure there were one or two, but they didn't make themselves known.

[**VW** addition: I apologise for forgetting to mention Kitty Grime, who wrote about jazz and was my good friend. She joined the staff of *Jazz News* shortly after I began to contribute to that little periodical and before that she worked as a publicist and general factotum for Johnny Dankworth and at Carlo Krahmer's Esquire Records. As a publicist at Decca, she was responsible for a number of unsigned pieces in their regular record listings. These, and Kitty's sleeve-notes for *Esquire* and *Jazz News* articles stand up today as intelligent, insightful writing on jazz. Her interviews with Charles Mingus, John Coltrane, Kathy Stobart and others, and reviews of records and performances by Joe Harriott and the Modern Jazz Quartet, were a significant demonstration of what a woman could do in those difficult times. She taught me a lot about how to "be" in the jazz world, and was one of the hippest people I ever knew.]

RW: So when you were a teenage girl finding your way into this music, what was that world like? And what were the people in it like in this country? The people associated with the Rhythm Clubs and so on.

VW: Well, I met some of them. I mean I was very lucky that I met so many people at an early age who were quite influential in the music, the people who wrote about music and the people who'd been record collectors and started the Rhythm Clubs in the 30s.

The reason I met so many people was because I grew up in a very male sort of household. My father died when I was about seven, so we were brought up by my mother — my brother and me — but she took in lodgers who were paying guests that lived with us. And as a result of that, I was exposed to many, many kinds of men that I would never have met in my normal sort of middle-class life, and it was through one of them that I got to know about jazz in the first place, one of them and somebody else, but that's sort of complicated. Before that, I really never had any interest in music at all. In fact I used to turn the radio off when music came on. I didn't like music, which is very odd. And I then met a boy, my first boyfriend, at a church fete. I was about 12 years old, and he liked jazz. He was slightly older than me. He played the trumpet and told me about Louis Armstrong. So that was how I got into it in the first place.

So where I lived in Streatham in South London, there was a shop called the Swing Shop, which was an extraordinary place. It was owned by a man called Dave Carey who was a drummer with Humphrey Lyttelton's band. I got to know him later on. But the man who ran the shop was called Bert Bradfield — and I knew this shop because I knew the sweet shop next door. The mother of one of my school friends ran the sweet shop, so I'd known it since I was about seven, and when I went in next door, I must have been about 12, I suppose. I said, "Have you got any jazz records?" And I guess he hid a smile because that was *all* they sold. He was probably relieved I didn't want the Beverley Sisters or something, you know. So he said, "Well there's one or two over there" — this was the second-hand racks, in the days of 78s. So I went through them, and the first name I recognised was Humphrey Lyttelton, so I thought, "Well, that'll do." And I said, "How much is it?" And it said 2s/6d. And he said, "You can have it for two bob." So I went home and that was it. Put it on the wind-up gramophone and my mother said, "What on earth is that?" And I said, "Oh, that's jazz," and that was the beginning of it all, really.

But because I grew up in this male household I was used to male ideas about things, culture and so on. Girls would not have done these things, like writing to people, not in the same way. Girls would have written fan letters to Johnnie Ray or Guy Mitchell or somebody, but not to musicians, or to other writers. And I don't know how it happened, but I was so convinced that I was going to write about jazz — I can't imagine why, I was so young — that I wrote to all these different writers. And it was through contact with some of them that I first found out about how the life was away from the records.

So I started to meet people and go backstage at concerts, and — sorry, I've wandered off — you were asking me what sort of people were they. Well, the record collectors mostly came from middle class backgrounds — though I don't know if that's actually true, because I always associate the split between the people who liked traditional jazz when it became more popular as being art school, middle-class, and the Modernists, who were essentially an extension of the dance band world, playing modern jazz. And their followers having been working-class people — and class, don't let's forget, was still very important.

So I met people who'd been in the war, in the Airforce, or who worked for the Civil Service, and they'd have these secret lives. They'd go off to listen to jazz, and when the American musicians came over, they loved hanging out with them. It was a relief from the Civil Service job during the day and the wife and meat-and-two-veg at night. And they could pretend that they were in New Orleans or Chicago on the South Side or something, and just hang out with the guys, and you saw all sorts of extraordinary transformations of people because of that contact, and then they'd go back to their ordinary lives.

RW: Your mum chaperoned you to concerts, didn't she, early on?

VW: Well some of them early on, yes. Not all.

RW: What did people in the jazz world make of this teenage girl with her mum? Were you accepted immediately, or did you feel there was any difficulty?

VW: Constant difficulties, because everybody is always summing you up as a "proposition", you know. I mean right from the earliest days. I should rephrase that: not *everybody*, because not everybody was like that. But there was a lot of sexual pressure from people, gradually more as time went on, so I had to deal with that, because it could get a bit overwhelming at times. But at the same time, we have a situation where there is a general lack of respect for women, you know, or girls. But there were also the people who took me seriously, and I single out people like Max Jones, who worked for *Melody Maker*, and Paul Oliver and Derrick Stewart-Baxter, who both wrote about blues. Stewart-Baxter wrote for *Jazz Journal*. All very nice people, and all different kinds of people. And Albert McCarthy who edited *Jazz Monthly*, who was an anarchist. Max had been in the communist party, but Jack Armitage and Jeff Aldam, people like that, were pretty sort of socialist-minded, I suppose, but they came from a fairly right-wing kind of background. A very mixed crowd of people.

RW: And you started writing to musicians in America. When you could find addresses.

VW: Yes.

RW: And it was writing to Jesse Fuller who got you your first piece.

VW: Well, I'd written to other people before that. And I'd had letters from other people too. People like Brian Rust, another person who befriended me — he was a discographer and he was a bit of a sort of, you know, devoted person to discography — and he worked for the BBC in the gramophone library, and he used to invite me to Broadcast House for lunch every now and then. That's when I was about 16. Very helpful to me. And he'd been to the States and had the addresses of lots of musicians [**VW** addition: People such as Polo Barnes who had worked with King Oliver, Omer Simeon who played clarinet with Jelly Roll Morton, and Nick LaRocca, of the Original Dixieland Jazz Band, all of whom replied to my letters]. And sometimes an article about somebody had an address, in *Jazz Journal*, or even *Melody Maker*. So I'd always write to people and say, "Can you send me a signed photograph?"

And I must tell you one of the most exciting things that ever happened to me. I can still remember coming home from school one day, I'm sure it was winter, because it always seemed to be in the wintertime, you know. You'd come in, it's freezing cold and there, on the hall table, was a letter with a New Orleans postmark. I can't tell you how old I was, but it was a letter from Lawrence Marrero, who played banjo with George Lewis and Bunk Johnson, in Johnson's well beloved revivalist band. And Marrero sent me a photograph and wrote me a letter —

I've still got it all somewhere. Obviously I know where the photograph is: it said, "To my pal, Valerie, best wishes, Lawrence Marrero." And then there's this New Orleans postmark and American stamp on the envelope. Do you know what that means to you when you're 15 years old? You're never going to forget that till your dying day, you know. It's a wonderful thing.

So I wrote to lots of different people and most of them actually replied — which is quite interesting given that people often say musicians don't write letters. So, Jesse Fuller — for those who don't know Jesse Fuller, he played guitar and he sang, sort of a folk musician. Not a blues musician. He wrote 'San Francisco Bay Blues' — which of course is quite a famous song — but he also played kazoo and harmonica in a rack round his neck. I believe Bob Dylan copied that rack and the whole set up. And Fuller had a thing he called the 'fotdella' which was a bass that he played with his feet. A bit of a piano and some piano strings, a dreadful thing, it was a thumping weight. It was like having a bass drum, you know, not like a string bass.

So anyway his address was published somewhere, so I thought, "I'll write to him," and back came this lengthy letter, all written in pencil, starting to give me the story of his life. So I wrote back again, and at one point I said to him, "Would you mind writing back in Biro, please? Because the pencil gets smudged." And he obliged, a very obliging man! And then I was ill for quite a while, and I thought, "I'm going to put all these letters together and do a biography, and tell his story." And I sent it to *Jazz Journal* and they published it. And gave me a record in exchange.

RW: As they did in those days.

VW: As they did in those days.

RW: And did that feel like a breakthrough? Did you feel that was the first step on a ladder, and were there steps immediately after that?

VW: Yes, yes I think so. That was very good. I wrote a lot for *Jazz Journal* — but it was part-owned or financed by Decca. I don't know if anybody knows this, but this is how it worked: if you wanted a record you just asked for what you wanted and they'd send off to the wholesalers and it would come directly from them. But it was not much fun working for Sinclair Traill. He was a very mean-spirited person.

But one of the people I got to know was Chris Barber, who of course is very well respected and admired for bringing blues and gospel artists to England. Muddy Waters and Sister Rosetta Tharpe and Brownie McGhee and Sonny Terry and so on. And I was talking to him one day and I said, "I really want to write about jazz one day," and he said, "Why don't you write for *Jazz News*?" And *Jazz News* was owned by him and Harold Pendleton, and they also ran the Marquee together, which was then in Oxford Street, and the National Jazz Federation. So I said, "Oh, could I do that?" And he said, "Yes, just send something in." So I interviewed a drummer called Herbie Lovelle, who was here with Buck Clayton's band. They were touring, with Dave Brubeck and other people. And so I sent it in and the editor said, "Yes, we'll use it."

By this time I had just left school, and I was studying photography nearby the *Jazz News* office at the Regent Street Polytechnic. And so I went into *Jazz News* and I said, "Is it OK? Is it going in?" He said, "Haven't you seen it, darling? It's in there." And there it was. This little piece that said, *Herbie hits out at US music racket*. When I gave it to Herbie, he said, "Oh God, I'll never work in the States again." But he's on one of Aretha's most famous singles, "Running out of Fools", and played with Dylan and everybody, as well as playing jazz. So that was it. And I started writing for *Jazz News* — who wanted an idiot like me to write things for about a pound a time. Or maybe a guinea. Maybe.

RW: You were studying photography. Were the photography and the writing about jazz separate things at that point?

VW: Yes, I think so. Because I didn't really want to be doing photography. I liked photography but I wanted to be a writer. I wanted to work in Fleet Street, by that time, to be a news journalist, really — but for some reason or other I ended up studying photography. It's a very long story. And I was quite good at it, but I didn't finish the course and I didn't like being there. But I carried on doing it, and have always done it.

RW: And then did you begin to see that as a kind of adjunct to the writing?

VW: Yes. At *Jazz News* and *Jazz Journal* and also *Jazz Monthly*.

RW: Were there other writers who also took photographs at the time, or was that something unusual?

VW: I think there probably were but I can't think of anybody off-hand, no. So people liked me because I did both, but it was a blessing and a curse at the same time, because people think of me as a photographer, and nowadays I want them to think of me more as a writer. And they don't seem to have any knowledge of that whole era, of all those little magazines and *Melody Maker* as well, and everything like that.

RW: You spoke of the people who accepted you and were helpful, like Max Jones. Were there people who were actively unhelpful?

VW: [Laughs] Oh God. Well, there's a whole retinue of people over the years, "Oh here comes that chick again," or something like that. Or one musician's wife — who will remain unnamed. I was very friendly with Memphis Slim, and he took me to this musician's house one night for dinner, and his wife said, "Don't bring that girl again." I don't know what I was supposed to have done. I hadn't done anything. I think either she wanted Slim's attention or she wanted to flirt with him, or else she thought I was, you know, beyond the pale because I was apparently going out with a Black man. Although I wasn't. It could have been any of those things.

But there was this very odd thing that used to go on. Not all these musicians I knew were Black, but most of them were, and so people rushed forward, mostly white men, rushed forward to welcome in the great stars. And women rushed forward to welcome them in other aspects — possibly, more entertaining aspects. There was a lot of cross-cultural exchange in those days. But men who saw these people as their heroes, they could take their wives with them but the wives were very much there in a wifely capacity, and so any woman who was around who was not somebody's wife — it sounds awful but it's just the way it was — was seen as a slag, or a sort of obstacle, you know. And one of the people who was connected with the tour (again I'm not going to go into detail about who it was) — he was the first person who helped me get back-stage — but as soon as I got published and became fairly well known, he became hostile, and made life very difficult for me. He once had me thrown out of the Hammersmith Odeon when I was taking pictures. Another time Buck Clayton was involved with this woman he was with for a long time, and this guy would always say to him, "Don't bring her with you." "Don't let her come," he'd say to other people. So it was just a mixed attitude to women. Race was at the bottom of it, I think, but not always. It was difficult, really.

RW: But in the world of collectors and critics in Britain at that time, was there any sense of "Let's keep this woman out of our boy's club"?

VW: No, not exactly, but it's the same thing that still goes on today. Which is that they don't think of you when the time comes to invite people to something. I don't think people were hostile, but somebody would say, "Oh, what does she know about jazz?" Or "Everything she learned was in bed with musicians". Well, as my friend Kitty Grime said, "What better place to learn?" Which is true. When they sent people out to the colonies they always used to say, "Get yourself a mistress as soon as you get there, so you can learn the language." I rest my case.

RW: The language of love.

VW: Or something.

RW: I hate to change the subject.

VW: I'm sorry, I've gone too far. I don't know if I've gone too far, but that's the way it was. There's no point in sitting around pretending these things didn't happen. In every field of endeavour women have had to put up with shit, frankly, all the time. Not to put too fine a point on it.

RW: *Jazz News* always seemed to me to be a bit lighter on its feet then, to reflect the day-to-day world of the London jazz scene. More than *Jazz Journal* or *Jazz Monthly*, which were rather more academic, graphical, analytical things. But of course it didn't last very long, did it?

VW: No. The interesting thing was that when the Trad Boom came along, *Jazz News* actually went weekly. So there was quite a lot in it — but they had a Polish typesetter, so there was some very interesting typos. 'Memphis Slum' was one of them. Or else Bob Dawbarn at *Melody Maker* perhaps, with a photograph of Muddy Waters, in the note to the blockmaker Bob said something like, you know, "Muddy Waters do so-and-so mate", and it came out as "Muddy Waters blah blah, oh mate!" with an exclamation mark. I think that was *Melody Maker*. But there were all sorts of interesting things in these papers, and if anybody bothers to go to the National Jazz Archive at Loughton and finds copies of *Jazz News*, or perhaps the British Library, you'll have many hours of amusement.

RW: You were there at that very significant time when R&B came into play among jazz musicians like Chris Barber, and Alexis Korner and Blues Incorporated. That was a pretty interesting time, wasn't it?

VW: Yes.

RW: And you saw all the sides of that. You weren't somebody who just stuck on the jazz side.

VW: No, I mean that's one of the strange things nowadays — how the worlds of jazz and blues are so separate. In fact people remark on how strange it is that you have been interested in both, that you were hanging out with Champion Jack Dupree and also John Coltrane. Not that I was hanging out with John Coltrane, but you know. And it wasn't strange at that time. People had a thirst for this music, whether they knew it or not. They had a thirst for authenticity and for African-American music — and I suppose in another sense rock'n'roll provided this, and so it was all there for you, but...

So a lot of the jazz players started playing rhythm and blues. Graham Bond was one — so that people don't even think about him as originally a jazz player — and Dick Heckstall-Smith and then of course Chris Barber. He had a rhythm and blues band for a while. And people would play with each other. There was a lot of cross-fertilisation, and the papers at the time, like the *Melody Maker* and *Jazz News*, reflect this. Folk music is in there too. When Big Bill Broonzy came to England, somebody took him to a place off Charing Cross Road, where both jazz and folk musicians used to hang out with taxi drivers and women on the game and everything. They said, "Oh well, you can go there and have a meal and a drink after hours." And Dizzy Reece turned up, a Jamaican trumpet player associated with bebop, and after Broonzy had a meal and a few drinks, he started to play, and he played with Dizzy Reece.

Now who knows about that? And who would think about that sort of thing happening today? People would go down to the Mandrake and jam together. People think about the Mandrake as being where Dylan Thomas went, and Francis Bacon, people like that. An arts place. But Josh White would jam with people like Laurie Morgan on drums. That type of thing.

All sorts of cross-fertilisation was going on. And actually because I was a jazz person I missed a lot of it. I was around some of it, but I didn't pursue the rhythm and blues world as such, or the pop world. I mean I went to see Chuck Berry and people like that. But all the worlds were on your doorstep whether you pursued them or not, so you couldn't avoid them. Whether you wanted to or not, really. So you'd get people like Georgie Fame going to the Flamingo, and you'd go in there and the first record you hear is Lord Kitchener and, oh, what's it called?

RW: 'Dr Kitch.'

VW: 'Dr Kitch', exactly, yes. 'Dr Kitch'. And then the next record they played would be Dexter Gordon, 'Doin' All Right'. And Jimmy McGriff's 'All About My Girl'. Those were the records, and then Georgie Fame comes on and what is it? It's blues, it's jazz, it's rock'n'roll, it's rhythm and blues — and he knows all the right people, and he uses the influences and uses them well. A wonderful place to be.

RW: When did your response to Black music turn into an interest in Black culture more generally and in more depth?

VW: Well, very early on. Because one of my primers, if you like, was a book called *Jazz* by Rex Harris, who was one of the early jazz writers. He was an optician, and one of the Rhythm Club founders, and he wrote this book, which was published by Pelican. I read it from cover to cover several times. And of course it talks about the background of jazz and it talks about Africa and slavery and, you know, New Orleans and plantations and so on, and work songs. It's all there. Maybe we disagree with some of his conclusions today, we know more about certain things — that "up the river from New Orleans" business is no longer relevant in terms of history — but it was all there. And it seems to me that all the serious jazz lovers knew about this background and it was discussed. If you go back to the 1940s you'll find articles about it, and one or two articles about racism, too.

And from an early time when I used to go back-stage I would meet Caribbean people and African people and British-born Black people, who were all part of this picture. They've been written out of the history, and I'm doing my best to write them back in again. Some were musicians, some were just ordinary people, but I got to know a lot of them. And one of them — I think Max Jones introduced me to him — was a very well known man called Edward Scobie. From Dominica, a journalist and broadcaster. He'd been a trumpeter briefly himself at school, and he grew up part of his life in Harlem with an uncle who lived there, and then he came here with the RAF during the war. He was around the clubs and went on to broadcast, and was involved with a magazine called *Flamingo*.

I'm sorry, I've jumped forward. He was involved with a magazine called *Tropic* which was owned by a Jamaican and partly funded with Nigerian money, as far as I know. And Scobie said, "Why don't you write something for us?" And so I did. I wrote a couple of pieces and then he said to me, "Can you go down to the Marquee and write an article about Joe Harriott?" Well, I knew about Joe Harriott. I don't think I'd ever seen him. But Scobie said, "He's got this new music, this free-form music, can you write us a piece about him?" So that was in 1960, which is a long time ago — and I went down there, and Joe Harriott was engaged in a slightly strong discussion in the pub with the Marquee's manager about money, so I realised that wasn't going to go anywhere. So I talked to two other members of the band, and that's how I got to meet them. And I wrote an article about it, took some photographs — and it was published as a three-page spread. And so that was fantastic. I was really delighted with it.

Then when I left college, the first job I had was at the National Gallery, printing photographs in the bowels of the earth, a very fascinating place. And one day everybody was out at lunch and I wasn't supposed to answer the phone, but I did. And it was a man phoning up to order copies of some of the Hogarth prints from the 18th century that have Black characters in them. And it was Edward Scobie. So I said, "Oh, this is me, Valerie. I'm here working." He said, "Why are you working there?" I said, "Well, because I was supposed to work for *Jazz News*, but that didn't work out, and I seem to be working here." He said, "Why don't you come and work for us? Come and see us. Come tonight." And I went up there and the next thing is that I'm working for this Black magazine called *Tropic* — which was an extraordinary experience. It only lasted for a short time because they ran out of money. The Nigerians decided that they'd had enough. They weren't making anything back, I guess. But I spent about three months there, and nobody could have had a better education.

One thing that happened before it closed was when it was getting on for winter time. I can't remember the name of the organisation, but it was led by Colin Jordan, who was the successor to Oswald Mosley, and the magazine were always having trouble with these people — this was a little Caribbean enclave off Edgware Road — and they came by one night with a gun, I think it was a rifle, and they shot through the windows. So there was a pane of glass missing... that was an education. As was the fact they hadn't got enough money to repair the window, so it was all done up with hardboard and plywood, and it was absolutely freezing. And I had to sit there with my coat on all through the winter with a paraffin heater in the middle of the floor. And this is very educational, yes. The shop was on the corner of a road, and next to it was a café and a barber shop. There was a shebeen at the back of the café which I knew nothing about, and all sorts of other offices upstairs. Little hole-in-the-wall rooms, gambling and travel agents and a man that did pornographic photography. Can't get away from it.

Everything was going on there, but because I was sitting at the desk — the job I ended up with was answering the phone and two-finger typing letters — everybody under the sun came in through that door. Anybody going to the barbers would come in, and anybody going to the café. I learned to eat rice-and-peas and salt fish-and-ackee and drink, what did I drink? Guinness punch? I don't think so, but lots of tea with Carnation milk, and coffee. And that was another education, because you met all these people you would never meet normally. Actors, writers, artists, businessmen — and people who came there because they needed to fill in a form, and they couldn't understand it. They were either semi-illiterate, or they didn't understand things. So at 18 years old I found myself being asked to help people fill in forms, which I knew nothing about. But it certainly was a salutary lesson to realise that people couldn't do it.

So this gives you a background to the world of music and to Scobie. Though I realise now it wasn't only him writing them, I thought he was the person who wrote all these historical articles. He would write articles about Toussaint L'Ouverture and the Haitians. He wrote about Rastafarians, he wrote about Ira Aldridge, the actor, and his daughter Amanda Aldridge, she was a composer. And he also wrote about Edward Wilmot Blyden, who was one of the first pan-Africanists. All these kinds of people. So I learned about them — and then one day my cheque bounced, and I stopped learning for a while. But this was a basic education that's without equal, because you could go to university and learn about Black history, but you won't learn in the same way as experiencing a mixture. Ira Aldridge and then you've Rastafarians, then Blyden and Toussaint L'Ouverture, and then you have somebody saying, "Please can you help me fill this form?" And then you go and eat your rice-and-peas. So it's all very educational.

RW: Did you feel any tension within yourself about being a white person writing about Black culture, reflecting it and translating it for a wider audience?

VW: Frequently. Anybody who doesn't is a fool, I would say. At another stage in my life I got a grant to do photography, the only one I ever got, from the Arts Council. I'd photographed Black women in Mississippi, and had been in the South several times taking photographs, and this was something I thought would be a good subject for a book. And a man down there said to me — a white man, he was in authority, so I had to go to him for permission for something — and he said, "Why do you want to do that?" I said, "Well, it's what I want to do." He said, "When you say that, 'Black, women, Mississippi,' you get a certain picture." And I said, well, I didn't say to him, "precisely" — but that's what I wanted to say — and I said, "Oh, well I guess so." And then I got another grant, and I wanted to go back and do some more. And frankly, life in Mississippi was so, so dire. Education was not compulsory there at that time.

RW: When was this?

VW: 1974 and 1976. Mind you, I'd been down there before a couple of times. And when they spoke of Mississippi, the people there often said "The State that has four 'I's and cannot see" — which of course is very true. Poverty was so extreme, the way people lived. People were very generous to me and the friend I travelled with — but at the end of it I decided that I wasn't the person to do this book. Not that it should necessarily be done by someone Black, but it certainly shouldn't be done by an English person. I mean, I do feel that the outsider is sometimes the better observer than the person in the community, and we know this all through history, but on that occasion I didn't do it.

RW: Why?

VW: Because I didn't feel I was the person. I felt that I couldn't be authentic. My picture was me looking *at* them, not how it *was*. And I felt the same thing when I went to West Africa one time. I started to take photographs and then I couldn't do it anymore. A lot of people this happens to, it's not rare, but most people are arrogant and pretend it doesn't happen. I'm trying to explain that you don't always feel comfortable, and I certainly often hadn't felt comfortable writing about music — but people have said to me, "Carry on doing what you're doing because we need you." Even people like Max Roach — who would be very, very critical of any white person doing anything. And that was the response I got from people, that what I had to say was important, so if I had doubts in myself I was encouraged by the musicians to carry on. But, you know, we're talking about all sorts of things here. It's very difficult in your life, you can't compartmentalise things, obviously everything crosses over — but what I'm thinking in a Mississippi field is not what I'm thinking when I'm sitting at my typewriter writing about Albert Ayler, and it would be wrong to say that it's one and the same because it isn't. We might like to talk about a 'Black community', but of course that's absolute rubbish, there's no such thing.

RW: You started off with fairly traditional and mainstream jazz and blues, and you eventually made a kind of leap into modern forms of jazz. How did that happen? Was that a simple, logical thing?

VW: Well no. Early on I mentioned Bert Bradfield who used to run the Swing Shop. Well in those days, the days of shellac records, mostly 10-inch 78s, they got broken often. Very fragile. And he used to get records that were chipped and cracked, but still playable. If they got chipped, you'd play them without the first part. If they were cracked, you just put up with it. And one day he gave me some records by Bud Powell and Stan Getz, people I would never have listened to if I'd stuck with Rex Harris's ideas about jazz: Harris wrote that it all ended with Charlie Parker, you know. And of course that was that, and so I moved forward. And some people used to say to me, "Why do you like all this modern jazz, or whatever you want to call it?" Older people. And I'd say, "Well, you like the music of your generation and I like the music of mine." And, you know, people like Archie Shepp, Albert Ayler, well, they're slightly older than me, but people like Milford Graves and Lester Bowie were born the same year as me. So we're the same generation.

RW: It's funny that that music, which is now the best part of 60 years old, is still called the avant-garde.

VW: Not by me.

RW: No. And it's still scaring people. It's never quite been assimilated. It's never become part of the wallpaper in a way that earlier forms of jazz have.

VW: It's extraordinary, isn't it? The Sun Ra Arkestra under Marshall Allen, now over 90, has been having this enormous revival of interest in this country — and all sorts of people go down to my local club, Café Oto. And sometimes you can hardly get in the door there's so many people. And one of the saxophone players has started to live here, has a great love with somebody here, so he's part of the local wallpaper as well. So they all think it's the most wonderful thing, and of course it is, and it's very entertaining. But I was talking to a woman that I know who's a very good saxophonist whose playing shows moments of freedom, and I said to her, "Have you ever seen them?" So she said no, so I said, "The next time they come I'll take you there." So we went down there and she was up and down like a yoyo filming it on her phone, which I thought was terribly uncool, but there you are. And then she came, and she said, "Oh, isn't it wonderful, it's wonderful." So I said yes. She said, "Do you know what? It sounds wrong, what they do is wrong but, you know, it sounds right…" I thought, "I can't believe this woman is saying this today. That's what we've been saying since time began." Since ragtime was first heard, or a cakewalk was walked.

RW: Was it exposure to the music and the culture that politicised you, radicalised you?

VW: Oh God. You know, when I was at school I had a friend — fortunately still a friend — whose father had been in the Communist Party, and somehow or other we ended up joining the Young Communist League and going to meetings, and it was all above my head. I didn't really understand it. But it was a world that you're in. I mean some people weren't in it, but a lot of people were — and Communism, Marxism, was just sort of in the air. And out of that crowd of people I met others, and for a long time I used to go to meetings at this sort of Marxist art group — which was really about drinking beer in Clapham. It wasn't about anything much else. But that was a place that I used to go all the time and every week.

So I was sort of aware of politics. And there was a kind of movement afoot to have a sort of reading group — all terribly half-hearted and I was just on the fringes of it — but one of the books was called *A Star to Steer By*, by a man called Hugh Mulzac, who was the first Black man to be a ship's commander in the American navy. I found that book very fascinating. I think he was going to be the captain on Marcus Garvey's ship when Garvey had the Black Star Line, but of course that didn't come to anything. And years later, when my book *The Face of Black Music* was published by an American publisher, and I had a very good relationship with them, I said to them, "Are you going to go up to Harlem and sell it?" "Oh no," said this woman. This was in 1976 — and at that time, I should point out, from about 1970-76, round about that period, white Americans were in total fear of anybody Black who came within six inches of them. So there was always this sort of thing that was in the air. "Oh no," she said, "We're not, no." I said, "Well, why not?" She said, "Well, who would we get to go up there?" So I said, "I'll go."

So I went up. I knew there was the two or three book shops there, and one of them was in Lenox Avenue, the Liberation Book Store. And I went in there and, "Yes, what do you want?" It was very sort of like that. And so I said, "Well, I've done this book, and I thought you might be interested." Anyway, it was all very spiky and, you know, like that. But she said, "All right, well, we'll take a couple of copies." I said, "Not more?" She said, "That's enough," and I said to myself, "Woman, just keep your distance" — that sort of thing.

Anyway, I asked her name. And she said, "Una Mulzac." So I said, "Are you related to Hugh Mulzac?" She said, "My father." I said, "Oh, I read his book years ago." And from then on it was a slightly different relationship. And I used to go back there from time to time and see her. She was never exactly cuddly with me, I must admit, but I produced some postcards and she bought those from me and sold them, and I bought my books from her. And the other day I was reading something and the bill fell out and it said 'Liberation Book Store', you know. And I felt a great wave of fondness for it. But, what an extraordinary thing, that white people in New York were so terrified that they couldn't get on the subway and go up to Harlem. But that's the way it was.

So as you say, how would you not be politicised? You know, the other day I heard somebody talking about Steve Reich on the radio. And I interviewed him once for *Melody Maker* — and I'd just come back from Ghana, and he'd been to Ghana too, the same place as a matter of fact, and heard the same music. I was talking about a person who was playing with him — who happened to be an African-American who was a friend of mine. I can tell you this now because I feel I must. This was in Michael Nyman's house, and we were talking and I mentioned this man, and [Reich] said, "Oh yes, well of course, he's one of the only Blacks you can talk to." So I said, "Oh really?" He said, "Blacks are getting ridiculous in the States now." And I thought, "This is a man who's just done this piece called *Drumming* which everybody cites as a great thing. He's gone and ripped off stuff he's heard in Ghana — and he's telling me that Blacks are ridiculous in the States now." I rest my case. Wouldn't you be politicised?

A writer-photographer since 1960, Val Wilmer has contributed to Jazz Journal, Melody Maker, Down Beat, Spare Rib and The Wire.

Music, arts and sports journalist Richard Williams joined Melody Maker in the late 60s, going on to be its editor in the late 70s. More recently, he was artistic director of the Berlin Jazz Festival 2015-17.

I Learnt to Eat Curry Goat, Rice-and-Peas

Val Wilmer remembers the Black publications she first wrote for, in the early 60s

Ever since I started writing about jazz and photographing musicians, I've been asked why do you do what you do? In other words, what's a white girl doing here? It's an understandable question, perhaps — and an obvious one, should the questioner be a journalist in search of a quote. Perhaps. But most of the time, it seems to me to suggest astonishment that a middle-class white Englishwoman should have chosen to associate with a society other than her own.

It's certainly been a complicated journey, and not always easy — not least because of having to deal with questions of this nature. The questions still come — and continue to bother me. However, having referred at the conference to my association with a number of 'black' publications in my early days in journalism, it may be useful to elaborate here on how these connections came about, while providing an indication of how the experience affected me at the time, and continues to influence the way I see the world. It is mainly because of these exceptional early opportunities that I became involved in documenting the story of Black musicians in Britain a quarter century later.

If we are to believe the contention of the late Jim Godbolt in *A History of Jazz in Britain 1919-50* (1984), the contribution of (local) Black musicians to British jazz was "slight" (p.188). The claim is echoed in his *A History of*

Jazz in Britain 1950-70 (1989) where — with certain notable exceptions — it was "minimal" (p.120), though he did allow that the mid-thirties period was "enriched by the presence of West Indian musicians" (p.119). He provided a list of names of some individuals active in that period (a flawed list, since at least two of them had yet to arrive in the UK), and would change his stance slightly in the second edition of the *History* (2010), presumably after some prodding. Nevertheless, it is only recently, and following the production of evidence, that his original statements have been challenged.

At the same time, a tendency to exaggerate the extent of the local black input has begun to emerge, as Afrocentric partisans seize on a name here and there to exalt, getting the details wrong in the process. A recent book by Lloyd Bradley is an example of this. Because this author is completely unaware of the intricacies of popular music in Britain in the pre-war, wartime and immediate post-war periods, *Sounds Like London: 100 Years of Black Music in the Capital* (2013) is laden with inaccuracies and misconceptions. Furthermore, he fails to credit the research work that provided him with his material, or to identify a single source — an omission especially galling to me since, in many cases, those sources are articles written by me, for *Mojo*, the *Guardian* and the *Independent on Sunday*. Other writers, and even musicians, continue to perpetuate erroneous views. A common mistake is the merging of two musicians who share the same name. The Jamaican trumpeter/ bandleader Leslie Hutchinson, known latterly as 'Jiver' (a business name he disliked), has nothing to do with Leslie Hutchinson the suave cabaret artist and pianist from Grenada known as 'Hutch': their personalities, politics and relative success could not be more dissimilar. But hey, none of this is particularly surprising because the story itself is complicated, and to this day few people have dug sufficiently deep to pretend any grasp of accuracy. The small group of individuals working in this field are aware of one another's contribution.

In attempting to tell aspects of the story of Black musicians in Britain, I have employed a variety of means. These include writing biographies in two standard sources, the *New Grove Dictionary of Jazz* and the *Oxford Dictionary of National Biography*, as well as numerous articles and obituaries in the specialist and national press. In addition, I have recorded several lengthy oral histories for the National Sound Archive of the British Library. I became involved in this work in the 1980s, inspired by getting to know Jamaican musician Louis Stephenson, a London resident since 1935, and through meeting Peter Fryer, author of *Staying Power* (1984), the standard work on the history of Black people in Britain. At this time there was very little interest in the subject, and some of the negative comments that greeted my ambition were astounding, especially from within the jazz world. But I persevered and continue to do so. However, given the received notion of the history of jazz in Britain, I doubt that I would have embarked on this project had I not had the privilege of an early education in the black community.

I began listening to jazz as a teenager in the 1950s, and moved into the London scene on leaving school. A strip cartoon by Yorkshire cartoonist Dave Robinson illustrates the complexity of the picture at the end of that decade as I recall it. It depicted an encounter between a (serious) white jazz enthusiast and a (conservative) black man. "Must be hell to be black in this country," opines the white man, only to be stunned by his new friend's enthusiasm for warm beer, the climate — "and Victor Sylvester!" Even as a youngster, I recognised this picture. Any attempt to engage an African student or the average West Indian in a conversation about Jelly Roll Morton or Charlie Parker was generally futile, as most metropolitan jazz fanciers knew. As for Sylvester (correctly Silvester), the leading proponent of strict tempo ballroom dancing, he was still a popular figure despite the emergence of rock'n'roll, and was held in esteem by many newcomers for whom the local palais was often their only social outlet. But while encounters of the kind Robinson depicted were not rare, neither were they entirely representative, as I discovered when I began to move in African and Caribbean circles and met individuals who liked jazz. Furthermore, while Robinson's drawing may have raised a chuckle at the time, it was only a cartoon — and, as I was to discover, the artist himself knew better.

'The West Indianisation of Dave' was the title of a fascinating memoir of Robinson's experiences in the Caribbean community, where he hung out at parties, played the bongos, drank Guinness punch and all the rest. This article appeared in *Tropic* (1959-60), a new monthly publication aimed at a 'black' readership, to which I, too, was a contributor. *Tropic* was published in London and backed by Nigerian money. It had a Jamaican proprietor and was edited by Edward Scobie, a journalist from Dominica who wrote about black history. Scobie was a former RAF officer who had been England since the war, and I probably met him through Max Jones, doyen of jazz writers and a staffer at the *Melody Maker*. Both these men influenced me greatly. I was 18 years old and already published in a couple of jazz magazines when Scobie accepted two of my interviews for *Tropic*. He followed up by asking me to write a piece about saxophonist Joe Harriott and his new 'free form' music. I sallied forth, pen and camera in hand, to listen to Harriott's group at the Marquee in Oxford Street, and met the musicians. When Scobie printed my story over three pages, it launched me into the big time — in my eyes, that is. The rest of the world paid little attention.

The magazine had offices in a street-corner shop-front off Edgware Road. I ended up working there typing letters, answering the phone and trying to keep warm behind a bullet-scarred window, the startling legacy of a fascist attack. In the three months I spent there, I learnt to eat curry goat, rice-and-peas, and drink coffee thick with Carnation milk, while helping recent arrivals to fill in forms. Many of the people I met at *Tropic* became my friends, among them two Jamaicans: trombonist Herman Wilson who came here in the same band as Joe Harriott, and Boysie Grant, an older man who sang on the first bluebeat band record to enter the charts. Another was Adam Fiberesima, a composer who played piano in a Nigerian nightclub while studying at college with his countryman Fela Kuti.

Jazz was not part of everyone's story, but as Black music it had cultural significance. I soon found that the music, and the fortunes of its creators, informed the lives of many of the people I was getting to know, and, in the process, it gave me a new way of seeing. The other contents of the magazine were informative too, helping place the music in a context apart from the English jazz world — something I don't think I would have discovered had I remained the other side of that shattered window.

I was learning on the job — literally. I was not 'of' that world, but I was definitely in it, and what I came to understand, while sitting at my desk, wrapped up in my coat and green mohair sweater, has informed my work ever since, even when there seems to be no obvious connection.

Tropic was not the first Black publication in Britain — credit for that goes back to 1912 and the *African Times and Orient Review* — but like earlier efforts, lack of finance ensured that it would be short-lived. Scobie had lived in New York as a youngster before coming to Britain, and began contributing to the African American press soon after his RAF days, mostly notably to *Ebony* and the *Chicago Defender*. He was well-connected, and by 1961 had found another local outlet in Britain. *Flamingo* (1961-67) was another monthly, which arose from the ashes of *Tropic*, although this time its ownership was white. Chalton Publications produced separate British and USA editions for a readership that reached across Africa and the Caribbean, and it was edited jointly, by several journalists.

In 1964 I spent six weeks in West Africa for *Flamingo*, but before that Scobie commissioned me to write a number of articles for a series entitled "Caribbean Musicians in Britain". My interviews with Coleridge Goode, Frank Holder, Pete Pitterson and Herman Wilson followed Scobie's own piece on Joe Harriott and an essay by Jamaican journalist Dick Pixley about Vincentian trumpeter/poet Shake Keane. Later on, when John Harold, a white Englishman with a West African background, became an editor, I did a long piece on "Jazz and the African Beat" and wrote about the South African singer Danny ("Moon River") Williams, and two Nigerians: Fiberesima, the composer, and trumpeter Mike Falana. *Flamingo* published articles on African Highlife bands in this period, several of which I saw when they came to London to play for student dances. I. K. Dairo MBE, Nigerian pioneer of juju music, was the undoubted star. I interviewed him in Streatham, sitting at my mother's kitchen table.

Chalton closed down most of the *Flamingo* editions prior to 1966, when the magazine was sold, to an East Africa-based American trader, an unscrupulous man who brought out a handful of issues before running it into the ground. The magazine was greatly missed, not least by its contributors, black, white and Asian, and some of us continued to meet at our local, the Albion in Ludgate Circus. I went on to collaborate with two Nigerian journalists, and together we produced articles for *Drum* magazine when it opened a London office, and for an agency called Africa Features, owned by the same company. Eventually I worked under my own steam for the agency, as a writer and photographer, and while my articles were by no means confined to music, I did manage profiles of musicians, among them Adam Fiberesima and drummers Bayo Martins and Gaspar Lawal. I also wrote about one of my trips to the USA where I encountered African retentions in the Deep South. All this material was syndicated across the African continent and published in some unlikely places.

Parallel with all this activity was the appearance of several titles published by Aubrey Baynes, an early circulation manager at *Flamingo*. Baynes, who came from St Vincent in the Eastern Caribbean, was one of the many ambitious individuals I met at *Tropic*. I wrote three articles for his *Daylight International* (1963-64), although these were not about music. In 1965 Baynes and the Guyanese writer Jan Carew were associated with a short-lived publication called *Magnet*, the launch of which was attended by Malcolm X, less than two weeks before his assassination. *West Indian World* (1971-85) would be Baynes's enduring memorial, and this, together with the earlier *West Indian Gazette* and *Caribbean Times*, marked the arrival of a weekly community newspaper as opposed to a periodical. By mid-decade I had stopped writing for Black publications, with a handful of exceptions. I had made three visits to New York in the 1960s, while writing about music and photographing musicians for jazz magazines, and I now began to concentrate on working as a freelance for *Melody Maker*, a much-respected music weekly with a large circulation. These are some snapshots of those early days.

A writer-photographer since 1960, Val Wilmer has contributed to Jazz Journal, Melody Maker, DownBeat, Spare Rib and The Wire.

Hundreds of Records, Just Hundreds of Records

Penny Reel looks back at nearly six decades of Jamaican ska, and how this happiest of musics had a darker social backdrop, a sound and a context that no one was writing about in the early 1960s

I still think that ska music in its original form is the most joyous music ever made. Ska music determined the careers of many aspiring hopefuls, and really put Jamaica on the map.

When I first heard proto-ska, in 1960, it was shuffle and rhythm and blues, but with a difference, the backbeat. You could always identify a Jamaican record by its backbeat, and this would come to the fore when ska was born, around 1962. It held for the next four years before transmuting into rocksteady and then reggae, but that's another story. It is the period between 1962 and 1966 that I wish to discuss here, emphasising the joyousness of ska.

It was Island, formed in 1962, with 'Independent Jamaica', by Lord Creator (Kentrick Patrick), that benefitted most from this sudden emergence of ska, and its second release, Owen Gray's 'Patricia', produced by a Chinese-Jamaican citizen, one Leslie Kong, which played around a stall that sold the record, and had a sizeable West Indian crowd. These were the days that one literally hung around a stall selling records.

Leslie Kong also ran the label Beverley's. Derrick Morgan was the main catalyst for Beverley's success. Morgan, who had released records before for various companies, such as Smiths, Duke Reid, Coxsone Dodd, Prince Buster and others, was in the vanguard of this label's success, supported by others like Jimmy Cliff, Desmond Dekker, Andy & Joey, and Robert Marley. Derrick had hits with 'Gypsy Woman'. 'Housewives' Choice', 'The Hop', and 'It's True My Darling', often accompanied by Patsy, a female singer. These were well produced records, and very different to what had gone before.

Ska is, simply, two verses, an instrumental break, and another verse. Most ska records pursue this simple theme.

The thing that gets me about these records is the instrumental break in the middle. With Coxsone, this instrumental break was often played by a saxophone (Roland Alphonso) or a trombone (Don Drummond). With King Edwards, it was usually played by a trumpet (Baba Brooks) and a harmonica (Charlie Organera). About half the records released were instrumentals. With Beverley's, which were much better produced than the earlier records, this was performed by trumpet, harmonica, saxophone, trombone, etc, played by the same musicians. They lost their muddy sound and were much brighter than before.

There is also Prince Buster, although he came a bit later, and proved the most innovative of them all. This was the scene around 1962. Pre-eminent were singers such as the aforementioned Derrick Morgan, joined by others, like Eric Morris, Roy Panton, Lloyd Clark, and many other aspiring hopefuls. All were teenage, many as young as 13. The thing that underpinned these records was the brilliant instrumentation of them.

This was all brought about by the Declaration of Independence from Britain, in August 1962. It produced a period of hopefulness for Jamaicans. This lasted until 1966, when the problems between the PNP (People's National Party) and JLP (Jamaican Labour Party) came to the fore. This produced a very different kind of music, rocksteady, that was slower and more in tune to the dances. For the first year after 1960, all these records were released on Blue Beat in Britain, whoever they came from, and Rio, with Island joining in 1961. Previously, these records by

Chris Blackwell were released on Starlite. Prince Buster was to go and release records on Blue Beat for the remainder of his early career, later on Fab and Prince Buster. Coxsone, who had released records on Blue Beat, switched to Island. King Edwards stayed with Rio. Duke Reid also joined Island. Others like Moo's, Smiths and Eddy Seaga's Whirl, who had started alongside the others, were gradually out of the music by 1965. Edwards didn't last much longer than that either.

So the scene around 1965 was predominantly held by Coxsone and Duke Reid, with upcoming productions from Beverley's, Randy's, Moody's, Crystal (Derrick Harriott) and Linden Pottinger's High Note.

This was what precipitated one of the greatest musical confrontations in ska, when Prince Buster accused Derrick Morgan of being a "blackhead chinaman", because Morgan recorded with Leslie Kong, probably because he was paid more. And Derrick responded with 'Blazing Fire', a huge hit for Beverley's. This would continue over five or six or seven records. These records had immediate effect on the burgeoning ska scene.

The rivalries between the sound systems, especially Prince Buster and Coxsone Dodd, was to produce many records, quite apart from Derrick Morgan and Prince Buster. Delroy Wilson, who was 13 at the time, weighed in records written by Coxsone and Lee Perry to attack Buster. There were tracks like the Duke Reid-produced 'Downbeat Burial', an attack on Coxsone, and ripostes by Coxsone such as 'Poison on Bond Street', Duke Reid's home.

As a youth, living in Britain, I was mystified by these attacks, and yet intrigued. It was all clothed in the joy I mentioned earlier. In addition to this there were anonymous attacks on persons unknown by the singers, including tracks like 'Ungrateful People', by Shenley Duffus, 'Prince In The Pack' by Delroy Wilson, and 'Spit In The Sky', also by Delroy Wilson. He was given these songs to sing by the older Coxsone, and Scratch. I doubt if he knew what he was singing about. Things got really nasty towards the beginning of the rocksteady era; then there were actual guns and firebombs used against each other. Fights were common. Duke Reid, Edwards and Prince Buster railed against Coxsone for much of the early part of the decade. The three former were JLP; Coxsone was PNP.

Politics played a huge part in this. Seaga, who was to become the Prime Minister towards the early 80s, was the housing minister and probable CIA operative. In West Kingston in the 50s, Back O' Wall, the area of Rastafari settlement, was notorious as the worst slum in the Caribbean area. In 1963 Seaga was elected to office representing the JLP, and was appointed minister for development. He has never lost an election since. Between 1963 and 1965, he razed Back O' Wall and Dungle, and built the Tivoli Gardens, known as Rema and Jungle, housing JLP supporters in these new estates, much to the chagrin of the PNP. It was all-out war. These urban developments were behind most of the changes in Jamaican society at this time, and many rocksteady records refer to them, albeit obliquely and in a more personal manner.

This conflict has proved enduring ever since. Even now, in the early years of the 21st century, repercussions continue. Rocksteady proved the end of ska, and with it went the joy in the music. Ever since then, it's been pure conflict, which has lasted 50 years.

When I was 12 in 1960 I discovered a stall run by a Jewish man, named Nat. He sold Blue Beat. He was the first man to sell Blue Beat in this part of London. He had five records only, they were the only five records that were released in Jamaica at this time. There was a Higgs and Wilson, 'The Robe', there was an Alton and Eddy, 'Muriel', there was a Beresford Rickets, 'Glory Alleluiah', there was a Laurel Aitken, 'Boogie In My Bones', there was a Jackie Edwards, and there was an Owen Grey.

And then within a couple of years there were hundreds of records, just hundreds of records. It's since been known to me that Jamaica released the third largest number of records after England and the United States. Now that is incredible, because it's an island of two million people. But nobody was writing about it in the UK. The main musicians for this were the Skatalites: Tommy McCook, Roland Alphonso, Don Drummond. They made the majority of the recordings. And the singers were people like Delroy Wilson, Alton Ellis and Errol Dunkley. And they released hundreds of records, I mean, thousands of records. And this continued till the 1980s. They released over a hundred records each week. That is fantastic to me, that these people should have made great records, constantly great records. I could play you them. They were just fantastic. Ska. And then it became rocksteady and then reggae. But ska was how I got into it, and ska is still my favourite music of all, and so has continued.

The late Peter Simons (who died as we were taking this book to press) worked in production on it in the 60s and 70s, and — as Penny Reel — wrote on reggae and early rock'n'roll for Pressure Drop, Let It Rock, NME, Black Echoes and Select.

'Dangerous, Paul'

Jon Savage explores the conflicted response of the pop weekly Disc and Music Echo to the music, trends and trips of 1966-67, in the spring and summer of psychedelia

"We've had bad publicity, bad records and atrocious lyrics like the Smoke's 'My Friend Jack' and the Pink Floyd's 'Arnold Layne'. I'm sick of these songs. I refuse to play any of them." — Bob Farmer, 'Simon Dee digs the amazing march of SQUARES!', *Disc and Music Echo*, 8 April 1967

In the week of 24 June 1967, the *Disc and Music Echo* charts were full of the new breezes sweeping pop culture. Procol Harum's 'A Whiter Shade of Pale' was at #1, keeping Engelbert Humperdinck's dreary 'There Goes My Everything' off the top spot. The Kinks' wistful, expansive 'Waterloo Sunset' was at #5, one place above a direct product of the new pop condition: Traffic's 'Paper Sun', with its bleak lyric illuminated by frequent application of the still other-worldly sitar.

At #8, the Supremes were sourcing contemporary art trends with 'The Happening', while at #10 the Young Rascals were 'Groovin' on a summer afternoon. Further down were strange noises like the Troggs' psych move, 'Night of the Long Grass', Cream's 'Strange Brew' — an early rock staple — as well as the Monkees' collaged, impressionistic 'Alternate Title'. The highest new entry was the Small Faces' 'Here Come The Nice', which on closer inspection revealed itself as a hymn to a speed dealer.

In the album chart, *Are You Experienced?* was at #3, bumped down a place by that hardy perennial *The Sound of Music*. The Beatles were at their fourth week at number one with *Sgt. Pepper's Lonely Hearts Club Band* — the album that had definitely proved that their withdrawal from live shows and their new shaggy image had not dented their popularity one whit. However they hadn't totally withdrawn from the media, and thereby lay the problem.

Sometime in the late spring, Paul McCartney had given an interview to *Queen* magazine in which he admitted to taking LSD: "After I took it, it opened my eyes. We only use one tenth of our brain. Just think what all we could accomplish if we could only tap that hidden part!" This quote was picked up by *LIFE* magazine for Thomas Thompson's article of 16 June on 'The New Far-Out Beatles', subtitled 'They're grown men now and creating extraordinary musical sounds.'

On 19 June, ITN interviewed a defiant member of the world's biggest group at his home in Cavendish Avenue. McCartney admitted to taking LSD "about four times". His final comments were at once perceptive, combative and disingenuous:

Q: "But as a public figure, surely you've got the responsibility to..."

PAUL: "...No, it's you who've got the responsibility. You've got the responsibility not to spread this NOW. You know, I'm quite prepared to keep it as a very personal thing if you will too. If you'll shut up about it, I will."

Five days later, *Disc and Music Echo* published an editorial, 'Dangerous, Paul'. Citing a London doctor and Jonathan King (!) on the dangers of LSD, the uncredited writer opined that McCartney could obviously do what he wanted: "As long as Paul's personal habits don't send a million people on a dangerous course, he is, of course, free to mess around as he pleases. It's his life." However he also had a responsibility to the public: "The danger is that fans who follow the star's example could land in serious trouble."

The Beatles had always rightly disavowed any need to set an example — by refusing to hide their cigarettes in press photos, for instance – but the magazine had flagged up an important issue. Fans did pick up the drug messages that saturated psychedelia and some were encouraged to experiment. Thus *Disc and Music Echo* felt impelled to issue a warning: "DON'T FOLLOW PAUL'S EXAMPLE BLINDLY. THEY'VE SET MANY GREAT TRENDS BUT THIS IS A HIGHLY DANGEROUS ONE TO COPY."

Despite such confident assurances, *Disc and Music Echo* was caught in a serious bind. During 1966 and early 1967 — after the April 1966 merger of *Disc* with *Music Echo* — the breezy tabloid had positioned itself as the market leader in the crowded weekly music-paper market. By 1966, both *Melody Maker* and the *New Musical Express* were bound by outdated formats and design: despite writers like Chris Welch and Keith Altham, they were struggling to adapt with the fast moving pop climate.

Aimed primarily at young women, *Fabulous 208* was super pop but had no charts. *Disc's* nearest competitor, *Record Mirror*, had the most comprehensive singles reviews, and great writers like Tony Hall and Norman Jopling. Even so, *Disc and Music Echo* trumped them all with excellent colour reproduction, a lively chart format on page 3, reader involvement, eye-catching cover lines and up-to-date features. It also had two of the UK's best pop writers, Derek Taylor as the US correspondent, and Penny Valentine.

Disc and Music Echo was strictly chart-based: who was in determined the news pages and features, as well as advertisements and features like page 3's Hit Talk, where a pop star of the day was encouraged to comment on the hits of the day (sample comment from Dave Dee in the issue of 24 June: "Fraid I can't find anything at all to say about the Troggs"). Pride of place was given to Penny Valentine's singles reviews on the penultimate page: as ever, album reviews were hidden next to the magazine's postbag.

That was both a blessing and a curse. For much of 1966, this frothy superpop approach had worked. The charts were, for much of the year, filled with innovative singles. Even the placemakers made decent records: Cilla Black's 'Love's Just A Broken Heart' for instance. The full colour covers reflected this richness and diversity: the Troggs, Bob Dylan, the Walker Brothers, the Who, the Beatles, Cilla Black, the Kinks, the Rolling Stones, the Small Faces, Paul Jones.

Sometime in the autumn however, this apparent unanimity began to break down. The problems were threefold: the Beatles' withdrawal from the stage in September took the heart out of British pop; the capital of Anglo-American pop culture moved from London to Los Angeles (and thence to San Francisco); the wages freeze and increase in the price of singles tipped the market more towards adults than teenagers. In early October, Jim Reeves' 'Distant Drums' went to number one and it didn't budge for weeks.

There was also a sense, epitomised by the comparative failure of the Rolling Stones' obtuse, if not nihilistic 'Have You Seen Your Mother, Baby, Standing In The Shadow' — which only made #5. In *Disc's* postmortem ('Stones — What went Wrong?'), Hollies drummer Bobby Elliott put his finger on it: "The record was basically above the fans' heads. It was too hippy and those photos showing the Stones in drag put the youngsters off a bit. The Stones need slowing down — I think they've been going too fast."

There was also a profound mood of disillusionment among the pop fans from around the country interviewed by *Disc's* staff writer Bob Farmer that late autumn. Most of the Newcastle teenagers he talked to — around 80 percent — said that they wanted to leave the UK: "I'm going to France to work at Christmas," said a 19-year-old salesman. "This country's no good for me." "Britain's just embarrassing," stated a 20-year-old graphic designer. "I was due for a rise, didn't get it because of the squeeze so I want to go abroad."

As pop modernism began to fragment under the impact of drugs and its own acceleration, the musicians were seen as over-reaching themselves. A test case was the Yardbirds: with two high profile and highly regarded top ten hits in 1966, their third single of the year was eagerly awaited. However 'Happenings Ten Years Time Ago' was a complex, troubled piece with a tricky riff and a chaotic, air-raid siren guitar solo. Progressive, but evidently not for the general public.

The usually benign Penny Valentine savaged it in *Disc*: "I have had enough of this sort of excuse for music. It is not clever, it is not entertaining, it is not informative. It is boring and pretentious. I am tired of people like the Yardbirds thinking this sort of thing is clever when people like the Spoonful and the Beach Boys are putting real thought into their music.

And if I hear the world psychedelic mentioned I will go nuts." In pop terms, she was right: the disc struggled into the mid-40s and died.

A major factor in this was the divisive impact of LSD. Much of the pop press was hostile to psychedelia, a word that was just beginning to enter common parlance. While the *MM* and *Record Mirror* attempted to get to grips with the new styles, *Disc* held off. As the balladeers began their grip on the charts, the magazine was reduced to special pleading for the likes of Val Doonican: "Ludicrous? Perhaps — but Val's so likeable nobody should knock his right to have hit records."

Pop was at war with itself, in the pages of the very magazines that had once cheerily reported it week by week. The week after the Val Doonican interview, Pete Townshend slammed the new trend towards ballads: "There's a place for everything, we are told, but I feel disgust at the people who buy these dreadful records." Townshend reserved particular venom for Tom Jones' 'Green, Green Grass of Home': "It's sentimental crap. We're living too much on sentiment and if this is what people want to hear, I give up."

At Christmas 1966, the top three were 'Green, Green Grass of Home', the Seekers' 'Morningtown Ride' and Val Doonican's 'What Would I Be'. The lower half of the ten were filled with Motown classics like 'You Keep Me Hanging On' and early psych artefacts like 'Sunshine Superman', 'Good Vibrations' and 'My Mind's Eye'. The split was being enacted in the charts and, by the end of 1966, this was about more than just another fad or fashion: it was about a generational shift.

The problem was that drugs heralded a new phase in youth culture. This was baffling to many, particularly as the once cheery/cheeky pop stars began to expound on the meaning of art and life. For instance, judging by the oddly written copy, *Disc* found Donovan's 'Sunshine Superman' — then at #5 in the charts — completely baffling: "Doing all the talking was Donovan — In Wonderland, naturally, and ensuring that if BBC Television's adaptation of *Alice* had him turning in his grave, Mr Lewis Carroll must be by now in convulsions."

Donovan further expounded his theories on pop to *Rave*'s Alan Freeman: "I call it the most important communication of today, because it's listened to. They extract the feeling from it. And there's one subject, really. It's truth, compassion, softness. I'm very pleased and excited to be part of a movement like that. But we're working under the eyes of a world that doesn't completely understand. Only the young eyes understand that there is a change. And in that change is this movement that began six or seven years ago."

At the end of the first week in January 1967, *TIME* published a cover story on 'The Man of the Year', which it defined as "A generation: the man — and woman — of 25 and under." The cover image showed a Caucasian young man and woman, together with a black and an Asian youth. Robert Jones wrote "that generation… will soon be the majority in charge. In the US, citizens of 25 and under in 1966 nearly outnumbered their elders: by 1970, there will be 100 million Americans in that age bracket."

Over six pages, *TIME* surveyed this global phenomenon: "In other big, highly industrialised nations, the young also constitute half the population. If the statistics imply change, the credentials of the younger generation guarantee it. Never have the young been so assertive or so articulate, so well educated or so worldly. Predictably, they are a highly independent breed and — to adult eyes — their independence has made them highly unpredictable. This is not just a new generation but a new kind of generation."

Emboldened by this cohort confidence — purchasing power morphing into the first glimmerings of political power — cutting-edge pop stars began to test the boundaries. It had happened in 1966 with the Beatles, the Rolling Stones, Bob Dylan and even the Kinks — with the BBC banning of their "sick" video for 'Dead End Street' — and, as if on cue, the first big kerfuffle of 1967 involved the Rolling Stones who, after their "drag" video for 'Have You Seen Your Mother, Baby', seemed intent on causing offence.

It's strange to read all the fuss about 'Let's Spend The Night Together' — now considered, if at all, as a 70s party warhorse — but there it was: 'Have the Stones Gone Gimmick Mad?' asked *Disc*, before declaring that the record was "certain to have headmistresses, archbishops, MPs, mother's unions, Mrs Mary Whitehouse and John Gordon raising a rumpus or at least locking up their daughters." Jagger defended the song, a direct and upbeat declaration of love and lust: "It's a happy song about proposing to a young lady."

On 22 January, the Rolling Stones refused to appear on the finale of the *London Palladium* TV show ('Stones in TV Rumpus'). On 12 February, after a murky set of circumstances that involved the collusion between the police and the *News of the World* with which we are now familiar, Mick Jagger and Keith Richard of the Rolling Stones were arrested and, with the gallerist Robert Fraser, arraigned on drugs charges — setting the scene for the summer's pop *cause célèbre*.

The first three months of 1967 saw the release of several records that fell foul of the authorities: the Smoke's 'My Friend Jack' and the Game's 'Addicted Man' (drugs), Pink Floyd's 'Arnold Layne' (transvestism). Meanwhile *Disc and Music Echo* was very busy with the Monkees: the charming Beatles-lite who flourished while the real thing was out of the way. When the Beatles eventually returned, they found that they were entering a very different pop climate.

The big pop shock of 1967 was the fact that Engelbert Humperdinck's 'Release Me' held the new Beatles single, 'Penny Lane'/'Strawberry Fields Forever', off the top spot for several weeks. On 18 March, the top ten contained two separate versions of 'This Is My Song', a song written by Charlie Chaplin in 1966 intended to evoke the 1930s; the Seekers' 'Georgy Girl', and Vince Hill's 'Edelweiss' — a Rodgers and Hammerstein song from *The Sound of Music*. It felt like a counter-revolution.

That week, *Disc*'s Bob Farmer essayed a definition of the phenomenon:

"They don't go to discotheques, indulge in freak-outs, or overrun airports. But they're everywhere among us. They've taken our chart away from us and made it their own. Who are they? Some say they're the over-twenties. Much more to the point, they're the mums and dads of Britain. Flocking in their thousands to record stores around the country every week to put people like Engelbert Humperdinck and Petula Clark and Vince Hill and

Whistling Jack Smith and Val Doonican and Ken Dodd and Clinton Ford and Larry Cunningham high in our hit parade. Young fans are furious about it; the artists are indignant about it; and people like Vince Hill are cackling heartily about it."

The only major new artist to make a dent in this tsunami of schlock was Jimi Hendrix, who — although well covered by *Disc* — might as well have come from outer space, with epithets like "incredibly ugly", "obscene", "vulgar" and "the Wild Man of Borneo" freely tossed around. His new hit, 'Purple Haze' was quite obviously a drug song in feel and execution (*"you've got me blowing my mind"*) but he deflected any criticism by claiming that it was "All about a dream that I had that I was walking under the sea."

For those in the know, coded drug references had been contained in words like "mind" and "dream" but, in spring 1967, after the Rolling Stones' arrest and with the spread of underground culture, *Disc* decided to take a stand. "Drug Takers Are Fools" opined Cliff on the front cover of the 29 April issue, and the next few weeks were taken up with a healthy discussion on the topic. As if overnight, drugs had become a hot pop issue — and the pop press would never be quite the same again.

"A famous pop star found guilty and fined for illegal possession of drugs," wrote Bob Farmer that week;

"Groups searched at airports. Stars stopped and questioned by police in the streets. To cap it all, fuel to the flames fanning public opinion added by irresponsible groups recording blatantly obvious drug discs often with insidiously tempting lyrics. Not only are a fair proportion of pop stars taking drugs (naming names would lead to libel action), but they are actually guilty of glorifying it.

"*Disc* has decided that the drug menace and its infiltration on the pop scene needs public examination. To discover just how deep the drug roots go in pop, to detect how harmful drug taking can

79

be, to discuss but not dictate what your attitude should be. Now the rumours have reached such magnitude that it's impossible to ignore this slur on the pop scene. This week — the first part of a three-part focus on drugs and pop — we put the case for the prosecution of the drug peddlers."

First up was Cliff: "Drugs are for fools. They can kill. I couldn't take drugs because I'd be defiling my body — a temple of God." 'Beatles 'drug' song is BANNED!', *Disc* announced on the front page of the 6 May issue, before delving into 'The Dangers of LSD'. "People who create under drugs are failures," stated Jonathan King while Paul Jones actually talked sense: "How hypocritical to decry drug-taking when you can walk into a bar and drink some drinks which are really dangerous when taken to excess."

A week later, Bob Farmer helpfully ran down the pharmacopeia for *Disc*'s young readers: the headline 'Names that spell danger' framed definitions of LSD, cocaine, marijuana, amphetamines etc. Farmer quoted a "well known London doctor": "Drug-taking in pop is much exaggerated. I have plenty of pop stars on my medical register but none of them are drug addicts. You just can't stay in pop and take drugs. You'd keep on being late for rehearsals and dates and the whole scene would bust up."

In late May, the Beatles did a series of interviews for the release of *Sgt Pepper's Lonely Hearts Club Band*. Ray Coleman tackled Paul McCartney on the ban of their supposed drug song: "If they want to ban 'A Day In the Life', that's their business. Drugs must have been in their minds — not ours. And the point is, banning doesn't help. It just draws attention to a subject when all the time their aim is to force attention away from it. Banning never did any good."

Two weeks later, on 10 June, Procol Harum's 'A Whiter Shade of Pale' leapt to #1 ahead of Engelbert Humperdinck: interviewed in *Disc*, the group pronounced the music to be "like mass suicide". In the same issue, 'Our Man in America' Derek Taylor lambasted the BBC ban of 'A Day In the Life': "I had forgotten how absolutely rotten the BBC could be. Forgotten those gibbering, quaking, syllable-by-syllable vowel-swallowing Bishop-pompous emotion-bereft voices..."

Taylor talked about the old England — "the international kingdom of

Moronia"— and the new possibilities: "The really creative work, it seems to me, comes from a handful of young or youngish people, whether they're musicians or film-makers, painters or writers. Those who fiddle around the fringes are as frightful as ever. Turn off your mind, relax and float downstream. Then unfloat and turn on and start getting something done. The time is now."

Disc followed up this explicit piece of drug propaganda with a toe-in-the-water description of psychedelia on 17 June, no doubt influenced by the continued popularity of 'A Whiter Shade of Pale' and the smash success of *Sgt Pepper*. Commercial pressures meant that the trends had to be covered, no matter how divisive or harmful they might seem. As Penny Valentine noted in a review that week: "Curiouser and curiouser how records now are getting more and more involved."

The paper's approach was, to put it mildly, extremely conflicted. In the week that it slammed Paul McCartney for admitting that he had taken LSD, it ran a long Derek Taylor article about the Monterey pop festival: "All of us were back in the light and the colour and the music and the people — fragments of the substances flowing out of the universe into what began as rock'n'roll and which is now the happening. I have nothing more to say. Just that it happened in Monterey and it mightn't have done…"

In the centre pages, Penny Valentine conducted a survey of "Flower Power": "The message is: lay down your arms, scream no more, be peaceful, and kind to your web-footed friend and anyone else that comes your way. Beauty is the password — and flowers are how to spell it," she enthused. "And to end with I would like to hand the most beautiful flower in the world to Derek Taylor. Who, even if he wasn't a fellow columnist, I would think has more colour and beauty in his words than all of us put together."

That was too much for Dave Dee, who in the next week's issue launched an "amazing attack on the 'Hollywood Hippy' scene", in particular Derek Taylor ("the triumph of the mediocre"): "I don't think either *Pepper* or 'Whiter Shade of Pale' really mean anything. Like a glorious sunset they just are. Somewhat random and extremely beautiful. But they are not a guide for loving, they are not an alternative to politics, warfare or anything else for that matter. As such they are an escape like LSD is an escape…"

That same week, *Disc*'s readers gave their verdict on Paul and LSD. Apart from one conspicuous libertarian ("It's Paul's life. He can do what he likes"), most agreed that he was "completely irresponsible" and that his words would influence fans to take the drug: "He must know other kids will follow the trend," wrote M. Hancock from East Barnet; "I still enjoy their sound, but as for admiring them, I'm afraid hundreds of fans including myself have been sadly disillusioned."

On 8 July, *Disc* reported the aftermath of the Rolling Stones' guilty verdict:

"*Jagger 'handcuffs' sales boom

*Who rush-release 'tribute' single

*Flowers planned for Judge Block

*Procol in 'peace' concert move."

"This case has been a showdown between the Establishment and the youth of this country," stated one Ian Ross ("owner of a firm that makes mod gear"): "I think it would be helpful to retaliate by a peaceful demonstration. The idea is a vast concert to raise money and send flowers to the judge with a message of forgiveness and a suggestion that, perhaps, he should read the Sermon on the Mount to himself."

Meanwhile, the Dave Dee affair rumbled on, with Derek Taylor's acidly cosmic rebuttal ('Dear Dave Dee, Dozy, Beaky, Mick, Tich and Ghostwriter: I don't know that I have anything to say to you') and various pop star replies. Pete Townshend: "I could never get so aroused about Derek Taylor's writing — although I could easily get aroused by the way that Dave Dee sings!" Graham Nash: "What IS Dave Dee on about? If he's feeling that puritanical, why does he behave so suggestively on stage himself?"

In the same issue, *Disc* ran a feature on Pink Floyd: "The people who put colour into the pop scene — a crazy kaleidoscope of flashing chemicals and colours as part of a psychedelic type stage act that's even brought the Beatles along to observe the action." There was also a rundown of the new West Coast groups, "the complete new sound that is broadening the outlook of American teenagers," which included the Doors, the Byrds, Love, Moby Grape, the Seeds, Buffalo Springfield and the Electric Prunes.

Clearly, by the second half of July, psychedelia was in the ascendant. The three covers after 15 July featured the Beatles, Pink Floyd and Scott McKenzie respectively. The paper reported on Traffic — "living a hermit-like existence at Stevie's cosy cottage hideaway in deepest Berkshire" — as well as Pink Floyd: 'Freak out comes to town'. It polled Rolling Stones fans for their reaction to the court case: almost all expressed their support — "The Stones fans will stick by them," replied Terence Redpath of Bermondsey.

'Is Flowerpower really gripping Britain?', asked the cover headline of the 29 July issue. The top ten for that week showed 'All You Need Is Love' at #1, with 'San Francisco' at #2, 'See Emily Play' at #6 and 'A Whiter Shade of Pale' at #8. Inside was another feature on Pink Floyd and an examination of Flowerpower, pegged on the smash success of Scott McKenzie's single: "There are a growing number of flower children who are quite seriously thinking of it as a new way of life, an alternative to being a Mod."

However, as Penny Valentine found when she went out and met the general public, it was not sweeping the nation: "Surprisingly few of them had HEARD of Flowerpower... most dismissed it as a fairly harmless craze, and in a rather tired way obviously thought it was all part of nothing to do with them. Basically they all though the actual IDEA of handing out flowers and wanting peace was a nice but impractical one. It was the clothes and the connection with drugs that worried them most."

By late in the year, however, things were getting back to normal, whatever normal was by that point. The issue for 9 December had the Dave Clark Five on the cover, and big interviews with Cliff Richard (his Sunday routine) and the Beatles (the Maharishi). There was a small piece about the Grateful Dead, while readers' letters praised Dave Dee for praising the likes of Des O'Connor and Engelbert Humperdinck and other "established entertainers" who had "SAVED pop from its 'in-crowd'."

Clearly, a section of *Disc* readers opted to reject psychedelia and all its works. In December, the singles chart was already moving on from the high summer of 1967: the top ten was again full of ballads by Val Doonican, the Dave Clark Five, Tom Jones, Cliff Richard and Engelbert

Humperdinck. But the tensions between pop and underground were becoming unsustainable: not only did the magazine continually reflect diametrically opposed points of view, but the writers were not in sync with each other or the readers.

In the inaugural Hollywood Column by *Teen Beat*'s Judith Sims, she praises the Grateful Dead — "They dance and laugh and carry on and 'take you to another place' when they perform" — while declaring that she "can't get excited about Engelhump or Tom Jones". Elsewhere she slags off the Cowsills: "The American groups held in highest esteem by the largest masses almost always have that sanitary, squeaky-clean look which Americans insist on calling 'all-American', as if we invented soap."

But the British charts of that week were full of Tom Jones and Engelbert Humperdinck. So what was Judith Sims there for? Was it to express her own personal taste, report on latest developments, to highlight a new and different culture or guide the magazine's readers to a more enlightened, 'better' kind of music? This uncertainty was reflected in the readers' letters: the Beatles are "scruffy and unkempt", Engelbert's TV show was "not nearly long enough", while a lone reader praised the "beautiful music" of Pink Floyd.

Pride of place, the 'Disc Star Letter', was given to Long John Baldry — then at #2 with the lachrymose 'Let The Heartaches Begin' — to defend himself against the charge that he had "gone commercial". "There is no limit to the material I use," he wrote; "Although it is a ballad, it has a bluesy feeling and is not much different to my previous work." But the mere fact that he was being accused of being "commercial" and his need to respond showed just how far pop had divided — into hippies and squares, into Us and Them.

Reading the music press week to week in the first half of 1967 is a window into a fascinating period of change. The split in a formerly uniform pop culture — the unitary forward motion of Pop Modernism — is laid bare for all to see in an immediate and barely filtered form. Indeed, the attitudes and statements contained in *Disc and Music Echo* are contradictory, illustrating the resistance that many teenagers, journalists and indeed artists had towards the new psychedelic form. On their own terms, they were right.

Disc and Music Echo was caught in a cleft stick: having to report on what was in the chart, while intuiting that psychedelia meant, if not the death, then the waning of their power. As pop moved to rock, and singles to albums, it would need a new kind of writing to encapsulate the experience and deliver informed criticism. This would take time to develop in the UK — both *it* and *Oz* were still in early days then, *Rolling Stone* had not yet launched — but would render the high 60s pop press irrelevant.

Indeed, *Disc* would not survive beyond 1975, when it merged with *Record Mirror*. For a while, however, in 1966 and early 1967, it was a true barometer of the changes and tensions in British pop. This function would be taken up at different times and by different publications in the future: the *NME* and *Sounds* in the late 70s, in particular *Smash Hits* in the early 80s. A proper study of these apparently ephemeral publications is mandatory for any understanding of the period's youth/pop culture.

Jon Savage wrote for Sounds and Melody Maker in the 70s, and The Face in the early 80s. He is the author of England's Dreaming: Sex Pistols and Punk Rock, Teenage: the Creation of Youth 1875-1945 and 1966: the Year the Decade Exploded.

OVERGROUND/UNDERGROUND

"Jann Wenner was the first person I ever knew whose entire luggage as he travelled round the world was one tiny little case, and a lot of credit cards"

— *Tony Palmer*

"The Idea Was to Have an International Culture Magazine"

An extract from Jonathon Green's 'Days in the Life: Voices from the English Underground 1961-1971' (Heinemann/Minerva, 1988)

MILES: After the Albert Hall poetry reading we did begin to believe that we could change the world. I wrote about this in an editorial for a magazine called *Long Hair* which was published by Lovebooks Ltd at the end of 1965. In parenthesis it was called *NATO: North Atlantic Turn-On*. There was an enormous amount of Ginsberg in it, and the name came from Ginsberg. Because that had been the thing that struck him most about England, the long hair the men had. I was suggesting that it was time that there was some kind of cross-pollination of ideas between all the people then involved in the scene in London. There was a lot going on: in fashion, rock'n'roll, theatre, movies, poetry, literature. What we wanted to do was to put these people in touch with each other; there was actually a need, quite a strong need, for some sort of vehicle for their ideas. That was what we were preaching at the time. It seemed to us that a cross-over of ideas between all these different groups would be a very beneficial thing. The next issue we did appeared in a different format: it came out in a small number of copies and we handed it out at the Aldermaston march in 1966. And that was called

The Longhair Moon Edition of the International Times. Or *Longhair Times. it*, of course, grew out of this. It had in it an essay about LSD by Harry Fainlight; it had a competition paid for by Paul McCartney, who offered a hundred pounds or two hundred pounds for some film script for some weird thing he wanted to do with Jane [Asher]; a facsimile of a John Wilcock column in the *Village Voice* about the US underground. [...]

PAUL McCARTNEY: Putting money into the counterculture was doing things about changing the world, politically. Once it came to standing up, to being a political candidate and actually running for something, we ran for cover rather than running for anything. But when it was just Miles and I and he was pasting up *it* and I'd be helping him with a photo or sifting an article or something and Sue his wife would be bringing in the tea — that really is what I like. I thought it was good, interesting, some nice stuff in it. [...]

MILES: So Hoppy [John Hopkins] and I wanted to do this paper, but it was clear that we couldn't do it ourselves, for a start we both had other jobs. We decided to expand Lovebooks Ltd and take on new directors. We took on Jack Henry Moore, Jim Haynes and Mike Renshaw, who was the hip accountant who knew how to handle the eccentric artists. Haynes had an enormous number of contacts and he seemed like a good person to bring in the more cultural side of things that we knew nothing about. He came down here in 66 to do a season at the Jeanetta Cochrane, the theatre attached to the Central School of Art. And the producer of that season was Jack Moore, an American who'd been in the Fantasticks in New York, then come over here. Very gay. We had good contacts on the experimental music side, this guy Alan Beckett who Hoppy shared a flat with was very keen on avant-garde jazz and lots more. Through Peter Wollen we knew Cornelius Cardew, the John Cage influence. Another guy was Victor Schonfield who was involved in avant-garde music but who I'd known in Oxford around 1960 when he was the main pusher, hanging around in a dirty mac selling ten-bob deals. We had a good collection of people but we needed money. Jim was very good at getting money. He knew people like Sonia Orwell and Victor Herbert...

SUE MILES: *it* started because everybody said, "Let's do something." We had no concept of how difficult it was. It was letterpress. You couldn't get plates made. Censorship was really heavy: you had printers ringing up and saying — 'I'm not printing words like this — I've got women working here!' and all that kind of stuff. People going in the middle of the night and setting the type when the owners weren't there. The printers still had to lay it out — we didn't know what to do, there were no art directors. Jim [Haynes] had a friend here called Bobo Legendre who lived above a fish shop in Shepherd Market, Southern American, rich. He got money out of her, and money out of Victor Herbert, the pyramid-selling guy tied in with Bernie Cornfeld. So Jim was this kind of go-between: on the one hand there were these hairy loonies, which was us, and on the other were these rather establishment, rich characters. Jim was pulling money out of them and for them it was all rather "Let's be like the Sculls or Guggenheim in New York: patrons to the arts." So the first typewriter *it* had was George Orwell's, given by Sonia, which promptly was lost — or sold. […]

JIM HAYNES: I suggested that we launch *it* at the Roundhouse and I got the Roundhouse from Arnold Wesker. I called up Arnold, who I knew through theatre connections, and said, "We're having a little party to launch a paper, can we borrow the Roundhouse?" And he said, "Well, I guess so. I'm going to be in Budapest giving a lecture." I said, "I promise we won't make a mess and it'll just be blah-blah-blah," and he gave me the keys. And we did the party, which was the first big event ever at the Roundhouse. Centre 42, which he wanted to do, didn't happen. The difference between his approach and mine was that he had a big sign outside saying 'Centre 42 needs £540,000'; I wanted £5. "You got a building? OK, let's use it. Let's start making it happen, let's do events in it…" The launch party did make money. Maybe £1,000, and it launched the paper, and launched the Roundhouse as a space.

MILES: It was a complete fire trap. It hadn't been used since before the war. The balcony was completely unsafe — Gilbey's Gin used it as a store. It hadn't actually been used as a roundhouse since the turn of the century. In fact it was never used as a roundhouse for locomotives — it was for the winding gear to pull the trains up the hill from Euston Station, and once steam power was strong enough it became redundant. It was grimy and very, very cold, cos it was October. We had the Pink Floyd and the Soft Machine. The Floyd got £15 because they had a light-show and the Soft Machine only got £12/10s. It was the first big gig for both of them. The Soft Machine had an amplified motorcycle as part of their act. This guy called Dennis put contact mikes on the motorcycle and revved it up, wearing a long cape, a head-dress, something like that. They gave girls rides around the outside while the Floyd played. At the entrance there were big trays of sugar cubes that people were offered — although actually there was nothing in them at all. But an awful lot of people managed to trip out on them. Kenneth Rexroth covered it for the *San Francisco Chronicle* and said that the band didn't show up but the audience between them assembled a rough and ready pick-up band which made these awful squawking noises, which was what he felt about the Pink Floyd. He thought the whole place was going up in flames, a complete death trap. Everyone we knew was there. McCartney dressed as an Arab... the most wonderful sight of all was Antonioni and Monica Vitti who was wearing this tiny little outfit... There was a giant jelly, about six foot long. Unfortunately the Pink Floyd's van ran into it so very few people saw it in its original glory. It was cast out of a bathtub.

CHRIS ROWLEY: A friend of mine took me along to something that turned out to be the *it* opening bash, in early October at the Roundhouse. There was a giant jelly and Mike Lesser crawled through it. It was a cold, damp interior, very dark and musty. The Pink Floyd set up and had a little screen about the size of a painting on which the blob-show was projecting. All these little groups from all over London were massing together. First of all they'd done it at the poetry reading or the Dylan concert, where they'd seen each other. But at this *it* thing they were actually rubbing up against each other, sharing joints, talking frantically about turning on the world. Everyone had made plans of various kinds and they all babbled away furiously about either electrifying the skies so that messages of love and peace could be beamed off the clouds, or turning European universities into a vast library of worthwhile information and so on. It all seemed like jolly good fun and a good idea at the time. It was remarkably optimistic. When had there been such vast quantities of raw optimism among any group? Perhaps not since 1914 when the lads went off to die. [...]

JIM HAYNES: Jack and I knew Tom McGrath and we tracked him down and found out he was living in Wales in the middle of nowhere doing God knows what and we sent him a telegram that said, "Come to London, you're editing a new paper." He came to London and he was the editor for the first ten issues or something like that. My vision of it was that it would be a European paper which would try to create a kind of underground consciousness throughout Europe. We'd get writing from Warsaw, Stockholm, Paris, Berlin, what have you. To a certain extent that happened. People reporting on what they were doing and trying to bring people together. [...]

MILES: *it* was originally run on the classic sexist role divisions. That was the way Sue and I lived: I went to work and she stayed at home. Ridiculous. But we did try to change as soon as we found out about these new ideas. When we were in Endell Street we divided the editorship three ways: we had a hippie one issue, the next issue would be a woman and the next issue would be a black. Courtney Tulloch was the token black who edited every third issue.

SUE MILES: My job on *it* was the advertising. I got four quid a week. Christopher Gibbs, whom I worked for later, bought out of solidarity a subscription for each of his five banker brothers and they all wrote saying, "We'll sue you if you ever send this filthy rag to us again." One of the things someone did was to grind up the mummified Egyptian shrew mouse that Christopher had on his mantelpiece and pretend it was dope. Christopher said, "I hope you got very high, because it was a very rare hit, man."

MICK FARREN: After *it* started to come out I ran into a few people who said, "Go over to the Indica bookshop," which at that stage had just moved into Southampton Row, and I went over there and I bought a load of stuff and there seemed to be all these people hanging out. Then I started going in there quite regularly. Miles was always bouncing about with the Beatles and stuff, though I didn't actually get to know him. I went on reading *it* for a while and hanging out and then I got into a long conversation with Tom McGrath, who was the first editor, basically complaining that there was no rock'n'roll in it. It was very old-fashioned. There were all these old geezers: Jim Haynes, McGrath; the only one with any life in him was Jack Moore. Apart from Miles interviewing the Beatles in succession there was nothing in the paper on music. There was nothing about what was going on with all these people I'd seen wandering about. It was still talking about Jeff Nuttall. "Fuck Jeff Nuttall," we cried, "there's all this strange shit. My friend Alex has this large sphere built out of plastic dispenser cups that is now seven foot across and he can't get it out of his room — this is more interesting than Jeff Nuttall." […]

MILES: At the time *it* started we knew we had a constituency — basically the people who'd gone to the Albert Hall poetry reading, 6 or 7,000. We probably printed about 15,000 of the first issue and there weren't many returns. *it*'s print curve began around 10,000 and went up to peak in May 68 around 44,000. There were a number of campaigns: one was the 24-hour city, to try to make London more lively, to change the licensing laws, have public transport running 24 hours a day — in other words, to return London to the state it was in before World War I. We had no clear idea of what we wanted to create, because there hadn't been that kind of mass youth culture before. Even in America the underground press had only been going for about five months. It was very much the Lower East Side drug scene that we were emulating — *EVO [East Village Other]* was just a bunch of stoned freaks. It turned out that we did hit the right chord. We were fortnightly more or less: sometimes three-weekly and occasionally monthly. We addressed ourselves to the mythical community that we thought was there and it didn't take long for that community to begin feeding back. The 'What's Happening' column filled right up and this cross-over really began to happen between the dress designers in the King's Road and the happening artists in the East End and so on. All kinds of connections were made. Quite amazing. How it really happened, I don't know. We were the forum; it wasn't directed by us in any sense, we didn't create the scene, but were used by it, and *it* was very useful in that respect.

SUE MILES: The original print run on *it* was 2,500, and at least 1,750 never left the cardboard box. The media grabbed it. You had Swinging London, then you had us. We were all on David Frost all the time. That was the one thing the underground press was brilliant at — we were fantastic self-publicists. Wonderful. Hoppy — who else would dress as Superman and try and run up Nelson's Column? And I suppose there wasn't very much real hard news going on. Reasonably affluent time, England wasn't fighting any wars, there were no big political issues, the whole thing about disarmament had gone pphhtt. The Labour Party were in power and for a while you had this period where the government were more progressive than the electorate. They'd brought in homosexual law reform, abortion law reform, and the end of capital punishment — issues that if you'd gone to the country on consensus you wouldn't have won on.

CHRIS ROWLEY: Issue One of *it* had appeared in October 1966. I hung out at the office, did a bit of street-selling (they never paid me a penny for it, but I never did it for money, just went to the clubs, got free drugs . . .). There was the office bookshop — Indica — where Miles had this marvellous mixture of Tibetan poetry, science fiction and William Burroughs. I spent a lot of time in there. Miles turned me on to various things, he'd point to various books and say, 'You ought to try this... I read a whole gamut of stuff: Burroughs, *Last Exit to Brooklyn*, all sorts of classics of the time. It was all getting very interesting. I became *it's* ipso facto office boy. I did various jobs, pushing things through mail boxes, that kind of thing. This was in Southampton Row, in the basement of Indica. One day I was in there and Alex Trocchi was there and he made this enormous show of shooting up, letting the blood run down the arm, trickling onto the floor, tying off, the whole thing.

Everyone else left except me, and I just sat there chewing my sandwich, drinking my coffee and goggling: this is, like, the real thing at least! A real tourist sight.

DAVID WIDGERY: We always laughed at *it* in our political wisdom —because they wanted to do such 'reformist' things as get the tubes to run late at night. That was such an American thing: New York has tubes that run all night, why don't we? [...]

JIM HAYNES: The only politics in early *its* was extreme libertarianism and the bias towards an individual's right to do with his or her mind and body what he or she wanted to do. Sexually, drugs, reading, no censorship, smoke anything, inhale anything, inject anything: it's your life, baby — do it. And that really, really upset people: the drug part. The fact that we were not anti-drug made us implicitly pro-drug and to a certain extent that was right. The bizarre thing about it is that I never used drugs, never smoked, never injected, I am not a drinker and never was, didn't smoke cigarettes, my favourite drink was orange juice and here I'm writing this incredible libertarian defence of your right to do it.

DICK POUNTAIN: We terrorised the early *it*. When they were still at the Indica bookshop one of the earliest King Mob/Situationist actions was going and breaking in there and scaring the wits out of them. Nothing violent, just language and posture and we stuck the Situationist poster up all over the place: a cartoon about the futility of politics and everyday life, a bit like the storyboard for a Godard movie. Our basic statement was that they were agents of the spectacle and they were all going to be co-opted. This was also the time when the graffiti started going up around Notting Hill. "The tigers of wrath are wiser than the horses of instruction," all those.

Chronicler of the underground and historian of slang Jonathon Green wrote for Friends/Frendz, International Times/it and Rolling Stone UK.

How Well Did the Mainstream Press Cover Rock and the Underground in the 60s?

Tony Palmer: *The Observer (1967-74), The Spectator (1969-74), films and TV documentaries, including All You Need Is Love*
Jonathon Green: *chronicler of the underground, historian of slang*
Mark Pringle: *chief archivist at Rock's Backpages website*
Panel chaired by **Esther Leslie,** *professor in political aesthetics at Birkbeck*

EL: Welcome back to the second panel. To start, I want to ask each of you an introductory question, because I don't think you know each other. You come from different places, different orientations: Tony, working more with mainstream press and TV production, Jonathon, more around the countercultural press, and Mark is now an archivist of rock writing and perhaps a reader at that time. Could each of you say where you were, what your relationship was to this field around 1967-68, the early part of our period.

    TP: Well, I'm so old I'm afraid I predate that. I think I was first recruited, if that's the right word, by an amazing music critic called William Mann, who worked for the *Times*, who was in fact the first music critic I think of any sort to try and analyse the music that the Beatles wrote. I was still at university, but I had met Mann through Benjamin Britten, oddly enough. Bill wrote to me and said, "We need a critic who will work for the *Times* who can write about the music that I don't particularly know — and don't particularly like," he said. I said, "Well, I'm hoping to be an academic, so you've got the wrong man," but we kept in touch.

Mann told this story to David Astor, the very distinguished editor of the *Observer*. So when I finally left university and came to London in 1966, Astor wrote to me and said would I like to join the *Observer* as music critic number two? Music critic number one being a man called Peter Heyworth.

Now I was by then working at the BBC, but this was an offer you couldn't possibly refuse. Because it looked as if I was going to appear alongside Kenneth Tynan, the great drama critic, and Caroline Lejeune, a great film critic, and so on. And I thought I must have a go at this. I did know quite a lot of people in the pop music world at that point.

So I was given the job of reviewing or writing about everything that Peter Heyworth didn't want to write about. Which was a fantastic opportunity for me — for example, I wrote about the last ever performance, in the Talk of the Town, now the Hippodrome, of Judy Garland, and I also went to a concert on acoustic guitar in the Purcell Room, by someone at the time totally unknown, David Bowie. Also through various other connections I met a guitarist who is playing tonight at the Albert Hall, although he certainly wasn't then, called Eric Clapton, which introduced me to Cream, and so on and so on.

I just wrote every week about what they asked me to write about, as well as things that I had noticed and thought were really interesting. Through Eric, I met Jimmy Page, and I think I wrote the first ever review of Led Zeppelin, long before the first LP. So that was my introduction.

The big problem — if you can put yourself in the position of somebody trying to write in that sort of newspaper — was trying to find a language that didn't offend absolutely everybody in the rock world, although it did offend an awful lot of people, which would also not completely offend everybody who would normally read the *Observer*. Thank God I didn't work for the *Times* then — I have done since — because had I done so, I think I would have been in even bigger trouble.

I hadn't been there very long, perhaps every Sunday for about three months, when I was suddenly summoned by David Astor, who is very tall and very patrician. He had a pile of letters on his table, and he sat me down — he was very courteous — and he said "I think we have to discuss what it is you are writing." I thought, "Right, that's it, I've been fired even before I've got going. Never mind, it was a fun experience."

He read one of these letters — from a woman, I don't want to call her 'Outraged in Tunbridge Wells' — and she said she was absolutely profoundly shocked that this dreadful noise was been given credence by a paper like the *Observer*, and she wanted Mr Astor to know that she was cancelling her life subscription. He put that on one side and then he picked up the second one, and I thought, "Right." I was on the point of saying, "Well, I'm very sorry, it's been very nice to meet you, goodbye." But suddenly he said, "Can you write a lot more of this? This is exactly what we need." So that was how I got started.

JG: How did I get started? Well, as you may know, I edited a book called *Days in the Life*, and one of the things that became very obvious to me about the counterculture as represented by those I interviewed in *Days in the Life* was it was middle-class and they had mainly been to Oxbridge — so I fitted the bill. The reason I say that is because — I would suggest like a lot of the people — I did not join the counterculture to bring about what we called the 'Rev-O', because none of us actually knew what the Rev-O was. The Rev-O of course being the Revolution, with a capital R.

In my case, I had written a pop column for the university newspaper. I've never read it since — I shudder to think what it was like. It was reviewing records and the odd performance — we had Hendrix, we had the Who, we had all sorts of people turned up.

In I think the beginning of 1967, there appeared in England this magazine called *Rolling Stone*, UK *Rolling Stone*. Looking back, what Jann Wenner, the editor, did was very smart: he started off with the 'Groupie' issue — I think it was issue 27. It had the Plastercasters, who as some of you know would memorialise the penises of their favourite rock and roll stars in plaster and then do whatever you had to do to set these phalluses up. It was about as sensational as you could get at that stage — very very large-S small-s sexy.

The other thing of course that *Rolling Stone* did was this. I'd previously only read *NME* — or in fact mainly *Melody Maker* — and it seemed to me what you mostly got from rock and roll musicians in *Melody Maker* was a reprocessed press release. Which on the whole was, "What's your favourite colour? What girls do you like? What girls do you not like? Do you have a pet?" And so on.

What you didn't get was some guy from San Francisco or New York or wherever it might be expatiating for four long multi-columned eight-point pages, at great depth, and of course being taken terribly seriously. Now people may have opinions on whether they *should* have been taken seriously or not... but it was fascinating — and it gave the music that one loved a whole new dimension. One read *Rolling Stone* as a kind of a bible, it was another league. And it was also America! And there was once a time, and I think Tony will remember this, a time when America was something you aspired to, rather than disliked and attributed evils to demonise. The America we grew up with in the 50s, which was the great golden land. And one of the reasons it was the great golden land was that it was bringing you rock and roll.

So what I wanted to do was join *Rolling Stone*. I joined by sending them a couple of articles, purely on spec. One was about the recently deceased Brian Jones, and one was about the Soft Machine album, not the first one, the second one. On the basis of this I was asked to go into their offices — which being enormously countercultural were in Hanover Square, about 50 metres away from *Vogue* as the crow flies. They've since knocked the building down. It was extremely smart – and allegedly that sofa over there was the one that Mick used to screw Marianne on, and that sofa over there was the one that he did something else on, because Jagger was always involved.

Earlier the same day I had been to the *Sunday Times*, asked by a man called Michael Bateman to come in and perhaps work on the Atticus column. So Fleet Street was also beckoning. But various circumstances combined against this: Bateman never kept a diary, his PA was away and there was a temp, and I was a frightened young man. So after waiting in the hall — the *Sunday Times* being of enormous all-inspiring importance at the time, with people looking at me as if I wrote on green paper with lines — I fled. Subsequently I found out that Bateman was indeed planning to give me a job, and the guy who got the job became an incredibly famous foreign correspondent and was shot dead, I think in Guatemala, 20 years later.

So I, on the other hand, went over to Hanover Square where Alan Marcuson, who was then editing *Rolling Stone UK*, gave me a joint and said, "Do you want 20 quid a week, you can be news editor?" This was something of a shock to me. And I would stress yet again that qualifications — as far as I'm aware — did not come into it.

MP: I was a very small kid. In early 1966, just before my eleventh birthday Hendrix's 'Purple Haze' pretty much changed my life. Basically I hated it for about two months, and then a big light bulb came on: "This is the greatest noise I ever heard." I was music-obsessive. At 12, in 68, I started at Holland Park Comprehensive. Every day I would get the 31 bus up to the top of the Earls Court Road. There was a newsagent there and I became a print obsessive. *Melody Maker* every Thursday. I had a brother, five years older, who was bringing *Oz* into the house, and *International Times* and later on *Friends/Frendz*.

I'm very glad Jonathon mentioned *Rolling Stone*, because it gets glossed over. I think *Rolling Stone* was the major source of rock and roll writing, from certainly 1968 onwards, when it was widely available. You could buy it in W. H. Smith's, it was well distributed. I would go in there and also buy *Black Dwarf* and *Red Mole*, or was it the other way round? Anyway, yes, I just became a complete print obsessive.

Not necessarily music print, because I bought the underground papers not for the music coverage — because regardless of what everyone says, the underground press really wasn't music press. It had music in it — Mark Williams running the 'Plug and Socket' section — but I bought *International Times* to read about Vietnam, about Paris 68, about psychology and R. D. Laing, all that sort of stuff. It wasn't primarily about music. The underground was surrounded by music, and music was a major part of the underground as a social movement, but the underground press wasn't music-driven.

Rolling Stone was the exception. It was loosely an underground paper — but very, very music. Music was central to what *Rolling Stone* was about. So it was my source of music information, rather than *it* — though people like Miles, Mark Williams, Jonathon and so on were writing very good stuff about music in *it*. So basically I was consuming print from all of these directions.

Then 15 years ago — many, many, years later — Barney Hoskyns came to me with the idea of setting up the website *Rock's Backpages*, an archive of pop music, rock music, journalism, however loosely you want to use the term. And since then basically every week I read and proof read 25-30 articles from the pop papers, from *Record Mirror*, *Disc* and so on, from the early 60s pretty much up to the 90s. We have a younger assistant who deals with more modern stuff because, you know, I don't understand it.

TP: I was just going to add one thing, since you mentioned *Oz* magazine. My involvement took a serious lurch to the left, I guess, because I had become, very soon after he came to England [in 1966], a great friend of Richard Neville, who edited *Oz*, and also Jim and Felix Dennis of course. I lived then in Ladbroke Square, Notting Hill Gate, before it was really fashionable, and Richard lived across the other side of Notting Hill Gate, and he was always being threatened by the police, one Inspector Luff who lived just down the road.

Anyway one night, at two or three o'clock in the morning, Richard was knocking on the door saying, could he come in? "Of course!" And he had just been busted and he escaped through the back. He lived in a basement flat, how he got out I don't know. He was about to be had up for the possession of various substances, and the hearing was in the Magistrates Court the following morning and would I go along and support him? So, I said, "Of course," because I was vaguely thought to be respectable. Ho ho.

So I went, and that morning was incredibly shocking — I wrote about it at length in the *Spectator*, not so long afterwards. Anyway, one thing led to another and eventually as you know, *Oz* magazine itself was prosecuted and the three of them were had up at the Old Bailey. I went as his bailee, because I had been his bailee at the Magistrates Court. It was all of £100, I was looking at the bail sheet only the other day.

I only had to be there on the first day of the trial, and the jury had by then been chosen, and I just sat and listened. I had never been in the Old Bailey before. And for some reason I was requested to come back on the second day as the bailee — I think because they thought Richard would do a bunk, which was the most unlikely thing imaginable.

On the way in I bought lots of newspapers to read about what they had said about the trial on day one, and that was in a way the most shocking thing, because the tabloid press had written this up in a way that bore no recognition whatsoever to what had actually happened inside Court Number One. So I'm now making notes about what is happening and compared it again on the third day, and became so hooked on this that I said to Richard, "I'm going to write all this down," — I thought just for a column somewhere maybe. But of course I eventually then wrote a book about the *Oz* trial. To the fury of a man called Geoffrey Robertson, God bless him.

Anyway, Geoffrey Robertson said, "This is my book, this *person* —" he actually wrote this in his first book, " — this *person* was of no consequence, and he had no right to write this book, it was my prerogative, I should have written that book." Well, Geoffrey, you didn't, I did. So, that in a way both cemented and undermined — can you both cement and undermine? — my relationship with all of that media. I was very grateful, because they were extraordinary people, and all the others that were to do with that trial, like Caroline Coon. A lot of very, very, remarkable people.

JG: Can I note one very important thing about what the relationship really was between the underground and music. On the whole we were incredibly ignorant — and if you extract *Rolling Stone UK*, which whatever one thinks of it was trying to emulate *Rolling Stone US*, or at least theoretically so — there was no real expertise. Yes, Barry Miles at *it* was talking to his friends who happened to be called John and Paul and George and Ringo — and maybe Mick as well, but I don't think any of the other Stones. But these were more conversations than interviews. As for rock journalism as such, and underground press journalism as such, let's be honest, I can count the real journalists on possibly a rather attenuated single hand.

But the point was that we needed the music business because the music business were the only people who would advertise with us. So you would have these wonderful ads which they pandered to us and we pandered to them. Like the famous one from CBS, this huge, vast, international or multinational: *The Man Can't Bust Our Music.* My arse. Nonetheless I remember this ad, and how we giggled and how we laughed — and how we loved the £70 we got for it.

When we were thrown out of *Rolling Stone* in Hanover Square, we obviously had to go somewhere nice. So, we went to a flat — again this is the counterculture — owned by a man called Bobby Steinbrecher, who I never met, but he had dimmers in the head of his bed, and the room started dark green at that end and faded gradually to white at this end. This was definitely a "shag pad", I think the slang has it.

But we got our £70 cheque and we got out and we took it to the bank and cashed it. So where are we? We're behind Harrods. So what do we feed the nascent revolutionaries with? We feed them with whatever was in Harrods food hall that day, that you could get for 70 quid. We needed the business on that level, so we kowtowed to CBS. But as you say quite rightly, if you wanted rock-and-roll stuff you were not going to go to the underground press.

Friends had started off as *Friends of Rolling Stone*, until the lawyers came in and we found ourselves as *Friends*, and then *Frendz*. We were already moving away. I was re-reading Alan Marcuson's interviews about it in *Days in the Life* yesterday. He had come from a more politicised background, from South Africa, and had been involved to an extent in politics there, and he wanted a more political magazine. That was what *Frendz* set out to be, a more experimental magazine.

Meanwhile Mark Williams started a magazine called *Strange Days* — which was all music, because Mark was always much more interested in that. But I gave up pretty quickly on *Frendz*. A guy called Dick Lawson was the music editor, he did most of the interviewing. Trouble was we were amateurs. There weren't people like Charlie Murray at that stage, who were fanatics, dare I say. There was Penny Reel, who turned up and we were too dumb to appreciate it, who started talking to us about something called reggae, and as you may remember, we didn't really take it on board very much.

Penny Reel (from the audience): It was very middle-class then. I was the only working-class person there.

JG: Penny was probably the only working-class person in the counterculture I'm afraid. But, you were an expert, that's my point, and we were not.

PR: I loved my music from the age of nine, you know, I would go and watch it in the town then.

JG: Yes, but this didn't mean anything to us.

TP: As Jonathon said, there was enormous pressure coming from the record companies to promote their artists. I wasn't being told by an editor to do this or that — but for example if Judy Garland is performing, then obviously I wanted to go and write a column about it. Apart from that, I was given complete freedom. When I began to write — in a relatively uneducated way — about the various rock stars whose music interested me musically, that's what I did.

But talk about being in the right place at the right time! I can't believe my luck of being dragged down to the Brighton Dome by somebody called Ginger Baker, who said you've got to hear this fucking new group mutter mutter. All I wrote was, "I saw this group in Brighton Dome and I was totally blown away, I thought this is three of the greatest musicians I've ever heard." It was my job to report on what I saw.

MP: [One thing which] I think speaks to a lot of this is the apparent lag between the creation of rock and roll as art and the writing about it. Basically what you have is an evolutionary process. So you've got *Rubber Soul* and *Revolver*, and whatever you think about the Beatles, the fact is those records changed the nature of the discourse of the actual music. There's no doubt this was serious in a way that even the greatest, the most lovely and beautiful pop music that we all loved was not. This was a substantial change, and somehow people had to go and find a way of describing it — and this was a very difficult process. Especially for the mainstream press, because writing about pop music was simply something that the mainstream press, up to that point had just simply not done.

TP: I think I was the first. Geoffrey Cannon was very close behind me.

MP: Geoffrey Cannon, absolutely. And as you mentioned William Mann was writing about it. Writing in such a serious and convoluted way that most of us pop fans simply didn't understand a word of what he was saying. So in a sense the importance of the underground press, both *Rolling Stone* from America and the writing that was in the English underground press, was that this was probably the first attempt for people to try and address the music on the terms in which the music was then starting to be made.

In my job now I read *Record Mirror, Disc and Music Echo* and *NME* from the 60s, and it's pop music, absolutely chart pop music, whether black or white, written about as pop music. Then suddenly albums like *Revolver* come out, and they don't really know how to deal with it. Good writers like Peter Jones and Keith Altham writing more about this one album than they usually write — the usual 50-100 words capsule reviews — and here they are writing 500 word reviews. But they're writing it track by track. "It's a beaty little toe-tapper with an interesting guitar solo." They want to take it seriously, they want to write about it seriously, but they haven't got the language for it, because they are set in their particular pop-music journalist ways. What the underground press did, I think, was liberate everyone to try and find new ways of describing the music.

TP: Yes, I agree absolutely. Here's a perfect example of this evolutionary process, of trying to write about this extraordinary cultural phenomenon in a way that took it seriously, but didn't alienate the people who were either making it or loving it. One of the most notorious columns that I wrote caused terrible outrage on all sides of the fence. I can almost quote the opening lines verbatim, it was as a result of the Beatles' White Album. I said, "If there is still any doubt that the Beatles are the greatest song writers since Schubert," and I then went on to justify it by saying they both wrote for money, they both wrote in the morning, so it was performed in the café in the afternoon, they had no concept of the historical value of what it was they might be doing. It just came pouring out.

Now of course I was lampooned for that, both by the underground press, particularly in my favourite magazine *Oz*, and I think also the *Rolling Stone* had a go at me. Did you have a go at me? You probably did. Justifiably, justifiably.

JG: It's too long ago.

TP: Yes, that's true, we're still friends. But the interesting thing is that now, 40 or 50 years later, we wouldn't think twice about that as an interesting comparison.

MP: I think one problem though was that once people started writing about rock and roll seriously, they wrote about *all* rock and roll seriously. Most rock and roll doesn't deserve that kind of treatment. The *NME* doubled, literally doubled in size between 1970 and 1972. *Melody Maker* was already a pretty packed paper. You had wonderful writers — I mean Richard Williams, Michael Watts, two of my absolute favourite writers, *Melody Maker* is somewhat unfairly maligned given the apparent triumph of the 70s *NME* — but a 4,000 word interview with Rick Wakeman? You want to slash your wrists.

TP: He doesn't know 4,000 words.

MP: Well, believe me, Chris Welch could turn in 4,000 words. So the writing became really bloated, and funnily enough just as the music became critically bloated. It's no accident that prog and 4,000 word *NME* pieces grew hand in hand. For my job now, I'm often finding teen magazines — for example, *KRLA Beat*, which was a free sheet given out by a radio station in Los Angeles, with 500-word pieces written by 19-year-old girls interviewing Herman's Hermits, and they have more energy and more excitement in those 500 words than 5,000 words on Yes, or whatever. The pop-writing baby got thrown out with the rock and roll serious bathwater there.

JG: Because we took the music seriously, we took the musicians seriously. And while maybe Lennon and McCartney and one or two others — Pete Townshend I remember was good, you could never shut Peter Townshend up — could get on their hind legs and become the Philosopher Prince, here's some cornfed boy from the mid-west who had gone into it to get laid, and was doing that very successfully. and you're standing on the top of the Hilton in Park Lane, with some band — I think it was Chicago — and they didn't want to talk to me. They had been told they had to talk to me, they didn't wish to. I didn't know what the hell to ask them, because I didn't know enough about the music. It was a nightmare. But I'm sure that like Chris Welch I churned out my 1,000 words.

But the strange thing was that Philosopher Prince was the marketing position that their PR people would take: *Go out there and say things for the kids, man.* They didn't care about the kids. The only person who very much cared was McCartney, when I interviewed him for *Days in the Life.* He said, "Everybody thinks John was the cultured one, everybody thinks John. But, it was me, it was me." Well, John was dead, there was nothing I could do, you know. But: "I was much more cultured, look I made the wrapping paper for Indica." Fine, yes, good, well done, whatever.

I mean, there you are, one minute you're writing your popsy little pop column in Oxford and then you're in Pete Townshend's garden or sitting in the Speakeasy. First time I met Mark Williams was, you know, "I'm going down to the Speak, anybody coming?" I thought, "Well, I don't know what the Speak is, but we're going." The next thing you know Keith Moon was throwing champagne bottles at me. It was wonderful. Jenny Fabian, the queen of the groupies. How could this not be fun? Anyway this was, as I say, not terribly revolutionary. But to be fair, we wanted more from these musicians than we had any right really to ask — because very few of them could come up to the act.

TP: That's absolutely true, but I think there's one very interesting thing you said there. Again looking at it from my perspective [as a mainstream journalist], and making an attempt to understand why these people were special. That really was the thing that blew me away. Just going back to Cream again, you couldn't ignore the fact that these three individuals were phenomenally gifted musicians. I mean as musicians — as technicians and as musicians and the improvisatory quality of what they did was breath-taking — it didn't always work, sometimes it rambled and went on and on and on, but it was absolutely breath-taking.

Now, my job in the *Observer* and later the *Spectator* was to try and make an audience that would quite happily go to a concerto for toothbrush and piano leg, and think "This is art, this is culture, this is the best art can achieve," to also take seriously what these people were doing. And that was tricky. Though in a way it was made slightly easier because I was also working at the BBC.

JG: Yes, they wouldn't read us, that audience would not read *Frendz* or *Oz*. They might have us on their coffee table.

TP: Yes, exactly. But I remember at the BBC I did a weekly show called *How It Is*. Which incredibly enough was an arts magazine programme between 6-6.45pm on BBC1, can you imagine that now? And it was clearly dealing with rock and roll as often as I possibly could. And at a quarter to six I had to present to the office of Paul Fox — who was then the Controller of BBC1 — and reassure him nothing too dangerous was going to happen. So of course I swore my life away, "Nothing dangerous is going to happen." Luckily there was a very great Director General at that time, Sir Hugh Greene, who agreed, and wanted everything to be moving forward.

So, for example, we did a section from *Hair*. Now I don't need to remind you that *Hair* has odd words in it like cunnilingus — and they sang it, and we thought "Christ, this will be the end of civilisation." You could imagine the questions being asked in parliament. We commissioned Adrian Mitchell to write a poem attacking Vietnam. So it really was a kind of underground attempt to unnerve the establishment. But in those days the BBC had the courage of its convictions.

The centrepiece of each show — which I pinched from *That Was the Week that Was* — was that we had a very staid BBC announcer, Ronald Fletcher, and either side of him were Richard Neville and John Peel, they would have a real ding-dong about what they were preoccupied with that week. With Ronald Fletcher — the face and sound of the BBC — saying, "Gentlemen, do you really think that's not a bit excessive?" You've got Richard, quick as a flash saying, "No, absolutely, this is what we *should* be talking about." Every week I was told, "I don't want either of those two people ever to appear again." But we kept them on and the BBC survived.

My proudest achievement was a film called *All My Loving*, which I was persuaded to make — and the BBC were so shocked and horrified by it that eventually it was put out after the epilogue. In those days, in 1968, when television came to an end, there would be a vicar or a parson who would bless us all and send you off for your cup of cocoa at 10.30, which is when they closed. They were so worried. [Controller of BBC2] David Attenborough said, "As long as I'm in control of television this film will never be shown, only over my dead body." Luckily he and I are still great friends now. But they announced that it would be shown *after* the epilogue — and of course, you know, we knew that would be a source of enormous publicity for us, which it was, it got a huge audience.

But the point of the story is that the only thing really that was on the BBC at that time which dealt with rock and roll and pop music in a totally utterly inadequate way — apart from *Top of the Pops*, and that's a separate issue — was something called *Juke Box Jury*, run by a man called David Jacobs.

All My Loving went out at beginning of November, and I went to a Christmas party at the BBC. And David Jacobs came over and he jabbed me, I mean really hurt me, and said, "You've ruined my career." I thought, "What, I've never met you!" Which I hadn't. So he trundled off, and then somebody else who was there who knew me and Jacobs came over and said, "What did you say to David Jacobs?" I said "I've absolutely no idea. He said, 'You ruined my career.'" He said, "Oh you don't know?" I said, "What don't I know?" One week after *All My Loving*, the BBC finally realised there was rather more to rock and roll than *Juke Box Jury*. *Juke Box Jury* got cancelled.

MP: People ask about the demise of the music press — and I think the adoption of pop writing by the broadsheet press in particular, significantly contributed to that. When you, Tony, were writing for the *Observer* and Geoffrey Cannon at the *Guardian*, and a handful of other people, there was very little writing about pop music, which meant that the music press could flourish in relative isolation. And there was a huge demand for this information — there were one or two television programmes, but not the massive coverage that we can get today. So particularly around 69, 70, when the *Melody Maker* in particular started writing about rock seriously, this allowed it to flourish. Then sometime around, I guess the 1980s, suddenly the music was written about all the time in the broadsheet press. And I think that is quite significant that for a lot of 14, 15, 16-year-olds, they could get the information needed about record releases and they could get reviews, in the daily papers their parents were buying. So the demand for specific music writing in a separate press was certainly less.

JG: I wonder whether that's part of a more general thing with the counterculture. Because we may have done it very amateurishly, but certainly at *Friends* we would deal with green issues, things of that nature, health issues, drugs — taking a very libertarian view, I suppose — but what gradually happened as we moved into the 70s was that the mainstream press, inevitably spearheaded by the *Guardian*, started to take these things on board, and threw expert people at them. I wonder to an extent whether this adoption of music writing by the wider and, dare I say, more expert world, was one of the reasons one could say why the underground was no longer relevant. It had done its job and tiptoed off into the wings.

Now obviously that doesn't include something like *NME*, which flourished enormously — albeit on the backs of Nick Kent (who I hired at *Friends*, we never got on), and Charlie Murray who was an *Oz* schoolkid, etcetera, and Mickey Farren. It's something I noticed in *Days in the Life* yesterday — that although Miles was writing, there was really no rock and roll in *it*, apart from these chaps Miles knew, because it was basically a European-focused beatnik magazine, and that meant jazz.

Mickey turns up around 1967-68, and in the *Days in the Life* interview he said, "I went in there and I saw all these old men and I said, 'Where's the fucking rock and roll?' They said, 'What is it?'" He basically took it from there. But *Rolling Stone, Rolling Stone UK, Frendz* — that was a logical progress, and we moved away from music. But Mickey was saying, "This is what people want in a countercultural magazine, where the hell is it?"

MP: Absolutely. I think the other thing is there's a sort of false memory about music in the underground press, which is created by all these disparate writers coming from the different underground papers and arriving under the same roof at the *NME*. So suddenly these people — who would write maybe two reviews a fortnight or something for *it* or

Frendz, where they had had no editing — were now being asked to churn out 3,000 word interviews and 400 or 500-word reviews every week. So from 1973 onwards this concentration of writers from all the underground press into the one music paper has given everyone the impression that the underground press was *full* of music writing, because these were all underground writers. But in fact they were all put together in the same place and given five times as much to write.

JG: I mentioned Mark Williams's *Strange Days*. This isn't in any way to impugn Mark, but setting *Rolling Stone* aside, it was the one deliberately British underground *music* paper and it failed utterly. The fact is there was not an audience in that category. People didn't want it through the agency of the underground press, I think. As you quite rightly said, it's a false memory and there wasn't as many as people may remember. But, again, we were sufficiently mainstreamed to know that you would sell more copies if you put a well-known rock and roll face on your cover than if you didn't.

MP: Interestingly *Oz* had virtually no writing about music at all. It's really startling.

JG: What you get is Germaine writing about Cock Socks…

MP: Absolutely, you'd get that — and Michael Gray wrote some sort of 5,000 word thing on Dylan in a fairly early *Oz*. Felix Dennis used to write a couple of reviews a month. A tiny amount — it's really only when Charlie Murray arrives that things changed. *it* had significantly more music writing than any of the other papers. And even then that was towards the back of the book, after a 3,000 word article on sexual health or macrobiotic food or all the other subjects that those papers are really about.

But in a way false memory and forgetting are the nature of pop music. That's what's good about it, it moves on, it keeps reinventing. I don't actually have a problem with people being forgotten. We now have the *Mojo*-fication of music, with everything endlessly revisited and dug out, all kinds of mediocrities and obscurities from the 60s being treated as a Festival of Great Gods. Which in a way I think is antipathetic to the spirit of the music they are making, which is, to some extent about disposability. It's about chuck out that 45, chuck out another — and now suddenly we're in a sort of post-historical world where everything has to be endlessly kind of revisited and filleted. So, yes, I think there are some values to forgetting people.

EL: So why did the *Observer* or *The Times* want those things if they weren't recuperating what the counterculture was writing about? Or was it something else they wanted?

TP: That's why I said carefully at the beginning, I thought David Astor was a remarkable editor and David Attenborough at the BBC was a remarkable Controller of Television, in that they saw something which they didn't really understand, but they were aware that there was something important about it. Something which we should take note of, and try and take seriously. Attenborough is a man steeped in music, he knew what great music was. I don't think he thought that the rock and roll coming thundering over the horizon was great music in his terms. But he heard something that he thought, "This has to be listened to carefully, treated with respect, and treated with the highest possible musical standards." But to that extent we have to be very grateful to individuals. You rightly mentioned Jann Wenner. Without Jann Wenner, *Rolling Stone* probably wouldn't have happened in the way that it did.

MP: Jann Wenner started something which was brilliant. But his own personality was why *Rolling Stone* became what it was. The way it changed, the move to New York was all about becoming a celebrity culture magazine.

JG: The reason we fell out with them at [what became] *Frendz* was basically that we wouldn't simply, you know, reflect that. Wenner wanted an eight-page insert which basically had as many mentions of Mick Jagger as possible. He was not getting that. We were starting to put in stuff that he didn't like — and the doors were shut. There was a notorious party where everybody got spiked — and what was worse was they were music business executives who got spiked. It's all in *Days in the Life*. And that was it really. The business cannot be insulted in this way. But we had pretensions to counter-culturality.

We couldn't write about it, we couldn't get it right, but the fact is that the umbrella of what we'll call the counterculture — we will not call it the underground or indeed the alternative society, the counterculture — the huge big unifying visible thing was rock and roll, and everything else was adjuncts. If you wanted to get your message across, you had to splash rock and roll, and we did that.

But Mark is absolutely right, *Frendz* probably had more rock and roll than most of them because it had come out of *Rolling Stone*. But you can watch it evaporate. And of course what happens if it evaporates is we didn't get the advertising — and then you don't get the paper, and that did happen. We had Alan Marcuson's rich father — who, you know, he made socks in South Africa, so it was in the millions — and that kept us going, but realistically...

TP: Jann Wenner was the first person I ever knew whose entire luggage as he travelled round the world was one tiny little case, and a lot of credit cards. I had never seen anybody operate simply on credit cards. But he did something of enormous importance, which I cannot underestimate, which was breaking the door down.

MP: In 1968-69, *Rolling Stone* would have about five or six pages of music news and major interviews, almost every issue, one major interview, maybe two with musicians. There would be other stories, political stuff and so on and so forth. That increased later and was very good, with Hunter S. Thompson, Joe Eszterhas. And then you got pages, five, six, seven or eight full size pages of 500-word reviews at the back. The one place which you could read a review of all the albums released pretty much in any given fortnight. So it was really a substantial music magazine — even after the *Frendz* fiasco happened, and it was all hived off. But American *Rolling Stone* was really easy to buy in the UK, certainly in London. You could buy American *Rolling Stone* in W. H. Smiths in a way that you couldn't buy *it*, for example. *it* was street sold.

JG: As was *Oz*. Felix Dennis started off as a street-seller. But the important thing is that the atmosphere at that time was that all of the magazines that we've mentioned — good, bad and indifferent — were a required read. I mean I was in my mid-20s, and I thought I must go and read this, I want to know what is happening. There was an appetite for trying to find out what was happening.

EL: The *what is happening* is interesting, because it isn't just music. I mean partly it's just a case of knowing who has released this and that, but it's also social significance.

MP: It was part-and-parcel of the counterculture.

TP: Yes, it was collectively that all of those people thought they were going to change the world. Well, they didn't — and that's a separate and very complicated question to even begin to consider. But, there was a feeling that revolution was just around the corner.

JG: And music was part of it.

TP: *it* had that slogan, was it Plato? I can't remember, "When the sound of the music changes, the walls of the city shake." *it* had that splashed under the masthead.

MP: I discovered an Atlanta underground newspaper called *Great Speckled Bird* recently, and one thing that I found very interesting is that the difference between England and America is striking. Because in a way we were dancing in England. It was hugely pleasurable, there were few immediate threats. In the United States, Bobby Kennedy and Dr King had been killed. If you couldn't get a college diploma and were working-class or black you could be drafted to Vietnam. The revolution there was serious, the Students for a Democratic Society were a much more muscular beast than any political organisation in this country. You read *Great Speckled Bird*, and their offices are firebombed, all kinds of things are going on, the street-sellers are being busted and beaten up and locked away for five or six days. The underground in America was under immense pressure and threat in a way that in England…

JG: We were *ersatz*, it was as simple as that. We were *ersatz*, we loved it, but, no, we had none of it. I mean the missing word is Vietnam, and Civil Rights of course, yes, and it all seems to me, you know, one looks for little allegorical things, but in Grosvenor Square in March 1968, there was a proper violent confrontation between the authorities, the police and the demonstrators. The whole of the year through to October there was this build up, build up, build up — if you thought it was bad that time, this time it's going to be even worse. What actually happened, they ended up singing 'Auld Lang Syne' together. I mean you didn't sing 'Auld Lang Syne' in Chicago.

And America had Weather Underground and we didn't have that. Well, we had the Angry Brigade — which I know came from the French word which means Angry Brigade, but nonetheless always seemed like a joke to me — but that's bye-the-bye. It was *ersatz* — which is really what *Days in the Life* is about, dare I say — but it's also about young middle-class people having fun, as so many youth cults, so many youth movements boil down to. Now it's of course completely beyond me, so I can't compare.

MP: And there was no risk of Barry Miles or yourselves being drafted to go and fight a war. With *Great Speckled Bird*, two of their senior writers both got their draft notices, had to feign psychiatric illness in one case or claim to be homosexual in the other.

TP: Were you old enough to have the threat of National Service?

JG: Oh no. When I arrived at Cambridge, sorry about that, I'm being made to feel terribly guilty about it, I was the first year that wasn't. But the year in front of me were.

TP: To his credit Harold Wilson kept the UK out of Vietnam.

MP: What Penny Reel is saying is sort of to do with this. That actually the one section of society — in London particularly, but in England throughout — who were under immediate pressure was the black community. And it's to *it's* credit that they wrote quite extensively about that, about the Mangrove trials and so on and so forth.

JG: I think *Frendz* covered that too, I think it was covered. Well, it was our turf. It was Portobello. As you say, it was to our credit, but it was the local turf, wasn't it? Danae Hughes wrote a long piece on Michael X.

Penny Reel (from the audience): Michael X had nothing to do with the black dialogue.

JG: But to a lot of my readers Michael X had the Black House, he represented the real counterculture.

PR: He didn't have grass-roots black support.

JG: No, no, but he was a good con man. And to go back a bit, when you read about black music — and maybe I'm just extrapolating for myself here — but a lot of people writing about it in the underground didn't realise that the slang that we were using, *heavy, groovy, out of sight, dig it man*, was all 1930s, 40s, American black slang. And I think a lot of us probably didn't realise that the music we loved so much had also come from this background. Again it was this ignorance. But people like Charlie Murray did know this. And then it began to get more skilful.

In Lieu of Actual Money

Mark Williams explains how the underground press was funded

Nowadays punters have a love-hate relationship with the record industry, mainly because it's dominated by streaming and download services — which consumers love because they get their music cheaply if not *gratis*, and musicians hate, for the paltry royalties they receive for their creative toil. But back in the late 60s we who slaved away at the countercultural coalface loved the record business because without it... well, without it we probably wouldn't have had a coalface to slave away at.

Looking back through my yellowing, flaking copies of *International Times* (*it*), for which I was the first music editor back in late 1968, it's clear that it relied for perhaps 90 percent of its advertising revenue on record companies. Which is why the *ad hoc* committee who owned and ran the paper decided to instigate an entire section — wittily christened 'Plug & Socket'— to corral all the nefariously capitalistic advertising into one place, along with the content which was at least nominally in the music industry's thrall, leaving the rest of the newspaper to get on with the important business of changing society.

At the point I was invited to be this section's editor, my entire background in journalism had been sending badly typed reports of the gigs I'd been helping to run to raise funds to start the Birmingham Arts

Lab. Light years away from today's high-pressure world, where a degree in media studies, a lengthy unpaid internship and a mummy who hobnobs with the editor's mistress might — just — get you a job as a junior hack. But those were different times, so without a second thought I moved down to London and quickly immersed myself in the underground movement (music division).

The bands that I loved when they played at our Birmingham gigs — Clouds, Family, Peter Green's Fleetwood Mac and the like — were staples of a music scene only tenuously allied to the ideals espoused by the underground press (which in 1968 was still basically just *Oz* and *it*). I had never written a feature for a magazine, let alone edited one, but — as I quickly discovered, when thrown in the deep end — there was much more to the job than bigging up the music I personally liked.

There was, for example, the important business of reviewing the slew of albums that arrived on virtually a daily basis. Many came in enticingly substantial cardboard envelopes, though the more assiduous PR flunkeys turned up in person at the offices, then located above a fish-and-chip shop in Covent Garden, bearing armfuls of albums and a mantra that varied little in its gushy assurances that the artists concerned were "very concerned about extending artistic boundaries, oh, and peace, love and understanding." At first I was innocently accepting of this cod-ideological banter — which combined with worthily worded press release promo-flak — but soon developed a cynical carapace, aided not a little by *it*'s regular contributors and reviewers, Mick Farren and (Barry) Miles, both of whose counterculture credentials ran considerably deeper than mine.

By virtue of their greater musical knowledge and standing in the society that the underground press promulgated — a paradoxical space, both closed and open — both Miles and Mickey had first dibs on the records they wanted to write about, or at least take home and get stoned to. So I was often left with the likes of Elton John and the Edgar Broughton Band — and the chance to trudge along to the Record & Tape Exchange in Notting Hill once a month with carrier bags full of unwanted swag which I could somewhat guiltily sell. (It wasn't till much later, as a *Melody*

Maker writer, that I realised virtually every music hack in London was doing the same thing.)

The revenue from off-loading review copies was handy to the point of being essential while working at *it*, because wages were unpredictable to say the least — in some cases consisting of half an ounce of Moroccan Black to dispose of as we wished, *in lieu* of actual money. This was less a statement of the paper's philosophical bent and more of a practical convenience because — and there's no judicious way of putting this — one or two of its benefactors were dope dealers and its finances were consistently precarious.

As has been pointed out elsewhere, the underground press emerged almost entirely as a consequence of the IBM golfball typesetter and the development of relatively cheap web-offset printing, together circumventing hitherto traditional hot-metal composition and letterpress printing, which were effectively controlled by aggressively protective unions on the one hand, and a small cabal of print barons on the other. And though mutually and doggedly incompatible, both these forces represented vested interests: the 'establishment' that the underground movement was all about overthrowing — albeit in a somewhat nebulous way.

it and *Oz* could lease the IBM machinery; the trouble arose with printing companies, who never shared our cultural and quasi-political views, and whose shareholders were often freemasons malignly susceptible to the influences of local cops, politicians and other defenders of moral rectitude. As one of the few staffers who owned a driving licence, I would regularly deliver the 'boards' — meaning the artwork — to far-flung printers in South Wales or East Anglia… only to be greeted by sheepish print managers who'd been leant on, and could not accept our seditious and sordid propaganda. At which point, as the bearer of bad tidings, I'd have to drive the company's Mini pick-up (don't ask) back to town in the wee small hours. Sometimes we had to forego a deposit already made; more often it meant that Dave, our business-cum-production manager, had to scrabble around at the last minute desperately trying to find a replacement who, aware that one of his peer companies had turned us down, could cynically demand top dollar and a down-payment to print the next, inevitably now much delayed, issue, often to a different page size. The income from sales was also unreliable. Indeed, my less-than-illustrious publishing career had begun as an *it* street-seller in Birmingham, a small army of whom were dotted around the country. These street sales underpinned the even less dependable sales from head shops and London newsstands, and meant that the paper's finances were always shaky — hence the occasionally unconventional wages-in-kind.

The establishment of Plug & Socket was intended to alleviate all this, and to an extent it did. But thanks mostly to John Peel (whose *Perfumed Garden* show on Radio London spawned a column of the same name in *it*), a large chunk of our constituency were more interested in hippie music than in hippie proselytizing. So record companies were happy to book full-page adverts, as they also were in the less frequently, and indeed less regularly published *Oz* (whose legal and printing problems were even worse than *it*'s).

Sometimes the cash-flow situation got so desperate that Dave had to scamper around record companies' offices to get instant cash payment for their ads, which he did with a firm charm and zero embarrassment. But there was often an assumed *quid pro quo* on their part — which certainly embarrassed me when I found myself obliged to scrawl a lengthy feature on Elton John or Deep Purple to ensure the vital ad revenues kept rolling in.

There was an increasing reliance on events advertising, too, which meant covering things like CBS Records' Rock Machine gigs at the Albert Hall or the Rock Proms at the Roundhouse — a rather far cry from the more laidback, innovative and eclectic entertainments offered at earlier underground venues like Middle Earth and UFO between 1966-69. In some respects this suited me personally, because I had free entry to virtually anything I wanted to see, which — given my wide-eyed and even naïve enthusiasm for all things rock-ish, from Soft Machine to Hendrix via Traffic, Beefheart and the Floyd — was virtually everything. And once in, I'd be glad-handed by beer-buying press officers. Even so, as I neared the end of my tenure at *it*, I felt a growing moral discomfort with the way that big promoters and record companies were dictating what we could listen to, and where. Indeed I myself clambered on my high horse in *it* #79 (May 1970): "We're herded around from circus to circus, the attractions offered seem to get mightier… and as the complexity and capital outlay of each new event increases, so too does the polarity between audience and performer."

Tired of the pecuniary unpredictability and the ideological infighting, I left the paper soon afterwards to launch *Strange Days* in late 1970, my own rather amateurish imitation of America's *Rolling Stone*, which lasted just four issues, and a little later, a motorcycle magazine — *Bike* — that 'Dares To be Different' (not anymore, as it's still going strong and I still contribute). My taste for music journalism resumed in the mid-70s as a contracted freelancer for *Melody Maker*, and later as editor of the strike-breaking *New Music News*. But while I quickly discovered the deadline disciplines that *it* largely lacked on these latter titles, the tunes I was obliged to dance for the record companies and gig promoters weren't very different from the ones I pranced around to in my days on the underground press.

Mark Williams was music editor at it, and wrote in the 70s for Melody Maker and Rolling Stone. He founded New Music News, as well as Bike, several other motorcycle magazines and most recently, the quasi-literary Classic Motoring Review.

And at that Point I Joined the Psychedelic Left...

Charles Shaar Murray interviewed in November 2016 by Mark Sinker

CSM: I was a schoolkid in Caversham in Reading, reading and listening and profoundly wishing I was somewhere less whitebread lace-curtain and boring. I wanted to be living in London, with my Own Pad — mingling with interesting people and sampling the joys of sex, drugs and rock and roll. I wanted to be either a writer or a musician. I wanted to be one of the groovy creatives.

MS: And in Caversham you knew about such people how?

CSM: It started with pop papers: *Fab 208*, the *NME* and the *Melody Maker*. I was just fascinated by the music, and wanted to discover what this stuff was all about. And having a historian's bent, I researched stuff.

MS: What did "researching stuff" mean in Reading?

CSM: It meant being exposed to some fairly cool records because my best mate up the road had a fairly cool older sister. And it was through hanging out round her house and borrowing her records that was when I first heard Dylan, the Stones, Georgie Fame & The Blue Flames Live at the Flamingo. Getting the first Stones EP, and it said on the back, and I'm quoting from ancient memory, "The Stones are Britain's leading exponents of Chicago Blues." And I thought, "Chicago Blues, so that's what they're doing — I wonder what that is?" So I went to the library and got a book on the history of the blues, and it was like, "Oh my God, this wonderful music that I love so much is a by-product of slavery and oppression! That can't be right! How dare they treat the people who make this beautiful music like this!" And bang, music and politics arrived simultaneously. From one line on the back of a Stones EP. Liner notes by Andrew Loog Oldham.

MS: So you were travelling back and forth from London?

CSM: Well, I came up to London a few times a year with my parents, before I was judged old and responsible enough to come up by myself. I'd seen the odd copy of *Oz* and *it* in Reading, but their distribution was really sporadic — so what I'd do in London was try and find places that sold *Oz* and *it* and *Rolling Stone*, and I would try to stock up on these as best as I could. I started checking out *Rolling Stone* probably in 1968.

MS: At the conference everyone was talking about the 'underground' as if it was something that everybody understood — including me supplying its title — but there must have been a point when it hadn't really started yet.

CSM: It was a lot of different scenes that found common ground. For example, when what used to be called the R&B boom started in the UK, what happened was that blues became a kind of *lingua franca* for musicians from the folk, jazz and rock worlds. Because they could all find a bit of common ground playing blues — so the music that was created, my pet phrases for this is that it was based on "creative misunderstandings of the source material". Similarly what the underground was was a new kind of spirit — caused by social circumstances that we can get to in a moment — which involved people in fashion, in fine art, in theatre, in film… And I guess what maybe *they* had in common was that they all went to see the same bands. So this music was the glue that united all these people from different disciplines.

In the early 60s, we were only just seeing off post-war austerity — and it's a total cliché to say that the art schools had a lot to do with it, but the fact that people from the working class and lower middle class could now receive the kind of education that had only been available to the children of the wealthy, barring a few scholarships. It meant that people with immense intellectual and creative potential were suddenly exposed to stuff which could enable them to realise and explore that potential. These people weren't thick, these were people whose situation had enforced artificially narrow horizons on them. And suddenly you had musicians, designers, fine artists, commercial artists, dancers, actors, all responding to social and economic change — and the reason I think of it as such a brilliant time, even though I was just a kid outside with my nose pressed up against the glass, was there was what Patti Smith called the *"sea of possibilities"*. Suddenly, it was like this tiny little grainy monochrome picture went *zhzhzhhhzhxxch!* Like the *Wizard of Oz*, the small black-and-white image becomes a great big Technicolor image with all these weird things in it. And we got these incredible cross-fertilisations… and it was simultaneously — and I'm either repeating myself or quoting myself — a plot by the kids of the middle classes to explore the mysteries of the aristocracy and the proletariat, and a conspiracy between the working classes and the upper classes to destroy the bourgeoisie.

There were some wild cards in the mix, the Krays and all that shit, but essentially people were meeting and mingling, on a more or less equal basis, who 20 years earlier would never have met at all, because there would have been no context for them to meet in. And everybody nicked a few of everybody else's tricks. Another reason I think it was such a great time was that there was the looming threat of nuclear war, the Alan Moore clock another minute and a half closer to midnight, so there's the pressure of imminent doom and at the same time this extraordinary sense of expanding possibilities, and the idea that we may not be able to save the world with guns but we can save it with culture! And at that point I joined the Psychedelic Left — to which I still owe allegiance. Alliances with the Boring Left are always short-term and tactical.

Basically it was like, "Hey, these are my people! I must join them!" And as soon as I could I ran away and joined the circus.

MS: So first your nose is pressed up against the glass, and then you pass through.

CSM: Schoolkids *Oz*! Richard Neville changed my life. And Felix Dennis and Jim Anderson. But answering the ad for Schoolkids *Oz* was the absolute tipping point. Because my exam results were shit, I even got turned down to study American Studies at Aberystwyth. So I was saved from university — which meant when I arrived at *NME*, I had a head-start on a bunch of people who were still doing degrees they never used.

MS: How long a gap was there between Schoolkids *Oz* and *NME*?

CSM: Two years. Schoolkids *Oz* is 1970, the trial is 1971. And in 1971, I went to America. I had American relatives who were quite well off — basically all our relatives had more money than we did, we were the poorest branch of both families. I'd first gone to America in 1968, first stop Chicago, a week before the Democratic Convention. I said I wanted to stay and join the demonstration. My relatives said the middle-aged Central European equivalent of "Fuck *that* for a game of soldiers" and immediately packed me off to the next relative in Cincinnati. I was very impressed by that fact that one of my Chicago relatives' friends lived in the same apartment block as Dick Gregory. Going up to their flat, and lo and behold, two doors down in his denim fatigues, was Dick Gregory saying "Hi!" I was the sort of English kid who, in 1968 at the age of 17, would know who Dick Gregory was.

MS: Routine access to Dick Gregory in the UK was surely limited then?

CSM: The thing was, I'd never seen or heard him perform. Another weird thing about our house was we didn't get TV till I was 16. This meant two things: one was that I had to go round other people's houses to watch my favourite programmes. I'm sure some of them got heartily sick of me turning up on the doorstep for *Ready Steady Go!*, *Star Trek* and *The Man from U.N.C.L.E.* But hell, I had records before we had a record player. I would walk around with records under my arm and stop people in the street, ask if they had a record player and ask if I could come in for half an hour and ask if I could listen to my record. That's the kind of funny kid I was. But it also meant that, for entertainment, it was down to reading. I read all sorts of stuff. In the end my parents would give me their library card — I'd go down to the library in the morning, take out six books, read them, and next day I'd go back and take out six more. They had to let me into the adult library by the time I was 12 because I'd read everything in the children's library.

MS: So after Schoolkids *Oz*, you start working with Richard Neville and others in his flat, to put it together.

CSM: I did, but there was quite a lot going on. I went back to the States in 1971, for the summer — and my nice relatives gave me a three-week go-anywhere-you-want Greyhound bus pass. So, with a cheap acoustic guitar, a suitcase, and not very much money, I spent five straight days and nights going to San Francisco. I had letters of introduction from Richard Neville to various underground press people, I had one for the *East Village Other* and one for the *San Francisco Oracle*. So I got to San Francisco, turned up on the doorstep of the *San Francisco Oracle*, and went "Hi! I'm from London, from *Oz* magazine. Here's a letter from Richard Neville, can I crash?" Spent about a week in San Francisco and its environs, hitched around California — spent time in San Diego, met a bunch of people on the beach, from somewhere I'd acquired a roll of amphetamine tablets, I can't remember where I got those, but I was crashing in their house, on their living room sofa, but I remember waking up and there was this plate of cookies on the table. I thought, "Oh, these look nice, I'll have a couple of these." They were special cookies! *zhzhzhhhzhxxch*, all this! [*waves hands around*]. Then from San Diego crossed over into Tijuana…

So in lieu of university, I got a place at the National Council for the Training of Journalists course in Harlow — so I spent five days a week in Harlow, where I got good marks in English and really shit marks in shorthand and local government law. But apart from instilling in me the virtues of accuracy and story-structure, they were grooming me for a career I knew I wasn't going to have. Because I was continuing to write for *Oz*. Because after the Schoolkids issue was done they said, "Hey, if you want to carry on writing stuff for us, you'd be very welcome." I got bunged a few quid now and then, bought meals and drinks, and given drugs — which seemed like a good idea at the time. So I wrote a bit for *Oz* — and hanging out with them I met all sorts of people, the other underground press people, the *it* mob. I think [Barry] Miles was still around at that point, Mickey [Farren] at the height of his White Panther phase as John Sinclair's representative on earth. And I started meeting heroes. I did interviews with Al Kooper and Johnny Winter,

Muddy Waters, Keef Hartley... And I also met people like Brion Gysin and Alex Trocchi.

Then *Oz* launched a very ill-fated side project called *ink*, a fortnightly newspaper edited by John Lloyd, who at the time was a long-haired revolutionary — and later ended up as a sort of stern Gordon Brown-type Labour right-wing economist. But the music editor was Charlie Gillett, and he was just on the point of leaving when my first submissions came in. He liked them, and said, "Look, I'm not staying with *ink*, I'm moving over to do this new thing called *Cream* [not *CREEM*], with a guy called Bob Houston." Bob was an ex-assistant editor of *Melody Maker*, who doubled as a sub on the *Observer*'s sports pages, was an old-time hardcore Red Clydeside guy. And sometimes I'd be delivering copy to Bob — which in those days meant physically moving around bits of paper you'd produced on an acoustic typewriter — at some pub round the corner from the *Observer* on Saturday night. He also edited *The Miner*, which was the newspaper of the NUM. Sometimes I would go to deliver copy to Bob, and he'd be round the corner from NUM headquarters.

So I'd be suddenly walking into this smoky beery environment, with basically a bunch of grizzled Scots trade unionists. [By now I'd moved from Reading to London], and was getting experience of social strata you don't encounter in Caversham Heights. So I wrote some stuff for Houston's *Cream* magazine, where he said, "If the regular press is the overground, and the underground press is the underground, then *Cream* magazine is ground level." It was a place where writers from the underground press and writers from the regular music press could each do stuff that wouldn't necessarily fit in their regular environment. It was at a *Cream* editorial meeting I first met Neil Spencer and Ian MacDonald.

What was also interesting to me was that the membrane between what was underground and what was mainstream seemed utterly permeable. Music that one week was in the clubs — the hippie clubs like UFO or the soul or reggae clubs, or ska and rocksteady as it was then — and then suddenly it could be on *Top of the Pops*. So one minute the likes of Desmond Dekker or Dave and Ansel Collins only existed in West Indian

Clubs. Or the likes of Pink Floyd or Jethro Tull or whoever only existed in the hippie clubs. Then suddenly they're mainstream, they're on Radio One, they're on *Top of the Pops*.

MS: Was that something you felt conflicted about, or simply excited about?

CSM: You mean like in Pete Townshend's song, "*Sadly ecstatic that their heroes are news*", from '5.15'? No, I was good with it. The idea that Dylan could be a pop star, I thought this was great. Every time someone from "our lot" breaks through into the mainstream, it is Raising the Consciousness of the Masses, Maaaan. Seeing Pink Floyd or Arthur Brown on *Top of the Pops* when three months earlier they'd been playing the Middle Earth Club, I thought this was absolutely brilliant. I thought it was a metaphor for how our ideas and our ideology were going to transform society. In the end society ended up transforming them. But that was me as an idealistic teenager.

MS: "Raising consciousness" always seems an interesting phrase to me — because it's somehow left unclear what it is exactly they're becoming conscious of.

CSM: Well, you know, the wonders of the All-Being and the need for all people to live in peace in harmony with each other. If everybody smoked spliff, dropped acid and listened to loads of Jimi Hendrix and *Sergeant Pepper*, and had tons and tons of sex, then paradise on earth would be achieved! And it was, in my flat. For a few hours at a time.

MS: But with someone like Dylan, if you're listening and thinking through what he's talking about, he's not a hippie idealist…

CSM: No! And neither was Frank Zappa. He hated hippies, he said he was a Freak. He was speaking for Freaks, not hippies — he despised hippies, he thought they were a bunch of mindlessly consuming sheep, and the only difference between them and straight society was that they consumed different stuff. Some of which was his, but there you go. [*Zappa voice*] "Everybody in this room is wearing a uniform, and don't you forget it!"

MS: I get a sense with magazines like *Oz* that it's a group of people learning as they go along, educating themselves in public. And readers reading them as they're discovering, and learning about things this way.

CSM: Yeah. What you find in *Oz* is that there's an awful lot of strands of underground opinion represented. You'd get hardcore Trot stuff from some people, real Angry Brigade blow-stuff-up people, you'd get the macrobiotic people, you'd get "Oh fuck, we haven't got a cover photo, get somebody's girlfriend to take her top off, snap! That's it, we'll get Martin Sharp to do some doodles round the edges, whatever." The underground was not remotely a monolith. It was so fissiparous — is that how you pronounce it? A word you see written down more often than hear in conversation — and so disparate that it was amazing that it hung together even as long as it did. There were the peace-and-love crowd, there were the armed-struggle crowd, and there were an awful lot of people that Mick Farren and Edward Barker called 'boggies', lumpen-hippies in greatcoats whose only aim in life was to find enough cheap drugs and cider to be as far off their heads as possible. And then they would try to batter themselves with the loudest possible music. They were basically regarded as the flotsam and jetsam.

But the people I hung out with were not lazy stumblebums. They were highly active, creative people with very lively minds, who were always doing something — someone was opening a shop, somebody was designing clothes, somebody wanting to start a magazine, somebody was promoting gigs. They were people doing stuff, they were not lazy stoners. Those are the people I moved with, and when people talk about hippies, those are the people I'm thinking of.

MS: There's this interface in the underground between liberals with an experimental bent who are generous about intellectual debate, and people who are like "Bring it on, let's bring the state down." In his essay, Mark Pringle mentions reading *Black Dwarf* and *Red Mole*. They're not music papers, obviously, but people are talking about music there as well.

CSM: Remember that there was briefly an interface between hardcore radical politics, and some of the music scene. Lennon gave a couple of interviews to Tariq Ali, and so on. I think a lot of people on the left had this idea that they could use radical rock musicians as Pied Pipers to recruit the yoot dem into the struggle. *Plus ça change*: I remember the last interview I did with Joe Strummer, he said every time he got to a Clash gig, there'd be telegrams from the SWP waiting for them. The thing is, no matter how political musicians can be, they are musicians first and activists second. Joe was saying, "We're for the Revolution and all that, but for fuck's sake, forget about all that marching up and down for a while, relax and smoke a bloody joint."

MS: In Nigel Fountain's book on the alternative press, he quotes Neville as saying, "We wanted everything in *Oz* **to be written as well as everything was in the** *New Statesman.*" **This startled me — wasn't this what you were getting away from? Were you reading** *New Statesman* **or** *New Society* **or** *Private Eye?*

CSM: If you've seen the very early issues of *Oz*, they were a sort of cross between the hipper end of the *Statesman* and *Private Eye*. But it was all happening in the world of drugs and rock'n'roll, and long hair and very fancy shirts. I would read *Private Eye* occasionally. The *Statesman* I never saw. In our house we got the *Telegraph* as our daily paper and both the *Sunday Times* and the *Observer* at weekends.

Remember in the 60s I was a kid from a decidedly non-wealthy background. The reason I have this BBC Home Service accent, acquired from the radio, is that my parents, both being refugee foreigners, [*Central European accent*] *talked like zis.* You've got to remember the times, you've got to remember that most of both sides of my family disappeared during World War Two, while my parents got a pretty good welcome here — a warmer welcome than their equivalents are receiving now, despite all the so-called progress made in the last 70 years. They thought, "You never know when the British are going to go mad and declare a pogrom, so we don't want him to be identifiable by his accent."

MS: Is it fair to say that the underground was OK-ish, if naïve, on race politics but not great on gender politics?

CSM: Pretty much. My standard take is that women had their 60s in the 70s. I remember the issue of *Oz* immediately after the Schoolkids issue was what was referred to in the office as the 'Cunt Power' issue, but emblazoned on the cover as the 'Female Issue' — and it was guest-edited by Germaine Greer. So at the age of 19, I was hanging out, mouth shut, ears open, on the fringes of the editorial meeting with the regular *Oz* crew plus Dr Greer. And this is prior to the publication of *The Female Eunuch*. So I was getting a sneak preview of what would be the feminist discourse that dominated the 70s. And afterwards I nervously approached La Greer — who incidentally had appeared in *Oz*'s Groupie issue, unzipping Viv Stanshall's fly and flashing a nipple at the lens — and said, "What difference is feminism going to make to me?" And she said [*Germaine Greer voice*] "Well, you'll feel a slight tingling in your balls." And I thought, "OK, I look forward to this."

But during the 60s, the role of most women in the hippie world was to look fabulous in long diaphanous dresses, roll a lot of joints and produce exquisite little vegetable messes for any number of people at short notice.

(Part 2 of this interview can be found on p.175)

Charles Shaar Murray first wrote for the Oz Schoolkids issue in 1970, before becoming a staffer at NME in the 70s and 80s.

THE HIGHEST TIMES

"I hadn't quite arrived at the stage where I could appreciate bald guys with trombones" — *Charles Shaar Murray*

The Trades Meet the Underground

Richard Williams: *Melody Maker, Time Out, arts and sports journalist, artistic director of the Berlin Jazz Festival 2015-17*
Charles Shaar Murray: *Oz, NME, Q, Mojo, Vogue, Guitarist*
Mark Williams: *it, Strange Days, Rolling Stone, Melody Maker, New Music News, Bike*

RW: This is Charles Shaar Murray, that's Mark Williams and I'm Richard Williams, absolutely no relation. We don't have a moderator, this is free form.

CSM: As a person generally not capable of speaking in known human language at this hour, I was hoping to get discreet prods from offstage to trigger those failing brain cells.

RW: Perhaps since I'm the kind of representative of the straight trade press, I assume, I should start. We've been asked to talk a little bit about ourselves, which we can do briefly, about how we became involved with the music press. I got chucked out of school, played in a band for a year, joined a local paper at the age of 18, did my four years of golden weddings and funerals and juvenile court, and because nobody in charge of local papers at the time knew what pop music was, I got a pop column, in which I could write about the Velvet Underground or Albert Ayler as well as the sensations of the day, and thus compile a healthy list of cuttings which got me a job at the *Melody Maker* in 1969, a paper I'd read since I was about 12, along with *Disc and Music Echo*. Actually I thought I wasn't good enough for a job at the *Melody Maker* at the time, so when I was about 17 I applied for the *NME* — and got turned down.

CSM: Well, that's how it was then.

RW: But eventually I landed the big one and I spent four years there.

CSM: In 1960, when I was nine years old, I bought my first *Superman* comic, and on the back there was an ad for all these wonderful things you could buy or be given as prizes if you participated in child capitalism and sold lots of seeds out of a catalogue. And one of these was an Elvis Presley guitar, and there was a little cartoon of somebody playing an acoustic guitar and waving it about a bit. So I said to my dad, "Who's Elvis Presley?" and he said, "Ach, some idiot from America," and I was still intrigued. This was 1960, I was nine years old, Elvis had been in the army, so pretty much all of his great records had been made when I was a toddler, and the next best thing seemed to be Cliff Richard and the Shadows — or some strange American records that you very rarely heard on the radio. But I developed a taste for this stuff, and then Beatles, Stones, Who, Motown, all the rest of it. I got more and more fascinated, I was reading all of the weekly music papers.

The *Melody Maker* at that time had good stuff in it, but also an awful lot of stuff about bald guys with trombones, and I hadn't quite arrived at the stage where I could appreciate bald guys with trombones. In 1967 I discovered the underground press, and suddenly, *whoomph*, there was this whole other dimension that went with the music I loved, the radical shifts in consciousness, the politics, the fact that print didn't have to be black-on-white all the time, that orange, green and purple had their role and possibly on the same page. In 1970 the editors of *Oz* ran a little ad saying, "We want our readers 18 or younger to come and do a special issue, because some of us here are feeling old and boring." And even though I was about to turn 19, I thought, right, I'm not turning this one down, so I went along, got involved in the *Oz* Schoolkids issue, shame and scandal in the family, continued to write for the underground press, and a short-lived magazine edited by a renegade deputy editor from *Melody Maker* named Bob Houston, which was called *Cream* (as distinct from the US magazine *CREEM*).

Then in 1972 I got headhunted by the *NME* which was about to expire from bleeding out its readership and wanted a radical makeover. And somebody there figured that what they needed to reinvent themselves was me and a bunch of people like me, or sort of like me-ish, and I was thinking, "Oh no, man, I'm selling out to the straights, maaan!" and then I remembered that I had a pair of boots at the repairers for two months and a pair of trousers at the dry cleaners for two and a half, because I didn't have the money to get them out, and I thought, "Sod it, I want to play on the big stage," joined the *NME*, brought in as many underground press types as I could persuade to collaborate, and they tell me the rest is history, but I really was there, so I can't remember it.

RW: I'd just like to say about Bob Houston, it was his job I took at the *Melody Maker* when I joined, his leaving was the vacancy I took. He was an amazing man, a Glaswegian, and he spent quite a lot of his subsequent career simultaneously editing the magazine of the National Union of Mineworkers — and something called *Majesty*, which he created, which was a monthly magazine about the Royal Family. Just fantastic.

CSM: I learned so much from Bob. He kind of resembled an unmade bed with a beard and he was the guy who told me, "You've got all the words here, Murray, now it's time to get them in the right order."

MW: It's me now, isn't it? Well, it's a sorry tale. I left school unconscionably young at 15 and I was playing in various bands in Newcastle-upon-Tyne. My best friend there was a bass player called Keith Jackson, who later became Lee Jackson of the Nice, and he moved down to London to join Gary Farr and the T-Bones and was having such a great time from his flat above the 2i's Coffee Bar in Old Compton Street that he said I should come down and join him. Even though I had very little talent as a drummer, I did so, and really the acme of my drumming career was playing for Marc Bolan at the *NME* Poll Winners' Concert at the Empire Pool, Wembley. After that I was pretty rubbish in all the jobs I tried to get as a drummer, so I went to work at Selmer Music in Charing Cross Road, and I wasn't very good at that either, so I moved to Birmingham where I got involved with the nascent Birmingham Arts Lab, or rather fundraising to try and establish it, which involved running concerts every Friday night at the magnificently gothic Moseley and Balsall Heath working men's institute.

We had some pretty good bands: Family were fairly regular, Gary Farr, Clouds... Anyway, we raised enough money to put down a deposit on leasing a building and open the Arts Lab, and my work there was sort of done, because I was in charge of fundraising. But during that time, I was submitting little news pieces to *International Times* — in London, obviously — and I was also street-selling *it* in Birmingham, we sold it at the fundraisers. So after the lab was opened, I came down to London, never having met anyone from *it*, went to their offices in Endell Street and — extraordinarily — was offered a job as music editor, purely on the basis of these little news items I'd been sending. So of course I took it and that was my introduction to journalism. The editor at the time was a guy called Peter Stansell, a Yorkshireman, who had worked in local newspapers in Yorkshire, and he was incredibly helpful and taught me about journalism, really. Certainly about editing other people's stuff and trying to write some decent words of my own. *it* at the time was reasonably successful.

Anyway, I carried on doing that for a couple of years and then I got tired of it, really, and it got tired of me, and *it* changed considerably. There were revolutions within the ranks, something called the London Street Collective took it over for a while, helped by the Hells' Angels, and that was the writing on the wall for me, so I then left and launched a motorcycle magazine called *Bike*, although I was writing at the time for British *Rolling Stone* and then for *Friends*, and then much later after I'd launched the motorcycle magazine, I went to work for Richard on *Melody Maker* as a freelance, not as a staffer, although I did have a regular weekly column which occasionally got us both into trouble.

RW: IPC did not pay you in dope.

MW: Sadly they didn't. And I carried on sporadically — until 1980, when there was a strike at IPC, and the IPC music titles. As a consequence of that I was without a major chunk of income, so I went to my friend and colleague Felix Dennis, who as you may know was one of the men behind *Oz*, and who indeed went to prison over the Schoolkids *Oz* trial. By then I was editing another motorcycle magazine. I said, look, the *NME* and *Melody Maker* are off the streets and are likely to be so for some time, so let's start a music weekly, because apart from anything else, there'll be a ton of money to be made from advertising because the record companies have got nowhere to advertise. And — again, extraordinarily — Felix said yes, and we actually got our first issue out just over a week after that initial meeting. *New Music News*, it was called, and it's something of which I am intensely proud. A lot of the content was provided by people like myself who no longer had anywhere for their material to appear in *Melody Maker* and *NME*.

Mark Ellen was one of the better-known contributors, and the late Tom Hibbert, and we got it out every week, but it was just *ridiculously* hard work, because there was no structure to it and the resources were extremely limited. But it was pretty successful for a few weeks, anyway. A lot of the people on it, myself, George Snow, the designer, Michelle Mortimer, the assistant designer, Miles, had all worked in the underground press, it was very much done in that spirit. Eventually of course the IPC papers came back, and I again thought it was time to bow out. Felix wanted to continue it, we had a huge row over that because I just thought it was stupid carrying on, and I left and it struggled on for a few more issues. Then I went to work in Los Angeles for a record company called Slash, and there was also a magazine called *Slash* produced by the same company, and I did quite a lot of work for them too. But that was really the end of my involvement in music journalism.

RW: The end of the 60s was an interesting transitional time. When I was working for the local paper in Nottingham, and doing my pop column as well as the juvenile court, there was an alternative bookshop there — in the days when there were such things — and it was amazing because it had *it*, so I read your stuff in *it*. It had the *Village Voice*, the *East Village Other*, all those semi-underground things.

MW: *The Village Voice* was ground level, *East Village Other* was definitely underground.

RW: So it was interesting that they made it to places like that, and they certainly helped form my thinking. But the *Melody Maker*, when I got to it, was a pretty straight publication in many ways. We all had our staff photographs for picture bylines. One staff member, a chap called Chris Hayes, his photo had him in a tin hat with a gasmask coming out of an air raid shelter in 1941 or something. Another member of staff was a chap called Laurie Henshaw who'd written a famous review of 'Heartbreak Hotel' in 1956 in which he said, "There's no future in this sort of thing." So it was a real crossover between an old guard and some younger people. It was also interesting that — like both these guys — I'd played in bands. Certainly at the *Melody Maker* that was a kind of unspoken qualification. It recruited people from local newspapers who had proper journalistic training, that was part of the thing, but also they looked with favour on people who were lapsed or failed musicians who knew their way around an instrument or two.

MW: I think you touched on something that I also mentioned briefly, and that is that a lot of the people on the underground press — I would say the majority of them — had no journalistic training. The ones that did, like the aforementioned Peter Stansell, came from local newspapers. It was very much a matter of inventing it as we went along. In preparation for this, I was looking through some of the journalism in here [*indicates copies of* it], and they were incredibly long pieces — just people mouthing off extreme consciousness stuff, a lot of it.

CSM: It's often a lot easier to write a long piece than a short one.

MW: Anyway, as I say, we were making it up as we went along, but also we were incredibly open to anybody having any opinion and printing whatever it was that they submitted. We were barely aware of things like libel — which changed as the underground press transmogrified into the straight press, as we called it. I don't know whether you noticed that, Richard, when you started employing people like me.

RW: What, that you had no journalistic training? Yes. But luckily there were a few people around who understood the law of libel. Even before the *NME* began recruiting Charlie and Mick Farren and Nick Kent from the underground press, the weeklies were loosening up under the influence, no question, of the underground and semi-underground press. Pieces were getting longer — actually it was amazing how few constraints there were.

For me the joy of working on the *Melody Maker* was that I could write about whatever I wanted and it would get a page or a half page, whether it was, I don't know, King Crimson or the Spontaneous Music Ensemble. And for me what I loved about the *Melody Maker* was that it wrote not only about pop music, but about the blues, about jazz, country music, folk and even contemporary classical for a while. I remember Michael Watts going and doing a long, long interview with John Cage in about 1970, which was quite unusual for the time. The sense of freedom and flexibility was fantastic, even though we were working for a straight publisher and there were controls in some senses. And of course it became very much free-er after the *NME* went through its great convulsion in the early seventies.

CSM: What I recall most clearly was the guy who recruited me was the late and much missed Tony Tyler, aka the Looming Boomer. He was about six foot five inches tall and had a very loud deep voice. But one of Tony's aphorisms that always stuck with me is I think a perfect summary of what I, at least, was trying to do at *NME*. Tony said, "We don't just write about the music, we write about what the music's about." So it was a great opportunity to follow up cultural references in what were considered to be the important songs. And because the *NME* was in a state of total flux, it was a very fluid situation because nobody knew WTF was going on or what was about to happen, I thought, "OK, we have the resources of a major publishing company, we have a title which even in its decline is selling around 200,000 copies a week," which is the sale figures that nearly got the *NME* cancelled in early 1972, the sales figures that any comparable publication in this country would now sacrifice its unborn great grandchildren for, but I thought, "Here is the chance to publish an underground-y rock weekly under the umbrella of a large well-resourced and reactionary publishing company."

Bearing in mind that Norman Mailer once defined a democracy as a society in which you headed as far as you could into the distance and waited for somebody to stop you. That's more or less what we tried to do, we wanted to sing mightily, we wanted to cause trouble, I wanted to import more than just the personnel of the underground press. Because not only had the underground press at this point shot its bolt, but the establishment had effectively decided that it didn't want this stuff around any longer, and everybody was driven into exile: Felix to become a wealthy capitalist, Richard Neville back to Australia, different people into different jobs. And we had great freedom, because until somebody complained, we could do what we wanted. There was a bit of a debate about the use of the F-word, and Tony Tyler was saying, "You mean if we wanted to quote the lyrics of John Lennon's 'Working Class Hero' we couldn't, surely that's wrong?" And as Mark was saying a little while earlier, *it* was at that point totally in thrall to the record companies, because it was their advertising that was keeping the thing afloat.

RW: I was amazed you said that about *having* to review records…

CSM: It was one of the accusations people in the underground made about the weeklies, "Oh, you're just there to lick the arse of the industry, man!" and in fact we took a great perverse delight at the *NME* in kicking rather than licking the butt of that industry — in the complacent knowledge that, at that time, they needed us more than we needed them. There were occasions when record companies withdrew advertising. I remember Chris Blackwell pulling Island advertising on at least two occasions, once when our reggae guru Penny Reel tore Bob Marley and the Wailers' *Babylon by Bus* live recording a new one, and once when I was less than worshipful about a Robert Palmer album that Blackwell had produced himself. But they came back.

Because it's very difficult in this contemporary era, the world in which we find ourselves, to remember that back in them days, there was no internet, no cable TV, no commercial radio worthy of the name, very little popular music on mainstream radio and television. If the rock musicians and the rock industry and the rock audience all wanted to stay in touch, we were it. We had a virtual monopoly. I mean, the national press, the straight press very rarely touched on pop music as anything other than celebrity gush or *isn't it disgusting*. We were pretty much the only game in town and we took advantage of this to chew the hand that fed us off at the elbow as often as we possibly could.

MW: Can I just interrupt there, Charlie?

CSM: You can try.

MW: As you rightly say, you and Tyler and your cohort did radically change the — for want of a better word — the straight music press, but one of the big differences between it and the underground press was that the *NME* was still published by a big corporation. There was a safety net there economically, there were resources there, you could weather storms — or the magazine could. The underground press really was always living hand to mouth, as I touched on earlier. We really did compromise with our music section. I mean to begin with, I didn't really know any better, I just was learning as I went along, and we had to review albums in particular and occasionally interview people or do features on people really to justify the advertising. But without that advertising, we couldn't publish stuff about the Black Panthers. We couldn't publish a debate about — well, for example, there were a series of concerts at the Roundhouse called Implosion, and there was a big controversy about where the money was going from that, and we could libel, basically libel people. We could publish stuff that would get the police forces in certain far flung regions of the country to arrest street sellers.

RW: It's interesting that although we were the ones with the journalistic background, you were the ones who were actually doing the proper investigative journalism.

MW: Well, I mean, I don't know that it was investigative, it was a *bit* investigative, but it was necessary to make that compromise, that's all I'm saying. But at the same time, I was looking through an issue, here I was reviewing an album of Erik Satie music, immediately followed by a review of a Taste album. But also Barclay James Harvest. I feel embarrassed about that, but there we go.

RW: Lumpenprog.

MW: Lumpenprog.

RW: They're the ones who should feel embarrassed. But both the *Melody Maker* and the *NME* were owned by the same company, IPC, which was quite interesting.

CSM: It's a political metaphor, it's like in both the UK and the USA, both main political parties are owned by the same corporations.

RW: And of course we were making scads of money for them, because as you were saying, at the beginning of the 70s the *Melody Maker* was selling 200,000 copies a week. I got on the tube at Lancaster Gate every morning to go to work and on a Thursday, anyone under 25, any male, I should say, who was sitting in that compartment, would be reading the *Melody Maker*. And I'm sure you found the same thing later in the 70s with the *NME*.

CSM: I've met so many people who've said, you know, I made a special trip into the west end of London to this newsstand where you could get the *NME* still damp off the presses on a Tuesday night. We had an incredibly loyal and obsessive fanbase, for which I'm profoundly grateful — because some of those people grew up into positions where they could occasionally employ me — but people actually loved the paper. I've had people come up and say, I didn't know who William Burroughs was till I read about him in the *NME*. Part of the brief — which we inherited from the underground press — was to broaden the palate of cultural reference, and turn people onto stuff they might not otherwise encounter.

My sweetie uses the term "*NME* babies", meaning people who grew up on the *NME* and learned about stuff, be it Burroughs, Chandler, the Marx Brothers... or Victor Jara, Andrew Tyler wrote a great piece about Jara. Tried to get the broader political and cultural span that we brought with us from the underground to create a different kind of music paper. But there were limits. We managed to chew on the hand that fed us in terms of calling bullshit and shenanigans on inferior or vapid music that was being hyped. But we never had the resources or the facilities to take on the business part of the business very much — because that's where IPC's patience with us would have run out. On the rare occasions that we did do it, it took months and months to get those pieces done, because it was a very different proposition from sitting in the review room with a headful of illegal chemicals thinking of ways to be funny about a hopeless album. This was taking on people who would either sue you or break your legs. And we weren't quite that resourceful and we weren't quite that brave and we didn't have quite the backing from our owners, who periodically stepped in to remind us that they were our owners.

MW: When you say stepped in, in what manner was that?

CSM: Well, anything that was really contentious — as opposed to pop weekly, letters-column controversial — would have to be run past the lawyers, and there would have to be a notification up to board level. And a lot of the time it would come back saying, "You can't prove this to the satisfaction of our lawyers," because they could weather some diva of a record company boss pulling a few weeks' worth of ads out, but when you're talking heavy lawyers from corporations bigger than them or possible physical reprisals by the less delicate end of the music business, that's where we were told to bring our toys back into the playpen.

MW: Two things we haven't mentioned about what we were doing as individuals: I think we were doing two things, we were enthusiasts, we worked for music papers because we loved music. The music was the thing that I was really interested in. Which is probably why I ended up on the *Melody Maker* rather than the *NME*, which is not a judgment at all.

CSM: But the *NME* was not yet itself, whereas *Melody Maker* was itself.

MW: That's true, that's true, but we were propagandists in a way, we found things that we liked and thought it was our mission to tell people about them, to spread that enjoyment. And that in a way developed later on in the 70s and 80s. When you look back at some of the writing it can be a little bit embarrassing. On the other hand because it's so kind of effulgent — but on the other hand we were very interested in writing style, and there we were on weekly music papers: most of us had read Tom Wolfe or Hunter Thompson, in my case LeRoi Jones and A. B. Spellman, people who influenced me, and we were bringing that in. Especially in the *NME*, but also in the *Melody Maker* in a different kind of way, we were bringing that into writing about pop music, basically. And that's why, the 70s particularly was such an interesting creative cauldron. You could kind of do anything in stylistic literary terms in that vehicle.

CSM: It was playground time. And also because we were a weekly you had to crank a lot of words out very quickly, many, many thousands, and there were artificial aids involved, and one of the ways to keep yourself amused when you're having to, for example, review a large pile of mostly duff singles every week, was literary pastiches. I started doing it in the style of H.P. Lovecraft or Arthur Conan Doyle or Len Deighton or Raymond Chandler.

MW: Did the readers get it?

CSM: Some did, some just enjoyed it, even though they didn't quite get what was going on, and others probably loathed it — but style was important and on the *NME* the informal hierarchy was based more than anything else on a combination of arcane musical knowledge and high style. There were some people who did excellent work in an unflashy way and were probably neglected as a result, both by editors and readers, but high style was considered important. It did get out of hand occasionally. I remember subbing a piece by Nick Kent once and crossing out 17 words and substituting 'that' — but then Nick was also a freelance and was getting paid by the word, and occasionally his brain would stop to consider the next thing he wanted to say, but his hand would keep on going, everything handwritten. Some of the secretaries made an extra bit of lunch money because they eventually stopped being persuaded by Nick to type up his copy unless he paid them.

MW: Also as a reader of *NME* in particular at that period, I felt there was a certain amount of wilful obscurantism. The lure of the obscure seemed to be strong amongst the writers. Is that true or was I just ignorant?

CSM: Do you mean obscure in terms of touting seriously arcane music or obscure in terms of style and vocabulary and reference?

MW: Both.

CSM: I would say that that didn't really become part of the mix until the arrival of Messrs Morley and Penman, which was late 70s through 80s. I mean, the 80s was a very painful period which I try to avoid even thinking about.

MW: Yeah, musically it was dire, I completely agree.

CSM: And a political nightmare, the kind of political nightmare into which we're about to re-enter. Can I just say the only thing I really have to say about the election is prepare to think of the last five years as the good old days?

MW: Yeah. I can't equate that period of *NME* too closely with what had happened in the underground press. Which is kind of the reason we're here. I think the subject matter in the underground press or the music bit of the underground press was a mixture, I was saying earlier, of having to pander to some extent to the commercial requirements of the music industry and again, our own musical tastes, which were sometimes quite obscure and heavily influenced. Something I did want to mention is the heavy influence of America and American underground music as it then was, or it was then referred to.

CSM: And American political rhetoric. Ladies and gentlemen, John Sinclair.

MW: Absolutely. And what was happening with underground music in Britain did inform British bands to an extent, particularly guitar players. There were a lot of Jerry Garcia soundalikes or people who were trying to play like Jerry Garcia, and play very fast, basically, and with greater or lesser success. So the underground and underground music did influence what was happening in Britain musically.

CSM: There were quite a few bands who came out of the underground scene who achieved a great deal of pop success. Pink Floyd had hit singles, at least in their Syd Barrett period — but it was not out of the ordinary to see people like Fleetwood Mac or Jethro Tull on *Top of the Pops*, sandwiched between a couple of the latest tinsel sensations, or what we used to call granny ballads. That was in the days when people the age I am now had terrible musical tastes, as opposed to the wonderful music tastes that people of my generation mostly have these days. The greatest underground-to-mass-pop trajectory was Bolan. That was an archetypal journey. He started out as this sort of — didn't Chris Welch from the *Melody Maker* call him the National Elf?

MW: But he was a mod before that.

CSM: But he wasn't successful when he was a mod. It's like Bowie, all the things Bowie did before he had a hit, all the transitions he went through, not out of any art theory about shifting persona but simply trying to come up with something that sold.

MW: Well, I think he was a commercial opportunist, Bolan, personally. I don't think he ever had any what I would call alternative criteria. I mean, I don't blame him for that, but I would never think of him as an underground artist.

CSM: He was somebody who worked as an underground artist because opportunities elsewhere were not forthcoming, and parlayed it quite nicely. But then I don't think the quote-unquote "underground" was actually as important as the fact that the music press helped support the underground press. It was a conduit to an audience that was considered important. If you look back, you'll find that all the main record companies had their quote-unquote "underground" subsidiary label. EMI had Harvest, Decca had Deram. Philips Fontana, as it was then, had Vertigo, Pye Records had the Dawn label. They all had their little *faux*-independent subsidiaries via which they attempted to court this significant new audience.

RW: It's worth remembering too at the time we're talking about, the music business was absolutely at its height and fantastically prosperous. And we benefited from that, not just in having jobs that were somewhat dependent on the existence of this culture, but we also got to fly all round the world at their expense...

CSM: ...and then come home and slag the acts off. How we laughed.

RW: Yes. I got flown once, totally against my better judgment, instinct, taste, everything, to see Peter Frampton at Madison Square Garden. I went, stayed a couple of nights in a hotel in New York, went to see him at Madison Square Garden. It was as dreadful as I thought it would be, and I said to the very nice PR guy, I said afterwards, I can't possibly write about that, it was total crap. I know there were 50,000 people going berserk and he's just had a double platinum album, but it's rubbish and I'm not going to write about it. He said, fine, that's OK, but presumably he got on his ledger that he presented to his boss that he'd taken so and so to New York to see Peter Frampton and nobody ever checked the cutting.

CSM: Or alternatively he could play the hero and say, "He was going to go back and write two pages tearing Peter a new one, and I talked him out of it."

RW: We did get some great trips out of it.

CSM: Like good leeches, we grew fat on their blood before we chewed their arms off. Of course the boot is on a completely different foot now.

The music press is... well, is there one? I mean, the *NME* is a dodgy website run by 12-year-olds and everything else has disappeared. I used to be quite proud telling people, yeah, I used to write for the *NME*. Now people either go, "well, there there, there are pills you can take for that," or "What's the *NME*?"

RW: There is no music press as we understood it, that's what you're saying.

CSM: I haven't gone so far as to say there is no music press as we understood it, but by the time I'm 75 I probably *will* be saying that, and Pete Townshend will be 80 and still jumping in the air.

RW: Well, I don't know about jumping, unless he's got a trampoline.

CSM: The man's 70 and he can still do scissor jumps now that I would never have attempted even when I was notionally young and notionally fit.

MW: Did you ever have any sense when you started that this would occur or was it just day by day?

CSM: My project when I started was to be either dead or a millionaire by the time I was 30 — and neither of those things happened, so I guess you could say I was making it up as I went along.

RW: I wanted to be a journalist for sure, and I think I knew that that was what I was going to be probably all the way through. But this was a particularly interesting kind of journalism to be in. I remember Ray Coleman, [who went on to be] editor of the *Melody Maker*, when he was still a *Melody Maker* reporter sometime in the early 60s, went for a job on the *Daily Telegraph*, and the editor of the *Telegraph* at the time said to him, "Where have you been working?" And he said, "The *Melody Maker*," and the *Telegraph* man said, "Why did you leave journalism?" I never really felt that, I felt that what I was doing at the *Melody Maker* was a kind of journalism, and maybe I thought I'd go back to straight journalism or non-musical journalism after that ran its course or whatever, so it was part of what I was going to do.

MW: You and I, Richard, have both been editors as well as earning a living as writers. I wonder whether you, like me, preferred being an editor?

RW: Not for a minute. I did 20 years of editing and in the end I found it very attritional and wearing and not what I wanted to do. I went into this because I wanted to be sent on a plane to write about something different, not to sit and scratch out 17 words of Nick Kent's copy and replace it with the word 'that'.

MW: I always enjoyed editing, I felt it was a bit like conducting an orchestra. That sounds terribly pretentious, but bringing together lots of often disparate writers and chucking in some of my own and turning it into something. Like being a chef.

A Lot of Words Every Day:
Words, Words, Words...

Richard Williams was interviewed by Simon Warner in 2002, for rockcritics.com (edited selection)

RW: I was born in Sheffield in 1947, but I was brought up in Nottinghamshire. I did four years on the evening paper in Nottingham as a cub reporter on the *Evening Post* and the *Guardian Journal*, the morning paper which doesn't exist anymore. You had to work for both of them. After a couple of years, I got a youth column so I started to write about music; Nottingham had a lot of clubs. You could get to see Georgie Fame or Graham Bond or Chris Farlowe any night of the week. R&B was the music I really liked. So I had this column and youth page: a girl did the fashion and I did the music. In 1966-67 none of the editors or subs had a clue what I was writing about so they could not change anything. If I wanted to write 500 words on Albert Ayler I could. When *The Velvet Underground and Nico* came out in 1967 I gave a page to it. The good thing was that I pretty well had carte blanche. When the time came to apply for a job with the *Melody Maker* [in 1969] I could send them all these cuttings about Ayler, the Velvet Underground, and Jimi Hendrix, which formed quite a useful portfolio.

SW: Was Ray Coleman editor then?

RW: No, Jack Hutton was the editor then, but he left after about six months, taking with him all the people who went to *Sounds*. I stayed. I thought about going with him but then I thought, "I've come to London to work for the *Melody Maker*," so I stayed. Those who stayed got immediate promotion and raises. Within six months of going there as the most junior reporter, I was deputy editor. Under Ray Coleman.

SW: How old were you then?

RW: 22 or 23.

SW: Around that time *Melody Maker* was described as "the musos' journal." It had a particular character, a particular style.

RW: It was a very good time to be on it because music was being taken seriously and the more seriously you took it the more you were listened to. The *NME* at that point didn't know how to cope — it was a pop paper. It didn't know how to cope with what I would never call 'progressive' rock, intelligent singer-songwriters, that kind of thing, so we had two or three years when the field was ours.

SW: What sort of things were shaping and developing your writing at the time? Were you reading other journalists?

RW: I read a lot, I always did. I read *Rolling Stone* and *CREEM*, but I also read the *New Yorker* from the age of 16, *DownBeat* and *Jazz Journal*, but I had also read the underground press since 1966 — *Village Voice, East Village Other, it, Frendz*, and so on — but I actually have to say that at that point I was too busy writing to think about the quality of my writing very much. I think that's why a lot of British pop writing of that time does not compare very well with American pop writing, because the Americans were very much aware of themselves as literary figures, and became even more so. To begin with, we weren't at all. We were writing for weekly papers, which was demanding. We would have to write every day, sometimes, 10,000, 20,000 words a week — a lot of words every day: words, words, words. And in a benign kind of way you did see yourself as a propagandist, trying to get people to listen to good stuff, so of course you had to write persuasively, but the persuasiveness was more a function of enthusiasm than of literary polish. There were exceptions more and more as time went on. I think Michael Watts was a polished writer from the day he arrived at the paper, a very grown-up writer, with very much more of a literary quality. I was more aware of other people's literary qualities as an editor as well as a writer. I was thinking more about how our writers worked and fitting them in than I was really concerned with my own stuff, to my detriment as a writer. I think I should have done.

SW: Did you find as deputy editor that your writing chances decreased?

RW: Not really, no. I was more interested in being a writer than actually minding the store. I still wrote 20,000 words a week, easily!

SW: Were you shaped at all by literature? Were you shaped by fiction or novels in the way you approached your life or your passion for music?

RW: It played a part in my life. But I didn't think of myself in those terms. I thought of myself as a journalist. I didn't really think of myself as a writer — even if I admired (Kenneth) Tynan, for instance, very much, and probably loads of other people, and certainly a lot of American jazz writers. Beautiful writers, but I never thought of myself in that league. I think I was doing a job of day-to-day journalism.

SW: So you weren't self-conscious about this process in the way that Hunter S. Thompson or Tom Wolfe were?

RW: No. Whenever I tried a literary conceit I always felt vaguely embarrassed about it. I tried to write clear, functional prose. I was more interested in getting the music right, getting it across more than anything else, I think. I loved finding things — Marley or Roxy Music or Laura Nyro or Springsteen — and presenting it to people, saying, "Here's something you haven't heard, go out and hear it, you're probably in for a treat."

SW: Did you have confidence in your own critical ability?

RW: Totally. Always. I was lucky. I was brought up in a household where music was important. My parents weren't musicians as such, but my mother loved music, played piano when she was a girl. My father's a parson, ran the church choir, he was Welsh. So music was a very important factor in my life, and right from when I was 11 or 12, I was in a skiffle group, then a beat group, then an R&B group, then a folk group. After I got thrown out of school at 17 I spent a year mostly playing around the Nottingham area in a semi-pro R&B group called the Junco Partners.

SW: I think if you are going to be immersed in a subject you have to have some genuine self-belief that you're saying things that are valuable and valid.

RW: And it comes mostly out of enthusiasm. I never really got any great pleasure from taking somebody apart. I could do it, but I'd much rather tell someone about something I really like, that I think is going to be valuable and worthwhile, always.

SW: In the early 1970s there was an interesting development as *NME* did find its credibility with its various changes; *Sounds* was also on board. Can you say how you saw the emerging British rock press in 1972-73? There was a three-cornered battle that began around that time.

RW: The two important corners were the *Melody Maker* and the *NME*. Most of the *Melody Maker* writers were from a background like mine — local journalism — so they had journalistic imperatives.

SW: Chris Charlesworth? Chris Welch?

RW: Michael Watts, Roy Hollingworth, Mark Plummer, Colin Irwin, Jerry Gilbert and those people. That was something that Ray Coleman, who came from a local paper background himself, on the *Leicester Mercury*, encouraged. So we had that background and we also had the *Melody Maker*'s tradition of dealing with musicians as musicians rather than, as I suppose they'd be called today, style icons. Whereas the *NME* re-made itself, it came from a completely different direction, by getting people in — very talented people — from the underground press, like Nick Kent and Charlie Murray and the next generation that came in, particularly Ian MacDonald and Angus MacKinnon, very, very bright people; it secured a patch that was more aware than we were of music as fashion, or more interested in exploring it, a bit more aware. We were aware of it, but they were also able to operate without the consciousness of the sort of progressive rock dimension. They did not have to be nice about Emerson, Lake and Palmer or Yes. We had a tradition of supporting that kind of music. Personally, it was of no interest to me, but it certainly was of value to the paper. And it wasn't negligible, you know, [it was] legitimate. But the *NME* could be much more light-footed, I think, in that way by concentrating on those things. We wrote about the Velvet Underground in *Melody Maker* years before anyone did in the *NME*, but the *NME* was more willing to embrace that as the central truth of their existence while the thing that defined the *NME* was, to us, an interesting thing, but there were other things going on the world as well. The *NME* guys, they took people who were central to their canon, like Iggy Pop and Lou Reed, and they made the world around that, saw everything through the lens of that consciousness.

SW: The fact that you were both owned by IPC was a bizarre element in the story. What was the relationship like between the two publications?

RW: Very rivalrous, very competitive, some degree of antipathy, some degree of amiability. We were — and I'm speaking collectively rather than individually — we were dismissive of the *NME* for far longer than was healthy for us. And I think that was a big mistake — if these were mistakes — because I think the *Melody Maker* continued in its honest path and the *NME* had a perfectly legitimate role and viewpoint as well. They were just slightly different, and it was obvious which one would have more currency with the coming generation of music-paper readers.

SW: Just to sidetrack for a second. That comment you made, "I didn't drink with anybody" — just to explore that briefly. *NME* certainly made a virtue, they made a play of the fact that their journalists did mix with Jagger and Richard, Kent mixed with Iggy Pop. They drank and drugged together.

RW: And it worked very well.

SW: Was this something that you consciously avoided? Did you want to keep this world at arm's length as a writer?

RW: Yes, as a person more than as a writer. I loved music and liked musicians, I loved watching musicians, but I like being with my own friends. I don't necessarily want to be co-opted into and subsumed in another world.

SW: So you didn't see the cultural explosion, post mid-60s, as all-consuming and wanting to drown in it?

RW: It consumed me, but it didn't dictate who my friends would be. It didn't dictate the social milieu I would move in. I never wanted to tag along with all that. I wanted to write about it. Of course I had friends who were musicians, but they weren't terrifically famous ones. I would think I was more friendly with British jazz musicians — and, of course, there's nobody less famous than British jazz musicians, or less celebrated than them.

SW: You were made deputy editor on the *Melody Maker*. Did you then rise to editor?

RW: Not then. In 1973 I was offered a job as head of A&R at Island. Island was a wonderful label then, and Chris Blackwell, whom I'd met a couple of times, was a very interesting, charismatic person. I thought I'd quite like to get closer to the actual making of the music. Because I had always admired people like Nesuhi Ertegun and John Hammond. Producers, you know. I knew I was never good enough to be a musician — I never had any illusion — but I wanted to try that and Island seemed to be the ideal environment for it.

SW: That was the time when Bob Marley was being promoted and projected as a major new international talent.

RW: I'd written the first pieces on Marley on a trip to Jamaica. That's really how I got to know Blackwell. So yes, Island at that time had Marley, Roxy Music, Richard Thompson.

SW: Island did have a remarkable array of talent.

RW: They did. I had three years doing that, for better and worse. It was very interesting to learn from the inside how the business works, to learn what a deal was, to lose my illusions about the business side of things — that was good for me as a journalist. To see how a marketing campaign operates. But Island was actually growing too fast, and over the three years I was there it became a much less happy place, a much less co-operative sort of place. It's always difficult when companies are run according to one man's vision and inevitably according to his whim. If you'd started a company like that you'd want to have a say in what went on and wouldn't necessarily want to be argued with too much. It was quite difficult. I signed John Cale, Nico, a few other things, had something to do with Kevin Ayers. I got the Richard and Linda Thompson album *I Want to See the Bright Lights Tonight* released because it had been put on the shelf and forgotten about. Pete Wingfield — do you remember 'Eighteen with a Bullet'? — was my artist. But I don't look back on it as a particularly happy time, though it did teach me a lot about the business.

SW: So from 1973-76 you held this A&R role and then you left that behind.

RW: I'd freelanced for a bit. I had done that while I was doing my A&R job. I had been writing pieces for *Let It Rock* and *Street Life*. So I left Island and freelanced. But then Tony Elliott, whom I didn't know, was editing *Time Out*, the London listings magazine. He was the founder and the editor but he was going on holiday and wanted somebody to look after it, with a view to having somebody do the job permanently as a replacement for him. I didn't know whether I fancied it or not, but I did it and ended up having two very rewarding years there. It was a very turbulent, very political environment in those days, long before *City Limits*, its later rival, came along. So all the radical politics were concentrated on *Time Out*, with a strong news section — and we'd breach the Official Secrets Act every now and then. I went in as editor, unknown to virtually everybody there, so that was quite difficult, quite challenging. I did it for a couple years and enjoyed dealing with theatre, cinema, music, books, dance, all those things. It was fun to have a broad view for a change. And then Ray Coleman stepped down at *Melody Maker*, and I went back as editor at a very difficult time, 1978, when the paper hadn't quite grasped punk but hadn't shed its other old skin, and that was my job to do that. Very difficult because the *NME* by that time had such a firm grip on it. My idea was to do it by just getting better writers, the best writing I could, and some of the things we did I am very proud of.

SW: Did you have to let people go? Was that part of your brief?

RW: Not really, no. I did certainly de-emphasise some people. And then there were things that happened. IPC and Ray Coleman started what was supposed to be the musos' own magazine, *Musicians Only*, and Chris Welch went off to work on that. Other people came and went. I suppose I was after more of a *Village Voice* thing, and then I got to the point of doing a big re-design which was to be the big statement. Then there was a strike and they wanted me to put out a scab issue and I said no, and walked out. I was there from 1978-1980. Ray Coleman walked back in, having been nominal editor-in-chief, and tried to reconstitute the *Melody Maker* as he had left it rather than how I had left it, so I don't have a very happy memory of that. Two years of working incredibly hard. It was very nice to bring in James Truman, who's now running Condé Nast, Mary Harron, now a very successful film-maker, and various other people, whose work I was very proud of, but it didn't, in the end, work.

SW: You were the first presenter on that British television legend, *The Old Grey Whistle Test.*

RW: Yes. I did a year on it between 1971-72. I didn't enjoy it. The BBC paid me a very small amount of money. I didn't give it very much time. I spent a day a week doing it. I was paid £20 a week to begin with to write and present it. They put it up to £30 half way through the year. No wonder I didn't take it very seriously. I didn't like being on TV anyway. If they'd paid me £100 a week I suppose I might have been tempted to stay. But I'm very glad they didn't because I wouldn't have wanted to at all.

SW: When the UK rock glossy revolution happened in the mid-80s, I would have thought it tailor-made for someone with your talents and experience. I know you have done some writing for the glossies over the last decade and a half. I mean *Q* and *Mojo* and so on.

RW: I never wanted to go back into music full-time. The further away I get from writing about it, the more I listen. I just find myself buying albums — I don't get free records anymore — and I listen all the time, and one of the things I feel quite strongly about is that writing about sport is a lot easier than writing about music.

SW: As someone who has been a football reporter and written about music, do you find them different beasts?

RW: Very, very different. With sport you are not trying to convey the abstract all the time, not trying to tell people what colour a note is. I found writing about music — I didn't exactly run out of words, but I had a sort of exhaustion and I wanted to stop or cut right down. But with sport you always get a result, it happens in front of you, it's physical, you can see it. Sport reveals character, so it's interesting to write about. The way people play a game is generally the way they are as a person, and you can't say that about music. Stan Getz made the most beautiful sound in the history of music but he was the biggest bastard God ever created and you can't correlate the two things at all. Hendrix and Coltrane made very violent music, but they were very peaceful men, so you can't write about their music in terms of them or them in terms of their music. It would be very, very misleading.

SW: Would you be interested in commenting on Simon Frith's assessment of you as the best pop writer on this side of the Atlantic. Do you feel as if this is praise indeed?

RW: Yes! In my time I was right more often than anybody else. I was not wrong very much. If that is the criterion then fair enough. I think Nick Kent was a wonderful writer, Charlie Murray was a wonderful writer, Michael Watts was, a few others... I don't know if I was as good as that. They somehow got themselves into a position where they could devote the time to concentrating on long pieces very successfully, and I never did that. I don't think that I had a portfolio nearly as good as theirs. When I did *Long Distance Call*, that was an attempt to adjust that. I tried to find the things that had lasted and add some new ones, and give an account of myself as a music critic.

SW: Something Simon Frith said in his book *Sound Effects* was that most rock critics were interested in the sociology or the culture of the music they were listening to, but had little of the apparatus to appreciate the mechanics of rhythm, harmony and melody, the elements that are integral components. I feel when I read your stuff as if you're quite serious in the way you listen to the music. Would that be fair to say?

RW: It would certainly be fair to say that.

SW: Do you understand the music?

RW: I do, yes, I do. And I'm interested in how it makes me feel. If it was an early Who single, I'm interested in how that made me and a lot of other kids feel, or what it was about a Motown record that made a lot of us dance at a particular time. But I'm more interested in how it does that musically, I think. That's the underlying core at it. The way that the backbeat and bass line works, rather than something else. That's how I listen to music. I listen to the notes. In my time I have also toyed with the violin, the double bass, the piano, the alto saxophone and the cornet.

With the wind instruments I learnt, or taught myself, only just enough to know how they worked. I had piano lessons as a child. And I spent a fair amount of time with the violin and bass, playing in school and county youth orchestras. I also sang in various choirs. So with a bit of guitar and a lot of drums and percussion, I think I have a fairly broad-based knowledge of the mechanics of music. That certainly informs, although it does not determine, the way I listen to music. That's really what I'm interested in and perhaps it explains why my real heroes are people like Steve Cropper at Stax, Benny Benjamin and James Jamerson at Motown, and Al Duncan at Chess. Sub-cultural and sociological aspects are always fun, but the only one I was ever really a member of was Mod. And I loved that. That's still how I feel. I liked hippie music but I never wanted to be more interested in the audience than the musician. That's probably a lot of what's happened to music. Clubbing is all about the audience. I'm interested in music that breathes rather than repeats itself according to encoded digital signals.

Music, arts and sports journalist Richard Williams began writing for Melody Maker in the late 60s, going on to be its editor in the late 70s. He also edited Time Out, worked in television and for Island Records, was artistic director of the Berlin Jazz Festival from 2015-17.

Simon Warner is lecturer in popular music studies at Leeds University. His most recent book is Text and Drugs and Rock'n'Roll: The Beats and Rock Culture.

The Great Days Had Already Passed…

Mark Pringle on what it meant to be reading about music and related matters in the late 60s and early 70s

Between 1968 and 1972, my morning routine went something along these lines: get the old 31 bus from Redcliffe Gardens to the top of Earls Court Road where it meets Kensington High Street, then walk through Holland Park to school. By the bus stop was a newsagent, which proved a portal into an astonishing world of print.

My parents were middle-class socialists, school teachers with no interest in pop music or popular culture whatsoever. Printed matter at home consisted of the *Times*, somewhat bafflingly the *Daily Express*, the *New Statesman* and thousands upon thousands of books. I had an older brother and sister, and it was through them that rock'n'roll started permeating the household. The first record I bought with my own money was the Beatles' 'Twist and Shout' EP. The first album we bought collectively was *A Hard Day's Night*, our pocket money in shillings, sixpences and thrupenny bits piled on the counter (we were ninepence short — the man behind the counter let us off). But shortage of cash (my parents were mean with the pocket money) meant we had just a handful of records, and a cheap Dansette on which to play them.

Around 1966 my brother, who had been packed off to boarding school (John Peel's *alma mater* Shrewsbury), started bringing home interesting stuff: records by the likes of John Mayall and Cream, and at some point in the year a copy of a paper called *International Times*. Five years younger than him, I was soon sucked into all of this. While my sister ran home from Town Records in Chelsea's World's End clutching the Monkees' first album to her fevered breast, my world was turned upside down by Jimi Hendrix's 'Purple Haze', a record I hated for about three months until I suddenly *got* it. A friend of my mother had a stall in Kensington Market, and I was riveted by all these impossibly tall young men with vast clouds of hair. It seemed all too exciting.

Once I'd got on the 31 bus I'd race upstairs to do my homework and smoke the first fag of the day. Getting off at the other end, still woozy from the nicotine hit, I would invariably head for the newsagents. The first thing I discovered there was the *Guardian*. First, it just looked fresher than my father's *Times*. Second, it seemed to be written for someone vaguely resembling me, but older and far more sophisticated. I also started buying *Melody Maker*. This paper was packed with articles about the bands I had started listening to. It also had articles about the equipment, which spoke to my burgeoning obsession with the electric guitar. I was starting to find the stuff I needed, stuff that differentiated me from my parents.

The underground press was fascinating to a 12- 13- 14-year-old boy. My brother and I soon accumulated between us a decent collection of papers and magazines: *it*, *Oz*, *Rolling Stone*. *it* introduced me to such heroes as (Barry) Miles and Mick Farren, who I was to see fronting the Deviants at a free concert in Hyde Park in 1969, on a bill topped by the fabulous Soft Machine. That concert was a massive game-changer for me. As skinheads picked off stray hippies at the edges of the crowd, the hardcore hippies from the Endell Street squat crazily danced in front of the stage. A Hell's Angel "chick" (as they were then called) danced topless to the Deviants, and Robert Wyatt used the word "fuck" when complaining when someone interrupted his drum solo, asking him to pass on a message — probably something along the lines of "Can Karen come to the left of the stage? I've got her 'insulin'." Half-naked women! Foul language! Rock'n'roll! I was 13 and *hugely* impressed.

Oz was a mad mystery to me. Its hallucinatory graphics made it a challenge to read, but they just reeked of exciting transgression. My mother was appalled and our copies would often go missing. *Oz* really wasn't much about music, *it* seemed to have much more music writing in it, so the two complemented one another, *Oz* addressing my increasing interest in psychedelic drugs, *it* providing the interviews and reviews that my rock'n'roll habit now required.

Rolling Stone had a particular fascination. First, it was American, and yet widely available in London — even the Earls Court Road newsagent stocked it. And it *really* went deeply into music. Huge interviews with musicians, and long-form album reviews that I'd hardly seen anywhere else. Eventually it would curdle into hagiography, but between 1968 (when I first started reading it) and 1972 it was pretty thrilling. It also looked good. Actually all the underground papers looked good, but each with a particular style. *Rolling Stone* introduced me to writers like Michael Lydon, Jon Landau and John Mendelsohn. It took rock'n'roll *very* seriously. As it turned out, possibly *too* seriously.

Other magazines started appearing. At some point in 1969, *ZigZag* appeared on my newsagent's counter. I adored it immediately. It seemed to be the only paper writing about some of the bands my brother and I listened to, like the great Love. It also made me fall in love with bands that *I hadn't yet heard* like the Grateful Dead and the Stooges, and when I did finally hear them — bought with still-scarce pocket money from the Virgin Records branch in Notting Hill Gate, a place of beanbags and headphones and hippies — I loved them even more. Andy Childs, Pete Frame and John Tobler wrote with a glorious enthusiasm, and it all had a wonderfully home-made feel about it.

Alongside the music papers were *Black Dwarf*, and its successor *Red Mole*. These rags were closely associated with Tariq Ali, who I knew as the wild-haired, moustachioed leader of the Grosvenor Square anti-Vietnam protests of 1968. I was too ignorant to understand the Leninist/Trotskyist background, something I only learned much later. Initially attracted by the general drift of their politics, I eventually found the whole tenor of these papers too austere. But they were a barrel of laughs compared to the paper one of my teachers, Roger Silverman, used to sell us in class: *Militant*. Silverman, I subsequently discovered, was on the "editorial board" (i.e. the central committee) of Militant, the Trotskyist sect that hit the news in the 1980s.

By 1970 I had taken to avoiding school at all costs, and hanging around Ladbroke Grove with my pals, scoring dodgy quid-deals of hash from, among others, a certain Lemmy, then living in Lancaster Road. (One tapped on the bay window of the raised ground-floor flat, the curtain would be pushed aside by a scowling face: "What do you want?" "Quid deal, Lemmy.") A new underground rag appeared around that time, initially as a London spin-off from *Rolling Stone*. *Friends* (as in *Friends of Rolling Stone*) was very much a local paper for the Ladbroke Grove hippie scene, in which the likes of Hawkwind, Mighty Baby and the Pink Fairies would feature. Some writers familiar from *it* and *Oz* , such as Jonathon Green, wrote for it, and new faces appeared, like Nick Kent. We all felt that *Frendz* (as it became) was very much written for us, as we shambled up Portobello Road in our Civil Defense surplus greatcoats.

We were too young and stupid to realise that the great days of the London underground had long passed. We still had the drugs and the music, and *Oz*, *it* and *Frendz*, and we marvelled at the *Oz* Schoolkids issue (Charles Shaar Murray on Fucking to Led Zeppelin!), and felt righteous anger at the magazine's bust and subsequent trial. In 1972 I spectacularly failed most of my O Levels, was busted for hash in Holland Park, and bundled off out of London by my mortified parents.

Returning to London in 1973 after my brief exile, I went to a West London further education college in an effort to scrape together enough GCEs to get into Art School, and discovered that *everyone had stopped reading* Melody Maker*!* As my new set of friends discussed Can or David Bowie, the paper of choice on the student canteen table was the *New Musical Express.* I grudgingly opened it to discover that — *holy shit!* — all the writers I had learned to love had migrated to it: Miles, Nick Kent, Charles Shaar Murray, *even Mick Farren!* Taking their old underground irreverence, they had succeeded (under editor Nick Logan) in repackaging it for the increasingly grim 1970s. There was life after death...

Former Hot House guitarist Mark Pringle is chief archivist at Rock's Backpages.
www.rocksbackpages.com

The Use of the Word *Black* Had Become Very Powerful

Editor in his time of Sounds, NME and Record Collector, Alan Lewis also helped launch Kerrang!, Uncut and Loaded. But before all this he created and ran the ground-breaking monthly Black Music. Interviewed December 2016 by Mark Sinker

AL: I worked on a local newspaper in Uxbridge, in Middlesex, on the fringes of London. In terms of music I followed the classic Mod pattern — you started off going to gigs in places like the Marquee, saw early black artists like Muddy Waters and Howlin' Wolf who started to come over in the late 50s and early 60s. At the same time the Beatles and Stones were releasing their early records, often featuring songs that we later learned were by black artists. That piqued my interest, and I began to get a bit trainspottery, always seeking out the original version. At the same time I was taking a bit of interest in what was happening in America to black people, reading writers like Richard Wright and James Baldwin. But there was very little in terms of magazines or even books to give you that information, you had to seek it out.

On the jobs front, I joined the local newspaper in 1964 — and in those days you were given a very good training, taken on apprenticeships, sent on block-release courses to learn on the job. I was initially just a reporter but gravitated to being a sub-editor. In 1969 one of my colleagues on the local paper got a job on *Melody Maker*, and he called me and said "They're going to advertise for a sub-editor, why don't you apply?" I did, and got the job, starting around about the same time as Richard Williams, who sat next to me. I think Richard started the week before or the week after me.

After about a year, half the staff left to launch a new paper called *Sounds*. Richard and myself were among the few that remained at *Melody Maker*, and we all got promoted because there was no one else to bring out the paper. We found ourselves elevated fairly rapidly and I became chief sub-editor. And at the same time I started to review records. Richard had been promoted to reviews editor, and started giving me soul records to review — and I also started doing the odd feature. And in the end I did quite a few. I had the amazing luck to interview people like James Brown, Curtis Mayfield, Stevie Wonder, Tina Turner, Ben E. King, loads of people — but as you probably know if you've ever seen a *Melody Maker* from that period, you'd get amazing access to people like those I've just mentioned, but it would end up as a sort of half-page feature. It used to try to cram a lot in in those days.

In 1973, I was chief sub on *Melody Maker*, and writing, and it began to frustrate me that there weren't many publications that you could buy to learn more about black music. There was *Record Mirror*, which had a very good guy, Norman Jopling — I never met him, but used to read him avidly, and try and do the same for *Melody Maker* that he'd done for *Record Mirror*. And there were one or two fanzines. In fact we didn't even call them fanzines then — but there was a magazine called *Blues and Soul*, which was quite well produced, but the writing was pretty awful, skimpy stuff. To be fair it was probably the first stand-alone black music publication in Britain, but it wasn't very good. And then you had *Shout*. And for a trainspotter that was much better — it had really densely detailed articles. Again, the standard of writing not very good, and it only came out sporadically. But it did get the attention of serious soul fans. Anyway, against that background, I suggested to the editor of the *Melody Maker*, Ray Coleman, that there was a gap in the market. And that we could do a monthly magazine, and that became *Black Music*, and it was launched in 1973.

MS: So can you summarise in a sentence or two what the actual mission of *Black Music* was going to be?

AL: Well, the name at the time was quite political. We'd seen soul music develop as part of the black movement in America. And I think for most people it would still be called soul or R&B. But the use of the word 'black' had become very powerful in America for several years, through the Civil Rights movement. And it began to get a harder edge, with people like James Brown embracing black music as Black Power, and the political side of it was well. So it seemed appropriate to call it *Black Music*, to show a seriousness of intent. Our seriousness was mainly musical, not political — but that was the way the artists were beginning to address the subject. Of course a lot of it was superficial, to do with fashion as much as anything else — the Afros, the style of dress, the style of talk. But politics was bound up in there. If you've seen any copies of *Black Music*, there isn't that much about politics, but it's an undercurrent. And I suppose looking back, it was quite bold of IPC to go with a magazine called *Black Music*. Ray Coleman and his predecessor Jack Hutton had both worked on big evening papers, Ray was old school, had come up through local newspapers, I think he worked on a paper in Liverpool. So he was quite a hardheaded guy, and to be fair to him, I don't think he had any great interest in black music, but fortunately he saw it might have some potential. And I suppose he saw me as a safe pair of hands, because like him I had come up through local newspapers, and could do a bit of everything, writing and subbing and layout and design and everything. Perhaps he felt there was no risk — and also, perhaps more importantly, launching magazines in those days was a very cheap business. There wasn't much money at stake. It was brave of IPC Business Press to launch it, but to be honest it was dead cheap, because we had a staff of three. Nevertheless, to give them credit, it was quite brave of them, I guess.

MS: Who was the staff of three, apart from you?

AL: It was quite difficult to start off, really. We did place adverts, but we didn't get much response. I mentioned earlier the fanzine called *Shout* — well, one of the main contributors to *Shout* was a man called Tony

Cummings. I was aware of Tony and called him up, and he came in. So we signed him as the main writer. Then I wanted to get someone to write about reggae — and I felt some pressure, not external pressure but I felt myself that we had to have someone black. It seemed a bit of an anomaly to have a magazine called *Black Music*, using the imagery of black power and everything, and not have anybody black! But I have to say in those days there were no black music journalists. And very few black journalists period. It proved very difficult, and I was literally despairing of finding anyone. But the writer and broadcaster Charlie Gillett suggested a young writer — well, not writer yet, he worked for the Greater London Council, actually — called Carl Gayle. Carl had written a piece for *Let It Rock*, which was one of the early rock magazines, a pretty good one, as I recall. I think something about reggae, which I must admit I hadn't seen. Charlie said "He seems quite promising." And Carl was very young, and working for the GLC, in their road traffic department. So we met, and got on well, and he hadn't had anything else published. So it wasn't exactly a leap in the dark, but as he'd probably cheerfully admit, he hadn't exactly got a portfolio. So anyway, we got him onboard, and the three of us were given a rather gloomy room — in those days the *Melody Maker* office was in Fleet Street, nearly opposite El Vino's wine bar. The building itself was pretty grim, as I recall, and as we moved into it in the autumn of 1973, there was a huge industrial dispute going on the with miners, and the oil crisis, the Three-Day Week. The country was reduced to working a three-day week, so often we had to go home when it got dark, so this was going on while we were trying to launch the magazine. So it was quite memorable.

MS: Was it obviously successful right away, or did it have to struggle a bit to establish itself? Was it being stocked everywhere, or was it only on sale in London?

AL: No, it had national distribution, and obviously benefits from all the support that IPC could give us. I think it was modestly successful — it wasn't a huge success, I mean, we won a few minor awards. The only advertising was within the pages of *Melody Maker*, which was obviously worth having, but we didn't do any overt promotion, it was a very low-key launch by today's standards. But of course the technology was incredibly simple, we wrote it on manual typewriters, I laid it out and designed it —

because in those days magazines didn't have art editors, that was a bit of a luxury. It was very cheap to produce — we didn't pay Carl and Tony much for writing it. I wrote bits of it, a few other contacts that we gradually developed as it got going contributed, it was cheap to do. The initial sales were quite good, I think we averaged about 25,000 over the first few years. IPC were brave to launch it, but on the other hand it didn't demand many resources. And though we have the internet now, it was almost as cheap as desk-top publishing.

MS: Who was reading it? Were you establishing a readership that hadn't existed before?

AL: I'm not sure that we could claim that we were. I mean, at that time black music was very big, people liked Stevie Wonder, Isaac Hayes, and all these seminal figures, there clearly was an audience out there. Covering reggae in depth was probably an act of faith, we struggled a bit to justify the amount of resource we were giving it, because Carl wasn't really interested in any other music. It was quite interesting what happened with Carl — I sometimes feel a bit guilty, because I don't know whether I'd made his life or destroyed his life. After a few months, he was doing interviews and including a lot of Jamaican patois, and that was really the first time anyone had seen it used in a magazine, and it became his sort of hallmark. I can recall that Ray Coleman, who was my boss, was a bit wary of it — as indeed anyone might be, because it hadn't been done before. So sometimes we had to rein Carl's enthusiasm in a little bit, because you had some sort of structure to the features, and sometimes launching into a big chunk of patois was asking a bit much. But nevertheless we did it, and it became his whole thing, really. If you look at some of the issues of that period, they certainly give a flavour. He went from being, well, a fairly middle-class guy with a job in the GLC, to dressing differently. Years later, from what I heard, he became so immersed in Rastafarian culture that he moved to Jamaica and gave up writing about music. I was told he lives a fairly rural life, goat-farming or something. I don't think he has any direct involvement in music. So I wasn't sure if I'd helped him to this great liberation, or if he might have been better off to stay at the GLC. Only he can say, I guess.

MS: What was your approach to who you put on the cover?

AL: Trying to strike a balance between American soul and black music artists, and reggae — we didn't have many front covers devoted to reggae, maybe one in five, one in six? We went on a hunch, from the feedback we got. I suppose to be honest you could judge it a little bit by what artists were getting support from their own record companies. There was far more activity on the American soul side than there was on the reggae side, because at that point we had Bob Marley, and acts like Burning Spear and the Maytals. Thanks to Island Records and Chris Blackwell, reggae was beginning to get quite a high profile. We probably put slightly more emphasis on black American soul, but nevertheless there was a lot of Jamaican stuff there.

MS: 1973 is the year that there's a shift in the nature of [mainstream UK] rock writing generally, with people like Charlie Murray and Nick Kent arriving at *NME*...

AL: The same era I've been describing was the era of the arrival of the underground press, from 1967 onwards, *Oz* and so on. That shift happened while I was on *Black Music*, while I was in my own little ghetto. I emerged from that in 1975, when I was offered the editorship of *Sounds*. Which was launched in the era you're describing, in 1970, and adopted quite a few of the things that were happening. *NME* was the first to pick up on what the underground press had established. *Melody Maker* was a bit late to go down the same route, but it did so in the end. Probably more so in the writing than in the layout. The *Melody Maker* generally followed the old tabloid format it had had in the 60s.

MS: So in the next couple of years, more people start writing about reggae in other publications. Idris Walters at *Street Life*, but other places also, Henderson Dalrymple had a little column in the *NME*, 'Black and British', I don't exactly know how long it lasted. Penny Reel moved from *it* to *NME*. Do you think this would have happened anyway, or was it down to *Black Music* breaking the ground?

AL: I think so, yes. We did our bit, but we weren't on any particular crusade. The politics of *Black Music* rose naturally from what people said in interviews. We had an early front cover that said 'Do Black Musicians Get a Fair Deal?' As I say, the politics of it arose from the music, I can't claim that we were trying to impose anything on it. In Carl we had a distinctive voice, but it seemed to come naturally.

I can recall one occasion when the politics came in, during the first few months. We got a little of publicity, I did one or two interviews — and one of them was with BBC World Service at Bush House in the Aldwych, which was where the BBC ran this worldwide broadcasting system, broadcasting in about 50 languages. And I was interviewed by a man called Darcus Howe, who was already quite a tough spokesman for the black community, and I remember he gave me quite a hard time. Basically because I wasn't black, and what did I think I was doing editing a magazine called *Black Music*? I found it not easy to answer. He said, "You're a cultural imperialist" — and I could see what he was driving at, I knew there was a weird illogicality that I was editing a magazine called *Black Music*. I tried to point out that I felt I knew quite a bit about it, and if we could find more young black writers we'd be using more of them. But in London at that time there were virtually none. And it stayed that way partly because in black culture there wasn't a great tradition of the written word. That was simply the way it was. And because of other social issues and the education system generally, the system wasn't producing many young black writers of any kind, male or female.

So I think after I left the editor was Geoff Brown. Like me he worked at *Melody Maker*, in fact he was my assistant sub editor when he joined, and he was a big black music fan, but yeah, we were all white boys. But it wasn't out of choice. Finding Carl was partly down to Charlie Gillett, but he was obviously a major find. I don't think *Black Music* did get the credit it deserved at the time, but as I said, we weren't on any kind of great political bandwagon. We were trying to do that through the music — and the real pleasure was talking to black artists, both Jamaican and American, who were incredibly flattered that people knew that much about their music. In America there was no writing about black music at all, till much much later. No books that I can recall — well into the late 60s and early 70s, the only book that even remotely covered black music [that wasn't jazz] was called *Urban Blues*, mainly about chicago blues, by a man called Charles

Keil. Of course after that the floodgates opened. We tried to be a part of that a little, and hopefully played some part, I can't exaggerate it too much. I wouldn't claim we saw ourselves as part of any great movement other than to produce a good magazine about an area of music that deserved better coverage than it had had before.

Alan Lewis joined Melody Maker in 1969 and launched Black Music in 1973. He became editor of the weekly Sounds in 1975, was the launch editor in 1981 for Kerrang!, became editor of NME in 1987 and, as editor-in-chief, was closely involved in the launch of Vox, Uncut and Loaded. From 2003-11 he was editor of Record Collector.

CRUSADING

"The *NME* was an extraordinary tunnel you could crawl through every Thursday morning. A whole new set of possibilities opened up then. It was psychedelic almost" — *Paul Morley*

I Wouldn't Say that Hippie Had *Failed*

Charles Shaar Murray interviewed November 2016 by Mark Sinker.
(Part 1 of this interview can be found on p.123)

MS: Once you'd embarked on this career — you haven't quite arrived in London yet but you're writing for *Oz* and you're part of the scene — who are you reading?

CSM: I did my catch-up on the Beats, Kerouac and Burroughs. When I was in the sixth form the books that all us smart guys were reading were *Catch-22, The Naked Lunch* and Thomas Pynchon's *V.* I was also big on James Baldwin, I read all of Baldwin's books. I read Mailer, though I preferred his essays and journalism to his fiction, I always thought most of his fiction was awful, but as a political and social commentator — I mean basically I learnt how to describe rock concerts by reading Mailer describing riots in Miami and the siege of Chicago.

And also loads of crime — I was big on Hammett and Chandler; loads of science fiction — my first big SF hero was Alfred Bester — and tottering towers of Marvel Comics. I loved Stan Lee, Jack Kirby and Steve Ditko. And then via the underground press I discovered Robert Crumb and Gilbert Shelton. I was taking in a whole heap of different stuff, from the highest culture to the toppermost of the poppermost. Trying to process it, put it together, use all this stuff to create a worldview and a self-definition.

MS: An interesting difference between the UK and America is that America had, all the way through from the 1920s, a layer of magazines where you could write at tremendous length. At one end there was the *New Yorker*, but at the other there was *Esquire* and...

CSM: Oh yeah yeah yeah, and now we bring in the New Journalism! Even when I was at school, Thompson's *Hells' Angels* book was one of the big books. And later *Fear and Loathing*, but that takes us into the 70s. When I went to the States the first time [in 1968], the only Wolfe I'd read was *Kandy-Kolored Tangerine-Flake Streamline Baby*. In the States I got all the others, *Kool-Aid Acid Test*, *Mau-Mauing the Flak-Catchers*, *Pump House Gang*... Basically, until he mutated into a neocon — I mean I depart radically from Tom Wolfe politically, but as a stylist and as a pioneer of creative journalistic methodology, he was a great influence and a great model.

Thompson and Wolfe arrived in very similar places from very different routes and vastly different starting points. I guess one of the catalysts must have been Kerouac, because Kerouac's novels are very thinly disguised autobiography. Once you know whose these pseudonyms represent, maybe embellished to flatter the narrative, this is fundamentally what was happening.

MS: My friend Frank Kogan pointed me to something Richard Williams said in an interview (see p.155) — that, starting in 1972 or so, pop mag *NME* began transforming and pushing itself to prominence specifically via the Velvets: "We wrote about the Velvet Underground in *Melody Maker* years before anyone did in the *NME*, but the *NME* was more willing to embrace that as the central truth of their existence. The thing that defined the *NME* was, to us, an interesting thing, but there were other things going on the world as well. The *NME* guys, they took people who were central to their canon, like Iggy Pop and Lou Reed, and they made the world around that, saw everything through the lens of that consciousness." Is that accurate?

CSM: Partially. When I said earlier on about the membrane between the underground and the mass market being permeable, in a sense the ultimate expression of that was Marc Bolan. Who was then creatively trumped by Bowie and Roxy Music. And commercially by Sweet and

Slade. But the pivotal figure was Bowie. I was into the MC5 — there's possibly a disquisition to be written about MC5 people versus Iggy people. I was an MC5 person. It took me longer to get Iggy. I'd probably spent too long hanging around with jazzers for the extreme roughness of Stooges music, and the calculated *stoopid* (rather than actually stupid) lyric. The MC5 had their James-Brown-meets-Chuck-Berry soul band rock drive, and their flagwaving rabble-rousing lyrics, that made more sense to me. Also I wasn't fully plugged into the free records dripfeed yet, so it was mostly my own money I was spending.

Felix had the MC5 albums but he didn't have the Stooges albums. So I would play the '5 a lot, but I didn't really hear enough of the Stooges to get it. Velvets again, via Felix's collection — but it was Bowie that provided the bridge to the *NME*. And he brought Lou and Iggy with him. He got Lou his one and only proper hit single. He was the bridge. He made it possible to justify writing about Lou and Iggy. And he also got Mott the Hoople out of the dumper. Mott had been a hugely popular live band who'd never quite figured out how to make records which would sell outside their hardcore fanbase.

MS: I think I'm circling another question about consciousness. Richard says "through the lens of that consciousness" — so if you substitute Bowie into his quote, is there a way of saying what that consciousness is?

CSM: In a sense, Bowie and Roxy were an acknowledgment of, well, I wouldn't say that Hippie had *failed*, but that it had served its purpose. Bowie said to me in an interview once, "The rock'n'roll revolution happened, it really did, it's just that nobody noticed." Because the visionaries had set the bar so high that it would actually have been impossible for Hippie to do everything it wanted to. I saw this trailer for some BBC thing last night, and the announcer said, in her classic BBC voice, "Whatever you're into, you can do your thing!" And I thought, "This is pure hippie prattle, but now it's normal to talk like that." And also Bolan, bringing expressions like "rip off" and "my main man" into general discourse. Once upon a time only black folks said this stuff, then white hippies started saying it, and now everybody does. It's the way stuff burrows into the light. So basically, you were asking me what the underground is, and now — an hour into our conversation — I finally figured it out. The underground is where stuff grows, and when it surfaces, some of it will actually make small but possibly vital changes in the way everybody thinks and behaves and consumes. The underground is where things grow. Like a delicious carrot or potato.

MS: Who are you being edited by at *NME*?

CSM: Alan Smith was the actual editor, and there was this strange guy in a blazer called John Wells, who was left over from the *ancien regime*, but I think they'd pretty much got rid of him by the time I arrived. [Nick] Logan had moved to deputy spot. So Logan riding shotgun, with Alan Smith as editor. But it was Tony Tyler who went out and got me, and slung me over his shoulder and dragged me back to Long Acre. And not very long after I'd arrived they said, "Can you do us a piece about Iggy Pop?" and I said, "I *can*, but I know someone who's *really* into him, let me make a phonecall" — so I called Nick Kent, and I said "I think we're onto a soft option here, Nick. They want stuff and they can pay." I brought in Joe Stevens, from *it* and *Cream*. I'd bumped into him at the *Oz* office, he was this exotic American who'd been in jail in Ireland... Anyway I was supposed to be doing this piece about the MC5, for *Cream*. And they were playing the Greyhound in Croydon. Joe was dressed all in black, black jeans, black turtleneck sweater, black leather jacket, red henna'd hair to his shoulders, big handlebar 'tache and dark glasses. I was just about to go off to Croydon — he was known as Captain Snaps then, I'm not sure if he had his work permit sorted out. So it was like, "Hey Snaps! I'm doing a piece about the MC5, wanna come along?" So that was the first Murray/Stevens assignment. And we got on, so we worked together a bit — and as soon as we got an in at the *NME*, it was like I brought my photographer, Nick brought his, which was Pennie Smith. Robert Ellis took it very well: he was the *NME* staff photographer, and suddenly you had these two other people around, in their different ways both pretty formidable.

All part of my cunning plan, which was to use the *NME* brand-name and the resources of IPC to create the world's first mass market underground rock paper. And I brought in as many allies as possible, we got Ian [Macdonald], we got Neil [Spencer]. I think we were a bit of culture shock for some of the people already there, but most of them went with it. There were people who felt threatened, there were people who didn't like the direction — but the point is that sales went up.

MS: A year before *NME* had been in danger of closure. And there's this gamble — they're gambling on 'the kids', which is you. It's Alan Smith's gamble, basically.

CSM: Well, he was the editor. When I came along he'd been in the job almost six months. Originally *NME* was three months away from cancellation, then six months, then suddenly — well, not suddenly, it took a while to get the balance right, but those people who couldn't get with the programme left, those who could found they were having much more fun than they ever had before. And basically what we wanted was to cause trouble and have fun, to upset the applecart as much as possible — we wanted mass-market subversion.

MS: In Pat Long's book you say "Ian [Macdonald] was obsessed with stuff that bust the fourth wall of the paper." This seems like a pretty important element in *NME*'s success.

CSM: I was big on this, and you know what my inspiration was? Stan Lee at Marvel! Not the stories — though I loved those — but the way Stan addressed the readers. And also the way Frank Zappa would invite Mothers fans into the world of the Mothers… admittedly only seen from his perspective, not anyone else's. But Zappa broke the fourth wall between band and audience in various important ways, starting with the liner notes to *Freak Out*. The way Stan would answer the letters, the way he would address the readers on the Bullpen Bulletins page. What we wanted was to make every reader feel they were part of the gang, and in the club.

MS: And part of what the club is doing is discussing what's good and what's bad. You're revealing the process, but you're also saying, "This stuff is great, this stuff is bad."

CSM: You must also remember that there was no universal consensus. You do find people arguing different cases in the *NME*. There were acts that Steve Clarke liked that made me wanna puke and vice versa. The thing is, at the time, we are nearly all of us at one end or the other of our 20s — only a few of us are married or have regular partners. Consequently we spend a lot of time in each other's company. We hang out. It isn't like everyone says byebye at 6 o'clock and hallo at 10 o'clock the next morning. We would go out to lunch together, we would go to the pub after work together — we would meet at gigs or receptions, and we would hang out round each other's pads, drinking wine, taking drugs and arguing the toss about music till the wee small hours. And it would only stop when we ran out of cigarettes or rizlas. Somebody would have the new Marley album, the new Roxy album — we'd slap it on the turntable and we'd listen to it and we would argue about. We'd either establish a rift or we would come to a consensus. I'm thinking particularly of me, Nick, Ian Mac, Tyler and Neil. It was a social unit as well as professional unit.

And basically, when I went somewhere, whether it was to a gig or wherever, I would feel the phantom presence of a quarter of a million people in a cloud around my head and shoulders. I was thinking, "I need to communicate to these phantom people as much as possible of what I'm seeing, hearing and feeling. I want them to feel they're here with me." I wanted to bring the readership with me wherever I went.

MS: You've also said, "I'd rather lose a slow reader than talk down to a bright one." So there's an interesting tension…

CSM: Yes!

MS: You're bringing the readership along, but if some of them fall off the bus because they're not quick enough, that's also part of what has to happen.

CSM: It is. And the number of people I've met who tell me they've discovered something — not necessarily musical, it might be a book or a movie — via a piece in the *NME*, not necessarily by me, it could have been by anybody, they'd discovered something through the *NME* that they would not have otherwise encountered, and that this has made an enormous difference to their lives. People who've said, "I didn't really get the Marx Brothers" or "I didn't know about Chandler" or "I didn't know about Burroughs". In a sense, we were educating by stealth. By making stuff seem as groovy and fun as possible, we were trying to broaden things — to give our readers what it said on the tin, plus some other stuff they might not otherwise have encountered. And I'm still meeting people who come up and tell me about this. I'm standing by the bus stop laden with shopping, and someone comes up and recognises me and says "Oh, your review of blah-blah in 197blah-blah completely changed my life, man!" And I'm thinking, "Oh. Nice to meet you. Glad to have been of service."

MS: It looks as if the set-up of what was being judged good in 1972 has changed a lot by 1974, and again 1976, and so on. Over 10 or 12 years, it really shifts fast.

CSM: That is the wonder of the British scene at the time. I was always fascinated by how Americans saw this stuff. The US being so huge, simply because of the geography of the place, it couldn't support weeklies, like we had, for distribution reasons. That's why *Rolling Stone* was fortnightly. We thought that to Americans, the British pop scene must seem like the box that fishermen take maggots out of, these brightly coloured wriggling maggots all going [*maggot voice*] *mig-mig-mig-wig-mig-wig-wiggle*. Whereas to us, the American music scene seemed to be so slow-moving, it was all [*slow-motion voice*] *thiiiis aal-waaays seeeeems tooo beee iiiin slooow mooo-tion*. And because we're a small chunk of geography with very intensive media, and a really fast turnover of ideas, styles, fashions and so on. Trying to change the American music scene, well, bring on the ever-popular oil tanker simile. By the time the American mainstream music business had caught onto what we were doing over here, we'd have changed it. Americans found this really irritating. We thought it was really funny.

MS: Is there a point where you feel, OK, the underground — or whatever you were calling it — this has been happening, I've been part of it, and it's now beginning to fray.

CSM: It was the Isle of Wight festival [in 1970]. People were throwing full cans of coke at people who happened to be standing up in front of them. Everybody had been waiting for Hendrix and he was shit — if you've watched a lot of Hendrix you'll know that the Isle of Wight is one of the worst shows he ever did in his entire career. I thought, "Shit, man, I've only just arrived and the party's about to break up." And I had the feeling of being stuck in lace-curtain-land in Reading, watching all the festivities from afar — and I'd arrived just as they're starting to clear up, there's only a couple of chicken legs and half of a Watney's Keg Party Seven left.

MS: And your career as a writer largely comes after that. So as a writer and a critic you're processing the failure of something?

CSM: Yup. As I said earlier, I think the failure of Hippie was inevitable because the goals it set were mostly unreachable — and the ones it did succeed in reaching didn't become apparent until much later.

MS: You've talked about Mick Farren several times, but you've always just called him Mickey. Which suggests you were very close to him, and you feel he doesn't need explaining to generations to come. But I think he probably does...

CSM: Aaah, Mickey. If you want understand Mickey, you need to read two books and listen to one song. The books are *Elvis Died For Somebody's Sins But Not Mine*, which is the Headpress collection of his journalism, criticism and vulgar abuse — and the other is *Give the Anarchist a Cigarette*, his autobiography. The song you need to listen to is 'The Pilgrim' by Kris Kristofferson. Preferably performed by Johnny Cash. That is Mickey: "*He's a poet, he's a prophet, he's a pilgrim and a preacher, and a problem when he's stoned/he's a walkin' contradiction, partly truth and partly fiction, takin' ev'ry wrong direction on his lonely way back home*" *[sings several more verses of the song].*

That is your portable build-your-own-Mickey kit. He wrote a load of other books, but those are the essential ones. He's buried on Felix's estate. Mickey always had his inhalers, because he suffered from chronic asthma. And that turned into emphysema when he went to live in the States. At one point he was living in Hollywood with a Cadillac and a swimming pool, making $100,000 a year writing screenplays that were never produced. But then he got sick. And under the wonderful American medical system he couldn't meet his medical bills, so Felix paid for him to come back to Britain — he lived in Brighton. By this time he was very sick and chronically overweight. Neither of us are exactly chiselled, but Mickey was chronically overweight. And Felix paid for his funeral, which was about a year and a half before Felix himself died.

One of the things about getting old is that your world gets emptier, as the people you came up with split. My best friend died this year [2016], Bowie died this year. I've got this theory that Bowie was the secret anchor of the world — as soon as he died everything went to shit.

Charles Shaar Murray first wrote for the Oz *Schoolkids issue in 1970, before becoming a staffer at* NME *in the 70s and 80s.*

"A Battle for the Hearts and Minds of Young Working-Class Britain"

Ruth Gregory explores the weave of music and culture in the late David Widgery's political life

The music chosen to be played at David Widgery's funeral by his family — Juliet, Jesse and Anny — demonstrated the variety of his musical preferences. He was both knowledgeable and passionate about music, and the five pieces not only represent his indefatigable optimism for life and liberty, but also his broad-ranging appetite: *Kind of Blue* by Miles Davis, 'Strange Fruit' by Billie Holiday, the overture from Verdi's opera *La Forza Del Destino*, the Parry setting of the William Blake poem 'Jerusalem', as played by the Grimethorpe Colliery Band, and the 1956 version of Sonny Rollins's song 'Oleo', which features John Coltrane in the Miles Davis Quintet.

Between 1976-81, I collaborated with David in the organisation Rock Against Racism, and on more than 15 issues of our highly visual RARzine *Temporary Hoarding*. "It took until the end of 1976," Dave wrote in his 1986 book *Beating Time*, "for the little RAR group to hammer out its ideas and consolidate a core of visual artists, musicians and writers who could drive the project ahead. But for that group the feeling of fear and passivity against the National Front's advance was over… It was a piece of double time, with the musical and the political confrontations on simultaneous but separate tracks and difficult to mix. The music came first and was more exciting. It provided the creative energy and the focus in what became a battle for the hearts and minds of young working-class Britain." As I remember it we worked to a soundtrack of all kinds of music (as our slogan said: reggae, soul, rock & roll, jazz, funk and punk – our music). But it was the emergent British reggae — along with punk rock — which mostly influenced our creative process, because they both carried a gritty urgent beat, specific to that time, on our island's soil. As Dave put it: "We aimed to rescue the energy of Russian revolutionary art, surrealism and rock and roll from the galleries, the advertising agencies and the record companies and use them to change reality, as had always been intended. And have a party in the process."

In the spirit of punk's DIY ethos, *Temporary Hoarding* challenged the cultural status quo in music, writing and design. We did not see ourselves as some kind of artisan élite, but as part of a conversation between RAR, the bands and some 300 RAR groups around the country. In an era marked by an intersection between music and politics, Dave was free to explore the roots of cultural resistance to Empire and slavery. Even when not writing directly about music, his passion for it shone like an RAR star — and herein often lay his insight. The following extracts, taken from his published work, are intended to show how music and culture interwove with his political life:

Too much monkey business

"I have spent a deplorably large part of my life listening to music in dives. But I will never, ever, forget the impact of seeing Cyril Davies and his Allstars steaming into 'Smoke Stack Lighting' in the Ricky Tick Club in Windsor, the first R&B I'd ever heard live. Davies was a panel beater from Walthamstow who, alongside the sorely missed Alexis Korner, was a founder of British R&B and a Chicago purist. He humped over his mouth-harp, spat his lyrics and drove his band like a galley master. The noise was phenomenal, a humping, thundering blast (…)

"Under protest, we would even go to the soul and blues packages at the Fairfield Halls, Croydon. The bluesman used to sit down with heavy spectacles not present in the photos in our jazz and blues textbooks. But jazz became a somewhat unrewarding passion, always just out of tune on the radio, or on a new record you could not afford, or in expensive clubs full of older men knowing what to do and doormen asking your age. Worst of all, there was no dancing (except to 'Trad' which we despised like the musical Savonarolas we were). So you could neither take nor find girls.

"Which is why we ended up skipping our A-level Tudor constitutional history and going in a battered blue van to an R&B club in Windsor called the Ricky Tick and run by John Mayall, who used to live in a tree until it was declared unsanitary by Windsor rural district council. And where I fell for a music which, a quarter of a century later, I am still entirely happy to listen to John's son Gaz playing in a dive in Soho. I now also love the minor operas of Verdi, Orlando Gibbons and Irish traditional music. But R&B remains the root: passionate, sexy and highly political. So thank you, Chuck. And roll over Beethoven."

(Published in New Society, 1988; reprinted in Preserving Disorder, David Widgery, 1989)

Underground Press

"Finally all that was left was the music which middle-class London art students had adopted from the American urban black and synthesised into a weirdly defiant electric music. The cosy communism of the folk coteries engulfed by rock music which could draw half a million kids to one field in Britain and keep them there for a week of fine sounds from the bands and hippy platitudes from the promoter. It was these kids who accepted the attitudes which had once been the private property of a London avant-garde. It was these kids who naturally looked to the underground press for some of the answers so long suppressed by Fleet Street."

(Published in International Socialism (1st series), No.51, 1972)

Billie and Bessie

"The blues is a feeling. For most of this century, music has been the only vehicle black America has been permitted to tell its story, to say what it feels and what it wants. From the harshest of slave systems has come the most moving art produced by modern America. And the source of the power of the blues singers has been their ability to empty out their experience of suffering and longing in the most direct and emotionally forceful idiom.

"For what Bessie Smith and Billie Holiday have in common is not their victimhood — it would be sentimental so to suppose — but their understanding. They knew why America needed victims like themselves. They both could understand not only what it meant to be black when that was a considerable liability, but that it was white society which was deformed and lacking and not themselves (…)

"The classic blues were the first blues on record. They originated with women singing in the minstrel tradition as one of the acts in a touring variety show which, like the English music hall, might mix serious singing with freaks, jugglers and sword-swallowers. But in the 1920s and early 1930s, under the impetus of the record industry, these women singers became performers in their own right, shaping a distinctive body of singing associated with the names of Gertrude "Ma" Rainey, Bessie Smith, Clara Smith, Bertha "Chippie" Hill, Lucille Hegamin and Victoria Spivey. Miss Spivey, the Texas-born pianist and singer, was an especially prolific instrumental blues songwriter. Her 'Dopehead Blues' is one of the first songs to deal with cocaine addiction, and 'TB Blues', recorded in 1927, is an open protest against racism. It was she who 'discovered' Bob Dylan, strongly influenced his writing and issued his first recording on the Spivey label. She died in October 1976 in Brooklyn."

(Published in The Wire, 1984; reprinted in Preserving Disorder, David Widgery, 1989)

Howling to the Beat

"The Beat mission was, in an almost classical sense, romantic and it is probably best to see the creative outburst in North American painting, music and poetry in the 50s as the third and possibly greatest wave of romanticism.

"For only a few streets away the Abstract Impressionist painters were making the first major break in the use of pictorial space since Cubism. And down on 118th in an after-hours dive run by Henry Minton and famous for its collard greens and Creole sauce, the young black virtuosos of bebop were, literally, turning jazz upside down.

"From Minton's Gallery Six and the Beat HQ on East 7th St was emerging the romanticism of the nuclear age, recoiling from modern capitalism, classicism and 'cool' with wildly emotional art which was in each case revolutionary in its formal innovation. And in his North American romantic agony Ginsberg quite literally put himself through the extremes of drug experimentation, sexual iconoclasm, incessant travel and insanity to find and formulate his own visions of human possibility. What remains inspiring is that his quest did not peter out after his first great, howling outbursts, organised on the page almost as Parker might phrase a solo or Pollock hurl himself at a canvas."
(Published in Socialist Review, No.81, 1985, as 'Writers Reviewed: Allen Ginsberg')

Letter from Britain:
RAR/ANL Carnival 1, Victoria Park, London (30 April, 1978):
"It was a most exciting-looking demonstration. Trafalgar Square, the site of so many grey occasions, was raked with colour. Yellow Anti-Nazi League (ANL) roundels, punk-pink Rock Against Racism (RAR) stars, dayglo flags oscillated in approval to the speeches. Giant masks of the Nazi leaders, streamers, Lone Ranger masks, steel bands and reggae and punk from flat-bed trucks, and thousands upon thousands of plastic whistles formed slipstreams of colour and sound. It was a carnival, a positive, joyous carnival against the 'No Fun, No Future' philosophy of the NF. Behind various scenes a lot of countercultural know-how had come together again.

"The politics of musicians performing free at the Victoria Park spoke out not just as representatives of their rock and roll generation or in solidarity with fellow-musicians but to start repaying some of the dues any musician owes to the black roots. RAR started in a spontaneous protest against some off-the-cuff racialism from Clapton and Bowie. But it's grown into something much bigger, a rank-and-file rock-and-roll roots-music movement against the NF, respectable racism and superstar cool. With help from the music press, goodwill from the bands, a natural empathy with the emerging UK reggae dimension and a record for putting on A-1 gigs, RAR provides some sort of a way for musicians of the new wave to keep in touch with their audiences and their ideals instead of spiralling off into superstar insanity.

"Best of all Steel Pulse, the first UK band to level with the JA sounds in music and politics too. The Pulse's 'Ku Klux Klan' is not only a masterpiece of electronic sound and multi-rhythm but a brilliantly wry and defiant lyric about the return of organised racialism. The concert ended with a jam round a white reggae riff which had Mick Jones and Danny Kustow, the two best white guitarists of the new wave, dropping power chords into a chant by Steel Pulse, 90 Degrees Inclusive, and Jim Pursey of Sham 69. It flowed because just as white and black UK kids in the 60s related to the sounds of the black cities of North America to fashion their music from, they are now listening where the black struggle is fiercest and the music most intense, the Caribbean and Africa.

"The punk-gay-reggae line up was amazing but is real because it expresses the common experience and defiance of inner city life; street heat, maximum unemployment, sexual ambiguities, fuck-all future, corrugated iron and the NF biding their time."
(Published by Radical America, Vol.12 No.5, 1978)
All extracts © David Widgery's estate.

David Widgery wrote for the New Statesman and Oz (where he was a co-editor for a time), as well as ink, Time Out, City Limits, Socialist Review and the British Medical Journal. He worked at Bethnal Green Hospital from 1972, and then as a GP in the East End until his tragic early death in 1992.

Ruth Gregory was on the RAR Central London Committee, and co-edited Temporary Hoarding with David Widgery. They later collaborated on various projects, including his book Beating Time. Ruth's work and archive formed half of the exhibition A Riot of Our Own at Chelsea Space in 2008, at the East End Film Festival in 2010 and No Turning Back at the Migration Museum, in September 2018. She is currently designing an archival website for RAR-RAP (Rock Against Racism — Research Archive Project).

Could Have, Should Have, Didn't

Forty years on, Idris Walters remembers Street Life, a magazine that mattered a lot but didn't last

And you may ask yourself
How did I get here? (Talking Heads)

Street Life, a fortnightly countercultural newspaper, burned all too briefly from 1975 through to 1976, whence it vanished without trace. In hindsight, it was a case of could have, should have and, finally, didn't. But I should confess at the outset a shameful fraudulence concerning this memoir. My involvement was as a distant contributing editor, a very insignificant role. Looped out, I knew nothing of the editorial, publishing or managerial decision-making at the paper, and cannot claim any forensic insight as regards its workings other than the intensely personal.

I had, in any case, abandoned London prior to *Street Life*'s first issue, in order to escape the noxious effluvia of burning bridges and the 60s hippie after-party which had taken a palpably dispiriting turn and become hazardous to the general health and well-being of the Alternative Society we had cherished for ten years or so.

During previous years I had written for a number of design and music periodicals — *Sounds, Let It Rock, Melody Maker, Black Music, Building Design, Design Magazine, Progressive Architecture* and so on — but had developed, as an enthusiast, a reputation for covering reggae music, an extremely niche pursuit in those days. *Street Life* at its inception drew upon an existing tribe of "usual suspect" rock writers in London... but my distance from London precluded any great awareness of the editorial structure.

Long gone were the golden years when rock music pulsed at the beating heart of a unifying turbo-charged force for change across the full spectrum of post-war behaviour and creativity. The US/UK counterculture, with rock music as its rhythm section, had begun to subside into a dismal spasm of sclerotic self-parody. Record companies, predictably enough, had established a self-serving agenda and would no longer be creatively led by the musicians themselves, as had so exhilaratingly once been the case.

Leaving for the North, I was also in flight from the prevailing contemporary art circus. With a friend from Architecture School we had been peddling a series of conceptual/installation art projects, and, short of encouragement from the ICA, the RCA and a number of cool-hungry colleges, we had met with very little meaningful response. We were tired of deaf ears and stony ground. It should be born in mind that this was a good ten years before the YBAs and the Turner Prize, and long before the Saatchi phenomena made irritating art spivs out of all of us. These new art forms, prior to being seen as a curious branch of the marketing industry, had evolved from event structures, acid tests and happenings out of the New York loft culture, as well as a growing taste for 'Art *and* Music' festivals within the countercultural movement.

But I digress. Creative writing had been very much an integral part of the emerging alternative society here and in the US. From the wormwood-addled attics and cafés of Bohemian Europe, from Céline and Rimbaud, to the wild-eyed streams of headlong consciousness of the Beat Generation, through Burroughs, Kerouac and radical writing by way of Hunter Thompson and Norman Mailer, had morphed into what became known, oddly, as The New Journalism in the late 60s. These latter heroes, word sculptors and crazed proselytisers had found a reliable berth at Jann Wenner's *Rolling Stone*.

It is a remarkable entertainment that a two-word phrase from an ancient proverb — suggesting that continuous movement insures against stagnation — should emerge in a variety of song lyrics from the likes of Hank Williams and Muddy Waters, should be used as a band name for what was to be the "greatest rock and roll band in the world" and that a Nobel Prize for Literature laureate should incorporate it as a *leitmotif* in what is often accused of being the best rock lyric ever composed. *Rolling Stone* had selected its title well.

Streetlife but you better not get old
Streetlife or you're gonna feel the cold
(Joe Sample, Randy Crawford)

There is no doubt that *Street Life* was an all-too transparent attempt to emulate Wenner's masterpiece in a British equivalence. Since its inception in 1967, *Rolling Stone* had quickly become essential reading for the suddenly stoned amongst musically liberated British youth. Plainly, *Street Life* failed to complete this transfer. Whether this was down to a tragic collapse of cool or poor management probably matters little. Could have, should have, didn't.

The *Rolling Stone* ethos seemed to show that rock journalism could be the next best thing to musical priesthood itself. A British version seemed, at the time, to be an excellent wheeze.

I remember crowding into a tiny room up on the North Sea coast with a new-found group of musician friends I was to run with subsequently, to catch the *Old Grey Whistle Test*, which coincidentally on that night, with the gulls complaining, the wind howling off the sea and the foghorns blowing free jazz, would review the first issue of *Street Life*. We were suitably bemused when I got a mention for a short piece about dub reggae which I had contributed, in response to some wonderful Augustus Pablo white labels which I had recently acquired.

I ought to point out that I was no musician. I fell into the "those who can't play had better write" group. I was a triumph for enthusiasm over professionalism, but I had, in fact, mastered the blues harp at grammar school. My harmonicas had been confiscated on numerous occasions as a result of my discovery that the school corridors made excellent echo chambers and I had found The Sound. The big Sound I had heard from all the great blues players. I had learned the water trick and throat patterns and I could roar raw right down to the bottom. I had no musicality to speak of, but I could blow sufficient.

But I digress. I was shortly to write a feature for *Street Life* concerning this particular group of musicians, then called North Star. The idea was to compile a road diary logging the disreputable adventures of a never-to-be-signed group of chancers gigging around the North armed only with an offal-smelling ex-butcher's Transit and a will, like so many others, just to be a band. We were indeed simply "the group", backing strippers, taking ourselves very seriously, surfing sofas, growing even more hair and generally wrestling the dream to the ground. The piece was published and appeared fresh on the newsstands the day we arrived home from a highly educational residency at a night club in Salamanca. General Franco had just died and Spanish youth was celebrating. This was fame indeed.

But I digress. It is a common scientific conceit that close observation fundamentally changes the thing observed. A major feature of The New Journalism was that the writer/observer wrote himself, with specific literary effect, deep into the narrative as part of the story. Hunter Thompson and Richard Brautigan were particularly adept at this exercise and, later on, the *NME* would speed-rush through the idea with vigorous effect on its own succeeding generation.

How does it feel?   (Bob Dylan)

Street Life could have been, should have been a handy springboard for an indigenous British gonzo. It wasn't.

Looking back, its branding was weak. Graffiti art had gathered substantial momentum as a New York art form in the mid-70s, but the rather lazy single-colour schoolboy graphic in the *Street Life* logo fell far short of its potential and, while the page layouts and illustrative content were acceptable in a conventional sense, the overall image/look of the magazine was somewhat anaemic.

Street Life's graffiti wall — an oval shaped brick pattern in a single red, with a freehand title font at a jaunty angle — I still feel to be undistinguished. Ovals, like circles, tend, unless artfully counterbalanced, to sit uncomfortably on a page... since they lack the impulse of direction. The brand effect is one of stasis, going nowhere, gathering moss.

In the original, *Rolling Stone* had chosen a comprehensive retro, almost Victorian style for its logo and layouts, visually continuous with its San Franciscan psychedelic musical compost.

Street Life
Street Life
Street Life
What a Life   (Bryan Ferry)

One other idea pursued at *Street Life* springs to mind. This was to interview prevailing rockistocrats on subjects and enthusiasms other than music. To this end I spent a civilised morning discussing Pop Art with Bryan Ferry at his palatial London residence, complete with maid service. Bryan had been taught by Richard Hamilton, and maintained a keen interest in contemporary developments in art. The piece was printed with *faux*-Hockney-style illustrations, and I was looking forward to approaching Jeff Beck to talk about hot-rodding. But *Street Life* collapsed and the idea was stillborn. Could have, should have... tragic.

To sum up, *Street Life* was, in my timespun romantic recollection at least, a missed opportunity to provide a healthy outlet for British counter-cultural creative writing, whether on rock music or not, and suffered most probably from comparison with the sheer quality and verve of its American inspiration. I suspect there were also financial issues and managerial disputes way beyond my corporate status. Given the understandable reverence owed to the *Rolling Stone* gold standard back in the mid-70s, it is alarming how that august periodical would develop over the ensuing 40 years, into the deeply embedded media behemoth it now appears to be. In the late 60s and early 70s the *Rolling Stone* strapline — "all the news that fits" — took ownership of the Zeitgeist with pinpoint accuracy, and attracted a loyal readership which saw itself as the rampaging vanguard of musical, imaginative and therefore societal change for the general good.

While there is nearly half a century of post-truth in this brief memoir — ghosts, shadows, the past as a Fourth World dictatorship — it is, with some affection, that I conclude that *Street Life* could have, should have... but sadly didn't.

In the mid-70s, Idris Walters wrote for Street Life, Pulse, Sounds, Melody Maker, Let It Rock and Black Music, as well as Design Magazine and Progressive Architecture, before returning to the practice of architecture and architectural illustration.

On Learning Not To Be a Snob

A voracious reader of the music press from an unusually young age, Marcello Carlin explains why the Melody Maker meant the most to him in the 1970s

As 70s readers of the *Melody Maker* go, my story may not be the most typical, primarily because I took after my father and listened mainly to jazz. In fact I was something of a snob about it to start off with — but the paper gradually took me somewhere else; somewhere better.

My father was a lifelong subscriber, and I remember first looking through its pages in late 1969, when I was five years old — I was a precociously early reader, with all the drawbacks this can entail later on. For a year or so I followed it intermittently — along with *NME*, *Disc and Music Echo*, *Record Mirror*, as well as subscribing to *Record Retailer* for the charts — it would become *Music Week* in 1972. (My father also subscribed to *Jazz Journal*, *Jazz Monthly*, *DownBeat*, *Coda* and *Gramophone*.) But before long I found myself much more interested in comics than music-writing: *Beano*, *Dandy*, *Donald and Mickey*, *Archie* and so on. I would not return properly to the music press until the autumn of 1973 — the event that changed things being the broadcast on BBC2 of Mike Oldfield's *Tubular Bells*, which my father loved.

Pop or rock hadn't really filtered into my consciousness until the mid-70s, and I still rather sniffed at it. Though I knew to be prepared when faced with the primary-school playground challenge. "Who done 'Metal Guru', then?" I made sure that I knew damned well who done 'Metal Guru' — and also where it was in the "Hit Parade." I was listening to Radio Luxembourg for the Top 30 and Radio 1 at Tuesday lunchtime — after the two-year break it all seemed very fresh.

But as a young jazz fan, *Melody Maker* made much more of an impression on me than the *NME*. I guess this is because right through the 70s it still somehow seemed to see itself as a jazz paper first, and everything else second, even though *MM*'s covers were dominated, as were *NME*'s, by huge, narrow black headlines outlining this rock band's tour dates or that rock band's shock split.

As the 70s wore on, I found myself becoming more and more interested in what was then happening in jazz and improvised music, not only in the lofts of the Lower East Side or in Chicago or St Louis, but in Britain too — namely the abrupt explosion of young talent which seemed to have converged upon London from all directions; from Sheffield (Derek Bailey and Tony Oxley), from Devon (John Surman and Mike Westbrook) and of course from South Africa (the Blue Notes and the Brotherhood of Breath). And thanks to a few open-minded, open-hearted and well placed individuals, there was genuine interaction between the free or free-ish jazz of the time and what was still termed progressive rock: Soft Machine, Nucleus, King Crimson, with such pluralist midwives as Keith Tippett, Robert Wyatt, Robert Fripp and Joe Boyd. Jack Bruce, John McLaughlin and Dave Holland were building bridges to the likes of Miles Davis and Tony Williams in the US. A lot of it seemed to have the same musicians in common: Mongezi Feza, for example, or Gary Windo (who played with Centipede and Matching Mole, but also session sax on a lot of glam classics, including Gary Glitter).

My father didn't have much time for glam (or later punk) but would buy pop or rock records if jazz people played on them (Nick Drake, John Martyn and so on). I still arrogantly considered myself a discerning jazz fan — but I applauded the fact that all these strains of music appeared to be coming together, fusing and co-existing. I didn't know it yet, but I was a nascent pluralist. And the first writer of note I spotted in *Melody Maker* was Steve Lake, a young lad from Chelmsford who had started out loving rock, but was buying Spontaneous Music Ensemble records by the time he was 16. I came across him in about 1974, interviewing Ornette in a New York loft, and being told, to his (Lake's) astonishment, that the great saxophonist's favourite group was Poco. Maybe you can't take Texas out of the Texan.

As time passed, Lake gravitated more towards the progressive European or Europhile side of contemporary jazz. Major labels had only released such records as tax losses in the first place, and had by this time largely dropped the artists in question. So the music's progress depended on the close observation of exotically named independent companies: Incus, Ogun, FMP, ECM... These labels put out records that were mostly impossible to find in Glasgow's record shops, and needed to be obtained via mail-order, frequently from the labels themselves. And Lake was on top of all of these with his marvellously descriptive reviews, raves which virtually demanded that you go out and find this music.

It didn't last long. Infamously, in late 1975, Lake performed a hatchet job on Patti Smith's *Horses.*To me, this was a key record in terms of building a bridge between two different manifestations of the 'New Thing' — free jazz and New York punk — and it seemed to me that he had missed the point entirely. His jazz reviews continued with increasing infrequency, but by the time he had disappeared to Munich in the late 70s to help out at ECM, it wasn't really a surprise.

Melody Maker was a large paper to digest. There were bulky sections on both jazz and folk, as well as innumerable classified ads right at the back, including recruiting for bands and a detailed "technical" section for fans of amplifiers, mixing desks and so on. And I had begun to follow other fine writers, the pluralists, in fact. Such as the remarkable Karl Dallas, for instance, whose enthusiasm recognised no genre boundaries.

And then there was Richard Williams, who I had remembered from presenting the *Old Grey Whistle Test* earlier in the 70s. (I watched *OGWT* and *Top of the Pops*, as well as art review shows like *Aquarius* and the regular jazz slots. *TotP* had an albums slot at one time: one week Dudu Pukwana and Assegai were on it.) Williams had also been an odd-job jazz review man in the late 60s, but apart from a spell in A&R at Island Records — where he famously spotted and signed up Roxy Music — I had no real inkling of his writing capacities until he returned to the *Maker's* pages in 1976 as a rather stern columnist. He ranged all over the place, and wasn't slow to stamp down on anything he thought was a waste of time — you should see what he had to say about Tony Palmer's *All You Need Is Love* documentary TV series.

But Williams had a passion and, I now recognise, an impatience similar to mine with those cursed genre boundaries, which immediately made him the paper's most compelling writer. It should be remembered that throughout the 70s the editor, later editor-in-chief, was one Ray Coleman, not the hippest of pop spectators and a person who I felt was happy just to leave the bulk of his paper to those who knew what they were talking about (his own tastes were relatively middle-of-the-road, encompassing McCartney's Beatles and the Carpenters, as well as the odd curveball like Gary Numan).

This freedom, I think, worked wonders, though the working took some time. Caroline Coon was arguably on the ball with punk far ahead of anyone in the *NME* (though *Sounds* was ahead of either), but it was Williams who sold me the notion of punk as something to which I ought to attend. Reviewing 'Anarchy in the U.K.' and 'New Rose' in the same column, he correctly criticised the Pistols record for being too ponderous, too eager to be another "rock" record, whereas the Damned exploded with the damn-you joy of the truly new. 'New Rose' was the first single that I bought with my own money, purely because Williams compared Rat Scabies' cymbal-heavy drumming to Sunny Murray. (By now I was also reading *Black Music, Blues & Soul, Let It Rock, ZigZag* and the short-lived *Street Life*. But *Melody Maker* was the one that seemed substantial to me, in look as well as content; that felt as if it had something to say.)

Williams soon took over Lake's mantle as new jazz observer, and his reviews were just as compelling, if somewhat more sardonic — especially where ECM was concerned. The genial, permanently bereted veteran Max Jones continued to take care of all the old-school jazz, as he had since the mid-40s, while writer and photographer Val Wilmer provided ongoing commentary on what was happening in the States throughout this period. Other writers, such as good-time rocker Chris Welch, were very funny, but happily admitted that punk was not their thing — though in terms of where rock was headed, Welch was a very early champion of AC/DC. (And in 1978, he also wrote probably the most memorable line of jazz criticism in the paper: tasked with reviewing a Graham Collier album and not really enjoying it, he stops upon a free percussion solo and compares it to "a herd of cows tiptoeing through a plumber's bedroom on a warm July morning").

Eventually Williams was offered the editor's job, and as it was now the late 70s and the *NME* clearly held the critical initiative, he made several important appointments, notably hiring Jon Savage (as the paper's Manchester correspondent) from *Sounds*, 60s veteran Penny Valentine from *Record Mirror*, future Condé Nast supremo James Truman, future *Wire* editor Chris Bohn, and future film director Mary Harron. Also from *Sounds*, he poached Vivien Goldman — reggae at last getting its belated regular due in the paper! — and put the jazz pages in the hands of the old *Jazz Monthly* team of Max Harrison and Michael James. He even managed to persuade the *sui generis* Brian Case to transfer over from the *NME*. Every issue was now unmissable.

Once again, it did not last. Deep down, Coleman wanted the *Maker* to be a pop *Daily Telegraph*, and argued with Williams. There was a union dispute in 1980. By the time it was resolved, Williams had left and the paper had changed forever — and, for half a decade, for the worse. There would be a rearguard action later that decade, but the 80s *Melody Maker* was a different beast from that of the 70s. I continued to read it — and contribute in great part to its letters page — until the mid-90s, and then stopped doing so out of frustrated boredom. Jazz and folk had quietly been dropped from the paper altogether in the early 80s. Still, at its best — and without the sometimes fatal cockiness of the *NME* — the *Maker's* message was much more readily absorbed.

And I won't forget that Saturday at Glasgow's Mitchell Library in the very early 80s, when I was leafing as usual through the volumes of *MM* back issues from the early 70s, to see what I had missed, and found to my delight a rave review of Carla Bley and Paul Haines' *Escalator Over The*

Hill. I had discovered this double album in 1980, in the listening booths at the (now defunct) Bridge Street Library in the Gorbals, and become somewhat obsessed with it, obtaining a copy by mail order from Honest Jon's in Portobello a few weeks later — it had been deleted in 1979 and this was one of the last copies in stock anywhere. And here it was at release date, being effectively (and correctly) called the greatest piece of music that anybody had created. The reviewer? Richard Williams. Pluralists will out.

Marcello Carlin is a long-serving NHS professional who will write about music if the price is right.

Rhetorics of Outsider Style and the Implicit Politics of Critical Stance

Paul Morley: *NME, Blitz, media commentator*
John (aka Jonh) Ingham: *CREEM, Rolling Stone, Crawdaddy, Sounds*
Barney Hoskyns: *NME, Vogue, Mojo co-founder and editorial director of Rock's Backpages*
Panel chaired by Toby Litt: *novelist, senior lecturer in creative writing at Birkbeck*

TL: I'd like to introduce each of the panellists. Jonh Ingham almost certainly doesn't want me to mention which particular band he was the first music journalist to interview. When punk began he was a long-haired bearded interrogator who'd been chronicling rock and pop dynasties since the 60s. Always open to the new, his review of Patti Smith's *Horses* shows him to be a man of impeccable judgment — every word he says there was right. He's since done many things, including being head of content for O2, and is now head of creative products for Soundlounge.

To his right is Paul Morley, who via his sleeve-note epigrams for ZZT, especially Propaganda and Frankie Goes to Hollywood, was my first introduction to weapons-grade pretension. Of course I loved it and was warped for life. He's occupied a central position in the UK's pop-cultural landscape since the late 1970s, often moving the river rather than being swept along by it. More recently he's taken on the much contested history of Manchester and the North, and has also written an acclaimed book, *Nothing*, about his own anatomy of melancholy and suicide. He's described on the *Guardian* website as a rock and roll journalist, which keeps things simple.

And finally Barney Hoskyns. He has for quite a while been patrolling what you might call a Laurel Canyon of the mind, revisiting and reanimating the Californian scene from the 60s and 70s, a sound, a kind of light, an ethic, and a catastrophe that seems more and more distant and yet increasingly painful to think of, as a rebuke perhaps to the clinical global soundworld of now. He's also written about The Band's Woodstock, about Tom Waits' Waitsville, America, and Led Zeppelin's world. In 2016 he'll be returning to Woodstock again for *Small Town Talk*. Is he perhaps an analogue guy in a digital age harking back to these Californian sounds?

So my first question is, if you think back to the time you published your first review, did you think what you were doing was political? What was the meaning of it in terms of what did you actually think you were doing? Was it to do with you or was it to do with the scene?

BH: No, I wouldn't say it was political. I would say it's entirely to do with one's ego and wanting to see one's words in print. I wanted to be a writer. I wanted to be if not a great writer then at least a good writer, and I think that's probably all I've ever really wanted to be. So did I attach any political import to it? I think the honest answer is no. I loved music. There was some political edge to that love. My first piece was published in 1979, and there was certainly politics in the air — but I was a kid really, so primarily it was about me, me, me. That's really all the ego ever says: *me, me, me, me*. So I've tried to combat that over the years.

PM: My first review was Buzzcocks up in Manchester. And there was something in the air in Manchester that was abstractly about power being elsewhere. You felt that we were at the edge of a universe and other people were at the centre of it. So there was very much a sense of placing a lot of energy into how I was writing at the time, because I felt a kind of vast, wonderful resentment. Obviously I wanted to be a writer, I'd wanted to be a writer almost since I could think — and at that stage two things. First, to become a writer it was actually easier to get to the *New Musical Express* than it was to get to the *Stockport Advertiser*, oddly enough — because I was told that I wasn't qualified enough to get to the *Stockport Advertiser*. But I had the weird qualifications necessary to get to the *NME*, which I think was almost just a kind of energy, a kind of madness as well, and a kind of self-belief that was transcendent and incandescent.

And second, I remember in my interview for the *NME* — with the great Nick Logan — that I was complaining about two writers in particular, Nick Kent and Charles Shaar Murray, just for the sheer hell of it, because they were too old. And I always remember Nick's answer. He said, "My god, they're only 23." But back then age was a very different thing. So at 19, 23 year olds seemed very senior, very establishment. So it was never directly political, it was never directly or specifically or explicitly those kind of things, but it definitely had that air of belief that you could change. All my favourite writers had basically willed their universe into being, and I could see that you could do that with language, and if you connected that language to something that was happening — and I happened to luck into that because I was in Manchester when something was happening — that combination of wanting to will something into being, you could actually make it happen.

And that in itself is, I guess, a political act, because obviously by the very nature of that you're saying things can be different, there should be different possibilities, it shouldn't always lie in the hands of, in my case, the South or Londoners, abstract as that was. And occasionally I glance back without nostalgia at that Buzzcocks review — and what I notice more than anything is just a kind of manifesto, and for many years in a way everything I did was really just a manifesto for change, and sometimes just change for the sake of it. I was quite proud. Possibly what you were noticing when you talk about pretension. Because some of the writers that I really adored were people like Marshall McLuhan. I love the idea of really winding people up and provoking them, and changing my mind half way through a sentence just to put ideas out there. Because for me it was always about ideas, great ideas, and suddenly being a writer for the *NME* — which was at that point in a world that treated music as a matter of life or death — the *NME* was the centre of that universe, and suddenly I had the power to will my particular universe into being, which was incredibly exciting. And went to my head.

JI: Well, my first published piece was a live review of a Detroit band, Grand Funk Railroad, in a Detroit magazine, *CREEM*. This is 1970 and Detroit was the centre of rock and revolution in a very fractious America. I spent all my high school and most of my college years mostly in California, and — as you heard from the underground panel here this morning — the Vietnam war had a massive effect on everything. It really focused the world that you lived in. And the draft was affecting literally everybody around you who could not get out of it — and the first couple of years at college there were always guys just back from Vietnam, like 19, 20, and they were generally sitting at the back in a corner, very, very silent, looking very hollow, so you were affected by this all the time. Bank of America got firebombed in Santa Barbara. There was running street riots in Berkeley, where the National Guard shot and killed people over a square of desolate land called People's Park. These things affected you a lot.

So it was just in the air. You identified with it all because you were young and anti-war, and you could see this violence going on, the establishment pushing people back down. But outside of that I'd been reading *Rolling Stone* — from maybe issue 9 when it just sort of appeared somewhere, probably in a headshop in the town where I lived — and slowly it dawned on me these people were getting their records free. That seemed like a really good idea. That was the main reason why I started, just to get free records.

TL: So when you started, who were the people that you wanted to be like — or unlike? Paul, was the *NME* your first point of call, as part of remaking the world?

PM: Well, when I started reading full stop, and then reading about music, some of the more interesting, exciting and I guess in hindsight more experimental stuff always came from America, both in terms of what became known as the New Journalism, and then all these magazines like *CREEM* and *Crawdaddy* and *Rolling Stone*. It was tremendously exciting. And the one magazine then that seemed to have that in it was the *NME* — so from a very young age, being in the middle of nowhere, it was an extraordinary tunnel you could crawl through every Thursday morning when it arrived. A whole new set of possibilities opened up then. It was psychedelic almost.

More than anything it was the one way into a world of *writing*. More than a world of rock or a world of music. And in that sense, back then, by the very nature of making a decision about the kind of music you liked and why you liked it, that instantly incorporated your political belief. That's why it was a matter of life or death. It's something that's very difficult to explain now — that if you aligned yourself with a certain sort of music and hated this other music, that there was a reason for that beyond taste, and beyond just lifestyle. It wasn't just about the fact, "Well, I don't like that," it was actually a political decision you made that that music was not going to do anything good, that it was not going to help the world. That in fact it was contributing to everything you didn't believe in. That's a thing that's difficult to explain now.

TL: When you're writing a review or going to a gig to review, isn't this attitude — that I want to do something about this, either because it's shit or because it's fantastic and people should hear about it — isn't that the attitude that makes for the really great writing? Going in with an agenda, not sitting back?

BH: I think that's absolutely right. I've derived as much pleasure and satisfaction from really trashing something that I think shouldn't be well regarded. I still feel that impulse, at my august age. And there is as much passion in that as in wanting to do justice to something that has moved you profoundly. But to go back to your original question, I emulated writers who really made music and the environment around music and even the music business come alive on the page. I was really impressed by that. Different kinds of writers. It wasn't just the Lester Bangs noiseboy aesthetic. There were historians who I thought were exemplary.

I wanted to be as good as them. Simple as that. The Nik Cohns and the Ian MacDonalds. I'm not sure that MacDonald in his *NME* heyday was as great a music writer as he became. I think some of the writing he did about older music actually, everything from Steely Dan to Miles Davis — in his collection called *People's Music* — I think this is just some of the finest writing. Incredible writing in any artform. So he became a great critic. So I just wanted to be like, well, Kenneth Tynan was mentioned earlier. I wanted to be a great writer and I loved music, so that was the avenue for me.

PM: It's interesting about Ken Tynan, because obviously the idea of *being a critic* was important. I thought the idea of being a critic was incredibly glamorous and important in terms of contributing to the wider context of things, giving it a shape, finishing it off if you like. I mean, it's been decided that it was a kind of élitist position — but those of us that managed to get there had fought and scrapped and made it our kind of goal to do just that. So we sort of earned something to be on top of the pile, to be screaming that this is better than that, that the Fire Engines are better than Wigwam or whatever. Whatever strange battle was going on at the time. And in a way because we believed in it so much and meant it so much we deserved to be the ones — because everybody used to complain and say why is it *you* and not *me*? Well, it *could* be you, but you have to fight.

Now everybody's fought and everybody's got free records now. But back at the time that was part of the point, that you'd earnt it and there was a kind of weird structure you were part of — and even though you were sometimes opposing and sometimes nagging and sometimes being incoherent, whatever those words might be, they were all in pursuit of something that was important. And you felt that it was important because in the years previous to you you'd seen so much change so quickly — because of ideas and because of writers — and so you took your part in that. You decided they've managed to do this, they've managed to meet people as well. Which was absolutely the idea, as well as the free records. The first two people I interviewed as a journalist were Marc Bolan and Patti Smith. So I was arriving one week, and the next week actually being with them, and that was an incredible perk. But you took it seriously within that.

I wanted to write about these people and write about these things I loved in as original and as — I mean, obviously people felt I failed, and that was OK as well — but I wanted to be as original and fascinating and constantly changing as much as possible, not least because of these people around you, like Ian MacDonald, like Ian Penman, like Nick Kent,

Cynthia Rose. There were some fantastic writers, and you were constantly kept on your toes. And I loved that about it as well — a constant reaction, *Oh, they've written something better than I have, I have to be better than them now.* There was a constant wonderful tension. I mean, editorial meetings at the *NME*, they were battlefields of ideology, in terms of who was in that very small room.

TL: You all started out casually saying it was just *me, me, me,* and now we've got to battlefields of ideology. So what were the ideologies at these meetings?

JI: I was at *Sounds* 1975-76. Vivien Goldman pretty much had reggae completely to herself — and advisedly so, she's brilliant at it. Geoff Barton pretty much had all the bands no one else wanted to touch, which became all the *Kerrang!* bands, Purple and Sabbath and KISS and god knows who else. And then there was another three or four of us fighting over the same five names that everybody wanted to interview or go and see. Neil Young, the Stones — I can't even think of half of them now.

The interesting thing from what we're all saying is you're trying to find a balance between a critical approach that's a serious approach — to analyse these people and go in with agendas and dismantle them intellectually and properly — and at the same time, as Paul said, everyone's in competition with everybody else. If Charlie Murray wrote that, then I'm going to do better this week. There was a lot of that going on. And you're fighting all the other people over those same stories. Around the end of 1975 I found myself getting really bored with just about all of it — everyone sounded flaccid and tired and old, and there was nobody new coming out. One day in the *NME* I saw this very small review about a band called the Sex Pistols. Just the name was enough. It was like "Sex Pistols, that's the best name I've heard in years. Who are these people? Where do I find them?" I want to go and check this out.

I finally saw them around the beginning of April in a strip club on Brewer Street and already anybody who's touched them says they're terrible — which was kind of interesting because they were like a young band. They had a good rhythm section. The guitarist played good rhythm guitar. All the songs sounded the same but not quite. You could tell some were good and some weren't. Then they'd do things like a Small Faces cover and a Monkees cover, which was quite funny in the context. And John is just going on at the audience, all 20 of them, "If you don't clap I'm wasting my time." It's just completely funny. But somehow it clicked for me, and that was when I made the shift and like, OK, there's my agenda, this is the new stuff.

I took a big step back and looked at it because I thought if I do this as a proper critic and do it the traditional way, anybody who likes reading that stuff is going to hate this, because it's just so aggressive and negative compared to what you're seeing for the previous 15 years. What if I write about it as an advertising campaign for 15-year-old boys? *This is the most exciting thing you're ever going to see.* And that's exactly what I did for the next year. I knew I was onto it when around June — I'd probably written about them twice since then — anywhere I'd go, a record company or just on the street meeting people, they'd ask, "How's your band the Sex Pistols doing?" And that's when I knew I had it. So then I *really* went for it.

TL: Weren't you worried you were undermining your chance to interview Sabbath or whatever, because they'll say "Don't send the guy who likes that punk band?"

JI: I was quietly taken aside by people and told to drop all this because I was ruining my career. I'm a really stubborn guy so I was just like, "You don't tell me what to do." I knew better than everybody.

PM: That is an interesting tension — that you were sometimes committing yourself both in terms of what you were selecting as something you were going to write about, or in how you wrote about it. I remember when I started writing about the Fall, that almost was the very end of my career at the *NME*. For about eight weeks I didn't get another commission. Because no one in the south could understand what I was talking about, because I tried to write it in the style of the Fall! Which was probably technically a mistake. But that was often how I wanted to represent my love for music — to not necessarily fall in with the narrative. Which was already beginning. Which later became *Q* and *Mojo*. So there was an ideological battle already.

I wasn't particularly interested in that storyline and the way that was going, a kind of almost academic approach to the history of music. I was more interested in a much more chaotic thing, always undermining whatever the new trends might be. So writing about the Fall in the style of the Fall upset my editor at the time, Phil McNeill, and he didn't ring me up for eight weeks. I understood that. But that was the tension. A kind of ideological battle.

And also, as Jonh was implying, it was about certain sorts of music — and again I suppose I'm clinging loyally and obediently to this panel's title. The sound that a guitar had begun to make, that certain bands were beginning to make seemed so static, seemed to be representing the status quo and everything we now much more coherently and regularly call sexist and racist. And eventually we called it *rockist*. And in terms of the band I was writing about, Buzzcocks, it seemed absolutely that the reduction of everything to a single guitar note was almost a kind of cleansing, an ideological cleansing. It was like an ideological reaction to all those dragons and Roger Dean covers and huge extended solos and box sets and the bloated, complacent nature of this thing, which had started so much shorter, faster, wittier and quicker in the 50s and early 60s — and I felt that the writing, and a lot of other people were feeling this at the time, had to fall in with this as well.

So it did become an ideological battle. At the *NME* editorial meetings you'd have a guy called Steve Clarke talking about Fleetwood Mac, and I was going on about Subway Sect. Right there is war, and *blood will be drawn*. Because it was a matter of life or death, and in a sense I think quite rightly. Some ideas are better than others and lead to a better truth, and it's more than political, it's about life itself.

TL: He's taken it to a better truth. Is it a better truth? Can you get there?

BH: I think Paul was right that punk was a kind of purging, it was an ideological purging. When I think back to when I started at the *NME*, which was 1981, I always think it was a lousy time to be writing. You weren't riding the crest of the Zeitgeist. And politically I felt meek and guilty because I was middle class and I'd been to Oxford. I felt I had to keep my head down really. I'm much angrier about politics now than I was then. Then I just felt scared of being outed, I think, in a way. But when you talk about punk and what that represented, the purging that it represented, I think what's important to acknowledge when you talk about

Roger Dean covers is that rock had become as bloated as a merchant bank, frankly, by 1975. It was the nadir year.

This thing that had started at some sort of grassroots street-punk level, these guys were now riding around in individual limousines, and it was obscene. I was, what, 15, 16 in 1975, and consciously I felt this was revolting. There was no alternative to Fleetwood Mac. And then we started reading about CBGBs, and so forth. So it did become, yeah, an ideological crusade — except I also felt some guilt because I still loved Todd Rundgren, and I know Paul did too, I don't know about Jonh. But by 1979 you couldn't really admit to any of that stuff. And the truth was I fucking hated the Clash, and I still hate the Clash. I quite like the first album. And even more than the Clash, I hate blokes who love the Clash. Is that ideological enough for you? I hope it's cantankerous and contrarian. What they came to represent — which was just this sort of right-on politics that I really took exception to.

TL: But they did have an ideological take. They were probably some of the best-*read* punks. Is that one of the things that pissed you off? Did you think it should be a much more instinctive form, and that the bloating there is that it's overthought?

BH: I just hated their little cut-off shirts and arm bands.

JI: But this is the thing though, you talk about best-dressed punks —

TL: I said best-read.

JI: — being in the States and looking at English rock and roll, American rock and roll, once we got past Elvis and Buddy Holly and all those 50s guys with those amazing clothes, by the 70s it was all denim and beards and very kind of, I don't want to say proletarian, but it was very *dull*. Rock and roll had always been about style and flash. Pete Townshend in a suit of lights, the Jimi Hendrix Experience, the way they're all dressed in Granny Takes A Trip and all that — this was an essential part of what made rock so essential. So then in punk, the managers behind them, McLaren and Bernie Rhodes and those guys, they instinctively understood you've got to have the clothes to go with the sound and the whole package. So it's funny that you say you don't like the way they look — but the fact that they had a very distinct style and look is half of what makes it so exciting.

PM: The other thing is because of the nature of the managers and because of the nature of what was happening, the Clash were what we would now consider to be a boy band. There was a boy band element to them. What was interesting is that at the time, in the late 70s and the early 80s, there were lots of groups representing things then happening in Britain — as much as they were about their music, they were also a kind of documentary about what was going on, through what they looked like, how they spoke, how they conducted themselves, what they were doing, the noise they may or may not have made — the different forms of a documentary. In the Clash's case this was a sort of tidied version, more middle-of-the-road, but necessary. It was BBC One, oddly enough. And you had to go further out — to Spike or to Living TV — to get the Josef Ks and the others.

But if you saw the Clash in America it was different from seeing the Clash here. I spent a couple of weeks with the Clash in America and it was very different — because the slightly showbiz politics that they enacted made sense over in America, and started to dent things a little bit. Whereas in Britain I remember there was a kind of annoyance. And because it was a matter of life and death, and because you took precedent seriously, you just remembered that Joe Strummer had been a pub rocker. Which might mean nothing to people now, but at the time it was horrendous. It was like saying he'd once played with Cliff Richard. There was a kind of weird code: Joe Strummer was a pub rocker therefore he doesn't quite mean it. You needed to almost burst out of nowhere and have no background — even though some of them *did* have a background. But the beauty of what you really were looking for is people that seemed to have gone *Voom*, perfectly, out of nowhere. Obviously they had influences, but their influences were so uncanny and idiosyncratic that they seemed completely fresh. It was too obvious with the Clash where they'd come from.

TL: But the clothes of spangly stars like Todd Rundgren, or whoever, someone distant, and punk clothes, which are accessible, isn't there a split here? If you're wanting change and saying that punk was a better truth because it was a more street truth, why don't we have someone like Little Richard, someone that extreme, as if they're from another planet?

JI: There's only one Little Richard.

TL: But there's a whole history of Sun Ra, Funkadelic, that idea of *I'm completely alien to you, I'm coming in from another place...*

PM: Dave Vanian of the Damned was otherworldly immediately. John Lydon when he went into Public Image, they were otherworldly — and it was still show business. It was still about the extraordinary nature of seeing someone so different, and representing it through performance. I never thought of it as unglamorous. I never thought of it as being particularly street. That wasn't what I was interested in. I was interested in it being brilliant, original, provocative ideas turned into performance — and at that time the best way of finding that happened to be in this area. Mark Stewart, quite a few of them, I found them incredibly powerful, and in that tradition oddly enough. Whereas the other groups that we've been talking about, the bloated ones, I didn't find show business really coming from them — for all their silver capes! They might have had the silver cape of Little Richard but they didn't have the ideas of Little Richard.

To turn an idea into the guitar sound of the Gang of Four, *that* was glamorous. And that was coming from Little Richard in a sort of zigzag way, but it was still in the tradition of what you're talking about. You just had to reapply how you thought about it and realise you weren't necessarily going to get it in that way. And why should you? It was 15, 20 years on — and back then there really were 15 and 20 years. Not like now. There was 20, 30, 40 changes going on. So for me it *was* in the tradition. I was seeing and hearing Little Richard in those little skronky guitar sounds of those early bands. To me it was incredibly glam. Mark E. Smith was incredibly glamorous. To me he was as glamorous as any of them. But basically this is glamorous because also it's the unexpected and the surprising, and that is inherently glamorous.

TL: Jonh, did you feel you were at the centre of things in America in 1968? Did you feel this thing of having missed it, that it's never going to get better than this?

JI: I didn't think in those terms. In 1968 I was living midway between San Francisco and LA, and the epicentre was San Francisco. So I was aware of all the bands in San Francisco by the end of 1966. I remember to this day a guy walking into the room I was in carrying the first Jefferson Airplane album. He was the school folky, and he's going, "You've got to hear this, this is amazing." And the first Mothers of Invention album about three weeks after. Why did he buy it? Because it had two records. "It's a double record man, look at this thing, this is incredible." So in that sense, yeah, I felt like I knew everything was going on that was like the cutting edge of then. Going to see the Grateful Dead and, I don't know, 100 people there. All of whom hated them. This is the irony — the Grateful Dead have become the representative band of the Summer of Love and hippies, and nobody liked them at all at the time because they were so far out, so experimental. It was almost like a jazz band, because there were some serious musicians in there and they would just do weird things all night.

Then I guess LA took over as a centre from, say, 1969 — and you saw everybody because all the British managers realised they could make their bands there. It was such a huge country, all their bands could tour three times a year. The number of times I saw Jethro Tull support somebody else, oh my god! I went from quite liking them to really hating them. So yeah, in that sense you felt you were in the epicentre of everything. And people like Dr John doing the Night Tripper, and he was second on the bill. Nobody knew who this guy was. And the headliner was Alice Cooper, who nobody knew either. The only reason I knew is because now I was a rock critic and I got into all that stuff free. Alice hadn't had a hit. All that stuff, cutting-edge, absolutely.

Did I think it was never going to get better? No. Of course it's going to get better. Every week there's a new band coming out with something strange to say. As Paul is saying, you're seeing somebody new with different ideas, it's all over the shop in the late 60s and the early 70s in that respect. And if you look through any of *MM* or *NME* or *Sounds* through that period, you'll see 15 reviews of 15 completely different styles of people, and that's the currency everybody's listening to, by and large. You didn't think in the way we do now, where it's very commodified into genres. From Van Morrison to Neil Young to Captain Beefheart to Fleetwood Mac in their blues period to, I don't know, just on and on and on. And that was just, "Yeah, I like them, I don't like them," that was it.

BH: I think I did feel slightly that I had missed a boat. I remember it was a real *event* when Paul did the singles column at *NME*, for example. These little things in their little homemade sleeves were real events, and I really understand what he's talking about, the glamour. He made them really important, and they were really important at that time — and I mustn't forget that, and I don't really forget that. But the boat for me was probably the 70s. That was my decade. It began with me hearing 'Hot Love' on the transistor radio, and it kind of ended with, I don't know, *Fear of Music*. The 70s is the decade that I go back to, from some kinds of bloated prog rock that I like to Talking Heads, via The Raspberries and Donny Hathaway. I mean, that's where I go back to. That's where I want to live in terms of my own pop culture.

TL: Do you think it was a better time and the ideals were better?

BH: No, not the ideals. I think it's as unfashionable as loon pants in a way, but I like it because it's the 60s utopian dream going a bit sour and a bit overripe — but it's also young men and women growing up a little bit and suffering a bit, and that's what I like. I can't get with the whole 60s, "We're young and groovy and we haven't really had any feelings yet." By 1971-72, these are people who've been bruised a bit. I'm more interested in that. I'm interested in pain. Always loved pain. There isn't enough pain in the 60s for me. There's pain and decadence and some degeneration [in the 70s] before the purging, and I'm interested in that.

I'm aware of our theme, *rhetorics of outsider style*, and actually what I'd like to talk about and hear about from everybody is that there was this tipping point where up until a certain point, on the *NME* anyway, you could get away with murder. By which I mean you could drop Roland Barthes and Derrida into the text, all the stuff it's become infamous for: Morley and Ian Penman. There's a certain notoriety to it. The fact of the matter is that we had a lot of power. You could write stuff. I was always amazed that my stuff just didn't get more edited. I'm looking at Tony Stewart here! I felt, "God, how did I actually get into print?" And it turns out all the readers were thinking that as well.

But I suppose what I'm interested in is at that point the writer was important, or thought he or she was important enough to be self-indulgent — and it all changed quite quickly in the 80s. By the end of the 80s it had utterly changed, and writers had been put back in their place, and we were all now expected to serve the music-industry machine. You just write your fucking 300-word review, tell the reader what the record is about and what it sounds like, and we don't want to hear the word "I" in it. I've got all the time in the world for Mark Ellen and Dave Hepworth, but there's a quote in Paul Gorman's book, *In Their Own Write: Adventures in the Music Press*, where apparently the first thing Ellen said to his newly assembled staff was that the perpendicular pronoun has no place in this magazine. So "I" was out. *Q* was the absolute reaction against that *NME* house style. That whole idea of Lester Bangs or Paul writing 3,000 or 4,000 words — in I think a really fascinating and original way — that was eroded quite quickly. I'm not saying that Paul was never allowed to write like that again because of course he was, but not in certain magazines, shall we say. Do you want to run with that ball for a second?

PM: Well, a lot of things occur to me — not least that for a while I did go out of my way to begin every piece I wrote with "I" and end it with "me". Not least because I could see this was winding up people like Mark Ellen tremendously. And what was interesting is I could never quite understand how just because they didn't say "I" or "me" that what they wrote wasn't actually still about them and their feelings. I could never get this, so I really ran with that one.

But it's funny, because of your enterprise, *Rock's Backpages*, where you do wordcounts, I was looking at some pieces I'd written — on A Certain Ratio and Cabaret Voltaire — and at the time I wrote them I thought they were what my features editor Tony Stewart had asked for, I thought they were 1,500 words long. And I'm always surprised to see that they were 5,000 words long. About A Certain bloody Ratio, who only nine people had heard at the time. But, you know, that freedom was important. It was the freedom to experiment, to try things out. Which sometimes went horribly wrong and other times went fantastically well — and you got some extraordinary pieces of writing coming out of the *NME* specifically. And photography as well, which was as important. In the wider sense, it was journalism at its finest.

But to this day I cannot understand how some of those issues ever came out. Running to the station with bits of copy as the train left, and they still hadn't got their cover feature, and I was chucking type written pages through the window. Two days later it'd become this immaculately laid out beautiful feature with great photography by Anton Corbijn. So it was a freedom to be creative that suited the times, I think. This is still me letting power go to my head, but I consider that the whole *Q-Mojo*-Mark Ellen thing came about because of who Tony Stewart had commissioned to write about Sting in India. Now, Mark Ellen, being of that ilk, was down to do the next Sting feature, and these kind of things mattered at the time. And I remember on the stairway when I told him it was me. But I like to think in his infinite wisdom, because it was India, Tony Stewart thought he'd send the writer to India to get the Indian thing going. So Mark Ellen hadn't got the Sting piece and his resentment was so huge, humungous, that he created and edited things like *Smash Hits* and *Q* as a sort of backlash to this outrage!

And what was funny as well at the time at the *NME*, *Smash Hits* used to be over the road. You could see into the window what *Smash Hits* was doing as we were smashing things, typewriters were coming out the window, and they were looking at us, and it did become an ideological battle. It was like two ships sailing; there's *Smash Hits* and there's the *NME*, and we're putting A Certain Ratio on the cover and they're starting to put this awful sort of teeny-bop stuff on the cover, trying to realign it and taking it away from the writer. They were going back to asking the musicians what their favourite colour was. And it was ideological. Mark Ellen was an intelligent bloke, an Oxbridge bloke, he knew what he was doing. He didn't want the kind of thing that had stopped him being able to interview Sting. He wanted to interview Sting.

So that ideological battle was taken, again, like I was saying, as seriously as life or death. And that freedom to experiment with your writing — which I think did represent some of the experimentation that was going on in music — was a really important element in terms of giving some of that music its context, and once it went the other way and it started to get what's your favourite colour again, it did lose a large amount of the necessary amplification for some of this music. Which obviously as a critic I would say is important.

JI: To what extent were you building on what Charlie Murray and Nick Kent and those guys had been doing stylistically?

PM: You'd never admit it at the time, because that was part of the battle and part of the those editorial meetings. I remember one near-fistfight about whether Joe Jackson or Joy Division should go on the cover. Joe Jackson won, which caused enormous sulking on my part for quite a few weeks. I sulked something terrible. An eight-week sulk. How could you do this? Because it seemed so important, and I still believe it was important at the time. Because, as you say, suddenly there was a lot of power. And although I didn't really understand it at the time — to some extent I didn't even think anybody was actually reading it, believe it or not, because you were just doing it in the moment — I realise in hindsight that it was an extraordinary amount of power. For a while a piece in the *NME* could actually get a record in the charts. Lower reaches. Maybe 98. But that wasn't bad at the time. Because obviously one of the big power struggles was against the establishment as represented by the BBC and Radio 1 as well. That was another political battle: you were opposing playlists, and a certain strange choice of music by mysterious figures in the middle distance, that you thought had no right to be choosing what people listen to. Sounds crazy. Now you can listen to everything whenever you want. But back then again there were these fights. You didn't want a certain sort of people to be choosing the music that people listened to.

TL: But isn't there a point where you made a conscious decision to *do* pop? To take gloss, to take presentation on and do something with it? With ZTT, and Frankie Goes to Hollywood. And didn't that legitimate it? Isn't there a turn towards "OK, I'm going to help produce the number one now, I'll be involved with that, I'll make it more intelligent or whatever"—

but in a way it swept onwards from that to Lady Gaga or someone, thinks she's saying something interesting but isn't?

PM: Well, part of everything going to my head is that I believed I was all powerful, and instead of writing about music I could suddenly write something in my bedroom that would become real — and unfortunately, in some senses, what I was writing in my little notebook, "I will now do this, I will now do that," *did* become real. So it really went to my head. Because I'd theorised in a way that I would about, say, A Certain Ratio or Cabaret Voltaire, now I theorised about an imaginary group in an imaginary situation, and "We will make this record," and it kind of came true. So at the time I felt that that power we'd got because we were working for the *NME* was real. It never occurred to me that it was just a complete series of flukes and accidents — and probably a few backhanders round the back door to Mike Reid, who banned the record we'd done. So I didn't realise there were other more adult things going on. I thought it was all down to the power of my extraordinary pen, as pretentious as it might have been.

But within that there was a feeling for a lot of people coming out of the late 70s, that instead of only reaching 100 people, as a lot of these great records were — fantastic pop records being made by groups that weren't hitting the charts— why don't we try and *make* it hit the charts. So there was a lot of disguising going on by writers and musicians and groups to suddenly have this music — which had previously been quite marginalised and avant-garde and in the middle distance — actually get onto *Top of the Pops*. This great moment when New Order or Siouxsie or Depeche Mode — or even Simple Minds at that point — were on *Top of the Pops*. It seemed like an act of invasion into a cosy world. Billy Mackenzie and the Associates seemed to be some sort of triumph, which confirmed how we'd been writing and what we'd been writing about. There *was* change, even though it was obviously establishment change, but it seemed like change. It seemed better and different.

TL: Doesn't that give up the outsiderness? Doesn't that mean that two weeks later the Associates will be on the cover of *Smash Hits* saying yellow is their favourite colour?

PM: It was all moving so quickly and you were making decisions so quickly that it didn't seem that way. I mean, even with Frankie my adverts were basically attacking Wham! and Duran Duran. So I was still making that ideological protrusion. And in a way it became too dominant. The manifesto situation dominated, and I look at it now with some embarrassment. But that was the willing of something into being — and I had taken it seriously, and that was why I had wanted to be a writer. So for a couple of weeks I *did* will it into being — and then George Michael was number one again and we had to start all over again.

TL: Jonh, there came a point at which you disengaged from the writing and moved on to other things. Was it the music or the political disengagement?

JI: I burnt out on the writing. At the end of the day there's kind of two stories if you're doing features: either you're on the road with a band or you're in the room with a band, and those two stories can get very old after you've written hundreds of them. Before Grundy nobody expected what did happen to happen — which was like the whole place knew about it in just one day, and suddenly every 15-year-old in the country had something to get excited about, for better or worse. The assumption had been that it would just kind of roll through 1977, and by about 78 or 79 would become really popular in a traditional sort of way. When it all blew up like that I thought, "This looks interesting, what can I do?" So there was a degree of that.

The photographers and designers who were caught up in it in the latter part of 1976 — like Linder in Manchester with record sleeves — decided to get into that kind of world and take the philosophies and the ideas in the air and apply them to how they looked at the world. In my case I decided that I'd get into management. First of all I wanted to start a record company because that looked like a cool idea, but a lawyer told me you've got a conflict of interests if you are a record company and manage a band. So we thought, "OK, let's manage a band," and I ended up with Generation X, so that's what I did for the next three years, four years.

TL: So you're also crossing over from writing to world-building. You're trying to make the band.

JI: Oh yeah, world domination in all things.

BH: They're all power-crazed. Get them out from behind the typewriter.

JI: Seriously though, you kind of get it from what Paul's talking about. Why do you want to get involved in doing these kind of things if you don't want to get the maximum amount of success from it you can? Because you've got to believe that you're working with the best people that are making the music, and that therefore they should be as successful in the biggest possible sense.

TL: But Barney, what you're specifically interested in, isn't it what success does? Isn't that darkening of the 60s into the 70s what the operation of success does to these musicians?

BH: To a large extent I think yes. I seem to return like a moth to a flame to that narrative. I don't know why. There's some sort of morbid fascination with it, I suppose. But to return to what Paul was saying earlier. You were talking about ideological battles with *Smash Hits* across the way. I remember there was a guy called Steve Taylor who had a late night pop chatshow called *Loose Talk* — and he wrote a piece [*we think for the Virgin Rock Yearbook — ed.*] rather grandly called 'The Death of the Swiftian Function', which basically said the *NME* was dead, the idea of the personality journalist was over, Nick Kent was over. We're in the 80s now: greed is good, the consumer rules, it's about expensive flashy stuff and having fun and going on holiday with George Michael or whatever. Just nutty stuff really. So even though the 80s produced some extraordinary characters — like Morrissey, Nick Cave, the late lamented Billy MacKenzie, these were extraordinary, eccentric characters in the middle of the sort of nightmare of Nick Heywood and Spandau Ballet. With all due respect.

TL: The long dark chunky cardigan of the soul.

BH: Yeah, it was. But in the end I actually felt myself surrendering to the inevitable. And there was a political component to that. Thatcher, Reagan, etc. Capitalist consumerism had won and there really wasn't any room or space anymore for a maverick voice in print. And everything became commodified and splintered into genres, and I felt myself retreating back into the things that I had loved when I was still innocent. So yes, I did go back to the 70s — I realise now that I thought, "Well, I want to write kind of books like Peter Guralnick. That's what I'm going to do. I'm not going to be Lester Bangs and stop taking drugs, I'm going to be Peter Guralnick, and I want to write about music that really moves me." Which was perhaps the beginning of what Simon Reynolds called Retromania. I think it started at some point in the 80s as a reaction to the awful synthetic, dead sound. To me the 80s were very synthetic, and by the end of the 80s I hated the sound of every record. I even hate the sound of Smiths records.

Apart from people like Tom Waits, who made interesting sounding records in the 80s, everything just sounded horrible and dead and flat and synthetic. So I went back to these little soul singles, to Macon, Georgia, and Muscle Shoals. And it might seem an obvious kind of nostalgia. So that was my stall that I set out, and in a sense that's what I've done since. The music that's excited me the most has not been all the Americana bands — for the most part they bore me senseless. So there is that interesting paradox. I think Burial is the most interesting artist this country's produced in about ten years, and I can't stand all those guys who want to be Neil Young.

TL: So *Rock's Backpages* is something that you've created. Are you saying, "OK, we're going to kind of time-capsule this because it's dead," or is it implicitly a challenge to someone to come along and do something now. To say, "OK, this is this period and now you have to do something else"? Or are you saying this is the best it's ever going to be, and we can now study it as a closed thing?

BH: Well, I don't think that music is dead.

TL: Not the music, the writing.

BH: Yeah. I mean, it's not about locking anything up. I think the commercial opportunity is that people are studying this stuff, so there's a sort of inevitability to that. But there was an evangelical aspect to it — which is this. At the end of the 90s, I got tired of hearing the same tropes and platitudes getting recycled in terms of the consensus around the evolution of musical history. Wouldn't it be good if you could actually just make this stuff digitally available? People can go back and see what Gram Parsons actually *said* in 1971, or Bobby Womack said in 1976. Let's make this stuff available. When I listen to a record by Bobby Womack from the 70s it's as alive for me today as it ever was. It's not a museum piece. I have an emotional relationship with it which is absolutely in the now. I really do believe that.

TL: *Paul and Jonh, how do you feel if you see your stuff on Rock's Backpages?*

JI: I think I'm still pushing forward because you've got to think that way. When I read a lot of the stuff back what surprises me is that it's actually way better than I think it was at the time. At the time I thought it was great, and then I'd look at it maybe ten years later and just think, "Oh my god" — and now some of it actually does hold up really well. What's interesting is that we're talking about the early 70s — and at least in my case, I don't think we had a blind thought about what was going to happen then beyond maybe next month. We loved getting high, and we were most of the time. You were in the thrill of it. There was a lot of competition.

But coming back to writing style: on the one hand, everybody was directly trying to better each other, but you were also looking at how people wrote. There was a lot of seriousness in what we were doing. You had those major stylists — Lester Bangs, R. Meltzer — and you would kind look at and see, "What can I steal from that?" Hunter S. Thompson was a huge icon for everybody, because it looked great. All he talked about was getting really seriously fucked up, and yet he'd write these amazing pieces, and you could never tell how much of it was true or not. So people would try that one on. Tom Wolfe's *New Journalism* omnibus really nailed it down as to what this style was all about — it wasn't completely objective, that it wrote about things which traditional journalism would never touch. "I" came into it a lot! And this was book of just amazing examples of that whole style, so that you could really pick and choose and figure out who you were in all of this. In that sense I think we all were very serious about what we were doing, even if on the surface it looked anything but. Plus you were writing tons of stuff every week.

PM: Every week. And you were serious about writing and structure and what it was you were saying and how you were saying it. And thinking about it, it is interesting that the momentum that was set up back in the 60s, with what Jonh's talking about — both the New Journalists and the new rock journalists — that momentum really swept us all through the 70s and 80s, all the way through to now really. You still feel that momentum. Except what's lacking is a sense of writing and the ideological life-or-death scenario — and I would obviously blame this going through the psyche of Mark Ellen, obviously. It's drained away a lot; it's become about rating and reviewing and favourite colour. Even the most interesting writing on the internet has lost some of the sense that it can be experimental, that it can be strange, that it can represent extraordinary times in a way that this writing did back then.

I mean, I hate the idea of what often happens in scenarios like this is it sounds like we're saying, "Oh, it was so much better then!" And of course it wasn't, it was just very, very different — and often we're just trying to articulate how different it was. But one of the things I do miss, as we go through something, is [exploring] it in terms of its impact on our consciousness and our reality and our environment. Which is more extraordinary than the local effect of punk rock. This is about reality itself, and the future. There isn't the momentum now that was set up by these great writers, that hopefully we all tried to inherit and sort of distort and turn into something else. That seems to have gone. And just when we could *do* with some of that kind of commentary and that kind of observation and that kind of interpretation — that gives the shifting reality something solid that we can hold onto to understand what's going on — it's all gone missing.

So the momentum has led to millions of people who think they're talking in that voice about similar subjects — but with almost nothing of the same sort of whatever you want to call it, ego or me-ness or ideology or interest in something other than just saying, "I like this, I don't like that." And this might be just because I still believe in that narrative, and I'm old-fashioned in that sense, but to me that's one source of shame, that I wish the momentum had led to areas where... well, I'm old-fashioned, I still believe in that romantic view of things, that when something strange and wonderful and bizarre happens, we have a load of great people, photographers, designers, writers, poets, playwrights all responding to it!

Whereas in all sorts of areas we still seem to be using industrial-revolution age language almost, or 70s language — and just at this moment when I would love someone to come along and do a piece of writing, in the tradition of New Journalism or the great *NME* writers of the 70s, I can't find it. It may be out there! But the fact I can't find it is part of the problem as well. There was a great *specific* amplification of energy in the 60s and 70s, and now that has basically mutated into a kind of chaos — and I would love another Ken Tynan, another Joan Didion to be out there somewhere, rather than being kind of nostalgic without even knowing it, for something that has been and gone and is of no use now.

THE ENGINE ROOM

"I landed in the middle of an editorial office where people were literally throwing pieces of vinyl around the space" — *Beverley Glick*

"The Look is as Important as the Noise"

*Tony Stewart recalls his time as writer and deputy editor at NME (1971-85)
— the strengths and pleasures of teamwork and the vital role of the visual in
the energies of a rock paper*

The week that I had my first-ever byline piece printed in the British music
press — a review for the fledgling weekly *Sounds* of ELP at Birmingham
Town Hall, published on 31 October, 1970 — could only be described as
bizarre, even in the surreal world of print journalism. Because elsewhere
I was writing about the difficulties of opening a public sauna in Burton
Upon Trent, Staffordshire (because of "the shocking condition of the
building"), the monthly meetings of Stretton and Yoxall Parish Council,
market prices (not city but fruit and veg — pomegranates at 6d and a
Cos lettuce for 1s 4d etc), and the funeral of a prominent local business
and sportsman who'd croaked in hospital after that delicate and unspoken
"long illness".

Such was life for an indentured cub reporter on local evening paper the
Burton Daily Mail, albeit a reporter with ambitions to enter the glamorous
and giddy world of the rock press, a reporter who was determined to put
into practice the advice of his English teacher Eric Taylor. "Another outlet
for writing," Eric wrote to me on leaving school, "would be for you to
become a specialist in a particular field. You might for example choose Pop
as you already know something about it… Even the stars of the Pop world

need constant publicity to keep them in the public eye and they will rarely refuse a request for an interview made by a journalist."

Half a century later, those words may seem a little naïve, but they were well meaning. Secondary-school teacher Eric, a former professional footballer, had a lucrative sideline as a health and fitness writer, and he also knew I played drums in various rock bands. How was he to know that between the journalist and the stars was the often impregnable barrier of a publicity machine, ferociously controlling who could or couldn't talk to their charges? And this *Burton Daily Mail* reporter who moonlighted as a stringer writing gig reviews for a collection of music papers — "the lowliest foot soldier" — certainly had no idea of that, either.

So when then-assistant editor of *New Musical Express* John Wells rang me in 1971 and asked if I could get an interview with Steve Winwood of Traffic — who were playing at the Belfry, Sutton Coldfield, on their 'Welcome To The Canteen' tour — I didn't see a problem. I went straight to the artist, bagged what is commonly known as a "front-page scoop", and was consequently offered a staff job on *NME*. It really was that easy. I started in September that year, moving from Burton to London with my small collection of vinyl albums and few belongings. I slept in the back of my car, on people's sofas or in their spare rooms for a few weeks... And never looked back.

For the next 14 years I would be intimately involved in one of the most defining and turbulent periods of the British music press. For me they were golden years.

In the early 70s, a collection of mismatched writers from different backgrounds with a passion for music came together in a bustling office in London's Covent Garden, fusing into a formidable team under the banner *New Musical Express*. I was probably one of then-editor Andy Gray's last recruits, joining an editorial team which included Nick Logan, Roy Carr, Derek Johnson, Julie Webb, Richard Green, James Johnson and staff photographer Robert Ellis.

Gray would soon be axed to make way for the brash, no-nonsense Alan Smith, who had only months... weeks... hours — depending on who you believe — to save an ailing *NME*. Once the definitive pop paper of the 1960s, enthusiastically covering every chart act from Cliff and Elvis to the Beatles and the Rolling Stones, by the turn of the 70s it had lost touch with a burgeoning, more serious music scene. Since 1967 there had been cataclysmic changes. In America, the Monterey International Pop Festival had featured the likes of Jefferson Airplane, Grateful Dead, Jimi Hendrix and Big Brother and the Holding Company (singer Janis Joplin). British music had seen the release of the Beatles' *Sgt Pepper's Lonely Hearts Club Band*, the Jimi Hendrix Experience's *Axis: Bold As Love*, Pink Floyd's *Piper At The Gates Of Dawn*, the Moody Blues' *Days Of Future Passed* and Traffic's *Mr Fantasy* — to name just five seminal albums. It was famously known as the psychedelic era — or sometimes 'progressive rock', at that time still an accolade.

1969 saw the Woodstock Festival. The following year in Britain there was the Bath Festival of Blues and Progressive Music in June, and the Isle Of Wight Festival in August. Together they presented a rollcall of influential acts, including the Doors, Leonard Cohen, Chicago, Miles Davis, Joan Baez, Ten Years After, ELP, Jethro Tull, Santana, Dr John, Frank Zappa, the Who and Pentangle.

Three-minute pop ditties, trilled by fragrant girls and clean-cut, well-groomed boys, slick as a lick of Brylcreem, seemed to have succumbed to the unkempt and great unwashed, swept in on long, intricate improvisational suites fuelled by hash and acid. But that blend of music and narcotics had largely failed to captivate *NME*, and in 1971 it was an embarrassing mishmash of musical genres, showbiz and pop pap alongside ineffectual flirtations with this more heady and serious music.

It was certainly no match for *Melody Maker*, which had willingly embraced these changes. The market-leader had authority as well as a team of eloquent and entertaining writers, particularly their lethal duo of Michael Watts and Roy Hollingworth, as well as the cheery and avuncular Chris Welch. They had a gift for writing about exactly the right acts. There was also *Sounds*. Launched in October 1970 by two former *Melody Maker* stalwarts — Jack Hutton and Peter Wilkinson — it was a young and refreshing voice, with an exuberant and talented team of writers, in what was becoming a vibrant and competitive weekly market.

But Smith was about to revive *NME*'s fortunes, along with his genius of an assistant editor Nick Logan. While Smith was an astute businessman who could deal with the commercial management of the paper and the vast profits it made for owners IPC, Logan was the creative eye, with a strong passion for words, photographs and layout. Succeeding Alan in 1973, he went on to become one of the paper's most successful editors, before leaving to conceive such seminal titles as *Smash Hits* (1978), *The Face* (1980) and *Arena* (1986).

In a matter of months, *NME* was a roaring success, recruiting from the underground press a Californian hippie called Danny Holloway, the infamous duo of Charles Shaar Murray and Nick Kent, and Mick Farren. With those writers came new photographers — most notably the reserved and thoughtful Pennie Smith and Joe 'Captain Snaps' Stevens, a garrulous American. Over the next few years, this motley crew were bonded by a team of creative, innovative, visionary, subversive and sometimes demented editors — including ex-military man and musician Tony Tyler and Cambridge drop-out and sometime songwriter Ian MacDonald.

Tony T and Ian Mac were both fiercely intelligent, with very wide cultural tastes and a wicked sense of humour and mischief. Formerly editor of *Beat Instrumental* and publicist for ELP, Tony had a sharp eye for talent both musical and journalistic. He was an early champion of Roxy Music and Dr Feelgood and played a significant part in hiring Nick Kent, Neil Spencer, Tony Parsons, Julie Burchill, Paul Morley, Vivien Goldman and Paul Du Noyer. He once had two radically different books in the *New York Times* best-seller lists at the same time, *The Beatles: An Illustrated Record* (1975) — a collaboration with *NME* colleague Roy Carr — and *The Tolkien Companion* (1976). He also wrote *I Hate Rock And Roll* (1984).

Ian, who I worked more closely with, was probably the more academic. He briefly went to Cambridge but dropped out after a year. He too would later write two strikingly different books — one a controversial study of the classical Russian composer, *The New Shostakovich* (1990), the other the highly-regarded *Revolution In The Head: The Beatles' Records and The Sixties* (1994). Sadly both had untimely deaths. Ian took his own life in August 2003, aged 54. Tony died of cancer on 28 October 2006, aged 62.

Like Smith and Logan and others, I had a background in local journalism. CSM and Kent by contrast arrived with an electrifying writing style inspired by the New Journalism of Tom Wolfe and Norman Mailer, as well as publications like *Rolling Stone, Cream, Oz, Friends* aka *Frendz*, US comics, hardboiled crime fiction and the unconventional generally, a terrain people called the 'counterculture'. They were aficionados of the cool and cutting-edge in music – Bowie, Bolan, Elton John, the Rolling Stones, Roxy Music, Iggy, Lou Reed, the Velvets, Captain Beefheart, the New York Dolls... They quickly became the star writers and the personality of the paper, barrelled along by the madcap irreverence and humour of Tyler and MacDonald.

Who knows how such a mix of personalities worked and flourished, but it did. All the same, given my own unglamorous beginnings, for at least four years I felt I was struggling to survive alongside them. (When Parsons and Burchill showed up in the summer of 1976, in response to the legendary "hip young gunslingers" ad for new writing talent, I would feel this even more. Suddenly I was made to feel old and out of touch. At 26, FFS!)

There was some praise, though. In July 1972 I wrote the first of a two-part story on Roy Wood leaving ELO to form Wizzard under the headline, 'Did He Fall Or Was He Pushed?', which Alan Smith told me was "as good as anything that appeared in *Rolling Stone*" — serious praise indeed. Wood's manager, the notoriously aggressive Don Arden (and father of Sharon Osbourne), took exception to the piece and turned up at the *NME* offices, berating me as a pox-addled, alcoholic junkie, and threatening me with serious physical harm. He also banned *NME* from ever mentioning his artistes again. Printed in the following issue, the second part of the feature was less, ahem, *controversial* — as Alan had asked me to be a little more diplomatic.

But it was only years later that I read the following observation from Tony Tyler, in Paul Gorman's excellent *In Their Own Write: Adventures In The Music Press* (2001), and realised that my approach wasn't as unappreciated as I'd imagined: "Perhaps the hardest job in rock writing is the interview," Tony T said, "and the best interviewer on the *NME* in my day was Tony Stewart, later editor of *Sounds*. He was so quiet and unforthcoming in interviews that his subjects would babble their heads off out of sheer nervousness, giving him great material to work on."

Probably my most notorious interview was with Queen's Freddie Mercury, in the edition of 18 June 1977 — as much for the headline and pull-out quotes Ian Mac put on it. 'Is this Man a Prat?' is one of those legendary headlines that is more famous than the article (as is Tony T's, alongside a picture of Bryan Ferry wearing South American dress in 1974: 'How Gauche can a Gaucho get?'). But as punk's musical anarchy was sweeping the UK, 'babbling' Freddie wanted "to take ballet to the masses".

Still, being "quiet and unforthcoming" didn't always work for me, as I discovered when I joined a taciturn, even grumpy Van Morrison on his homecoming to Ireland in 1979. We travelled together in a car from Belfast to Dublin, barely speaking during the three-hour journey. When I did eventually talk to him it was in front of a film crew, his platform to rip into me in probably one of my most uncomfortable and humiliating interview encounters. Payback was two-fold — first I refused to sign the release for the filmed interview to be included in a documentary that was being made (and it wasn't), and then I wrote a cover story for *NME* on 10 March, 1979, with the headline 'When Irish Eyes Are Scowling'. Feck you, Van...

With me on that assignment was Pennie Smith, who had an easy-going manner and could be completely unobtrusive as she snapped away, capturing crucial, unguarded moments. Not particularly technical, Pennie had a raw, artistic, bleached black-and-white reportage style that reprinted brilliantly on the shoddy newsprint of *NME*. Her picture of Paul Simonon of the Clash smashing up his bass on stage in 1979 would grace the cover of their *London Calling* album — and, in 2010, a Royal Mail First Class postage stamp. But there are many others — from Led Zeppelin to the Stone Roses.

The photographers at *NME* should never be under-estimated. If the writers signposted the way to the soundtrack of a generation, the photographers provided the showreel. Pennie and Joe Stevens — and later

Chalkie Davies — were visual pioneers who'd go on to form legendary teams, the former with Nick Kent, the latter with Charles Shaar Murray. In contrast to Pennie, Joe was an ebullient New Yorker who talked his subjects into his lens. He was an untutored, natural force of nature.

Together they brought the paper a style and unique look, which combined with inventive layouts had tremendous visual impact. Logan was a superb magazine designer, with a gift for headline-writing that drew readers in. But what I learned from Ian Mac in particular was the idea of a writer and photographer working as a team with a commissioning editor, a kind of triumvirate. He was my editor and we did some bizarre features including Lulu and Dorothy Squires. His excitement and enthusiasm were inspiring and contagious.

Probably the most memorable was the 'Schoolkids Tommy' cover story of 20 July 1974, with photographer Ian Dickson, which featured the youngsters of the Ryhope School, Sunderland. Ian and I spent two days there as six months of rehearsals came to a head, for their staging, over four nights, of Pete Townshend's rock opera *Tommy*. This was a unique piece: not simply an observational, fly-on-the-wall docu-feature, but an exploration of the British educational system and the conflict within the school. Ian Mac read as the pages came off my typewriter and became more and more animated, clearing space in the paper to run it at length. More than 6,600 words! We worked late into the night before press day at his London flat (which had a massive Scalextric in the middle of his living room floor). Again, his design, headline and pull-out quotes were key to its impact, including five pictures down the side of the centre-page spread, with caption bullets under each: 'The Director', 'The Music Master', 'The Head Of Art', The Headmaster', 'The Acid Queen'. (The 'director' being Malcolm Gerrie, an English teacher who later went into television, creating *The Tube* for Channel 4 in 1982 and televising *The Brit Awards* among other music programmes.)

I owe Logan, Ian Mac and Tony T an enormous debt for their inspiration and whatever success I enjoyed in the music press. In the late 70s, encouraged by deputy editor Phil McNeill and Logan's successor as editor Neil Spencer, I moved over to the commissioning and production side, when it was discovered I had an eye for design. I ended up working on countless covers and major features. But with such talented photographers as Anton Corbijn, Kevin Cummins and Peter Anderson — to name just three — the task was a delight. They would continue the tradition established particularly by Pennie Smith, with their images defining the look of *NME* into the 1980s.

Anton is probably the most celebrated, not least for his work with U2. He was the master of the black-and-white photograph, which was heavily stylised and theatrical. He once told me that he created the photograph's atmosphere in the dark room, working on the light and shade as he developed the image. Many are striking works of art. One of his most famous is Captain Beefheart shot in the Mojave Desert in 1980, holding his hat in his hand as he peers into the lens. Pennie Smith thought it very similar to her classic shot of Mick Jones used on the cover of her 1980 book, *The Clash: Before And After*. It is.

But then Anton probably felt Kevin Cummins' style could have been inspired by his own. Maybe it was.

"The fact that I was there for many defining rock'n'roll moments is a great testimony to the power back then of the *NME*," Kevin wrote in the introduction of his excellent *Manchester: Looking For The Light Through The Pouring Rain*, a revelatory 2009 compendium of his work, featuring Joy Division, New Order, The Smiths and Stone Roses: "Rock'n roll photography has been unfairly denigrated over the past few years. Many art critics dismiss it as juvenilia. However in my opinion the way we perceive our bands is often formed by the images we remember of them."

In contrast to Anton and Kevin, Peter Anderson was a raw and spontaneous photographer, with a powerful energy dominating his work. Like Joe Stevens, Peter was the captain of the snap, rattling off frame after frame, and capturing the moment. Even so, he also delivered beautifully composed cover shots time after time — and it was this versatility which made me invite him to come to *Sounds* with me.

Rock photographers — Anton and Peter in particular — were the inspiration for my book in 1981, *Cool Cats: 25 Years Of Rock 'N' Roll Style*, a collection of images and essays. As I wrote in the introduction, 'Putting On The Style': "Rock 'n' roll is a visual culture. The look is just as important as the noise."

Appropriately enough, the 60s chapter, 'The Total Look', was written by Paul Weller, an artist well aware of image and the power of photography. One of my most memorable experiences at *NME* was designing the cover for the 1982 Christmas double issue, with an exclusive Weller interview to mark the end of the Jam (my last major feature for *NME*). He decided he wanted to dress as John Steed from the TV show *The Avengers*, with a bowler hat, brolly and city slicker suit, and the session was artistically shot by Peter Anderson in colour. With the coverline 'The Gentleman Mod Comes Clean', it worked well.

Perhaps less illustrious with hindsight, one of my final *NME* covers and concepts, from May 1985, had the headline 'Watching The Detectives'. Heavily disguised, I modelled as a private investigator watching his victims, shot at night by Peter again. It was a moody, atmospheric and smoky image that tied together two major features – Gavin Martin's 'The Secret Life Of A Private Eye' and CSM's 'The Prime Crime Fiction Of Elmore Leonard'. Aside from a title that adopted the name of a famous Elvis Costello song, this hadn't much to do with a music mag, as I now see — but everything to do with a youth culture paper.

A couple of months later, Neil Spencer left and I applied to be his successor, as the next editor of *NME*. I resigned when I was turned down. For me, the golden years were probably over. Well, until the new challenge at *Sounds* began…

Tony Stewart was a writer with and later the deputy editor of NME in the 70s and 80s, then editor of Sounds from July 1985. He was creator and launch editor of Select (1990), managing editor of Rage (1991), and assistant editor and columnist at the Daily Mirror (1992-2014).

So Obvious it is Rarely Spelt Out

Simon Frith excavates the hidden "we" of strong writing

Rock critics, like rock musicians, are prone to cast themselves, in romantic terms, as cussed individuals. But, like music making, music writing is essentially a collaborative activity. It is possible in the digital age, I guess, for the words of bloggers to pass straight from writer to reader without anyone else intervening. But in the age of print this certainly wasn't the case. No writer reached a reader without working with one or more editors, subeditors, copy editors, copy takers, etc. etc. And writing almost always involved a fairly crude commercial transaction, a negotiation about how much one would be paid for what number of words. Even the most single-minded (or single-handed) fanzine publisher had to worry about printing, marketing and distribution costs. In the days before the internet (or the fax) 'writing' involved the telephone as much as the keyboard; a final draft was initially shaped in conversation. I stopped writing for the *Sunday Times* in 1987 when the Murdoch titles moved to Wapping not because of abstract principle but because my copy taker, whom I'd got to know well without ever meeting, was being made redundant.

That music writing is a form of teamwork is so obvious to writers themselves that it is rarely spelt out. It should be. All those interviews, reviews and features so lovingly archived by *Rock's Backpages*, for example, went through editorial processes. They were commissioned, cut and amended. They were made to fit — a space on a page, a house style, a collective ethos. When I now read my pieces in *RBP* I remember how they were shaped by other people much more clearly than I remember my own thinking processes.

Where do ideas come from? Not from nowhere, that's for sure. As a freelance writer I rarely had an idea for a story that I then 'pitched' to an editor in the way now taught in journalism courses. Rather, ideas would emerge from discussion or I'd get a call: "could you write something about X?" The best discussions happened at *Let It Rock* (1972-75). They resulted, among other things, in my interviewing people in whom I'd had little interest (Wishbone Ash, for example) or writing instathink pieces to fill up space. At *LIR* I became reviews editor and learned to edit other people at the same time as I was learning to be edited. Once I realised how much thought it took to match reviewer to record, to decide who could have what number of words, I became less fretful about accepting apparently arbitrary juxtapositions (*Raw Power* and *Tubular Bells*!) and value judgments. I began to understand that the constraints laid down by editors were the necessary conditions for good journalism.

The editors from those days I remember with most gratitude are Charlie Gillett and Dave Laing. Both knew a lot more about music than I did; both were enthusiastic for new and unexpected ideas; both were blunt in their dismissal of emotional posturing. Usefully for me, their guidance complemented my academic research training. They were more interested in evidence than rhetorical flourish; they were as interested in musical institutions as in musicians. The ideas that I had for my earliest articles and interviews were almost always a response to their suggestions.

Good commissioning editors were people I didn't really know but who could call up and ask for a piece on something that immediately interested me. The most challenging was Richard Williams, as editor of first *Time Out* and then *Melody Maker* in the late 70s. He exemplified the editorial skill of knowing what kind of piece a magazine needed and who could best write it. He could then somehow ensure that the chosen writer delivered exactly what he'd envisaged. Why else would I have written my

'Thesis on Disco' for *Time Out* (in 1978) in homage to Karl Marx's *Theses on Feuerbach*?

Editors of underground and left-wing magazines lacked Richard's subtlety. They tended to follow trends in which they lacked personal interest or else just wanted space filled cheaply; for everyone it seemed, from *Oz* to the *New Statesman*, coverage of rock music was necessary for attracting advertisements. There were exceptions. Tony Gould, at *New Society*, didn't have his own ideas for music features but was a wonderful person with whom to discuss mine. He had a much broader sense of British cultural history and argument than anyone else I then worked with. And some commissioning editors had a different sort of skill: they could persuade writers to contribute to their magazines for little or no pay. Martin Jacques, editor of the monthly *Marxism Today*, was particularly persuasive. The obituary of John Lennon that I wrote for him in 1980, at great speed because the magazine was about to go to press, subsequently became the most anthologised of all my articles. It took him longer to persuade me to accept the commission than it took me to write it.

From the very beginning of my rock-writing career I wrote about music for publications on both sides of the Atlantic and became accustomed to the rather different editorial treatments of my copy. In Britain what I wrote was checked for mistakes and typos but rarely considered in terms of style. At the *Sunday Times* (as in newspapers generally) articles were always cut from the bottom (if additional space for a late arriving ad was needed, for example). I learnt to shape my arguments so that they could be cut this way, the last paragraph the most expendable and so on. Otherwise the only significant edits that I can remember emerged from the paper's final 'lawyering' process. I once had to rewrite a paragraph about Elton John, for example, because it hinted that he might be gay; at the time such a suggestion was considered potentially libellous. Otherwise my *Sunday Times* editors, John Whitley and, latterly, Nigella Lawson, were supportive but essentially uninterested in what I wrote.

American editorial teams, by contrast, were very interested indeed, beginning with that bane of every writer's life, the fact checker, someone I'd never come across in Britain. And US editors, unlike UK editors, worried as much about how a piece was written as about what it said. The best such editors I worked with were Robert Christgau and Doug Simmons at the *Village Voice* in the 1980s. Christgau has certainly had more influence than anyone else on how I think about writing. This was partly a technical matter, again related to the space constraints, but the *Voice* editing process was also stylistic, involved helping a writer make an argument more effective, more personal and more pleasing. The arguments here might have been about small details — the use of brackets, dashes and semi-colons, for example — but they always involved self-justification. I partly dreaded the monthly transatlantic phone calls in which my latest *Britbeat* column would be dissected and improved, line-by-line, and partly looked forward to Bob or Doug's insistent questions: What did you *mean* by this? Is this word/metaphor/image *really* the right one?

One of the norms of academic life is that everything written is assessed. Student work is marked, academic publications reviewed. This doesn't happen much in journalism. Such protocols don't fit the rhythm of newspaper or magazine publishing. By the time a column is out the next one is being prepared. The only magazine I wrote for which had a review process was *CREEM*. Each month the editors would collectively discuss the latest issue, article by article. Their comments were then typed up and circulated to all staff writers. I found these reports fascinating less for the comments on my work (which were usually neutral, neither enthusiastic nor unenthusiastic) than for their revelation of *CREEM*'s ethos and how that affected its writers' sense of themselves.

In a 2002 interview on the website *Rockcritics.com*, John Morthland remembers his brief stint as a *CREEM* editor in 1974-5:

CREEM wasn't a place you could be a boss: it would never have worked and it wasn't my inclination anyhow. So I worked mainly at... getting a real solid deadline and production schedule worked out and cleaning up typos and making it look better and read cleaner... It worked out fine. Contrary to *CREEM*'s image maybe, nobody there objected to that, they were all glad to have that. Lester [Bangs] included. Lester was real good at deadlines and took editing well, I don't think he'd ever really been edited before at *CREEM*. And I didn't edit him as heavily as I did most people, but he didn't need as much editing as most people. I edited him probably more than he had been edited by anyone except Greil [Marcus] up to that point. But he welcomed it. He wrote really, really long, and I didn't mind that but I was not adverse to cutting and when I did I'd explain to him why and we'd discuss it, sometimes we'd put it back in.

The most significant word here is the "we" in the last sentence, though the editor I remember best from *CREEM* in the 1970s (my "we", as it were) is Susan Whitall rather than Morthland or Bangs. Whitall became a well respected features and entertainment writer for *The Detroit News* but she is rarely mentioned in histories of rock writing. As an editor, she worked, of course, mostly backstage, but then without such backstage people there would be no history of rock writing at all.

Sociologist Simon Frith is Emeritus Professor of Music at University of Edinburgh. In the 70s, 80s and 90s he wrote for Let It Rock, CREEM, Melody Maker, the Sunday Times, and the Village Voice.

Professionalising the Playpen: What Were the Editorial Pressures?

Beverley Glick: *Sounds (as Betty Page), Noise!, Record Mirror*
Cynthia Rose: *Melody Maker, NME, The Wire, City Limits, MTV*
Tony Stewart: *NME, Sounds, Select, Rage!, Daily Mirror*
Panel chaired by **Tom Ewing:** *Freaky Trigger, I Love Music/I Love Everything*

TE: Hello. OK, we're starting the final panel of the day, and now we're moving into that deplorable era when people were doing things like taking notice of the audience and wondering about the market. I am delighted to welcome Cynthia, Tony and Beverley, all of whom have experience on multiple sides of those editorial offices, as writers and as assistant editors and editors. To open the conversation, I think it would be good to go back and talk about your first experience of a music paper's editorial office, when you first found yourself in the world of editorial pressure as a writer, as someone new to the music press. What did it feel like? What was it like?

BG: Well, my first experience of an editorial office was in 1977 when I joined *Sounds* as the secretary to the editor, Alan Lewis. My first job when I left school had been in the civil service, and I landed in the middle of an editorial office that was so diametrically opposed that I nearly walked out on my first day. It was incredibly chaotic. People were literally throwing pieces of vinyl around the space. And I didn't know whether I could ever fit into this.

But eventually I did, and I actually made the transition from secretary to writer within about 18 months. I benefited hugely from the punk ethos — which was that anyone can get up and do it. I wasn't a trained writer, I wasn't a trained journalist, obviously. The only thing I'd ever trained to do was type — which was extremely useful as a journalist.

And I think that I benefited hugely also from the support of Alan Lewis, an editor who was meritocratic and could see the potential in me to tap into the Zeitgeist. And I grew into that role from an absolutely standing start. I don't think that, that could happen these days. I mean, these days, you have to have a degree to do anything, it seems. But in those days, if you had talent and creativity, then you could easily start writing for a music paper. Which is where I started.

And my first day in the office at *Sounds*, they were playing 'Looking Through Gary Gilmore's Eyes', by the Adverts, one of the great punk records. And I'll never forget that, it has had a lasting impression on me, and I think it spoke volumes about the atmosphere at the time. But it was also very tribal, and it took me a while to find my tribe. It wasn't until the early 80s that I found my tribe. I was accredited with coming up with the term 'New Romantics', for my sins. I'm not sure that's absolutely true, but Gary Kemp of Spandau Ballet says it is. So I believe him.

TS: I'll start at the ending of my career on the music press, because it gives a certain continuity to the afternoon. I never knew till today that Mark Ellen held such a grudge about me giving Paul Morley the Sting piece in India! So when Spotlight Publications or whatever they were called, *Punch* and so on, sold *Select*, the magazine I'd created and edited, to EMAP Metro — while I was on holiday in Dublin, as it happened — they appointed a gentleman called Mark Ellen as the managing editor. And in my absence, I was sacked. So that was the end of my music magazine career. When was the Sting piece, the early 80s, something like that? Wow. He held a grudge for that long.

But I'm of the generation, as you can probably see just looking at me, that started on *NME* in 1971. And I was a journalist and I'd been working in the Midlands at the time for an evening newspaper. And I was passionate about music. And *Sounds* had just launched — I think in October 1970 — and they needed somebody in the Midlands to write copy for them on local gigs. And I started doing that. Major gigs, obviously, but held in Birmingham and Coventry and so on.

And then I got an exclusive. As I didn't like *NME* I wrote for it under the name of Tony McNally. It was a horrible showbiz mishmash paper then, which was sinking without trace. And *Sounds* at that time was a brilliant, new, refreshing weekly music magazine, with serious writing in it. So I used my real name there and a pseudonym in *NME*.

But *NME* asked me to get an interview with Steve Winwood, who was touring with Traffic in England. And I just walked backstage at the Belfry in Sutton Coldfield, walked up to Steve Winwood, didn't know about PRs or anything like that, said, would you mind giving me an interview. A gentleman interrupted and said, "Excuse me, Steve's just about to do a gig, come back afterwards and ask again." And I asked him who he was. And he said, "My name's Chris Blackwell, I own Island Records." So I said, "Oh, OK, I'll do that."

Anyway *NME* offered me a job on the strength of getting that interview. Because I didn't know protocol, I didn't go through PRs. And I then managed to have a successful-ish career in music journalism by ignoring and defying PRs for 20 years, which I'm rather proud of. Which isn't the case now.

But walking into the *NME* office at that time was bizarre. One writer — who I won't name — was playing a tape of his sexual activities on tour with Creedence Clearwater Revival. Another, one of the female writers, was sitting in Nick Logan's lap. And a third writer took at least an hour out of his day to show me how to fiddle my expenses — the most important job when you worked on a national music paper.

And I think in that first week — it seems like the first week — I interviewed a succession of people: Sandy Denny, Julie Collins, Status Quo and Shirley Bassey. That gives an indication of how mixed up *NME* was at the time. And, of course, it was when people like Charlie Murray, Nick Kent, Ian MacDonald and Nick Logan — who was a visionary genius who can never be given enough credit for what he did to *NME* — obviously with the help of MacDonald and Tony Tyler, people like that, that it started to morph into something very special. It became a youth-cultural publication. And I'm incredibly proud to look back on those days and feel I played a small part in it.

And everything I did there was by accident. I became the live review editor by accident; I started to design the paper by accident; I became a sub editor by accident. And I've been a writer. That was intentional, actually, but I wasn't that good at it, really, so I was quite happy to move to a backstage arena. And then eventually I became the deputy editor, then failed to become the editor. And that's when I moved to *Sounds*. The day I resigned, *Sounds* approached me and asked me if I'd like to be the editor of that publication. And that's how I started in it all.

CR: So do you want to know what the first editorial meeting was about?

TE: That would be good! But mainly just what your impression was.

CR: Well, technically I was working for Richard [Williams] at *Melody Maker*, though I hadn't really started. We were doing a project for him, I was doing it with Ian Birch. And I was asked in for an interview at *NME*. And I went because I wanted to criticise the paper because I didn't like it. I already had a job, I was quite happy with going into *Melody Maker*. And I went, and *NME* offered me a job. And I told them I didn't like the paper and didn't read it, and why I didn't like it or read it.

TE: Why didn't you like it?

CR: I can't really remember all of the reasons, but I didn't read it. At the time I didn't really enjoy their particular version of the promoting of the cult of the personality of the writer. I'm interested in journalism, and I was then — and I always felt a lot of the journalism was a bit lacking in that era. There were a couple of people — who later I learnt weren't even in the office, actually, Julie Burchill and Tony Parsons – who were allowed to sound off about stuff they really didn't know anything about. So I told them all this, and they offered me a job. And then we started talking and I told them why I didn't want the job. And then they offered me a bit more money than *Melody Maker* and a bit more freedom, and this and that and the other thing. And I ended up going there.

So my first editorial meeting was really just the first Tuesday I would have been there. But actually the editorial meeting wasn't exactly where things got decided either. It was much more around in the office, around your desk, Tony, and around Phil McNeill's desk essentially.

And what people were saying earlier about the package that it was, that's what gave the writers the freedom that they had. This freedom was enormous, as long as you produced that amount of work, which was also enormous. In a sense it was plantation journalism: you put out a lot of words: you'd do a 3,000 word interview, you'd go to a press conference — which could have been about a movie, or book launch, or anything really — and perhaps a book review, a live review, an album review as well, all in that one week.

But the actual packaging of, say the singles page — whoever was doing it that week, Danny Baker or Paul Morley — was always a kind of work-of-art thing. And Tony would get [the artist] Ian Wright to do a portrait of whoever [the lead single was by]. It became much more the idea of how you put a concept together, and the concept of what the paper was — which was eternally debated, debated in the office.

One thing that hasn't maybe come through is that these were people who cared a *lot* about what they did, and about how well they did it. They were reading all the time. And everybody was a kid, so they were reading things for the first time. If they were going to America, maybe they were reading Raymond Chandler, Dashiell Hammett, LeRoi Jones, you know, whatever, Peter Guralnick, Charlie Gillett. Any number of things, as well as playing all this stuff. And these were people who knew about the black music behind the music, most of them, and cared about it.

So there was a whole lot of context that may have not come through — but it's the context that was being built in the paper that interested me when I was there. The fact that this was a place where people were shouting jokes back and forth, trading tapes, trading DVDs, talking about

TV programmes. There was constantly music being played, old music, new music, all kinds of music.

TE: So while the word chaos gets used a lot, it was totally productive chaos?

CR: No, it wasn't really as chaotic as all that. It was just a lot of back-and-forth between a lot of people of different backgrounds, different kinds of humour, different interests, different focuses in their writing, they were at different points in their writing. But everybody was starting out, basically.

TE: And how did management react to this?

CR: They weren't really a part of it, except for creaming off the money brought in from the paper's following, which there was, out there somewhere. Though every time I saw someone reading the *NME*, it was some trainspotter kid on the tube. It was a bit disappointing, actually, so I tried not to look too much.

TE: So, all of you, what would your ideal reader have been, given the things you were trying to build? "A market leading socialist youth paper," as one of you said in an email to me.

CR: It *was* a socialist paper. That's something that also needs to come across. It was a *very* political paper. I mean, maybe it was particularly my thing that I had different bits and pieces that I was allowed to commission when I first came in, and columns that I had to cover later. I covered anti-nuclear stuff for a long time, bits of news. I did stories about deaths on the YOP scheme, I was able to go investigate the death of Richard Campbell in custody. This was on top of all the rock stuff.

TS: Originally we were in Covent Garden in Long Acre, and the offices were like an apartment. So we just went into work and then went out to lunch and got drunk, and went back into work and fell asleep a lot of the time. And then we'd go out at night and work. And I remember the review room was next door to somebody's flat. And she was constantly complaining about the noise. So we had to move the review room into the middle of the office. And a couple of floors down, there was the advertising department, who we just thought were strange people. We didn't quite know what they did and we weren't very interested in what they did. And there was one management guy at that time, the publisher of *NME*, who had a little office in the same building, 128 Long Acre.

And then they made the mistake of moving us to King's Reach Tower, the IPC monolith on the South Bank. I forget which floor we were on, but it was very high. And Burchill and Parsons created the Kinderbunker there, which had barbed wire on the partition. And it had a sort of curtain, and you had to knock on the door to go in there. And Julie wouldn't answer the phone, she had a thing about phones.

And management quickly realised this wasn't a very good idea — by this time I suppose it was the mid-70s or something, and it was now quite a subversive paper. But it was also making a phenomenal amount of money. And the management took a great hands-off view. They just though, "Oh, let's not fuck it up, let's do whatever you're doing — as long as it's not in our building." So they moved us out to Carnaby Street, which is what they were talking about earlier when *Smash Hits* was opposite. And that really *was* an apartment. People slept there, and all sorts. And there was no management, and no advertising department.

CR: That's when I was there too, Carnaby Street. I wasn't in any of the other places.

TS: So the only time we were aware of the management was when there were strikes. And we were a very left-wing paper and because we were making so much money, our union — and we were all members of the union — had come over to us first, and instructed us to go on strike. And we'd willingly do it. And that was the time when the management would get involved and go, "Oh, hang on a minute, you're over in Carnaby Street?" Yeah, yeah, yeah, making a million pounds or more a year. And that's when it hit them.

And I think by the time I left *NME*, July 1985, the weekend of *Live Aid*, management were moving *Melody Maker* people in — and no offence to them, but management wanted to take control of *NME*, which was also *losing* money by that time. But for those 15 years it was brilliant. Until the strike, whatever year Ian Curtis died, it was that year, the really bad strike [*ed note: it was 1980*]. That's when I think management decided to do something about these subversive rebels occupying Carnaby Street.

BG: On the surface it might seem that *Sounds* maybe wasn't as political a paper as the *NME*, but under the surface it was. Perhaps it's easy to forget, given his subsequent career at *The Sun*, that Garry Bushell was initially a socialist; he worked for *Socialist Worker* before he worked for *Sounds*. And it wasn't maybe so explicit on *Sounds*, but it was implicit that everybody was left-wing, really. And much like on the *NME*, pretty much all the writers were members of the union.

And we had a similar situation on *Sounds*, I think in 1981, where we went on strike with great idealism for several weeks. And the management managed to cobble together issues with the paper — which I think really fatally damaged the title, causing huge amounts of ill feeling. Because every PR in London who normally couldn't get their bands in *Sounds* got their bands in *Sounds* when we were on strike. It was a very difficult time. And at that time, *Sounds* was approaching the circulation of the *NME*, but the strike absolutely stopped that. And I don't think we ever regained the readers' trust, certainly not for a number of years.

CR: We also had these editorial meetings. We would debate why we wouldn't take advertising from the Army, when of course the Army would *never* have advertised. There's politics and politics.

BG: Another thing around the same time as the strike was an article in the *Daily Mail*, which accused *Sounds* of being 'A skinhead bible of hate'. I don't know if anyone remembers that. This was in 1981 as well, off the back of Garry Bushell creating a genre of music called oi!, which was basically, from what I could tell, a lot of football hooligans with guitars. And quite often they were in the office, which I didn't particularly appreciate. So that certainly was part of the chaos for me.

TE: To go back to an earlier panel, Jonathon Green was talking about the underground press as almost a middle-class playground, a kind of politics that felt very high stakes, but perhaps wasn't quite as high stakes as they imagined, given the UK's absence in Vietnam and such like. In terms of the real world, it sounds like this had completely changed by the early 80s, when [the rock press] was very much more in tune with socialist politics and such like. Was there any relationship between the music elements and the political elements? How did it all fit together?

TS: You have to remember that in 1976, there was Rock Against Racism, and a tidal wave against fascism in this country, which is ironic considering where we are now. And I think *Sounds* had a circulation that matched *NME* for a great deal of time, even overtook us when we'd been on strike, for something like eight weeks. The strike also gave an opening to a weekly publication which exploited it [*New Music News*], which funnily enough featured Mark Ellen on the masthead. He keeps popping up, doesn't he, this gentleman? And they were in the building opposite. Of course, they wouldn't dare cross our picket lines.

I don't know whether it would be a capital P politics or a small P, but we were all aware of the culture and the environment, and the power that we had. And it wasn't just the power to put Dr Feelgood on the cover of *NME*, for example, and make them successful. It was the pieces that were written, it was informing people about particular views.

So we were very aware of the readership. And carrying *NME* around was a badge of honour. And those views mattered. For myself personally, I probably wasn't as politicised as somebody like Tony Parsons and Julie Burchill, or maybe Charlie Murray. I'm not sure about Nick Kent, but Ian MacDonald was politicised, and so was Tony Tyler. These are the people driving *NME* from behind the scenes, if you like. So when we had weekly editorial meetings, it wasn't just a battlefield of ideology over music, it was a battlefield over views and things that mattered to us, things affecting our lives. And that kind of stuff, racism particularly, affected our lives. How could a music paper like *NME* support things like Bob Marley, black music, soul music and then ignore the racism that existed in Britain at the time, and also the fascism.

But ironically, *NME* was at its strongest when there was a Labour government; two successive Labour governments in force. And I vaguely remember trying to do something about Thatcher's sweep to power. Which involved getting a Thatcher mask and dressing somebody up with an ice cream tray. I can't even remember what the feature was about, but I know it wasn't supporting the Tory party at the time. We certainly wouldn't have swept them to power if we had our way. And, of course, there was the miners' strike.

Another writer for *NME* was Chris Moore, X Moore, who was a member of the Socialist Worker party, and went on to form his own band. And he was a very political animal. He was given his voice in *NME*, willingly given his voice. The one who wasn't given a voice, ironically, was Garry Bushell when he came to *NME* looking for a job. Because there was a dubiousness about the oi! movement, who were seen as right-wing fascist bastards, basically.

BG: Yeah, it was a tricky time when all of that was going on at *Sounds*. I found it very difficult to defend the championing of the oi! movement. At the time, by the early 80s I mean, it had started to be very tribal, with different writers representing different genres of music, with *Sounds* being very inclusive in that way. You had Eric Fuller writing about reggae, Sandy Robinson writing about avant-garde kinds of American bands, Jon Savage writing about punk and post-punk, Sylvie Simmons in America. Some fantastic writers all writing about different genres. And of course Geoff Barton writing about heavy metal.

So now you had Garry and Geoff, heavy metal and oi!, fighting it out for cover space. And it became increasingly difficult to wedge anything in that was even remotely considered to be pop music. Because obviously this was a time when the great schism was forming between pop and rock, and when colour magazines were coming back. And the pop content was eventually taken out of *Sounds* and put into a very short-lived magazine called *Noise!*, which I don't expect many people remember, which I worked on. It was a kind of *Sounds* colour supplement.

But it was tricky for me because I wasn't seen to be a particularly political animal in the more obvious sense. The oi! thing I found very difficult to deal with because I couldn't defend it really at all to anybody that asked me about it. And at the same time I was being singled out as the woman who just writes about pop groups, the fluffy stuff — and what did I know about the Clash and the Jam? So it was a difficult balancing act for me at *Sounds* at that time.

TE: You all moved from writing positions to editorial positions. What were the expectations editorially, the pressures — in the sense of pressure both from above and from the readers? How did things change once you moved to an editorial position?

TS: I stayed in the office more. It's very difficult [to answer] because as I said, there weren't the pressures in *NME* from above, from the management. We were allowed to do what we wanted to do. I was rather relieved to stop writing, because as Jonh Ingham said earlier, you're revisiting the same house week after week after week, with different personalities, and you're having to write about music three or four times a week, you're out at gigs and you're reviewing albums. Of course a lot of people will think my God, that sounds like a doddle. And I have to say that I think it's just incredible that somebody has paid me to do this for so many years.

But I don't think when I gave up being a writer that there was any pressure from IPC management, because we were successful. And what I then wanted to do was to bring in the new guard, if you like. I encouraged Paul Morley a great deal, and Ian Penman. I indulged them: the 1,500 word piece that turned into 5,000 words. I didn't notice. But you didn't because the volume of words in *NME* every week was just incredible. And there were so many commissioning editors to put it all together.

And I'd never give up the live section, because that was where the lifeblood of the paper was. It was where the young writers came. Gavin Martin, for example, who's now the *Mirror* writer, I brought him to the *Mirror* when I took over *The Ticket*, their Friday supplement. He was 17 when I gave him a job at *NME*. And he loves telling the story that I had to wait for him to come home from school to get him to do some review or other. I can't really remember the details like that. There was loads of people. There were the 'hip young gunslingers'. The famous hip young gunslingers were Parsons and Burchill. But that ad that *NME* ran in the early 70s also produced Paul Du Noyer — a more stately writer, if you like. And we mixed all those people together.

And the idea was to bring them onto *NME*. And I loved facilitating that. That's what I became, a facilitator. And if you could get young talent into the rock press, into *NME* specifically, then we all had a future. And for a long time, we did have a future. So that was just exciting, it was brilliant. You learnt so much from all these people. Because there was incredible talent on *NME* and on *Sounds*, and on the other papers as well, on *Melody Maker* as well. I mean, there was a rivalry between us, we all stood for what we believed in, and that was completely separate to what *Melody Maker* or *Sounds* might believe in. But there was so much talent, and that was what was brilliant about that particular era.

CR: So I came into *NME* and was asked to edit a page. And through that I was able to meet people like [the cartoonist] Gary Panter, people abroad. This is when there were two phones in the office that you could call outside of Britain on, at either end of the office. So when you did a story with someone, about Marvin Gaye being shot, say, you were having to make your phone calls and then run to the middle of the office and confer, and then go back and call people, because of the time difference.

But it taught me how a paper was put together and what the expectations were, without me even realising this. The idea that typesetting played a part, that typefaces played a part, that headlines played a part, that straplines played a part, that captions played a part, that photography played a part, that the use of people like Ian Wright for illustrations could play a part. And this was the work of a whole lot of specific people who were our editors at the time, as well as Tony here and Phil McNeill being the linchpin people when I was there.

But what made a huge difference was that we had people of such quality — we had Ian Wright, we had Andy Murray, we had Anton [Corbijn] — and it did help shape everything. So you would go into your next job looking for that. And actually, a more important thing from my own background is that this was not from an Oxbridge point of view. If I'd gone into the BBC, say, where I later worked, there was a different concept of hierarchy and who's going to tell you what to do. And they would have been the sons and daughters, or the husbands and wives, or the cousins and the ex-schoolmates of people. But the people at *NME* were recruited because they were seen to be good at what they did, or potentially could become good at what they did. And many of them did.

Which is not to say there weren't things that we didn't cover. When I started there there weren't enough black writers — there weren't any black writers — and there weren't any women writers. But we brought in quite a few by the end, so it was starting to get more diverse, for want of a better word. People writing about Indian music, who weren't white people from a European background. People who were British Indian people writing about Cornershop, or whatever. People bringing stories in that wouldn't have been there before. But the management cared more about having someone who would not vote against them in the next strike — or not having a next strike — and so on.

BG: My first experience in a more backstage role was as a features editor of *Noise!*, which only lasted for six months. Which was really my first experience of market forces, too, because the reason it closed was that it was apparently not generating enough advertising revenue. But it wasn't really given enough time to bed in. That was a bit of a crazy time, I was really the only member of staff. I not only commissioned all the features, I wrote most of them as well. So it was an intense time.

After *Noise!* closed, I was absorbed onto *Record Mirror*. Rather reluctantly, because when I was at *Sounds*, I'd always considered *Record Mirror* as a poor relation — that rather old-fashioned title. *It's just a pop magazine*. It was all a bit snobbish of me, but I was reluctant to go there. But I didn't want to leave the company, so I went onto *Record Mirror* as an assistant editor.

And that's really where I learnt my trade, in what Tony terms the 'backstage area'. That's where I became a sub, that's where I learnt about design, that's where I learnt what makes a great layout with great photographs. And I started to operate much more in that way, though I still carried on writing and interviewing. But *Record Mirror* was much more governed by what would bring in advertising. By that point in 1983, it became much more about the market.

TE: So that's the encroachment that's being talked about, I guess. It struck me, hearing about the underground earlier, that there was a sense that anything could be covered. And in a way, the early 80s music press was a recovery of that. Is it fair to say that there was a much wider selection of subjects; that it was a way to dig into a lot more than just music? And was there a sense of disappointment that the readership might not be picking up on this? Especially if when you saw someone actually reading the *NME*, it was a let-down?

CR: No, because you got a lot of correspondence in the office from people. It's not like they rang up exactly — they didn't have the phone number that we had. And we all shared a desk phone: I shared mine with Chris Bohn, and then with Richard Cook. That was an interesting bonding experience. But you did get a lot of letters from people. From Bruce Pavitt, for instance, who went on to do Sub Pop, he used to send me stuff all the time. And I collected the fanzines that came in. Loads of people did fanzines, and I'd worked on this project with delinquents who were making fanzines as well, and then they would give me their fanzines. Because people really wanted to write. They would read the writing and they were the same kinds of kids, they were aspiring writers. And so they were really keen.

And the great thing about it, I thought, was that if you were in the office, there were all these different voices. These people defending what they wanted to write about, then writing about it. People going on the road with somebody who was interesting, or going to an interesting place. Albeit that six people who were 17 or 18 or 20 going to LA for the first time will each write a version of the same knock-off introduction to LA — before they get to the part about the music at all, you know — in the style of whoever they're reading about LA. We had a kind of samizdat network of people's copy. You would read it as it was being typeset, or before, the uncut version or whatever.

And that was always interesting. And there were lots of different people interested in different things. Some in the office wanted to really write about cinema, or incorporate it in what they were writing, and so on. And, of course, you'd see people at gigs. I mean, you spent your whole life waiting around for the show to start, and drinking. You would run into people from other publications there, and also the people reading the paper. I did have someone come up and bonk me on the head for a bad review as well, in a restaurant.

TS: I don't know if the audience did reject the cultural mix of *NME* in the 80s. I mean, it was very much a specific thing we wanted to do. If people were interested in music, it therefore followed they were interested in cinema, for example, or were interested in TV.

We did do some strange things. I've got no interest in football, I'm glad to say — but we once put a footballer on the cover of *NME*. I thought that was something different, quite brave. And it wasn't until I was interviewed for the editorship, which I didn't get, that the publisher actually said, 'Oh God, whoever thought of doing that?' And he blamed Neil Spencer, who was the editor at the time. But, in fact it was me that did it. And I went, "tut tut, shocking, shocking." We also put a snooker player on the cover, I think Ronnie O'Sullivan or someone like that. And I quite liked snooker at the time.

No, it was Jimmy White. [From the audience: The footballer was Pat Nevin.] [*No, it was Charlie Nicholas, Pat Nevin was some years later — ed.*]

And I remember there was a big hoohah — did Robert Elms write that feature? He played a part in *NME*, not least of all introducing us to Spandau Ballet. But the inkies, as they were known, were starting to get a bit of a reputation that wasn't so good. Was the generation as politicised as it had been during the 70s? Well, I don't know. Were they as interested? I don't really know the answer to that. The miners' strike in '74 brought down the Heath government. So there was quite a groundswell of left-wing support at that time, which fitted into the *NME* ethos, if you like. But then ten years later Thatcher defeated the miners. And that played a part.

CR: There was a big involvement in the miners' strike. The miners' wives used to come to the office all the time.

TS: Yes. But there were also other things that were going on in the music press. Nick Logan had launched *Smash Hits* in 1978. And ironically, this was would lead to a big hit on *NME*. As deputy editor, then editor, Logan had been the main architect of where *NME* was going [in the 70s]. Other people informed it but he was the main architect. He was responsible for *NME*'s success.

And then Nick, of course, launched *The Face* in 1980. Which was a revolutionary monthly music-style-cultural publication. And people suddenly discovered something called glossy paper, and they preferred that to the newsprint. But by then, the music press was probably a little bit old-fashioned, and I don't think it was down to the mix of the content. And reflecting on it, I don't know whether Jimmy White was right to put on the cover. There was much better snooker players than him at the time.

CR: *The Face* was directly across from us then, we could watch them laying out their pages when we were laying out our pages. A big difference, when it started out, was that it was essentially more or less a compilation of press releases. I was asked to fire Robert Elms the day I joined *NME*, for being too much of a press officer. Phil McNeill didn't want to do it. So I guess he went straight across the street. But that was a big debate, I think, with the management too. I think Neil Spencer encountered feelings about that, more than we got.

TS: Yes, I think Neil — who was editor of *NME*, up until 1985 — protected us. I was the deputy editor but I was more involved in the creative side of it. And I think what Neil did — and thanks to him for doing it — was protect us from IPC management.

I remember once seeing a memo — there weren't emails then — because I'd stayed in a hotel in London. Because we used to work ridiculous hours, and I lived in Kent. And it was from the publisher. And the memo to Neil was, "What was Stewart doing staying in a hotel in London?" I thought, well, fuck, that's a bit rude calling me my surname, so much for any respect from the management. And it was from seeing that memo that I realised they were a bunch of bastards at IPC, and I wouldn't have much time for them at all. But Neil, to his eternal credit, kept all that shit away from us, so that we got on with what we wanted to do, which was to create what we thought was the best music or youth-culture publication going.

CR: This is what I didn't get about being an editor. All this expectation. What you did learn one way or another was through arguing with the printers, that kind of thing. But the other side, which I just don't have a taste for, was having to play the *role* of the editor, meaning going on TV, giving interviews. I was more interested in what I understood, sitting across from you, Tony, and watching Phil; commissioning the photographers, talking to the writers, you know, shaping the thing, actually *editing*, not just *being the editor*. But there's a fair amount of being the editor required if you're going to fit the expectations.

BG: One of the things that I found difficult when I actually did become editor of *Record Mirror* was that, by that time in the mid to late 80s, the paper was really a bit of a mishmash. It had its pop roots, and also a strong tradition of covering dance music with James Hamilton, who was a very well respected DJ at the time. And I had to cater for all these different markets, which was difficult! It didn't give me much freedom in terms of trying to create a magazine that came together in any meaningful way, because we had to put in chart music, we had to put in dance music, we had to put in a little indie to keep the indie kids happy. And we had to satisfy the advertisers as well.

And I think it was much harder, on that pop magazine format, to create something creative. But, you know, we still felt passionately about producing something that we felt proud of. And we probably were sometimes a little bit disappointed in our readers, because a lot of *Record Mirror* readers were basically chart geeks. They literally collected the charts out of *Record Mirror* every week, because *Record Mirror* carried the official chart. So yes, that could be a bit frustrating. But it was still something that the team felt really passionate about, creating something that was true to their values and that they believed in.

TE: Did you see yourself in a tradition with the various undergrounds and the early music press? How much of it was continuity? How much was a break from what was happening before?

TS: We're talking about *Oz*, right, and things like that? Well, *NME* made a conscious effort. I wasn't part of it, I'm only speaking as an observer. I wasn't from the underground press, I was from a publication called the *Burton Daily Mail* in Burton-on-Trent, which was slightly removed. I went to journalism college in Darlington, though I shared a place with one guy called Tristan, who actually did write for *Oz*. And he was delighted that he'd done a review of the Incredible String Band and been paid for it. And I thought, God, can you do this and get paid for it? So yes, that was part of what prompted me, but not directly. Because I wanted to become a journalist, and I'd had it knocked into me, by my dad particularly, saying "Get a proper job." And I'm a failed musician as well, which a lot of people on the music press are.

So I think it was Nick Kent and Charlie Murray, and also the brilliant Mick Farren, who took the spirit of the underground press — that's where they'd been — and they helped imbue *NME* with that spirit. But there was a lot of things going on in *NME* at the time, you know. Charlie Murray and Kent, and Farren a bit later, they just had that sensibility and they were interested in pure music. A part of me was much more showbiz. I'm rather glad it was actually, because it served me well later. Paul Morley was saying earlier that a lot of it was showbiz dressed as something else, and silver capes and bombastic prog rock bands, etcetera. It was good to have that element. And I think Kent and Murray and Farren came to dominate *NME* for a certain period of time. And Parsons was probably very much inspired by that maverick attitude. And I think others were, Morley probably, Ian Penman. So yes, that did exist on *NME*. There was a link.

But there was also this other element. Because when I got my job on *NME*, it was very much this mishmash of showbiz. The editor was a guy called Andy Gray, an amiable Canadian gentleman who spent most of his time on the golf course. And the news editor was a guy called Derek Johnson, who spent most of his time in his garden. And I just thought this ain't very rock and roll.

So then the arrival of Kent and Murray — and Chrissie Hynde also appeared in the office as a writer briefly, which was quite entertaining. We saw David Cassidy in a completely different light after she went on the road with him. And of course other people that hung around in the offices also probably hung around the underground press, certain musicians who were dealing drugs at the time. Because as Penny Reel mentioned in his question earlier, there was a division on *NME* between which drugs people were taking. And this informed you as well. And I think the underground press people loved the harder stuff, and there was another group of people who preferred to chill out on weed. *[Sadly the tape recorders missed Penny's interesting question — ed.]*

CR: I think *CREEM* magazine in the States was a huge influence. And maybe the early *Rolling Stone*, which I've read a couple of vintage issues of. But I think many of the people who went on and wrote for *NME* were really influenced by *CREEM*. I think even Nick Logan was actually. I think *CREEM* was a huge influence.

And when I started doing 'A Letter from Britain' for them, I really enjoyed getting to know that, albeit on the phone. *CREEM* was really doing something unique, [from Detroit], a place with a huge musical history and a huge political history that mattered to the underground press people, that mattered in American terms, in American social history. And they tied it all together. And I think that went on even when they were putting the Ramones on the cover, or Boy George.

There's another difference about how UK acts covered in the UK press were perceived in America. They often went to America to break into music in a way they couldn't in Britain, and succeeded. Like the Eurythmics, for instance, who had fallen a bit flat at the time in Britain, and then came back from America really huge.

So those weren't necessarily things we were equipped to deal with critically at *NME*. It just wasn't the way that it was perceived. There was these two different audiences. Though I expect the *NME* — I don't know about *Sounds* — was fairly widely read through import in America, and influential as well. It would be interesting to find out where that lag was from the other side. It might have been like *CREEM* coming our way.

TS: Plus let's not forget fanzines either, they were really, really important, you know. That's where a lot of the *NME* writers came from during the 70s, the late 70s and even a bit later than that. James Brown, for example — not the soul singer but the guy who went on to edit *GQ*. He came to our attention with a fanzine. So that was a very important strain of writing that was absorbed by *NME*, because it was felt to be important.

BG: Yeah, same with *Sounds*. Quite a few *Sounds* writers came through the fanzines as well in the late 70s. So I don't think I could quite trace it back to the underground press as you were framing it, but definitely fanzines were hugely, hugely important.

TE: Was there stuff the fanzines were doing that you felt you couldn't do or would have liked to do?

TS: Well, they had no constraints, did they? *Sniffin' Glue*, Danny Baker and Mark Perry, they just did what they wanted. Which Danny then came to *NME* to do. He was the receptionist at first, as anybody who's read his autobiography knows, and he used to charge readers to speak to writers. Danny's always had a fantastic imagination. But that's what he could do. There was nobody to answer to.

And I suppose I've been a bit glib about the management influence on *NME*, because it did become very strong after that long strike that we had. And it led to a lot of people leaving *NME* — me, for example — and to the *Melody Maker* people being drafted in to *NME* to soften it down and, you know, to protect the golden egg, if you like.

And the other pressure, with a small P for politics, was the record companies themselves. When I was an editor of *Sounds*, the ad manager would come in to me saying, "Oh, you know, CBS are really bothered about the reviews on such and such, can you get them to tone it down?" And I used to say, "Here's a message for CBS, tell them to fuck off." Because I didn't think that had any place. And, of course, when the publisher found out that I was saying things like that, I wasn't very popular.

But you have to have integrity. Right up until my departure from *The Mirror* a year ago, there was a constant battle with advertising and what the advertisers were demanding of a national newspaper, for fuck's sake. And you just think, alright, Proctor and Gamble, you can pay for your Fairy Liquid ads or whatever, but you don't have a say in the editorial.

And this was the same record companies who were getting brilliant exposure. Graham Parker and the Rumour, for example, would never have been the success they were without the music press, *Sounds*, *NME* and *Melody Maker*. Phonogram Records would be on the phone, their ad department, about some naff old band they'd foisted on the public had got a bad review — and a deservedly bad review because they were a naff old band.

So you had to resist those sorts of pressures, much greater than any pressure you got from the management. At least at that time. I left *NME* was because of being on the wrong side of a picket line — the barricades, if you like — and I'm convinced to this day that I didn't get the editorship of *NME* because I was seen as a subversive left-wing troublemaker. Whether that's true or not, whether the person who did get the job in the end just purely on talent, I don't know, but I'd like to think I made my mark in that respect, anyway.

TE: One last question. In terms of editing or writing, what are you proudest of?

BG: That's a very big question. I think what I'm most proud of actually is being a champion for a number of bands, and probably not the ones that I'm more publicly associated with, which was bands like Spandau Ballet and Duran Duran. Of championing a lot of new music in the early 80s, especially at *Sounds*, but also at *Record Mirror*. And really being able to connect those bands with a new audience.

And that's really just going on the letters that I got from readers, thanking me for introducing them to bands that they would never have heard of otherwise. A situation that just wouldn't arise now: it's almost impossible to have anything be a secret now. The power that we had in those days was extraordinary — and I'd like to think that I used my power wisely. I might not always have done. I think I slagged off Gary Numan quite a lot. But I'm quite proud of the way that I used that power wisely. I'll take that with me.

CR: Well, I'm proud that I was the only person in the office who never wanted to be in a band, ever! But I'm glad that I had the experience, because it equipped me to do a lot of things later on that I wouldn't have been able to do. It gave me the curiosity to stay curious about things, to enjoy listening to people and to find real merit in doing that. And I really appreciate that — and I actually am really grateful that I learned in the way I learned, all those things I said earlier about production and the importance of those things.

TS: I'm proud just about being there, you know, during a period in the music press history that will never be repeated again. And playing a part — quite a small part — in facilitating a lot of really talented writers to come forward, and photographers. When I first commissioned Anton Corbijn to go and take some pictures of Bill Haley at some gig in London, and he went on to do such fantastic work with U2, I like to feel that we were helping him to make a name for himself. And he was presenting an astonishing range of work. Pennie Smith was the same, Kevin Cummins was the same.

CR: There was a lot of photographers.

TS: There was a lot of fantastic photographers. And when I went to *Sounds*, there was Ian Tilton, another brilliant photographer out of Manchester. So we brought those people together and just gave them a platform for them to express themselves. And, of course the artists. I'm not going to name some of the bands championed — but a Dutch yodelling band in the 70s, called Focus? No, thank you. But it was a brilliant era for the music press and I'm pretty glad that when I went on to be an editor that I resisted the management, and that I resisted the advertising departments. And eventually I fell on my own sword. You know, I was 42 when I left the music press and I thought that was OK.

My Lunch with Andy

Cynthia Rose on how she learned that journalism means more than typing

Maybe we still cling to calling it "the media". But what people now read for news and culture can come from anywhere. Unified by nothing, only one thing drives it: the nonstop, all-inclusive competition. To those who are creating a majority of its 'content', today's distracted readership is nothing but 'eyeballs' and clicks — and it's a landscape in which writers are minor cogs.

This world couldn't differ more from the ancient music press or, at least, from the *NME* where I worked. There no equivalent to the Like button existed and our staff saw its independence as sacrosanct. Far from anyone trying to please, we knew our editors often saw us as trying and difficult. But no one sought, needed (or cared about) approval.

Several factors underwrote that point of view. The *NME* was proudly a socialist music paper "for youth" but, more importantly, it was a market leader. Because we happened to enjoy a large circulation, the corporation behind the paper made good money. So whether or not anyone really agreed with our formula, in terms of what mattered to those higher up, it worked. At our level (if not that of all our editors), that result bought us editorial freedom.

It also gave all of us quite a showcase. At *NME*, if you did your work well, people who mattered noticed. The paper was monitored by its rivals, by editors at publishing houses and by the people commissioning TV and radio. So if your work shone (or if you clearly had ideas), freelance jobs and book deals usually came your way. Some of the most interesting work I did was not at the paper — yet, in another job, it would never have found me.

Working in the music press also gave you confidence. It was highly competitive and, week after week, your plate could be as full as you wanted. All of us were on the hook for "in-depth" features, but these were juggled with non-stop writing on records, books, gigs and movies. Distilling all of that into words was life, 24/7.

Every week we thought about and sized up what we heard and saw. Not only did we come to view all of it as related; we made a case for why that was so. These days, when hierarchies everywhere are collapsing, that kind of schooling has turned out to be useful.

Jobs in the music press entailed a lot of mundane detail. There was endless waiting and schlepping; plenty of sitting in airports, stations and venues. The logging of transcripts, in my case by hand, was seemingly endless. But, thanks to the paper's status, we had genuine access. Not for us pontificating on the basis of links and emails.

The narcissism which produced the selfie was inbuilt *chez nous* and *NME* was infamous for its "personalities". Most of the founding fathers were gone by the time I arrived, but their *modus operandi* certainly lingered on. Many a scribe aimed to live, dress and write like some kind of star. This seemed to be a legacy of the Swinging Sixties, when musical luminaries anointed the first "personality" hairdressers, cobblers and tailors. Eventually, star artisans of every ilk followed, from writers to supermodels and even typographers.

When it came to actual celebrity, however, we saw it. Our job made us witness to all its daily perks and details — from the girls and boys and drugs to the suites and chauffeurs. We also listened, over and over, as people told us how it really felt. In the case of someone like Dolly Parton or David Bowie, that experience could often be surreal. But it was never boring.

My lunch with Andy Warhol was a good example. It took place in Dallas, Texas — the site chosen by Andy for a rendezvous with his "dermatologist".

I had already heard a lot about Andy Warhol. According to Debbie

Harry, who I frequently interviewed, he was more orthodox than his myth might have you believe. Andy, she told me, habitually got up early, attended Catholic Mass and spent most of every day working. ("I think he's very much in control. So much so that it sometimes startles me.")

My memory of walking in and seeing him remains a vivid one. Sitting alone in a restaurant with all-white décor, he couldn't have looked much more like "Andy Warhol". From the black turtleneck to his pockmarked face and wig, every piece of that iconic image was present. But what struck me more than anything was his posture. It was impeccable; I'd never seen anyone sit that straight. This was due, as he later showed me, to a pair of custom-made corsets. One of these was pale pink, the other mint green. Two decades after being shot, Warhol's body still couldn't support itself.

Now Warhol lives on in countless tapes and digital files, machinery diffusing his flat, fey tones in perpetuity. You can also type his name into any search field and diverse queries spring up: "*Andy Warhol boyfriend?*", "*Andy Warhol Edie?*", "*Andy Warhol shooting?*". Yet when I disinter my own plastic tapes, it isn't answers to those queries I discover.

My day with Andy sounds like the relic it is. Not because Warhol-in-the-flesh was so witty (although he certainly was) or so oddly prescient (Debbie was also right about that) or so totally working-class. It's because there was nothing "virtual" about him. Every bit as present as he was on the day, Warhol audibly, if passively, takes charge. As I listen in — after decades — to us talking, the subjects bounce from lunch to the history of photography, from art deco to the finer points of libel law.

Warhol often hesitates, yet he is far from laconic. He has opinions on everything and most of them are erudite. As one might expect, too, he sounds very up-to-date. The artist so famed for his interest in the new sees plenty to praise in his Commodore Amiga.

Yet, as I keep on listening, something else emerges. It isn't the taste for novelty which makes Warhol singular. What does that is his total immersion in the present tense. Despite a clear fascination for image and self-presentation, nothing about Andy's presence is simulated or fabricated.

On my tapes he is canny and caustic, then reticent, then risqué. But, during every second, whether we're alone or joined by his entourage, Andy gives the conversation all his attention. This is his real art, the skill of paying attention; he wouldn't be that guy preoccupied with his mobile phone. It's the last comparison I expected, but Warhol had a lot in common with Madame de Sévigné. If his façade was totally as advertised that was where the symmetry with his legend stopped.

Fourteen months after our meeting, Warhol was dead. Now, thanks to the internet, anyone can access his most secret foibles. They too can learn he went to mass, worked long hours, volunteered at homeless shelters. But, for me, our lunch remains less a revelation than the embodiment of something basic: the story is never what you expect. In comparison to that exceptional guy I met, the Warhol Google serves me up is just a paper cut-out. Virtual facts and screens of text just can't compete with the randomness and detail of life.

One thing about the real, though, is predictable: it always comes with politics. Understanding that is part of *NME*'s legacy too. The paper didn't just sell because Paul Weller graced our cover. We also backed CND, the women at Greenham Common, the miners and the Labour Party. We were a union shop and, on one occasion, a majority of us voted for a strike of our own.

My first-ever news piece came out of that consciousness; it exposed deaths on the Youth Opportunity Scheme. Back then, most British school-leavers faced unemployment so, through 'YOPS', Thatcher offered them mandatory, short-term "training". Much of this came from small, local firms, places where employers were actually looking for cheaper labour. Because almost no oversight was put in place, over three years YOPS caused seven deaths on the job. Not to mention more than 9,000 injuries.

I still remember many of the kids I wrote about. One was mopping a factory floor with solvent when someone tossed a match. Another was cleaning a mincing machine, standing inside, when it got switched on. All of this occurred long before email, so I took the details by phone from parents around the country. Those who had no telephone answered with hand-written letters. Blurry, smiling photos slid out of the envelopes.

Those four years in the *NME* office certainly changed me. I gained the ability to better pitch a story and I learned to make it work at any length or format. I absorbed the importance of images, headlines and captions. I was able to hone a favourite skill, that of interviewing. All of this remains useful and engaging.

But what I really learned was something more important. Because, although skills and confidence are vital, neither will profit you if you lack curiosity. It's really curiosity that leads to the unexpected, to the telling detail or the heart of a story. Today, when I look around at the world of tweets and texts, that's the one thing I find absent. The *NME* turned my own curiosity into a reflex — and that made life enormously richer.

Without it, would I have worked "underground" in a Twinkie factory? Would I have listened when Chris Stein insisted I meet Jean-Michel Basquiat? Would I have ever set out to learn why James Brown screamed?

Would I have combed the Western hemisphere for Our Lady of Guadalupe? Would I have moved to Seattle on the advice of three oddballs (Kurt Cobain, a medical examiner and a skateboarder)? Would I have written a book with a gay, black, working-class artist?

Would I have met, in a tiki bar, the person I live with? Would I have landmarked a 1914 steam laundry? Would I have made a film about performance typing?

In short, could I have understood what Andy Warhol had to show me?

My time in the music press was just one link in a chain. But it was a critical one. Maybe there are no longer any jobs in "journalism". But real journalism keeps changing my life.

Cynthia Rose got her first press card at 20. Initially hired by Melody Maker, she joined NME in 1980 as Thrills! editor and worked for them until 1986. Now based in Paris, she works as a journalist, author and broadcaster.

THE MANY SHAPES OF THE WORLD

"By dubbing the singer 'Lord Frederick Lucan of Mercury', with one neat soubriquet *Smash Hits* could mock the group's cold aloofness, sense of entitlement and class privilege — and Freddie's moustache"

— *Bob Stanley*

Rhythms Would Skitter, Jiggle, Leap or Lurch

Mike Atkinson remembers James Hamilton, the pioneering dance-music columnist at Record Mirror

If you were planning a weekly music paper from scratch, you would never devise something as fundamentally fractured as the *Record Mirror* of the 1980s. Of the three sets of readers it attracted, only one would open their copies from the front. Here, in the magazine's first half, you would find the usual mix of news, features and reviews: slanted towards the more sophisticated end of pop, or the lighter reaches of rock, if largely lacking the questing spirit of the *NME*, *MM* and *Sounds*, the wit and access of *Smash Hits*, and the distinctive stylistic flair of all of them. If this had been *RM*'s sole stock in trade, the title could well have floundered and withered.

Meanwhile, in the back half, sales were buoyed by two other readerships, enjoying something the first group lacked: the sense of being right at the centre of things. For chart watchers outside the industry, of which there were plenty, *RM*'s coverage was unmatched elsewhere. It was the only non-industry title to list the official Top 100 singles and albums, it carried the most extensive US chart coverage, and by the mid-80s its other weekly

sales charts included indie, reggae, US R&B, 12-inch singles, CD albums
and music videos. And in the pages which immediately preceded it, James
Hamilton's dance section had successfully willed its own parallel universe
into being, offering a comprehensive and authoritative mix of reviews,
dancefloor charts and industry gossip that had become required reading
for nearly every DJ in the country.

Following a five-year stint (1969-74) at *Record Mirror*, reviewing
singles from the US, Hamilton re-joined the paper in June 1975, after a
ten month gap, for the launch of his own Disco Page. This was coupled
with the first ever national weekly dancefloor reaction chart, compiled by
submissions from participating DJs. Re-introducing himself to his readers
("Disco DJs, dancers, and super sharp record freaks in general"), he made
mention of his 1965-66 residency at The Scene in Wardour Street, playing
weekend all-nighters for London's prime mod crowd. ("I played nothing
but Northern Soul... on its first time around!") The first chart-topper was
Van McCoy's 'The Hustle'; the first review compared two versions of '7-
6-5-4-3-2-1 (Blow Your Whistle)', Hamilton preferring the "stompalong
chanter" from Rimshots, who "thump along more cleanly" than the
"messier arrangement" of Gary Toms Empire.

By describing tunes in these functional, practical terms, focusing
on dancefloor effectiveness more than lyrical message, a distinctive
reviewing style emerged: concise, largely impartial, and deploying a
particular vocabulary that accrued meaning through familiarity. Favoured
words emerged, forming a kind of shorthand. Rhythms would skitter,
jiggle, leap, lurch, stride, chug or roll; they might even canter. Structures
might meander, build or erupt, or they might be "episodic". Vocally,
something like Raw Silk's 'Do It to the Music' might be "gently chix-
cooed", Adeva's 'Respect' "stridently wailed", a Bobby Womack cut
"soulfully rasped".

Once attuned to the language, DJs could readily identify the tracks
that would most likely work on their floors, and punters could build their
wish lists with confidence. And really, this was the whole point; for as
James made emphatically clear on the first time we met, his prime purpose
was "to actually describe what the records SOUND like". While others

polished their *bon mots* and honed their snark, he built his own brand on factual accuracy.

To this end, and in the wake of a revelatory visit to New York's Paradise Garage in 1978, where he witnessed Larry Levan's beat-mixing style for the first time, James added a key new ingredient. In his first column of 1979, under the headline "To BPM Or Not To BPM", he announced that "all significant record reviews will in future feature the Beats Per Minute as an aid to the ever-increasing number of jocks who mix between records with similar rhythms," before giving a detailed instruction course in beat-counting. "Finally, the reason why so many of today's disco records — especially on 12in — have a thumping instrumental intro and rattling rhythm break about two thirds of the way through should be obvious," he concluded. "They're making it easy to mix! (Gah, penny's dropped!)"

Although not the first British DJ to beat-count his records — he readily conceded that Pete Waterman did it first, albeit using a metronome rather than a stopwatch — and although he didn't personally coin the term "BPM", James was unquestionably the prime mover behind this new approach. Priding himself on painstakingly precise timings, he would record every tempo fluctuation, to the smallest of non-decimal fractions, exceeding any practical need. (Gwen McCrae's 'All This Love That I'm Giving', for instance, weighed in at a boggling 111¼-112-114⅔-112-112⅓.) Sometimes, a particular BPM could signify a whole genre: 114 for jazz-funk, 129 for hi-nrg. And when steady pre-programmed beats began to propagate, the relief was profound. ("Somebody buy them a drum machine!" he wailed, no doubt soulfully, reviewing Level 42's resolutely analogue 'Hot Water' in 1984.)

The Disco Demolition Night riot of July 1979 might have dealt a death blow to the genre in the US, but we never got the memo over here, and the *Record Mirror* column — re-branded as "BPM", and now covering several pages — continued to thrive, without even a blip. In common with John Peel, whose time at boarding school in Shrewsbury overlapped his own, James remained open to, and enthusiastic about, any new development from the grassroots. Electro was eagerly absorbed, despite fierce resistance from old-school soul/funk jocks, as was chicago house and its subsequent derivatives. Pick any dance classic from the mid-70s to the late 80s — 'You Make Me Feel (Mighty Real)', 'Planet Rock', 'Holiday', 'Pump Up The Volume' — and you'll almost certainly find that James wrote about it first, often well before it fully broke. He got to 'I Will Survive' a month ahead of its chart debut ("Diana Ross-ish slow starting 117bpm loper gets kinda symphonic with more than a hint of 'Reach Out I'll Be There' to it"), and filleted *Thriller* for nuggets a week in advance, pegging 'Billie Jean' as a "tapper", 'P.Y.T.' as a "strutter" and 'Beat It' as a "whipper".

Having ridden the 1988 acid house wave with seeming ease, pausing only to pen a cautionary side-box on the perils of chemical over-indulgence, James started to lose all-encompassing relevance during 1989, as a new dance culture began to establish its own communication networks. By 1990, guest reviewers were muscling in on his space, without even the courtesy of supplying their own BPMs. Yet his niche remained a sizeable one, and big enough to ensure his survival when *RM* folded as a standalone title in 1991, continuing as a dance-oriented pullout in the centre of *Music Week*. He filed his last column in June 1996, just three weeks before his death from cancer, at the age of 53.

"No one has ever got close to him in terms of respect as a journalist," said Pete Tong, paying tribute on the front page of *Music Week*. "He was drawing on such a wealth of knowledge that even if you didn't agree with him, you had to respect his opinion."

6' 8" tall, with a patrician demeanour that put many in mind of James Robertson Justice, James Hamilton left behind a grieving widow — she was my stepmother, and they had been married for just over 18 months — a one-bedroomed flat in Harlesden, stuffed so full with records that kitchen fittings had been removed to make way for them — and a legacy that has never been given its full due. Coming onto the market as vinyl prices were bottoming out, his collection of around 250,000 records, too many to catalogue, were auctioned off in job lots for a fraction of their true worth. His memory lives on in discussion forums, a Facebook page, and the affections of all who encountered him.

Mike Atkinson's blog Troubled Diva, started in 2001, led him into freelance music journalism. He has written for The Guardian, Metro, Time Out, Slate and Stylus, and he is now building an archive of James Hamilton's Record Mirror columns at jameshamiltonsdiscopage.com.

A Utopia for Rock *and* Pop Fans

Beverley Glick, who wrote as Betty Page, describes her times at Sounds, Noise!
and Record Mirror in the 80s

In 1974, at the age of 17, I emerged from my pubescent glam-
rock chrysalis to become a floppy-haired butterfly in loon pants
nursing well-worn copies of *Tubular Bells* and *Close to the Edge*. I
also underwent a metamorphosis in my reading habits, abandoning
my weekly fix of teen pin-up magazine *Jackie* and graduating to the
relative sophistication of the *New Musical Express*. However at that
time I was a bigger fan of its Lone Groover cartoon than the prose of
its more earnest writers.

Two years later, when punk happened, I was working as a secretary
and singing backing vocals with a whimsical power-pop band called
Tennis Shoes. I liked the Sex Pistols — in a smug, ironic way —
but would never have risked adopting the look. The real irony being
that I would go on to benefit from punk in ways I could never
have predicted.

Tennis Shoes went on to be regulars on the London pub rock
circuit, making one independent single that was played by John Peel.
There seemed to be a chance of a major label deal, and it was with
that in mind that a friend suggested I apply for the vacant position

of secretary to the editor of *Sounds*, at that time Alan Lewis. I was initially reluctant — the salary was much less than I was earning at the time — but the promise of positive reviews outweighed my misgivings.

I got the job.

On my first day working for Alan in the summer of 1977, I stepped into a shambolic scene. The Adverts' 'Looking Through Gary Gilmore's Eyes' was playing at full volume, the office was littered with discarded press releases and several scrawny men were using vinyl albums as frisbees.

I thought I had made a terrible mistake. But after a couple of months, I settled into the chaotic rhythm and made friends with writer Tony Mitchell. As our friendship developed into a relationship, we started going to gigs together — Talking Heads, Blondie, Television, U2 — and I would help him write his reviews.

Happy to play muse, I had no ambition to be a writer. But one day, after we had been to see a minor Detroit combo called Destroy All Monsters, Tony announced that he didn't have time to write the review and suggested I take over.

I agreed to write the review under his name. But he insisted that the byline should be mine. Knowing I wouldn't get paid if I used my real name, Tony suggested the *nom de plume* Betty Page — in tribute to the 50s cheesecake model turned fetish queen who, at the time, was very much an underground figure. So I handed in my first live review, which to my surprise was published with very little editing.

I guess I shouldn't have been that surprised. *Sounds* had an extensive network of stringers, many of whom published their own fanzines but had little journalistic training. Enthusiasm and a finger on the pulse of the music scene were more important than conventional experience.

While the likes of Siouxsie Sioux had initiated the punk ethos of "getting up there and just trying to do something", I reaped the rewards further down the line, becoming "a fan with a pen". Tennis Shoes did not reap any rewards at all, and I quit singing soon after.

For a year after that first review, I lived a double life: secretary by day, rock critic by night. My company — Spotlight Publications — had no idea I was Betty Page.

They might never have known had Alan Lewis not invited me to be one of two female journalists to join the paper in June 1980 (the other was heavy metal fan Robbi Millar). After a battle of wills with the management (their argument being that allowing a secretary to become a writer would set an intolerable precedent), Alan won the day and Betty Page became a *Sounds* staff writer.

Alan was the sort of editor who could smell the Zeitgeist. At the dawn of the new decade he was well aware there were rumblings coming out of the London club scene and had his eye on Betty Page to be the writer to cover them.

Why me? Well, I had more of an appetite for pop music than many of *Sounds'* other writers but I was also a blank canvas, unsullied by the daubs of reputation or allegiance to a particular musical tribe. And it helped that I liked (somewhat saucily) dressing up rather than dressing down.

Spandau Ballet were the darlings of this new club scene and Alan was determined to secure an interview with them despite the fact that they loathed the rock press. Enter Betty, jumping through the hoops set by manager Steve Dagger.

Gary Kemp later wrote in his autobiography *I Know This Much*: "Betty Page, with her doll-like presence, became the only inky music press writer we would trust. Her *nom de plume* gave her cheekily decadent leanings away."

It is disputed, he goes on to say, but the resulting interview was "the first time I ever saw the phrase that would go on to name a youth movement. In *Sounds* that September 1980, she coined the name with the title: The New Romantics. It stuck."

That cover story — my first assignment as a full-time staffer — quickly established my reputation and I became *Sounds'* New Romantics/

Futurist correspondent, subsequently doing the first major interviews with Depeche Mode, Duran Duran, Soft Cell and many other bands that were lumped in with this "movement".

What it ultimately pointed to was a new wave of internationally successful pop music made by predominantly male artists who wore make-up, flamboyant clothes and toyed with gender stereotypes. As a teenage glam-rock fan, I felt quite at home in this world, with its frills, furs and frissons of taboo sexuality.

To me, the New Romantics represented a welcome blast of colour after the monochrome of the "Raincoat" bands (Joy Division, The Fall, Gang of Four, Echo and the Bunnymen and so on). To *Sounds*, they represented a dilemma: how to incorporate this blast of colour into a black-and-white publication?

For a couple of years, rock and pop co-existed in its pages. But the tectonic plates were shifting: new pop magazine *Smash Hits* had built up an impressive circulation and Spotlight wanted a piece of the action. Alan Lewis's answer to this was a glossy A4 colour supplement version of *Sounds* called *Noise!*

Noise! made its debut in May 1982, with Bow Wow Wow's Annabella Lwin as its front-page star. The cover lines listed no fewer than 37 artists, ranging from ABC to Bill Wyman via Iron Maiden, Mike Oldfield, Spizzenergi and Judie Tzuke.

Like *Smash Hits*, it featured song lyrics and colour posters but espoused the same cross-genre ambition as the *Sounds* mothership, covering chart-topping pop bands alongside heavy metal, punk, electronic and indie music. I initially came on board to write a column about the bands that had emerged from the New Romantic/Futurist nexus (I called it "Electrobop").

After encouraging sales of that debut issue, *Noise!* became a fortnightly fixture and I moved from *Sounds* to become features editor, although with Alan busy with *Sounds* and its heavy-metal offshoot *Kerrang!*, I was de facto editor.

It was a bold, anarchic experiment that launched a counter-strike against the emerging trend of niche marketing. *Noise!* embraced many musical tribes and created a utopian world in which both rock and pop fans were welcome.

This melting-pot philosophy worked well on *Sounds'* newsprint but seemed harder to pull off in a smaller, glossier format, with less physical space in which to cater for the different genres.

While I enjoyed the freedom to write about all of my favourite bands (as did *Sounds* writers Garry Bushell and Geoff Barton plus designer Dave Henderson and newcomer Bill Prince), advertisers were confused by the diffuse nature of the *Noise!* audience and their lack of support resulted in the publisher pulling the plug after six months.

I was heartbroken. *Noise!* had largely been my baby and I didn't feel Spotlight had given it a chance to thrive.

Then I was offered a transfer to pop weekly *Record Mirror*. Founded in 1954, it had been the first music paper to publish articles on the Beatles, the Stones, the Who and the Kinks and feature full-colour printing. However, when I joined in 1983 it had undergone an uncomfortable transition from tabloid to A4, with just a few pages printed on glossy colour stock and the remainder on black-and-white newsprint.

To a self-important former rock music journalist like me, *Record Mirror* seemed old hat and deeply uncool. But I got on well with editor Eric Fuller, who had been my reviews editor at *Sounds*. He took me on as assistant editor and I worked closely with chief sub Michael Pilgrim while — again — writing about the artists with whom I had become associated, from Marc Almond through to Ultravox.

Record Mirror had been publishing the official UK pop charts since 1956, the only publication with the rights to do so. As a consequence, the magazine's content was based around artists who had the potential of reaching the UK top 100.

Struggling to match the production values of its rivals at a time when design was as important as content, *Record Mirror* was in direct competition to the now hugely popular *Smash Hits* and newcomer *Number One*, which launched in May 1983.

Both were firmly aimed at the teenage market (which remained largely female) and unencumbered by the disc jockeys (who avidly followed veteran dance music expert James Hamilton) and chart geeks whom *Record Mirror* had long served.

By this time bands such as Spandau Ballet and Duran Duran had become established chart acts and the more successful they became, the harder it was for me to secure interviews with them. *Smash Hits* always trumped *Record Mirror* — and sometimes *Number One* did too.

Then there was the endless horse-trading with record companies — "If you do a piece about our latest signing, you might get an interview with one of our big acts!" — and deals where an interview would only be granted if the artist was featured on the cover. This slowly pushed *Record Mirror* towards covering newer, more easily accessible artists who hadn't yet troubled the charts — which made us popular with PRs but didn't always result in increased sales.

The magazine went through endless redesigns and repositionings — most notably in 1985 when Eric Fuller's successor Michael Pilgrim relaunched it as *RM* with Morrissey on the cover.

We faced a constant fight for readers and advertising revenue in an increasingly fragmented marketplace. It became clear that merely selling a magazine wasn't enough. Nearly all the weeklies were giving away cover-mounted freebies: *RM*'s included a series of interview flexidiscs and — in response to music videos becoming the new art form — an A5 magazine called *Vid*.

By the time I took over as editor in 1987, the pop boom had well and truly peaked, and hiphop and chicago house had started to inspire dance hits in Europe. Fortunately, *RM* had extensively covered both, so we were perfectly placed to capitalise on the approaching dance-music revolution while continuing to cover chart and indie pop.

With several constituencies to serve, I became engaged in a relentless juggling act. And with the coming of acid house, I could see that the music was becoming more important than the personalities making it. But there were only so many smileys you could put on the cover.

As 1989 dawned I was beginning to feel my time was up. The role of editor didn't suit my naturally collegial style and I had turned into a manager with a headache. I longed for the carefree days of being a fan with a pen that I had experienced in my early days at *Sounds*.

In the end, my body made the decision for me. I woke up one cold February morning and couldn't get out of bed. I was utterly exhausted.

After taking a month off, I decided to hand in my notice.

Two years later, I discovered that new owner EMAP had closed both *Sounds* and *Record Mirror*. The two publications to which I had dedicated so much of my life had disappeared on the same day in 1991. It was the swift and brutal end of an era.

But Betty Page would live to fight another day…

Writing as Betty Page for Sounds in the late 70s and early 80s, Beverley Glick worked on the short-lived Noise! before becoming editor of Record Mirror in the late 80s. She is very likely the inventor of the term 'New Romantics'.

Without Feeling the Need to Justify its Stance

Bob Stanley celebrates Smash Hits, the most successful UK music magazine of the 80s and 90s — and often the best

The fortnightly *Smash Hits*, which ran from 1978 to 2006, was the most successful new music magazine of its era. The late 70s were a boom time for record sales, but since the end of the 60s there hadn't been a decent publication targeted at 11-to-14-year-olds. This is the age at which pop is most captivating, when you want to learn as much as possible, and *Smash Hits* provided entry-level pop writing for music-hungry youth.

Smash Hits had its stylistic roots in the mid-60s, the last time that seven-inch single sales had reached peak levels. The monthly *Rave* and weekly *Fabulous* had been a pretty reliable *précis* of all that was hip and popular amongst teenagers. Unlike the inkies, they were aimed neither at the trade (*NME*), nor jazzers and folkies (*Melody Maker*). Instead they were read by, and largely written by, young women: future novelist Shena Mackay and pop star Twinkle's sister Dawn Ripley were at *Fabulous*, where Mackay was briefly editor. *Fabulous* took pop stars out bowling, or ice skating, and brought them together for photo shoots, as if pop was a big happy family. It was a terrific, affordable, colour accompaniment to 45s in plain company bags.

By contrast, the 70s offered slim pickings: *Music Star* was heavy on pre-teen idols like the Osmonds and wannabes like Darren Burn and Ricky Wilde; more successful was girls' mag *Jackie*, which turned to Pete Duel from *Alias Smith & Jones* as readily as it did to the stars of RAK and Bell. By the late 70s, pop fans had little beyond *Disco 45*, printed on something akin to school toilet roll, which featured nothing more than the lyrics to the hits of the day. By stealing this key selling point but printing it on glossy paper — and including full-colour posters — *Smash Hits* shut *Disco 45* down almost overnight.

Colour was an important issue, and possibly a reason why even now *Smash Hits* doesn't get the credit it's due: glossy versus inkie, pop versus rock, easy versus hard. *Record Mirror* had briefly been colour in the 60s, and would attempt it again in 1981, with eye-melting results that made you feel like you needed 3D glasses to read it, but it would be some years before print technology allowed *NME, Melody Maker* or *Sounds* to move fully away from monochrome. *Smash Hits* was full colour and high spec from the start, and very soon became the BBC of music publications — a measure of success and public awareness, a *Who's Who* despite its irreverence. It had to feature hits, acts its writers may not necessarily have liked, just as *NME, Melody Maker, Disc and Music Echo* all had until the mid-70s. It was providing a valuable public service.

It wasn't until the eras of punk and post-punk that *NME* began to feel it could dictate musical taste, the other weekly papers to some degree falling into line. Certainly by 1978, with *NME* no longer catering to those 14-year-olds as intrigued to read about Peaches & Herb or Andy Gibb as they might about XTC, *Smash Hits* was launched onto a clamouring, desperate market. *NME*'s initial shift away from Tin Pan Alley, towards a confrontational rock journalism, had primarily been Nick Logan's project when he became editor in 1973 — but the teasing relationship fostered between the paper and the stars sat more easily in his new, straight-up pop publication. Logan was the first editor at *Smash Hits*, followed by the catty Ian Cranna, and then in 1981 the furrow-browed David Hepworth. None were obvious choices for teen mag editors.

Little of this would be worth recalling if *Smash Hits* hadn't been the most invigorating new music magazine in years. Let's take a random issue, dated 6 September 1979: in an interview with cover stars The Specials, Jerry Dammers described the lift from Prince Buster's 'Al Capone' at the start of 'Gangsters' as a "musical quotation" (a pre-sampling notion which has stuck with me ever since); reviews included Joy Division's *Unknown Pleasures* ("the sound of feelings talking"), Chic's *Risque* ("so far ahead in the disco field it's just not true"), Talking Heads' *Fear Of Music* ("like an unnerving soundtrack, tinged with madness — Neil Young meets David Bowie"); and there was a fine appreciation of Eddie Cochran, written by Hepworth, and not remotely patronising,

It also felt like a safe place for girls. The inkies in the late 70s and early 80s were several shades of sexist — even hit-conscious, chart-friendly *Record Mirror* was happy to print pictures of anyone from Honey Bane to Tight Fit with captions to make you wince. *Smash Hits'* editorial stance avoided almost all of the era's sexism, knowing that it had a larger proportion of female readers than the weekly papers. Initially, it was still largely written by men, but Bev Hillier's disco column was very much a return to the uncynical breeziness of *Fabulous*, and a time before rockwriting existed. What mattered most to Bev was danceability: she wasn't blind to the lyrical banality of much of the music she was reviewing, and said that she preferred instrumentals. Her presence was benign but encouraging — in time, the magazine would foster stronger talents like Miranda Sawyer and the teenage Siân Pattenden, and the lack of the weeklies' editorial venom allowed their cheek and wit to dominate the feel of the magazine.

In effect, *Smash Hits* was anti-rockist without feeling the need, as the *NME* did, to analyse or justify its stance. Ian Cranna was one of the magazine's few writers to get bilious. Damning as he was of the amateurism of the Television Personalities and Desperate Bicycles (who nevertheless, astonishingly, merited a half-page review), he was far more hostile to the New Wave of British Heavy Metal. If any music struggled to get a fair hearing in the magazine it was heavy metal: reviewing a live album by Birmingham band Quartz, Cranna wrote, "The musical equivalent of the Flat Earth Society, heavy metal satisfies only those happy to gawp and challenge nothing."

This wasn't pretty writing — taking down the bad guys by ridiculing them — and was put into sharp relief by the good humour elsewhere. In other publications, Queen might be described as "posturing" (which carried a whiff of homophobia), "ersatz" (authenticity still being a big hang-up for many writers), and even "fascist". *Smash Hits* would never have been as openly abrasive, but by dubbing the singer 'Lord Frederick Lucan of Mercury', with one neat soubriquet they could mock the group's cold aloofness, sense of entitlement and class privilege — and Freddie's moustache. The writer behind this nickname was Tom Hibbert, a Winker Watson-lookalike who could be as cynical as the next Fleet Street writer (his books, given his talent, were all slightly disappointing), but able to channel his humour into mid-80s *Smash Hits* at a time when *NME* was riven by the hiphop wars and *Melody Maker*, just ahead of its late 80s renaissance, was unmoored and boring. Hibbert's surreal sense of humour and willingness to poke fun at "Dame" David Bowie and other untouchables was inspirational.

Today it seems strange that Paul Morley, gazing from his office across the street directly into the windows of *Smash Hits*, could see them as the *NME*'s enemy. On a fortnightly basis, in full colour, wasn't his New Pop manifesto largely being reproduced by his perceived rivals? Of course it's true that in 1985 Hepworth and Mark Ellen did leave *Smash Hits* to start another EMAP magazine that was retrograde, conservative, and the opposite of New Pop in every way — this was *Q*. By this point, Hibbert was steering *Smash Hits* into surrealistic waters ("Where's the cougar, matey?!"). This absurdism held it in good stead as pop fragmented in the 90s; it didn't shy away from significant coverage of acts like Manic Street Preachers, or nods to rave and riot grrrl. A KLF-themed quiz asked its readers "Are you an art terrorist?" A glance at an early 90s *Smash Hits* gave you a much more rounded take on pop culture than *NME* or *Melody Maker*, by this point the only music weeklies left.

There was a tendency in *NME*, and even among the sympathetic, to assume that pop didn't know what it was doing, or that its flashes of brilliance were wildly accidental. But there was nothing accidental or slapdash about *Smash Hits'* editorial sensibility. It made the Buzzcocks (no Top 10 hits, 'Ever Fallen In Love' giving them their highest chart position of 13) coverstars in 1979. The same issue featured a poster of ABBA, the words to Public Image's 'Death Disco' trailed on the cover, and (at a reader's request) to Rod Stewart's 'Sailing'. It was no accident that it treated these acts even-handedly — good humour aside, *Smash Hits'* legacy is as a leveller. It would have been no surprise at all if someone at *Smash Hits* had said that Tight Fit's 'Fantasy Island' single was better than *Led Zeppelin III*, and Paul Morley for one would have thought they were quite right.

Bob Stanley is a writer and film-maker, and a member of the pop group Saint Etienne. His book Yeah Yeah Yeah: The Story of Modern Pop is published by Faber & Faber.

On Being the Other Ian Penman...

Ian Ravendale talks about radio, Sounds, covering the North East scene and inventing Death Metal

You didn't have to be an intellectual to read *Sounds*. Or know about the nuts and bolts of music. Founded by a group of journalists who'd broken away from *Melody Maker*, with Billy Walker as editor, *Sounds* was first published in 1970. Alan Lewis became editor in 1975, and by the late 70s, as the first weekly to respond wholeheartedly to UK punk, it had established itself as the rock and street-level music weekly open to everyone. In effect — thanks partly to designer Dave Fudger — a fanzine with better printing and production, as well as, importantly, access to the stars of the day.

It was more down-to-earth than the *NME*, which found its post-punk niche via the arty ramblings of Paul Morley and the Ian Penman who isn't me. *Melody Maker* was still generally considered the musos' paper: it had an older, more serious audience, many of whom were in bands — or felt that they should have been — and lengthy articles about new mainstream stars like Elvis Costello and the Police rubbed shoulders with features on whammy bars and truck hire. *Record Mirror* — whose audience were mostly the 10-14-year-old age group — catered to the poppier end of the market. The other music weeklies were staffed by journalists who were the same age as their readership, and fans of the type of music they were writing about. But this wasn't entirely the case at *Sounds*.

Phil Sutcliffe was the paper's North East correspondent but moved to London in early 1979. Phil and I had worked together since 1975 on BBC Radio Newcastle's *Bedrock* programme, where I'd reviewed gigs and albums and interviewed literally hundreds of national and local musicians, and he suggested to *Sounds'* deputy editor Geoff Barton that I'd make a suitable replacement. We'd both also written for *Out Now*, a Newcastle-based music fanzine, so Phil knew I was up to it. I'd recently left the security of a full-time job to make it in media and his recommendation was greatly appreciated.

My writing career had started in the early 1970s with articles about comic books for fanzines. I was an avid reader of music mags like *ZigZag*, *Let It Rock, Disc* and *NME* and had actually written for a national music paper before *Sounds*. Just. The band Lindisfarne were reforming with their original line-up for what was meant to be a one-off gig on 23 December 1976 at Newcastle City Hall, the band's "home" venue. This sold out in about ten seconds, and two further shows were added. As Lindisfarne had been a chart band, I contacted *Record Mirror*, who said they'd take my review. The *NME* version of Ian Penman was yet to surface, and I was able to use my own name — as I had with *Out Now* and BBC Radio Newcastle. My relationship with *Record Mirror* started and ended with that review. I forget why — probably because they weren't too bothered about regional coverage at that point.

Come 1979 the *NME* had their very own Ian Penman, so I needed a new name. It was the tail end of punk, with Vicious, Idol and Rotten in the charts, so I toyed with 'Ian Neon' for a while. But in the end I went for 'Ian Ravendale' which I got from East Ravendale, a small village just outside of Grimsby where two of my oldest friends lived.

My first job for *Sounds* was a review of a Newcastle gig by the Tom Robinson Band, in the 7 April 1979 edition. Geoff Barton liked it, and I was off and running. *Bedrock* featured a weekly gig guide and I kept a diary of upcoming shows. I'd ring Geoff every week, go through what was happening in Tyne, Wear and Teesside, and he'd chose which gigs he wanted me to review — generally two or three. Unlike most of the other music papers *Sounds* was interested in local talent as well as the big names.

I was *Sounds'* ear to the ground in the North East, as Phil Sutcliffe had been before me. He wrote the first national articles about Penetration and the Angelic Upstarts, and I carried this tradition on, with the result that *Sounds* featured more North East bands on a regular basis than all the other weekly music papers put together. I went as far as Redcar, with 'Des Moines' (real name Nigel Burnham) handling Yorkshire and Mick Middles reporting in from Manchester and the North West.

I broke the news of Penetration's split, scooping the *NME* who'd been promised an exclusive and sent Paul Morley up to the Newcastle City Hall home gig where the band were going to announce the break-up from the stage. By virtue of our Wednesday publication — the day before the *NME*'s Thursday — we got the story out first.

Sounds was a weekly with a quick turnaround. Deadlines were tight and a big news story (such as the Penetration break-up) or an important review often had to be rung in and dictated to *Sounds* secretary Beverley Glick, who took copy quickly and accurately (see p.275 for Glick's story).

After a month or so working for *Sounds* I contacted *Pop Star Weekly*, a short-lived music paper (24 March — 23 June 1979) that was soon absorbed into *Record Mirror*. As Alan Lewis didn't like his journalists to be seen writing for other papers, I became 'Rick O' Shea' for the dozen or so reviews and articles I wrote for *Pop Star Weekly* that included reviewing disco bands like Gonzalez and Hi Tension and interviewing Child, the latest teenybop contenders. I'm pretty sure I wasn't the only one moonlighting from another weekly. I never did find out who 'Gay Abandon' was.

Geoff Barton was very good to work with. He was a graduate from journalism college and a big music fan, particularly rock. Despite its readership containing a very big contingent of metal addicts, most *Sounds* journalists weren't really rock fans, including me. As on the *Bedrock* programme — where some of my colleagues would only review or interview bands they liked — I was happy to write about any sort of music. Consequently Geoff often sent me along to review heavy metal bands.

The irreverent approach I developed was soon unleashed on the major bands who took themselves a bit too seriously. "Why is Ozzy Osbourne so cabaret?" I asked. Ian Gillan's stage act was "shaking his hair round his head, playing inaudible bongos, giving fist salutes and going 'Argghhh' for extended periods." I'd had my photo in *Sounds* a couple of times, generally in interview mode next to a band. Fortunately this wasn't often enough to be recognised by Ozzy when I later stumbled into the backstage area at Newcastle Mayfair. Or by Gillan at the hospitality area of the Loch Lomond Festival (which was a tent in a field). After I'd suggested that in a couple of years Saxon would be back in the Yorkshire Working Mens' Clubs from whence they'd come, lead vocalist Biff Byford was "looking for Ian Ravendale" — or so my mates in the Tygers Of Pan Tang told me at a gig both bands were playing. Fortunately Biff hadn't seen my photo and didn't find me. Saxon never (to my knowledge) returned to the clubs so we were even.

In 1979, as the other music papers by-and-large ignored ground-level rock, Alan Lewis had come up with the idea that these metal bands were actually a movement, rather than just a bunch of young bands (or not so young, in Saxon's case) who'd chosen rock, rather than punk or ska, or anything fashionable. Alan called this the 'New Wave of British Heavy Metal' — which instantly clicked with both bands and readers, some of whom had gotten a tad tired of the amount of coverage punk was getting. Geoff Barton then ran with it. He'd written about his trip to Sheffield to see the teenage Def Leppard and soon had me on the case in the North East, reviewing and then producing articles about Leppard's Geordie counterparts.

The North East had always been a stronghold for rock and heavy metal, so I was letting the rest of the country know about the Tygers of Pan Tang, Raven, Fist, Mythra, Venom and more. Wallsend's Neat Records had issued a couple of unsuccessful pop records and was going nowhere until label boss Dave Wood (who also owned Impulse recording studio) saw the Tygers, signed them and put out a quickly recorded EP. Jump-started by my *Sounds* articles, the record was on the radio, being written about and the band chased by major labels, eventually signing with MCA.

I wasn't just writing about HM bands. During my three-and-a-half years at *Sounds* I reviewed pretty much all of the North East outfits that I thought were any good, including White Heat, the 45's, It Hz, Deep Freeze and the Toy Dolls. Not forgetting the bizarre self-promotion machine that was (and still is) Wavis O'Shave. This promotion of local talent fitted in with the ethos we had on *Bedrock*, and I was happy to go with it. If I liked a band or thought a national audience would be interested and I could be positive, I'd write about them. If I couldn't, I wouldn't, figuring that writing something negative in a big-circulation music paper would do a struggling band major damage.

Sounds journalists were given a lot of creative freedom. For the heck of it I decided to write my 1980 review of a gig by North East singer-songwriter John Miles in cod Geordie, as a letter to him from an imaginary uncle. "'Ere why canny lad. Just thought I'd drop yer a line to let yer know what me and our Dotty thought of yer show," it started. I was half expecting Geoff to reject it but he didn't. Several years later I booked Miles onto a TV show I was working on. He didn't seem to twig on that 'TV researcher Ian Penman' was also 'Uncle Ian Ravendale.' One of the advantages of writing under a pseudonym.

Another review got me quoted on a number one record. After years playing every dive and punk club in the UK, Adam and the Ants had just broken big and were doing their first ever concert hall tour, kicking off on 23 March 1981 at Newcastle City Hall. As part of my review I wrote: "He's got the moves, they've got the grooves." Six months later 'Ant Rap' came out: "*I've got the moves, they've got the grooves*," sang the Dandy Highwayman. To this day I wonder if two lines qualify me for a co-write credit.

Geoff Barton moved across from *Sounds* to edit *Kerrang!*, the UK's first magazine exclusively devoted to rock, and I wrote the first full length articles about Raven and Venom for #3 in 1981. Yes, I'm responsible for Death Metal. *Sounds* continued to have a large rock and metal readership which stayed with the paper until it folded in 1991, but it wasn't quite the same for me after Geoff left and I stopped writing for it in September

1982, when I joined Tyne Tees Television. After a 30 year gap I'm back writing for music magazines like *Classic Pop, Vive Le Rock, American Songwriter, Iron Fist, Classic Rock, Record Collector* and more. And still waiting for the cheque for 'Ant Rap' to thud through my letterbox.

Under his real name of Ian Penman, Ian Ravendale worked for local and national BBC radio in the 70s. He then wrote for Sounds, Kerrang!, Pop Star Weekly and the local press in the 80s, before moving into television.

...AND ITS DISCONTENTS

"When punk happened, I was quite sharp and thought, 'Ah, this is my exit out.' My exit out of a world that I just could not imagine escaping"

— *Liz Naylor*

Did Punk Affirm the Underground's Values – or Challenge Them?

Liz Naylor: *co-editor Manchester's City Fun, writer, promoter, publicist, DJ, label boss*

Edwin Pouncey: *cartoonist at Sounds, Forced Exposure, The Wire; musician and writer*

Nigel Fountain: *L'Idiot International, Oz, Street Life, Let It Rock, co-editor City Limits with John Fordham, historian of the underground press*

Panel chaired by **Adam Gearey**, *professor of law at Birkbeck*

AG: To get things rolling, I'm going to link one of the themes concerning people yesterday through to the experiences of our panellists today: is the personal political, the notion that one's engagement with politics comes out of one's life experiences? And I'll hand over to the panel, to say what their personal trajectories are, or were.

LN: I was about 15 when punk happened. Prior to that, I felt absolutely trapped. I live in Hyde in Manchester. Which happens to be the murder capital of the Western world, given that it gave birth to the Moors Murderers *and* Harold Shipman. It's a really small place, so that's quite impressive.

And I was kind of stuck in this house with my mum. Val [Wilmer] this morning was talking about being on the fringes of a sort of communist or Marxist youth movement. That was my *dream*. But I wasn't, I was stuck in this world that felt very airless, and I had no access to culture. Nobody from our family had ever been to university, you know. I was very stuck. And I knew I needed to escape but I didn't know how.

And somehow when I was quite young, of my own craving for something, I'd discovered hippie music, I don't really know how. So I used to sit in my bedroom and listen to Jefferson Airplane. And it felt like a huge distance from me. I used to think, "How will I move to San Francisco, they're all dead, you know, how will I connect with something?"

So when punk happened, I was quite sharp and thought, "Ah, this is my exit out." My exit out of a world that I just could not imagine escaping. Then from the age of 16 onwards, I became involved in bits of the music industry and writing — putting out records, being involved with stuff, running a fanzine. But it's all been about my kind of inventing myself — me, me, me! — because I felt like I had nothing, no form of escape, no form of expression, so it was very much about that.

EP: When punk happened, I'd moved to London, I'd got a place at the Royal College of Art. And our halls of residence were right opposite the King's Road. This was about 1976, when punk really started happening. And the Sex Pistols were on at the 100 Club every Tuesday or Thursday, I can't remember which. We used to go down there and see them and everything.

Liz said she listened to a lot of hippie music, well, so did I, and I had the same dreams of going to San Francisco and wondering how wonderful it all was. But in Leeds, you were stuck in this horrible industrial backwoods-type place that was still living in the 1950s. So you only got glimmers of what living in London at that time must have been like. I'm sure it was a fantasy as well, I'm sure it wasn't all it was made up to be in reality.

But hitting London at that time, it was like having a second chance to become involved in a movement that was just taking over everything and firing your imagination up. I was pretty apolitical. I didn't really think about politics, I was just enthralled with the music, the look of it, the ideas that were going on. And I was interpreting these into the art I was doing at the Royal College of Art. I formed a band with some fellow students, and people outside the art college, called the Art Attacks. And we performed at the Royal College of Art. A riot broke out, typically. And we went from there. We decided, well, why don't we go and do this as a performance piece round the country? So we got on a bus and went and did that.

Anyway, it eventually all fell apart and I decided that the idea of being in a so-called punk rock band — although I denied it was a punk rock band — wouldn't work, and I decided to just go for my degree instead, which was probably the best idea really. They all hated us anyway.

So that's how I came into that scene. I used to go and see Crass, I thought that's what punk should be, Crass. All this farting about and pantomime dolling around and blah blah blah, and spitting and rubbish like that, that wasn't getting anywhere.

But Crass really nailed it. Crass really knew what they wanted. They wanted to overthrow stuff and they had really strong ideas. They had really strong symbols, they had really strong art. And it really hit you in the head and people were going, "Hang on a minute, wow, that's serious." But I could never be politically like that, I could never think as politically fierce as that really because it's just not in my nature. But they had it nailed and it was really good. And I still admire them to this day.

NF: As I cast my mind back, I find that the 70s was when I seemed to attend political meetings where people spent a lot of time apologising for who they were. And I would like to reassert this tradition this morning, inasmuch as my experience of music writing and music journalism was actually as an outsider. I didn't set out to be a music journalist and I was very rarely a music journalist. With the possible exception on *Street Life*, where I managed to predict that ABBA's 'Mamma Mia' was going to be a flop, which didn't prove to be the most accurate assessment.

I came into journalism in the late 60s. And my journalism, all the way through, on the magazines that I worked for then and later, was to try and produce a popular magazine which could pack some kind of radical punch. And by that I mean a left-wing punch, which has not always been easy — and has also produced acres of some very boring journalism on occasions.

I noticed once, when reading *1984*, that I am Winston Smith. Not in a melodramatic fashion — but I am the same age as Winston Smith. I grew up in that post-war world. So by the time that punk came along, I was already past it.

Now to explain why I was past it, I'd like to say a little bit more about the past. I am in many ways the classic kid of the post-war period. Well, not altogether typical because I went to a grammar school, which immediately marks me out as different to a large chunk of the rest of the population. But having decided by the age 14 that I wanted to be a journalist, when I left university in the mid/late 60s, there was a magazine called *New Society*, which I mourn to this day. Because it was one of the few quote "mainstream" unquote magazines which gave you the opportunity to write more or less about anything. I wrote about things like the National Front and the Monday Club, which was a right-wing organisation of that time. And I was also commissioned to write a feature about the Crazy World of Arthur Brown, who were considered — for about a week — wildly subversive. And I actually wrote about teen culture, but once again, not from within the teen culture. I was always the observer. At that time, I was a fairly pompous 22-year-old or whatever.

Now the other thing which obsessed me then, was indeed politics, which was my focus. And by the late 60s, I was a Trot. And I began working in the early 70s for a magazine called *Socialist Worker*, which some of you may have heard of. Before that, I was working for a magazine called *Idiot International*, the non-sectarian paper of the revolutionary left. Now I'll say this as an aside, which I always found rather funny — and as you may have noticed, I haven't got to punk yet — in order to try and make anyone buy *Idiot International*, which proved very difficult, particularly as the distributor was stacking all the copies in a warehouse in Old Street, we set up a section which was going to deal with rock. We were going to try and mix politics and rock in that format. This did not work.

But what friends of mine and I were doing was indeed trying to make some kind of combination between popular music and politics. And foremost in these activities — which is where we get a little closer to punk – was a dear friend of mine, now deceased, called David Widgery. In himself David was the link between the West London underground scene and more of an East London Trot scene, as a consequence of which various links were made. David was interested in those connections. In things like Allen Ginsberg and so on. Which meant when punk arrived, David picked up on it very rapidly.

In preparation for today, I looked at a piece I wrote in 1973. I noticed when I was here yesterday that the subject of the Pink Fairies will not go away. People seem to have experienced or suffered — however you wish to put it — the Pink Fairies over the years. I had actually blotted it out of my mind, but I found I had written this article, about the Pink Fairies and Hawkwind playing at the Empire Pool Wembley. And as I read it, all my horror of awful memories of this early 70s kind of period came washing back over me. You know, these endless bloody hobbits and psychedelic portraits of women with no clothes on.

And all this, coupled with this kind of psychedelic copy being generated, and all these dreadful albums, you know the stuff, *King Arthur and the Knights of the Round Table*, all the stuff covered perfectly by *Spinal Tap*. This kind of desolation was around at the time when I went to work on *Street Life*, which was supposed — as several people reminded me this morning — to be the British *Rolling Stone*.

Now *Street Life* was financed by Chris Blackwell. I *think*. One piece of investigative journalism none of us ever carried out was to find out exactly who had put the money up, but we did initially have a lot of money. And we produced this magazine, which was trying to deal with things like Magma. I don't know if any of you remember Magma. Fortunately, I have actually completely forgotten them other than the name. But the effect of all this stuff was that people were indeed writing more and more ponderous articles about more and more ponderous bands, as I saw them. And it was pretty tedious.

And what fascinates me about *Street Life* — which I managed to disinter from a very dusty cupboard this morning — was that the one subject *Street Life* did not address itself to was indeed punk. We were too old, we didn't get it. And anyway it was only just breaking at the point when Chris Blackwell pulled the money and *Street Life* went down the tubes.

But in the political world of the early 70s which was — well, I was going to say it was pretty dreadful but I wouldn't say the political world at the moment has turned out too well — but in that world, where the National Front were actually prospering and there was a hell of a lot of racism, and when the black and ethnic communities had not organised or got established, although they'd been here forever, it was a pretty febrile political atmosphere.

And this was the point where David Widgery embraced the idea that you could politicise — or a fairer way of putting it may be intrude into — the kind of new movements which were growing up. And that included punk. And crucially, of course, it involved speeches, no, not speeches, utterances made by Rod Stewart, David Bowie and Eric Clapton. I mean, I'm fascinated by the way that Clapton has airbrushed all this stuff out, actually. Clapton was making rambling addresses on Enoch Powell being right, and so on.

All this meant that, from my point of view, observing the rise of punk for me meant observing the rise of things like Rock Against Racism and the Anti-Nazi League — which was a manifestation of the political strand through which I had observed politics in my case from the 50s onwards.

AG: We're talking, politically or culturally, about the short decade from about 1968 to 1977, from the context of the underground press to punk. And you were all talking about different ways in which cultural resources present themselves to you in a particular time, a particular place. And Liz said about self-reinvention. You were saying before the panel that you saw the Fall in Droylsden, and that opened up your mind and it took you towards journalism. I was wondering if I can push you a bit on perhaps these specific encounters with specific bands or specific books which took you in the directions that your life took. I remember reading on your website, Edwin, that you come across a bundle of comics?

EP: Well, discovering underground comics was a real enormous influence on me, being interested in art. And also the Mothers of Invention, as a band, and Captain Beefheart, things like that. This kind of 'freak universe' that was out there, it was just so outside anything that most people would describe as being normal. I suppose the English equivalent would be like the Bonzo Dog Band. This is the 60s I'm talking about now.

So in a way, I wanted to transplant that kind of energy, which sort of illuminated my imagination, through into what I was seeing in the punk rock years. And I did that by drawing a comic strip called *Rock and Roll Zoo*, that was subsequently published in *Sounds* for most of that time. And that was like an underground comic, except in a corporately published rock paper. And it was like a weekly comment on what was happening in punk rock at the time. So yes, I suppose finding that batch of underground comics was eventually my main kicking-off point. It's what made me want to be a cartoonist.

AG: Is it true to say that the Fall at Droylsden Town Hall was that moment for you, Liz, or am I romanticising it?

LN: You're romanticising it. OK. This idea of inventing yourself, I think that makes it sound quite benign. Me and Edwin were talking about this before we came on. And I was interested that Nigel talked about being a post-war child. Because I grew up in a very traumatised household. So I often think, "What is it that drove me to go out on my own and find this kind of culture?" Because I literally did hit the streets of Manchester and found a book shop called Grassroots and bought a magazine called *Mole Express*, which was a well-known underground magazine.

I think, "What is it in me that sought that?" And I think it's just trauma. You know, I grew up in a house where people were quite shut down, to put it mildly, and everybody I went to school with read *Jackie* and liked *Starsky and Hutch*, you know, that was my era. It wasn't that I was particularly creative. I was quite desperate and I encountered culture in quite a random way — and in my desperation, took from it what I could.

And, you know, I was also a gay teenager stuck in my bedroom, and my otherness and weirdness, I needed to make sense of that. And *Mole Express* was like a sort of fanzine. How would you describe it, Nigel, *Mole Express*, did you ever come across it?

NF: Yeah, I did. It gets closer into the realm of London's *City Limits*, which I was involved with, which broke from *Time Out* [in 1981]. And there was this cluster of magazines [like *Mole Express*, which first appeared in 1970], which predated *City Limits*, a cluster of magazines that proved there was another bloody world out there. I'd make a general point about all the magazines I've ever worked on which were in any way dissident, the whole theory was, you proved to people sitting alone in your bedroom and all over the country who wished to overthrow the state by various means, none of which unfortunately worked... You know, it's the function of the media to prove to people that they're not alone, that there are other people who think like them. And that was true when I was reading the *NME* back in 1962.

LN: I loved *City Limits* because it was about books. I didn't know anything about books or films because that wasn't my kind of upbringing, and that was a way of me finding out about culture that I was interested in. Or I don't know if I was interested in, I just knew it was important. And I kind of suspect that if this was now, I would just be in my bedroom on the internet. [But this having to hunt for culture] literally forced me out of the house, physically.

And then my first ever punk gig was the Fall at Droylsden Town Hall. It was 50 pence, and I met somebody there who was selling a fanzine and I went, "Oh, I'll write for your fanzine." And that was my in. And I made sure I wrote for the fanzine, and then I took over the fanzine. So, you know, I was quite sort of aggressive about having *to get out there* and *connect with freaks* because I knew I'd die if I didn't. A bit melodramatic, but that's how it felt. I really did need to get out there and meet people.

And at the time, around punk, the music press wasn't that interesting actually. At the time, the music press was writing about music, and it was a way of finding information about music. I think post-punk the music press becomes more interesting, because people are bringing in different strands of culture. And it was *highly* pretentious, but it was a much more interesting music press post-punk rather than punk.

AG: One of the questions from the floor yesterday was about punk as ground zero, it obliterates everything that has gone before it and it recreates the future. But listening now there's this sense — you were saying you started off listening to Jefferson Airplane, Captain Beefheart.

EP: Well, those bands were the foundations for what punk became. Though people wouldn't really admit it. But what they were doing was radical, records like *Volunteers* or something. That really is a get-up-and-shout-it-out-loud we're-not-taking-it-anymore thing.

LN: How punk is Grace Slick, you know?

EP: How punk is Grace Slick? Well, to many not very. But to me, she was kind of a punk icon really.

LN: She's still punk. She's kind of fat and does really terrible art, and I think that's really punk. She's very unapologetic about her horrible art, and she sits there going, "Well, I do art." And she's great.

EP: They didn't really cut much mustard with hardcore punks. When I was in the Art Attacks, people used to come up to me and say, "What bands do you like?" And I'd say, "Well, actually I'm really into Todd Rundgren and I like the Beach Boys, and Jefferson Airplane. The Beach Boys' later stuff, obviously, from *Sunflower, 2020* type stuff." And they'd say, "You takin' the piss, mate?" And start having a real go because they just couldn't understand it. They hadn't heard that music. It was like, "Oh, they're obviously trying to take the piss out of us, they're trying to be stupid or clever, or something like that."

But what they didn't really realise was that is where the roots were of the music they were championing — though they were basically just a load of stupid media-driven puppets, who were going for the fashion angle, in my opinion, and trying to be outrageous, maaaan, and all this stuff. They'd really swallowed this whole fishhook of idiotic media garbage about punk rock and were acting it out on the street.

But to go back to my original point. Without those early influences, you know, the punk rock thing probably wouldn't have happened. And more importantly, the post-punk thing would never have happened. And I think what we were saying was that the post-punk thing was even more interesting than the actual punk thing. The punk thing laid down another set of foundations for the post-punk thing to come along. And then that's when things really started to get interesting, in my opinion.

AG: It's almost as if as soon as punk becomes a set of rehearsed moves, then it's not what it is, it wants to move on, it wants to create the next thing. That's authentically what it is. But your example earlier on of Crass, they were massively politically engaged against that kind of nihilism of punk.

EP: You see, naïvely, I keep thinking that people ask me these questions because they're interested in music, but they're not really. Like everybody else, they just want a statement to write in their little fanzine, so it makes them look cool — "oh, yeah, I'm really into Sham 69" or something, when I'm not. I can't stand Sham 69. Nice bloke, you know, Jimmy Pursey, really good bloke, but I'm definitely not going home to my teenage bedroom and putting Sham 69 on. I'm putting on, I don't know, *Blows Against the Empire* or something.

AG: Nigel mentioned [David Widgery] from an earlier period, who's working between the East London Trots and the West London music scene. Two energies that meet but are arguably quite disparate. And if you go back further, to what's happening in the States around the SDS, you have this same problem — how to bring together two subcultures that are key players? Did it all fail, all the dreams at that period dreamt by different people in different places, about the coming together of the energies of music and forms of left politics? The world didn't change, we didn't smash the state. Are we looking back on this? Are we critical about that legacy? And what bits can we appropriate? What can a present generation learn from these cultural experiences, these political experiences? Whether or not we want to fetishise punk — and I'm sensing that we don't — what do we carry forward? What are the positive legacies of this period, do you think?

NF: I think that's a bit of a "meaning-of-life" question, because it never stops. There's never a point where you can say, well, we've now achieved X, Y and Z. I mean, as I made clear, I can't talk about punk in particular because I never really followed it closely enough.

At the beginning of the 80s, I was on *Time Out*, and having cycled past Blitz [*meaning the club — ed*] on numerous occasions, one of the first things I did was commission a vastly expensive feature about the New Romantics. My thinking was, "What are we going to put in the paper next week, punk out of the window, New Romantics next"— this is what you do [*at a weekly*], bang it out, there's the cover. I'm aware that wasn't the way it was, and that you know, punk was growing, changing. But that whole series of progressive attitudes grow up over a period of the last 50 years. The only gay MPs in 1955 were being arrested in a bush in Hyde

Park, that's how it was. You now have people who are out, you have that whole change in attitudes.

I just want to put it in somewhere in the mix. About 20 years ago, I interviewed Abbie Hoffman, the great American radical of the 60s who I think most of you will be familiar with — who in some ways you could say anticipated punk, in the sense of his ability to create total outrage. And he was an extremely fascinating and intelligent guy. When I interviewed him, he said this, which was about the 60s: "We were right, God damn it, we may not have done much fact-checking but what we wrote turned out to be right in the big things. We fought apartheid in the south, we fought against the war, and we were right and we won." This to me is an example of someone who's a political activist who used the most wonderful techniques — such as arriving at the House Un-American Activities Committee dressed in American revolutionary uniform and blew away a whole series of conventions and attitudes.

And that was really important. As it was in the 70s. People like Burchill and Parsons accused the International Socialists and so on of trying to hijack punk — which is I think absolutely true. And you know, it *worked*. It actually did work very well at that time. So you win things, you win sometimes, you lose sometimes.

AG: I know you've written about the 'Dialectics of Liberation' Congress at the Roundhouse. Could I ask you about these switching sites between different forms of cultures? How significant was this event, given the stellar line-up of radicals, musicians, poets…

NF: If you ever see the film, it a great opportunity to see how straight people's haircuts were. That was 1967, at the Roundhouse. The role of the Roundhouse throughout that period is interesting, in London terms anyway — a place where a whole series of things were worked out, in terms of the launch of *International Times* in 66, The 'Dialectics of Liberation' in 67. There *was* an atmosphere around that you could explore new ideas, that certain old orthodoxies had broken down.

In terms of that conference, to be absolutely honest, the one line that I remember — it was widely quoted, and raised all sorts of bloody awkward questions — was when someone asked the black American revolutionary Stokely Carmichael what the role of woman in this struggle is, and he replied, "Prone." This created considerable stir in all sorts of ways. This was around the time the Woman's Movement was coming into existence, so it raised questions about male attitudes, and so on and so forth, and had a long lasting impact. The Woman's Movement in Britain grew within two years of that. Not, I hasten to add, as a result of Carmichael's observation. But people wanted to go to those kind of things, they wanted to explore new ideas. There was also the Anti-University. And The Arts Lab in Drury Lane, which I did actually go to. That to me was more important.

To use a pompous word, there was *praxis* in that period, and a will to change. And of course it does go on into the 70s, and into punk, which, as David Widgery wrote once — I'm sorry I'm quoting him so much but he was effectively my connection with punk — punk was the revenge of the hippies. David was wrong because it was much younger than that, but he was right in another way. Which brings out the idea that the hippies were a bunch of peace-loving, bell-ringing dope-smokers, which actually was very often the case. Although I'm not too sure they were good on the peace bit.

AG: This links with something that Liz said a second ago, about trauma and therapy within the culture. Perhaps the revolutionary ideas respond to a deep sense of socioeconomic trauma, which obviously plays itself out at an individual psychic level. And there's links to the anti-psychiatry movement as well. I'm wondering if that resonates with this idea of culture as a therapy, against loneliness.

LN: I think it's remarkable how close the Second World War was to the 1970s.

EP: Yes, I always keep thinking this, and how weird it was.

LN: Because I consider the 1990s like yesterday, but I work with people who weren't born then, and consider them a very long time ago. We grew up in an era where the Second World War wasn't very long previously. My mother still behaves to this day like the Second World War is still on.

EP: I was born in 1951, so about six years afterwards. Six years is nothing. I think it must have been so weird for our parents as well, to see their children grow up and then rebel against them ten years later. And they went, "But we've saved the world and you don't want it! What? What are you doing?"

LN: Rebellion is a form of acting out, isn't it? It's emotional acting out. I think for me, the interesting thing about punk and post-punk is it's a time of confusion, and there's almost quite an androgynous movement. It wasn't very blokey. And I don't know whether that was to do with the amount of speed that people were taking. But, you know, it's very unsexual — and then it all settles back down into normal sort of boy stuff.

EP: But to carry on this thing I've just said, "We've saved the world and you don't want it." Then punk comes along and all the people who created progressive rock are like "But we've changed music and you don't want it, you want to destroy it!" It's almost reflecting that same scenario, isn't it? Like crash and burn again, you know — let's do it again, let's just rip it up again, start again, keep ripping things up.

LN: I think one of the sadnesses is that that doesn't seem to particularly exist now, that sort of desire. I don't know. Or maybe it's too fragmented, maybe I don't understand where it exists, that desire to reinvent, to rip it up. It must be continuing somewhere, in little pockets.

EP: All I knew was that I was alone. I was alone in Leeds. I'd have *Trout Mask Replica* on and I'd try and drag friends up there to listen to it. And they'd sit there and listen to a side of it, and go, "Well, I'd better go home and have my tea now." So it was just really, really like you were just *alone*, you know.

LN: We're not coming out of this too well, are we? Like really sad, lonely people!

EP: Sad, lonely, pathetic people. Freaks. But I didn't have any other freaks I could relate to, you know what I mean, they were all just like totally straight and going off to university. Boring really. So it seemed like punk did give access to a lot of freak-dom. You did meet a lot of it.

LN: Or maybe they were just more functional than us, Edwin, rather than boring. Maybe it's about functionality, about being more able to be in the world. So to get back to my idea about trauma, there were people trying to work out something because they're not able to be in the world.

EP: Working out who you are, your own identity, that's it, that was basically what it was, that was the main part of it: who am I? What am I? What can I do?

LN: Can I just hijack this a bit? This was my experience — first I was a kind of punk, a sort of post-punky person, I ran a fanzine and then started writing for the music press. And then I became a publicist. I wasn't very good at it, but nevertheless I worked for several labels doing PR. And my experience of the music press — if we're talking *NME*, *Sounds*, *Melody Maker*, *City Limits*, *Time Out* — is that in the post-punk era it was very interesting and people were quite open. But it very soon settled into a cynical kind of Luke Haines-y type boys club run by people that were quite acerbic. It was quite difficult as a woman to go into the office of the *NME* and run this gauntlet of angry young men. And so Brit Pop was perfect for a time that had settled into a sort of blokey normality.

And that was the moment that I got very involved with riot grrrl. And in a way it was quite a painful experience trying to release riot grrrl records and deal with the really laddy music press. They were quite unpleasant. I had quite nasty personal run-ins with Steve Sutherland at the *NME* — who I'll gladly name as a complete cunt.

EP: I'll second that.

LN: So it really felt like a kind of collision again. Riot grrrl was a return to knowing we needed to change how culture, how music is written about. What goes on and how it's represented.

AG: One of the things that seemed to animate the underground as a culture or as a stylistic force was precisely this question: *how now do we write about music?* Given this culture, given this excitement, how do we change how we represent, how we write, take pictures, draw, what have you. In terms of your own engagement as musicians or artists or writers, or even your style of life. Obviously we're talking about quite a span of time...

LN: One of the Year Zeroes is *Mojo* magazine. So the sort of *Mojo*-isation of music where people actually write about music — which is a bit kind of juggling for radio, isn't it? To me, it's really *boring* reading about music. It's capital-C Culture, it's the Other. We started off talking about those strands of culture where the press was talking about books, music, influences. But at *Mojo* is it's kind of: *We're going to talk you through how the* *album was made.* And I guess if you're a musician, that's interesting, but I think it also sets up this thing where people who read it then aspire to be musicians. Which to me is a very pre-punk position of power — like, *oh, if only I could be Rick Wakeman.* But I can't.

AG: It's about modernism, isn't it? This idea of not being nostalgic, breaking it up, making it new. And the resistance seems to be to a nostalgic recycling industry: the box set, the complete-ist industry.

EP: Because there's nothing there. All the notes have been played, all the songs have been played, it's just all been regurgitated. It's like *World at War* being on a loop all the time, isn't it, really? You turn the TV on, and here's all the swastikas coming at you again in black-and-white, and Normandy, and everything like this. And you're going, oh, this again?! But everything that was really great and all the new ideas have seemingly just been done. All you've got left is Simon Cowell and all this other horrible stuff.

LN: I don't think Simon Cowell's the problem, I think it's Alan McGee. It's not Cowell, it's the rock industry.

EP: Jools Holland rules the blooming TV airwaves, we have to sit and listen to these parades of dreary boring awful 21st century music. Paul Weller's got a new album out. Wow. Hold the front page.

LN: We're like those two blokes on *The Muppets*, aren't we?

AG: To go back to what you said, Edwin, about we saved the world and you don't want it, that generational thing, in this political or cultural temporality, this timeframe that we've got here, it makes me interested in your views about the welfare state, and about your experiences of higher education.

And I'd like to bring Nigel in on this as well, because this theme of going to university — either as a positive or as a negative experience — has been one of the things being talking about. Thinking as a Mancunian myself, and the flats in Hulme where New Order lived, where Johnny Marr lived; everybody lived there, on the dole. It was more or less a rock and roll university, and all this of cultural energy was possible because at that point, you could get housing benefit, you could live on the dole in these rundown inner city places. When the history of our times is written, there's this contribution of the welfare state to punk, post-punk, to everything we're talking about. Not that I'm saying living on the dole was particularly, you know...

So my question, about cultural experiences and education — while you were experimenting, as an artist, as a journalist, as a writer, what have you, what were the networks that sustained you emotionally, physically and financially?

EP: Well, when I was at art school, I had a grant. You don't have those any more. I mean, I was very, very lucky, I was in the right period. Before that, I'd worked, I'd had a regular job in Leeds working in a department store. And I'd worked there for about four, five years before I decided to leave Leeds and go off on my own to live in Colchester, Essex, first where I got into the art college there, and then when I got a place in the Royal College of Art, I moved to London.

And there, I was lucky enough to get halls of residence. So I didn't really live in appalling poverty or squats or anything, but I knew a lot of people who did. The band we started, they all lived in squats and everything in Brixton. But I wouldn't say they were appallingly bad, falling down, terrible, unsanitary or anything. They were lovely, you know, great, just like regular houses that had just been left abandoned, and people had moved in and made them their homes.

So you were aware of it all the time. It didn't affect me, I didn't go on the dole really. Well, I did when term broke in the summer and then you had sort of a big holiday on the dole. You looked for work and you got a job or signed on. But in a way I was very lucky, I was cosseted from all that. So I'm not the best example to ask about it.

AG: Liz, does this spark anything, or am I romanticising?

LN: I did a Master's degree which I wrote exactly about this, and half of an aborted PhD. Owen Hatherley's written a lot about it, too. I do think a more interesting line of enquiry when we write the history of culture is to take into account things such as physical space — and the cost of physical space per square foot. And, you know, it's very relevant to what's happened to London at the moment. Nick Cohen called it Monaco without the sun. And we ought to be looking beyond London for what will be culturally happening in the rest of the UK. It's not going to be happening in London, is it? Because nobody can afford to live here.

And I lived in Hulme, you know, and nobody ever paid. There's a really great book called *Manchester Slingback* by Nicholas Blincoe. Sort of crime novel, but it's set in Hulme. At that point, Manchester City Council was a left-wing council that was in conflict with the central government, and not very interested in collecting rents. So Hulme existed, this big, sprawling housing estate which was beautifully designed to replicate the crescents of Bath, though done in a rather different way. But nobody was bothering to collect rents, so it became a really utopian-dystopian sort of city, almost on its own. Not utopian. And lots of really creative stuff happened there. After I moved out and it got took over by a crusty, ravey dance scene that went on until the 90s.

So to me, there's loads of interesting stuff about how the way people live in a system is mirrored in its culture. I'm going to bring Nigel back in again, because I loved *City Limits*. I moved down to London I think in 1985 and I'd read that the London Filmmakers' Co-op were showing something and I'd go. *City Limits* was almost like a directory for me. It didn't provide me with an ideological or theoretical lead, more like a very practical directory of where to find stuff.

AG: So, Nigel, when you were a student, did you have experience of student activism?

NF: None. I mean, we're dealing with very different generations. I remember once explaining to an American how I'd gone through the classic post-1945 settlement education, which meant if you're very lucky, you popped out at the end and you went to university. So it was indeed four percent.

When I went to university, I was politically liberal, I mean with a large L. And by the time I left university, I was beginning to transmogrify into a Trot. My level of political activism was minimal. I was involved in producing student magazines, but it was more or less the standard path that anybody of my generation went through, and I didn't then become radical at all. I did become radical by the late 60s, and that meant that I was in a fairly continuous political atmosphere where we were spending a lot of time going to meetings or various other things. So, you know, looking back, I found it utterly thrilling because we just spent a hell of a lot of time just sitting around talking, along with getting drunk and then indeed smoking dope.

But one of the things that I've been thinking about in this discussion, and in the whole conference, is that the economics of this whole period, from the war, changed so radically. I grew up in a generation where the economy was expanding, people were optimistic; to an extent children are optimistic. I start off in bomb-sites, I take them for granted, I then take other things being built in their place.

That's true in the late 60s. If you take the underground press in the late 60s, it is part of a culture which is *rich*, in many ways. When I interviewed people for a book about the underground, people said things like, "How did I get by? Well, Nigel, it was the 60s, you got by, didn't you." If you were going to squat, you were actually squatting fairly well. Risking getting into the grim-up-north routine, if you lived in Manchester, then it wasn't like that. When I first went to the north, which was in 63, I remember getting a train over from York to Manchester. And it was like going into revolutionary Petrograd — except there was no revolution. There was smoke everywhere and to me — as a kind of lower middle-class naïve kid from Southampton — I just found [being there] there utterly romantic. If you were living in bloody Salford, it wasn't too romantic.

So that's the background that I grew up in. And that's the key thing about why there was an underground press. The one I know about was from 66 to 74. And in the 70s, you begin to get wise to the fact that the world is getting rougher, tougher and more unpleasant for large numbers of people. And in many ways that hasn't changed — well, it has changed drastically in some ways — but the whole experience of the 80s of affluence increasingly concentrated on a smaller group of people, or a large group of people but with another underclass underneath it.

There was two things. One point is just to go back to what you were saying about the previous generation wondering why on earth they had been rejected. For me, it came at the moment of the old Merseybeats show of 1964 (which didn't have anybody from Merseyside on the show). The compere — after the audience had booed him in a witty fashion for some hours — said, "We sweated and slaved and went through two world wars to wind up with a bunch like you." Whereupon we all cheered. I thought this is a great moment actually.

The other moment for me about the way this culture works is when I found I was no longer a traveller on a train, I was a customer. And that was to do with the whole bloody way this society has commodified things. And we're going through it right now.

That was my background. In terms of what I was reading in the 60s, I was reading things like *Memoirs of a Revolutionary*, by Victor Serge, which to me opened up a completely different perspective and made you think outside the confines of your fairly narrow life. Mind you, I also enjoyed the opening sequence of *Breakfast at Tiffany's*, because it showed me there was more to life than Southampton High Street.

AG: Does anybody feel like summing up, or have anything to say that we've not touched on?

EP: I would just like to say about riot grrrl really, and what Liz was doing. I don't think we've really discussed much of the post-punk thing. I thought riot grrrl was a really good example of that, of punk not growing up but just evolving into something else. What I liked about that was it reminded me of no wave, the New York thing — which I thought was much more interesting than punk anyway. Lydia Lunch, Teenage Jesus and the Jerks, the Contortions, Mars, who were really, really experimental, DNA. This sort of New York art-punk-type stuff, like rejecting punk altogether and going into another way.

LN: It references jazz, doesn't it? A continuation from Val [Wilmer] this morning, avant-garde jazz.

EP: Something you can get your teeth into, rather than going on about, you know, "I am a plastic bag" or something, or "I live in a dustbin."

LN: Some great music has contained the lines "*I am a plastic bag*". X-Ray Spex! What a great song! But the trouble is that writing about that becomes very limited — which is what this panel, I guess, is intended to be about, writing. I think it's very difficult to write about music that is just kind of visceral really. Some music's just dumb, isn't it? But it's also great.

Grisly Titles

Liz Naylor unearths Spare Rib's struggle to decode punk 1976-80

So much of the 90s was about grandiose, often coked-up aggression, and Camille Paglia's writing hasn't aged well. But for all the self-serving posturing and hyperbole, she got one thing right, and said it well. The Robert Mapplethorpe photograph of Patti Smith, used for the 1975 Arista debut *Horses*, Paglia calls "the most electrifying image I have ever seen of a woman of my generation."

For those of us who encountered it in the mid-70s, this sparse black-and-white image, so dense in meaning — and part-realised by a gay man — was a new-queer explosion of a bomb, a radioactive event still emitting possibilities of a different way of being decades into the future.

The Paglia of the 90s is a professional feminist irritant making a career of annoying rival feminists, so perhaps you'd expect her to be out of step with a pioneering 70s magazine like *Spare Rib*. Even so, it's a surprise, looking back through the 21 volumes recently digitised by the British Library, covering its life-span from 1972-93, how rarely Patti Smith is mentioned. And fascinating to see how much *Spare Rib* struggled at the time with punk, missing its often contradictory provocations, its irony, kitsch and visual self-realisation. Yet here were the next-generational forms of third-wave feminist politics in embryo — though as it happens, any self-respecting angry young woman turned instead to the weekly music press for exploration of punk. But more of that in a moment.

Offering an alternative to conventional women's magazines, *Spare Rib* was first published in June 1972, the 'women's news magazine' — a monthly, coverprice 17½p — was so radical and inflammatory an idea that many newsagents at first refused to stock it. It wasn't until its fourth year that *Rib* used the tagline 'A Women's Liberation Magazine'. By the late 70s, it was a collective, running features on domestic and international politics, with an art section largely consisting of polytechnic Marxist analysis of novels, poetry, film or theatre, plus coverage of the endless agit-prop workshops and performing groups then flourishing in London. From the outset, it was more comfortable with the written word, and music coverage is occasional rather than central.

By the mid-70s this tended toward a mixture of female artists active in the UK music scene — Carol Grimes, Marsha Hunt, Maggie Bell with Stone the Crows, Elkie Brooks with Vinegar Joe — as well as black jazz and R&B artists from the US, no doubt reflecting the influence of the redoubtable Valerie Wilmer, a regular contributor. Further strands arrived from around 1974, with the womyn's lesbian feminist scene, notably the Michigan Womyn's Festival (1976). Plus such newer UK artists as Joan Armatrading.

There is *a lot* of Joan Armatrading in *Spare Rib*.

Reminiscing in 2010, Frankie Green, drummer in the London Women's Liberation Rock Band (1972-74), summarised the then-meaning of women's liberation for musicians: "[We] incorporated politics not only in the lyrics and style of what we played but in moving toward a different way of living, collective working, radical production values, creating political culture." Green would drum for several similar bands in this era, and a *Rib* cover story (#46, May 1976) titled 'Turn on to Women's Rock' confirms her description of a feminist approach to music: the Stepney Sisters (1974-76) "talk about rock, performing and collective work" with Marion Fudger, who asks the question "Feminism and rock music: can they be combined?"

At this stage, the bratty audio-visual shock of punk is still largely being ignored, as one might an unruly child or over-dramatic teenager.

In the fifth anniversary issue (#60, July 1977), there's a change. Nestled among articles on the Equal Opportunities Commission, Erica Jong, feminism in Spain — plus adverts for albums from Elkie Brooks, Dory Previn and Sandy Denny — there is 'Women in Punk', by one Su Denim. The article is extraordinary for several reasons. First, given the low-key bemusement to date, this four-page spread emerges from nowhere. Second, the layout is at odds with the usual 'community press' visuals: here islands of type are roughly cut or torn and pasted onto the backdrop of a greengrocer's brown paper bag, complete with its jagged pinked edges. It's like a punk fanzine smuggled between *Rib*'s pages: a series of mini-interviews, quotes lifted from the weekly music press, plus reprinted lyrics. The interviews are great: Susie McEwan, the "would-be drummer from The Toilets" is not a woman aiming to enamour herself with *Rib*'s readership. Asked if the band will be "all women", she states: "Yes, well it's a lot easier in a lot of ways. I mean we're not lesbians or women's libbers or anything like that."

Other interviewees are not, it must be said, people you'd routinely expect to find quoted in this journal: they include Wire's Robert Gotobed and Edwin Pouncey of the "Heart Attacks" (as they misspell the Art Attacks). Su Denim, it turns out, is the punk *nom de plume* of Marion Fudger, a fascinating *Zelig*-type figure in this world. Arriving at the magazine via the Beatles' Apple Corps and *Record Mirror*, she was the cover star of #6 (1972), the archetypal 'dolly bird' alongside John Cleese. By the mid-70s — as well as being on the editorial collective — she was in the Derelicts, a proto-punk band regularly active at magazine benefit 'bops', tantalisingly described as a "Trotskyist R&B band", which would bifurcate (1977) into the Passions and pragVEC — by which time Fudger/Denim was bass player in the Art Attacks, alongside Pouncey.

There are a couple of significant quotes in this piece. Frankie Green (by now playing with Jam Today) applauds punk for its "attitude for demystifying music: stressing that you don't have to be technically knowledgeable" but is concerned that "most of the emphasis is on style as much as musical demystification, and the presentation of punk is just as sexist". Meanwhile Sophie Richmond — of Malcolm McLaren's

Glitterbest organisation — thinks that "there's definitely a different attitude towards women, they're treated more as people in their own right... I think the reason they (women) look negative, shocking, outrageous or objectionable *is to see how far they can go*" [italics mine]. You can glimpse in this quote both the emerging visual aesthetic and a shift away from the collective struggles of second-wave feminism towards an identity politics.

But this is a pro-punk blip, and normal Armatrading-facing service resumes (interestingly, there's no letters-page response to the feature). In #66 (January 1978) there's an interview with Jam Today that largely revisits the concerns of the Stepney Sisters feature: the financial practicalities of being in a rock band, having a female sound engineer and collective working practices. But there is a live review of X-Ray Spex playing a benefit for the National Abortion Campaign. Poly Styrene, Jill Nicholls writes, "[has] a fantastic stage presence and witty lyrics (…) but even that got boring as the music thumped on."

This discomfort sets the template for the rest of the year. In #75 (Oct 1978), Nicholls reviews the Siouxsie and the Banshees single 'Hong Kong Garden' fairly favourably, but calls the "flip side" ('Voices') "ugly", with "pretentious words", warning readers that the imminent album contains such "grisly titles as 'Carcass' and 'Helter Skelter'". In #77 (Dec 1978) we're promised reviews of "new albums from Joan Armatrading and Crystal Gayle".

But by now the editorial collective was changing. Writing as Lucy Toothpaste, Lucy Whitman arrived from the proto-riot grrrl fanzine *Jolt*. Heavily involved in Rock Against Racism and Rock Against Sexism, Toothpaste brings a greater confidence and ease to writing about punk and new wave. The X-Ray Spex album, *Germfree Adolescents*, "captures the best of [the band] — manic wit, aggression, energy, fierce intelligence and Poly's tuneful screaming. I love it." Of the Banshees: "their songs are mostly about alienation and cruelty" (both #78, Jan 1979). This is an improvement, even if many of the more interesting post-punk musicians go undiscussed (no Kleenex, pragVEC, Delta 5 or Essential Logic). In #83 (June 1979; cover story the Yorkshire Ripper) Nicholls and Toothpaste interview the reliably defensive Siouxsie and the Banshees, a somewhat pedestrian examination ("with her tartan trews and windmilling legs and arms") that includes a predictable discussion about the use of the swastika and the aesthetics of shock. A more provocative comment by Sioux — about how "irresponsible and selfish a lot of women are in taking on being a mother" — isn't picked up on, beyond the response that Sioux is "trying to shake up those conventional expectations and responses". *Rib* apparently struggles to challenge the archetype of woman as lifegiver and carer, and certainly fails to grasp how punk and new wave might be resisting it.

Music coverage 1979-80 is a mixed bag of the genres that *Rib* was most comfortable with: soul, jazz and blues, plus in #85 (August 1979) a roundup of earnest US folkie-feminist records by Holly Near, Meg Christian and Cris Williamson — a truly terrifying triumvirate to those of us who have heard these works. There is the odd post-punk band (Raincoats yes, Young Marble Giants or Ludus no), but everything is still very much anchored to the message and meaning of the written lyric. Beyond the occasional passing comment, the visual self-determination of many of the women involved in punk or post-punk goes undiscussed, as does the emerging confidence of a queer aesthetic. For example in #94 (May 1980), a live review of the Raincoats and the Slits in Paris at the *Rock au feminin* festival describes Viv Albertine as "looking like a Toulouse Lautrec lady gone drastically wrong," with her "blue tutu and hair in a haystack" — that Albertine was thus adopting and arguably *détourning* the transgressive femininity of the prostitute is not explored further.

Present-day feminist website the F-Word has described the early *Rib* response as "stiff, formal and bemused, if not hostile". Interviewed in 2011 by Cazz Blaze for F-Word, Toothpaste/Whitman acknowledges this culture clash: "[I was] having to try to explain and justify punk to older feminists, eventually they came round actually... because, basically, when punk came along most feminists were utterly horrified. [They] thought it was yet one more manifestation of macho cock rock. They just thought it was horribly unpleasant and had nothing to do with feminism." In *Rib* #107 (June 1981), Toothpaste had written a lengthy feature on the topic: "When punk began, a lot of feminists were hostile to it... alarmed by the way some punks adopted Nazi regalia... Feminists and the left eventually became more enthusiastic and there are now punky bands... to be found within the women's movement itself." And almost as an afterthought: "(not to mention the dramatic change in feminist fashion, inspired by punk, which deserves an article all to itself)."

I mentioned the music press above, as being a primary source of our information. It's more complicated than that: in those early days, provincial kids like me often *saw* or *heard* punk before we read about it. I took things in via the legendary *Daily Mirror* splash, via John Peel. I saw Patti and the Pistols on Manchester's local TV show *So it Goes*. I stood in Underground Records, or Virgin on Lever Street, attempting a kind of transdermal absorption of the potency of certain record covers: *Horses, Blank Generation, Spiral Scratch...* This felt like an overwhelmingly sensory experience, and that's what made it so obvious the axis of my world had shifted.

In fact the music press had also struggled at first to understand the wider social significance of these tectonic shifts. Embracing the natural and valorising of the patchwork-shabby near-anonymity of the collective, *Rib* failed to sense a sea change from hippie. In its turn, the weekly rock press swerved from toxic laddish fetishisation and clichéd Colin Wilson-esque authenticity (the ubiquitous "street cred") towards a pervasive horror of intimacy. For respite there was always Vivien Goldman, Jane Suck, even Julie Burchill... But the 40th anniversary activity of 2016 — including endless male-centric books and *Mojo* articles — saw Viv Albertine depressingly, predictably and rightly having to amend the exhibit blurbs at the British Library, to re-insist that women also had a role in punk. As much as anything, the axis-shift had been about the ways gender registered, individually and socially.

"I get into so many genders I couldn't even tell you," Patti Smith had informed Amy Goss at *Mademoiselle* in 1975. In *Rib* #71 (July 1978), Pam Isherwood reviewed Smith at the Rainbow: "Her presence is total, she controls the band, the crowd, the world." What's key here is the recognition of Smith's self-actualisation, and the visual power of her physical presence. It's surely significant that Isherwood is primarily a photographer, part of the group that in 1983 would establish the women-only Format Agency. Certainly she recognises her own dissonance: "I started out feeling vaguely alienated, unaccepting of star performances, being more used to the accessibility of Women's Liberation Music Events, but as the show went on it became obvious why she has to become separate — the illusion wouldn't work if she was *one of us*" [my italics]. This is a world away from the earnest everywoman collectivism of the feminist music groups of the 70s.

Toothpaste had mentioned feminist fashion in passing (in fact in brackets) in her 1981 essay. This was a full year after the launch of *The Face* (May 1980), Nick Logan's (successful and influential) response to a youth (sub)cultural realisation, in punk, post-punk and beyond, that the visual element — your clothes, your look — were also there to be played with and decoded, as a conscious and active element in the play. Self-definition had always been a matter of performance — but by now, at least for a few years, writers on the weeklies and elsewhere were happily enjoying themselves exploring the rapid eddies of the self-aware evolution that this led to.

To return to 1975: the explosion of *that* moment and *that* image serves as an historical rupture that was simultaneously a unique event and yet connected to wider socio-political shifts. It can be seen as a point of clash, of confluence. Refracting the visual codes of the female and male outsider, to fashion something at once powerfully female and unutterably new, the Patti Smith of *Horses* remains a potent cipher of other possibilities.

As for 1976, just as the mainstream manifestation of its 40th anniversary seemed often to miss that visceral visual first encounter with the gender weirdness of punk, the response at the time at *Spare Rib* — hobbled by its unease at the role that performance was playing in this political identity shift — seems in retrospect oddly lacklustre, and a lost opportunity.

Notes: *the interview with Frankie Green can be found at womensliberationmusicarchive.co.uk. The F-word website's interview with Lucy Toothpaste is at www.thefword.org.uk/2010/03/women_in_punk_w/*

Liz Naylor was co-editor with Cath Carroll of Manchester's City Fun in the late 70s, wrote for NME and Melody Maker early 80s, and has worked as promoter, publicist, DJ, label boss and riot grrrl activist. She co-founded and runs Foundation for Change, a non-profit organisation that offers psychology courses for people recovering from substance abuse. foundationforchange.org.uk

An Oppositional Force Without Being Overtly Political

David Toop, improvising musician and historian, remembers the publications that shouldered open a space for his inclusive approach: MUSICS, Collusion – and The Face

To play free improvised music in the early 1970s was to shoulder great responsibilities. Extending beyond an economy of music and its training regimes, these responsibilities ultimately had purchase even on the spheres of those who attended upon music and its infrastructure, meaning such allies and/or necessary professional evils as promoters, publicists, administrators, funding bodies and critics, and even the audience itself. The implications and intentions of the music oscillated. Sometimes we focused on the state of politics, sometimes on histories of music, sometimes on workings of sound: this was a music created collectively, dispensing with composer, score, instruction, ideally without a leader (though in practice these ambitions took time to mature). In principle this was a music founded in listening and communality, in which individual expression could coexist with the creation of a mutually comprehensible language of exchange.

At their most expansive, these ideas were imagined as an agency to profoundly alter the conditions of music-making, the entanglements of human beings and the possible structures of human society. Though we resisted theory and dogma, Marx offered some clues; feminism and anthropology offered others. The major obstacle to these aims was a lack of general interest. As with many other utopian communities, past, present and future, audiences were tiny and agency was weak. If a music were deemed fashionable then interest might briefly grow, but any Zeitgeist-related excitement that had been aroused by free improvisation in the 1960s had subsided by the mid-1970s. The *Melody Maker*, a weekly paper whose ancestry lay in the coverage of dance bands of the 1920s, at first explored the scene with cautious curiosity, before withdrawing gradually, offering free improvisers a tentatively supportive coverage too sporadic to really help anything beyond a few individual careers.

In its unfamiliarity — particularly in its rejection of established forms, repetition and orthodox harmony — the music was considered difficult. Only through establishing a sustained discourse could these difficulties be overcome. That was the theory, anyway, so some of us made efforts to publish material that no existing company of any size would touch. Paul Burwell and I took inspiration from sound poet Bob Cobbing, whose Writers Forum press had been publishing poetry and experimental texts since 1963. Cobbing's philosophy was to circumvent the gatekeepers; do it yourself. So we published small books with his help and advice — my *Decomposition as Music Process* in 1972, Paul Burwell's *Suttle Sculpture* in 1974 and the anthology I edited and co-published in 1974, *New/Rediscovered Musical Instruments*, featuring the inventions of Hugh Davies, Evan Parker, Paul Lytton, Max Eastley, Paul Burwell and myself.

This last book was probably the reason why Burwell and myself were invited to the first meeting of a new venture, a magazine that came to be called (at Burwell's suggestion) *MUSICS*. Details of this meeting are now vague. It was held at the flat of violinist Phil Wachsmann and those present included the conveners — Evan Parker, Madelaine and Martin Davidson — and their invited guests, Wachsmann, Burwell, Steve Beresford and others, the memory of whose presence has slipped away into the shadows of that room. The original premise was that a magazine be launched to serve the cause of free improvisation: to air its philosophy, to review its records and gigs, to give pre-publicity to its events.

As the name implies, *MUSICS* was from the start a pluralist, more inclusive proposition. Many little presses produced specialist magazines and pamphlets at this time: dating from the 1960s, my own collection ranged from *Blues Unlimited* to publications like *Tlaloc* and *Kroklok*, dedicated to concrete poetry. Produced in the classic conditions for such publications — Gestetner stencils and typewriter, a kitchen table, a staple gun, glue and scissors — the first issue of *MUSICS* can be considered a transitional object. But after issue 2, with the departure of the Davidsons to New York State in 1975, the production of the magazine and its editorial policy began more closely to mirror the structural principles of free improvised music. The so-called editorial board, with all its pompous associations of academia, transitioned into a wasps' nest of collective reasoning, argument and group paste-up sessions.

A brief intervention by cellist Colin Wood on page 2 of issue 4 (October/November 1975) helps to illustrate this convergence. Under the title STOP PRESS REVIEW SECTION, Wood wrote:

Three years ago ten music students from Cologne sat in horse shoe, one end of fine Wren church in Smith Square, sang ninth chord all evening, sound mixed and rareified [sic] by man in nave.

Last Saturday ten religious men from Tibet sat on horse shoe in same spot, sang tenth chord all evening, no sound mixer.

The former refers to a performance of Karlheinz Stockhausen's *Stimmung*; the latter to a performance of Tibetan chant by monks from Gyütö Tantric College, then in Dalhousie, Himachal Pradesh. Both performances utilised the vocal harmonics of overtone singing. Many inferences are compressed into the satire of these two paragraphs, not least the distinction made by Wood between a group performance achieved without electronically amplified manipulation and a composed piece whose final outcome is decided by a single individual.

Much debate could, and did, rage around the validity of this type of comparison. Issues of power and legitimacy were at stake, with the Stockhausen example apparently sucking less powerful entities — group improvisation and musical techniques from non-European traditions — into a regressive, technocratic, authoritarian yet highly marketable model of practice. What was undeniable about the more collective, semi-improvised approach to publishing was that its discursive vitality combined with inefficiency to exhaust the participants. *MUSICS* lasted from 1975-79, at which point Steve Beresford and I decided to move on, deciding on a magazine of broader musical interest edited by a smaller group.

So it was that *Collusion* magazine was founded in 1980, with the first issue appearing in summer 1981. Initially we invited another *MUSICS* veteran into the group, Peter Cusack, along with Sue Steward. Sue had worked on issues 20 and 21 of *MUSICS*, and brought mainstream publishing experience, a feminist perspective and enthusiasm for Latin and African music to the new magazine. With hindsight, *Collusion* can be identified as an early adopter's guide to what became known as world music. In practice it was about diversity. Our target was genre, particularly the way in which musical genres were atomised according to age, race, class, geography, economic status, cultural and tribal allegiances, education and other demographic factors, all of which suited the selling of music as a commodity.

From within an unpopular and philistine Conservative government, Employment Secretary Norman Tebbit's response to the Brixton riots of 1981 was to suggest that the unemployed should get on their bikes and look for work until they found it. With this as the backdrop, our belief in producing *Collusion* was that music articulated political convictions. As much as it reflected social mores, the innovatory force of music played a significant part in shaping attitudes to issues such as race. In other words, music could be an oppositional force without being overtly political. So we ignored the practice elsewhere of matching content to release schedules or current fashions, and either wrote about or commissioned articles on music that we liked, embracing such unfashionable topics as country music, female big bands, music enjoyed by middle-aged Jamaicans, Japanese *enka* ballads and the Bay City Rollers — along with short, under-resourced investigative pieces on Pink Floyd's investments and the convoluted structure of the UK record industry.

Again with hindsight, this was polemical in intent. Alongside salsa, hiphop, Milford Graves and Diamanda Galas in the first issue there was Robert Wyatt on listening to shortwave radio from Radio Vietnam, Radio Tirana and Radio Habana, the anthropologist Barbara Peterson on social comment in Nigerian praise songs, Simon Frith applying Brecht and Eisler to the film music of Ennio Morricone, and Dutch improvising pianist Misha Mengelberg on the conservatism of music education. This approach was both ahead of the wave and part of it – though our allegiance to free improvisation and such contributors as Lol Coxhill and Ian Breakwell ensured that mainstream success was impossible. Worn out by the struggle of producing such an ambitious publication without financial support we closed *Collusion* after issue 5, in September 1983.

Inevitably, the eclecticism of the early 80s became an increasingly prominent selling point for magazines more astute in their commercial appeal, market knowledge and aesthetic sense than ours. By 1984 I was a freelance contributor to *The Face*, writing features, interviews and the monthly music column. The contrast (and lack of it) was instructive. For *MUSICS* and *Collusion* there was little sense of adjusting language or content aimed at a hypothetical reader. At *The Face* there were implicit boundaries, drawn less by editor Nick Logan or the features editor at that time, Paul Rambali, and more by the magazine's image. Once again, diversity was the key point. The mid-80s was a golden age for reissues of jazz, R&B, rare soul, psychedelia and early pop. This cornucopia was heavily featured in my column, up until the point when Nick Logan suggested that the balance of the monthly 1,000 word text had tipped too far into retro. The issue was resolved amicably when he suggested I list a small selection of reissues at the foot of the column. It was an editorial intervention, but far milder than those I would come to experience in broadsheet newspapers.

For the last issue of *Collusion* I had edited Steven Harvey's groundbreaking survey of the New York disco underground from c.25,000 words down to eight A4 pages. *The Face* ran a similar piece by Harvey shortly afterwards (Logan was not happy to be second), both pieces featuring photographs by Patricia Bates. The text used by *The Face* was less substantial than ours but Neville Brody's design far superior to my primitive cut-and-paste.

Whatever I had learned of design from my time at art schools in the 60s had been forgotten by the 80s. What was not forgotten was the experience of being caught up as a foundation student in the Hornsey Art School sit-in of 1968. Having co-produced a small magazine of poetry, record reviews and literary experiments called *ONE* in 1966, I was only too open to the idea of taking over a college (albeit temporarily) and working collaboratively to maintain functions ranging from canteen to classroom. In this sense, the appeal of self-produced magazines would be something that sustained political ideals of independence, collectivism and self-determination more far-reaching than simply writing about music.

David Toop was on the editorial collective for MUSICS and for Collusion, and a columnist in the 80s for The Face. He was written for The Wire since its inception.

Panel:
The Changing Make-up of Bohemia: Who Was Reading When?

Paul Gilroy: *The Wire, City Limits, Professor of American and English Literature at King's College London*
Penny Reel: *it, Let It Rock, Pressure Drop, NME, Black Echoes, Select*
Cynthia Rose: *Melody Maker, NME, The Wire, City Limits, MTV*
Panel chaired by **Simon Frith,** *Let It Rock, Melody Maker, Observer, Village Voice, Tovey Chair (now Emeritus Professor) of Music at University of Edinburgh*

SF: I wanted to use this introduction to draw attention to some writers who haven't been mentioned in this conference at all — but were certainly significant for me, because they also say something about the writing community I've seen myself as part of. The first — who was immensely important to my career and for writing in Britain about music generally — is the late lamented Charlie Gillett. The first thing I wrote in Britain was something I sent blind to *Cream* magazine, which I happened to see in a shop in Leeds. It got published and I never heard another word. Certainly no pay. But eventually I had a call from [*Cream* reviews editor] Charlie Gillett, who'd tracked me down. So next time I was in London I went to meet him and started writing reviews for him, and other magazines thereafter, like *Let It Rock*. Charlie Gillett was very much an inspiration.

Just as significant, the second person is Dave Laing, who was certainly part of *Let It Rock* but was also a link to the various more left political underground papers, the sort of magazines Nigel Fountain was talking about earlier. It's also worth remembering that Charlie Gillett's *Sound of the City* — which was a very significant book for people thinking and writing about the history of popular music — was actually written as a masters thesis at Columbia University. So Charlie, though not himself any sort of academic, did suggest that part of the interesting community for writing about popular music would be the academy.

I went to Berkeley as a graduate student in 1967 and quite early on met Greil Marcus, another graduate student. A lot of people were talking yesterday about *Rolling Stone*, and [its founder] Jann Wenner was actually then the editor of *The Daily Californian*. Berkeley was such a huge campus it had a daily student newspaper. When the *San Francisco Chronicle* went on strike so there was no local newspaper for the Bay area. Even at that stage an extremely skilled opportunist, Wenner realised that he could sell *The Daily Californian* as a daily newspaper to all the Bay area. So it was no longer a student paper, it became a Bay area paper. And as a result of that experience — of thinking not just about a student paper but something more national — Wenner contacted Ralph J. Gleason, who was a local resident, and formulated the notion of having a specialist magazine, in a sense a music paper, but also thinking a bit about the alternative San Francisco Bay area culture.

So though *Rolling Stone* wasn't an academic magazine, it had academic connections and academic writers. Certainly in terms of my own career, the academy has always been significant, and the writers that I actually read most at that time were not necessarily what we would think of as music writers. For example Stuart Hall at *Universities and Left Review* and later *New Left Review*. Nigel mentioned *New Society* this morning; writers there like Ray Gosling, academics writing about music like Howard Becker, Eric Hobsbawm writing about jazz under the name Francis Newton. I read these people as a model of what sort of writing I wanted to do, just as much as I read the underground press we were talking about yesterday.

The other important strand, which is where Dave Laing comes in — which again was touched on much more this morning — was Marxism and the politically committed notion of how to write about this popular music form, particularly in the context of the Frankfurt School, Adorno and all these sorts of people. The model Nigel gave this morning was Trotskyism. I was in a rather different strand, loosely related to communism but more a kind of independent Marxism. There was an organisation called Music for Socialism, which was in some sense a kind of alternative to the Trotskyist model. But also there was for two or three years a Marxist rock writers group which met pretty regularly and was again a kind of link between the sort of music papers that I was working for and the political papers that I was working for.

So there was a sense of community — and in an odd way the place for me that always summed this up was Compendium Books in Camden Town. Coming from the provinces that was the place you went to first — because you could see every consumable form: alternative and mainstream, Marxist left political, underground and everything else — and I got to know Nick Kimberley who worked there, and later helped run a reggae fanzine for a while, *Pressure Drop*. So there was a kind of bohemian community — I didn't actually know people in it very well, but I felt that it was the kind of place I belonged when I went.

The final point worth stressing is that musicians can be part of the community. My brother [Fred Frith] formed the band Henry Cow. They were heavily involved in music socialism as a kind of European movement. And there were numerous others. David Toop wasn't able to be here today, but the improvised music scene was very politicised, with its musicians' collectives. They ran a magazine, *MUSICS* — and then *Collusion* became a very interesting magazine. And these are rather different from the underground press in the sense that they were magazines for musicians wondering about how they could be political musicians.

So it's not exactly bohemia, but there's a sort of loose grouping of academics, Marxists, musicians, performers, all trying to work out ways in which popular music — which had always rather been despised by all these groups — could now, for various reasons of which the underground press was clearly a symbol, be thought of [as political], how could it work politically, how should you write about it and so on. So that's how I would place myself and the very loosely notion of what I meant by bohemia.

PG: I suppose I took bohemia in a slightly different sense because I imagined it was sort of code. An unlikely code for the changing character of British culture during the decolonisation phase on one side and the rise of civil rights and black power on the other. And it seems to me that one thing which flickered into life occasionally in our conversation yesterday and again this morning, of course, in that very delicate and engaging conversation between Richard [Williams] and Val [Wilmer], is how both the writing and the world of music it addresses respond to the presence of black people in this country.

Was it Richard Williams yesterday who talked about how in his development as a writer, he was thinking about what LeRoi Jones was writing — and I suppose I began to see how some of what was being worked out in the writing was a discussion of what white writers could say, and what their relationship to the world of music and world of culture from which it came was going to be. Especially if — and this wasn't something for everybody — if that culture and that music could not be rendered as exotic, but just become an ordinary part of life.

Now, I'm a little different age-wise from Simon, and I was living in London and trying to do music and being at school, wanting to be a writer. I grew up in a household of a writer, so writers were always there, books were always there. My mum's a writer — and when there's a writer in the household there is no household, there's just writing. So I will say I coveted that typewriter, and I was interested in what it could do in the world. And like the people who spoke yesterday, I was an avid reader of *Rolling Stone*, of *it*, of *Friends/Frendz*, of *Seven Days*, these things were the things I went to. And I went to them for the music! Though the *Rolling Stone* coverage of the Chicago trials also sticks in my mind very deeply, and the film reviews.

I also remember sitting in the public gallery of the *Oz* trial. I'd never been in a court before, but once I knew that was happening I went and sat there. And reading Val and Richard in the *Melody Maker* later confirmed to me that what was being worked out was a set of rules about who could speak about these things, and how they were going to speak, and in what spirit they were going to speak. And Richard mentioned A. B. Spellman along with LeRoi Jones, and those were people I was reading. And I was also reading Ralph Ellison and W. E. B. Du Bois, and finding out these things before I went to university and thinking about what it was to write about the music in that way and that spirit. Ellison's essays about music still move me more deeply than many things that have been written, and I think it's odd how deeply plagiarised they've been by so many people.

Anyway, I gave up my music for a bit and decided to go to university — and I was actually having a very difficult time and going to leave. But one of my teachers had been a supervisor of Ben Sidran's thesis — Ben Sidran from the Steve Miller Band, who had run away [to the UK] from the draft [in the US]. Anyway, his PhD thesis became his book *Black Talk*, and I remember sitting in a library and reading that and thinking OK. I thought it was an interesting way of writing about music in relation to the movement of history and the transformation of culture and the development of capitalism.

Someone spoke this morning about the free press. I think there was a layer of stuff being published that wasn't the *NME* — so I'm less inclined than some people here to cede the space to the bromantic ethnography of the *NME* office. No one's mentioned *The Leveller*, which goes alongside Compendium Books. There's a layer of publishing that's been missed out, and it would be good to address ourselves to that.

We can try a kind of thought experiment. The first edition of *Black Echoes* was in 1976. And Penny Reel's voice, very loudly. *Black Music* from 1973 — a sort of mainstream commercial experiment, I don't know where those are even archived. There were important things in those. [The TV] programme *Aquarius* in 1976, and Peter Hall, introducing reggae. And for me the model that I drew on, thinking about a being writer — I mean, obviously your voice and your style were important to me as a writer, Penny — but another name that hasn't really been mentioned here today, I'm sure some of you will remember, is the voice of Carl Gayle. Carl as a stylist. So I had been sort of trying to publish my work, and I could get it into little sort of leftie places, but when I went begging work from Vivien Goldman at *Sounds* she very politely told me to go fuck myself.

PR: And did you?

PG: Well, funnily enough, no. Anyway, that's another story. So there was a layer of people publishing in those independent spaces, people like yourself, Penny, people like Davitt Sigerson wrote some brilliant things in the early issues of *Black Music*. And also the framing and the scale of the project, the altitude of it. Everything I wrote later, in some of my more academic books, like *Black Atlantic*, came from that experience. I'm not going to lie. That's the truth, so there you go. I knew Charlie Gillett because I used to win those competitions on Radio London on a fairly regular basis, competitions for free records — which of course at that time we all wanted very badly. And actually I was playing in a band with his cousin. So we were always trying to solicit his help — and of course it was never forthcoming. But there were other writers in that world, in that space. Steve Barnard I think had been part of things. Penny here. Sebastian Clarke — now Amon Saba Saakana, and gone back to Trinidad. Imruh Caesar [Imruh Bakari], who's in West Africa now. And Chris Lane I think.

PR: Yes. The first person to write about reggae in England.

PG: He had a column in *Blues and Soul*. I put a page from one of his columns up on Twitter last night, so people could have their memories jogged about where to imagine the boundaries of that archive. I was living in Brighton when the punk thing started and wondering a little bit about it, trying to get in. I found that I could publish things in *Temporary Hoarding* or whatever — in the space that they made much more readily at Rock Against Racism. It was very difficult yesterday to sit here listening to Tony Palmer, I mean, respect to him, but going on about Eric Clapton, when the politics of all of this was defined by that affair. I mean, I know they're all in UKIP now. I understand the movement of that, the Countryside Alliance, UKIP, all the rest of it. But what cut through the politics — what's the title of this conference? *The changing politics of UK music writing 1968-85*. What slices that in half is Clapton turning round and saying Enoch Powell's the man. I know people are still in denial about that, because he's got very expensive PR. But he's not in denial. He employs the PR to clean it up whenever it bubbles. This new biography of Clapton — at lunchtime I walked over to Dillon's, as it used to be [*now Waterstone's*] to look at the music shelf. I checked the latest official version of Clapton's life about that affair, and it's the same old garbage. We owe the truth of that story to two novelists who I think both attended that gig, to Caryl Phillips, who comes from Sheffield — his family is from St Kitts — and Jonathan Coe, whose taste in music I don't share. So we owe them for recording it, holding onto it, making it a historical thing. The last thing to say at this stage is to note what Val said this morning, that white Americans find it difficult, even into the mid to late 70s, to deal with African American people. I would say that some of those dynamics were also going on here. And I'm not saying that the American racial *nomos* is the same as what's going on in London, obviously — thank goodness it's not. But things are not all right here. Things are not sold now, and they certainly weren't sold then — and there were a lot of people who positioned themselves as gatekeepers and custodians of this world of black music and wouldn't let people like myself in. I mean, I'm not saying I'm belligerent about it now. Happily, almost everyone's great friends. After 30 or 40 years you start to let these things go, if not before. But I just want it on the record that I found myself having the same stupid argument with all these people.

Not that they were misplacing themselves by writing about what they were doing — but that they had to be open to some demand for their accountability for what they actually wrote. David Toop, Charlie Gillett, I mean yeah, put the names in. I'm not going to censor things, I'm just going to say the truth. I'm not going to be Stalinist about it. Nick Kimberley. When you went into Compendium, Nick was there on the right hand side of the door. You couldn't get down the stairs without having to deal with him. So people write things and you want to say, well, actually what are you doing, what are you talking about? How is this OK? Isn't there a basis for a conversation that might be had about this rather than...? And I will also honestly wonder — and this is something else that hasn't been talked about — what kind of relationship the so-called black community has with its own history and its own culture. Because a lot of archive has not been maintained by [the Black Cultural Archive]. I know they've got their lovely building in Brixton now, from Heritage Lottery Fund and all the rest of it now, but a lot of this was not something that people were proud of, or wanted to celebrate or affirm or remember, and given the situation, of course, that was entirely understandable.

So anyway, I want it on the record, given we're all being taped, that I got really bored of having the same old fucking stupid argument with all these people, all these blokes, who were the kind of official guardians of what you could say or not say about black culture in this country [in the 70s and the 80s]. What does one do with that? I don't know how much that's an expression of deeper ambiguities in the underground and the counterculture. Somehow I don't think so — because if you look at those old films or if you think back to what was going on in Implosion [the club], or whatever, you'd get, I don't know, the MC5 and Funkadelic on the same bill. There was a sense of people sharing a space, even when you went into some of the places at club level. People would dance when the records were on. If there was live music they would retreat from live music.

So there were some deep things to say about all of that, which complicate the story a lot. I'm not trying to make another Manichean pattern, and I'm not trying to draw another either/or line. I'm saying that there's some real difficult questions there — and that nobody has an interest actually in facing them or bringing that history back up to light, but they're actually critical to understanding the development of the written archive.

CR: I think what Paul is drawing on to a large extent is also the fact that you miss out context when you just get one person's view of anything. Val and I were just talking about this — that sometimes today there is a sense that you can't go and find out for yourself, but in fact you always can go and find out. Not just the written source, but you can just contact people, as long as you're willing (A) to respect their point of view, and (B) to really listen to what they have to say and then go on to verify it, to check it out, to follow up what they suggest. I think that's what I learned from the whole thing — so it would be crazy to give people a list of anything I read. More important are the things that helped make sense out of what I started to find out — and I think a lot of that may have come from the punk ethic as it filtered through stuff later. It certainly filtered through the workplace. It gave people the idea that they could do stuff themselves.

When I was at *NME* I worked with a group of delinquent kids making fanzines, because that was a way of dealing with writing for them, and their point of view about it was really interesting, I learned a lot. Later on I went on a thing in the Appalachian Mountains with a poet who was working with kids that couldn't read, and teaching them to using strips of words with colours and papers and so on. So there are always different things that affect how you approach things. Probably what affected me most was how I was taught to analyse things, and that was because I went and got myself instructed — by someone who made me read Marx. His name was Gavin MacKenzie, he was then a young Marxist scholar. And I read a lot of Raymond Williams, who had a huge influence — and who I later sought out and met and got supervised by. Those kinds of things are available to anyone who wants to pick up the telephone and really be a bit tenacious. I don't think the same thing can happen through emails. I just don't think it can.

The same thing's true about people I hired. When I was able to hire writers I would call you, Paul, and get Armond White's number, say — whoever I was interested in through what they'd written, or whoever I thought would know somebody I wanted to contact, and then I would ring that person up or get in touch with them, however possible. It is always possible to do that. But it's not possible to apprehend what really happened at a certain point in time if you don't have a few basic tools — for me, it's political. If you have a closed mind or you have a preconceived idea of what a story is, you're not going to find out what the story was. That's really all I have to add to what you guys are saying.

The thing about Compendium Books is really important, though. When I was a student coming up to London — and afterwards when I was just looking for interesting stuff to read — there were readings at Compendium. The main thing was that it was a friendly place. No one was snotty. No one looked down on anybody else, and Nick [Kimberley] was really helpful and really welcoming to everybody, all kinds of people.

And that's aside from him being a good writer and interested in music. Just as a guy who worked in the store, he was always helpful, he was always friendly.

PR: I've got an unusual experience, my life story. I was born in a one-bedroom flat in Stoke Newington in a building owned by the Industrial Dwellings Society. It was a red brick Edwardian block that my father moved into from the East End in 1903 or something. My mother was born there. My dad was born also in the East End, in New Street opposite Liverpool Street Station. He was an amateur boxer. You wouldn't believe it because I'm a wimp. My dad tried to teach me to box, but I was always left-handed, so I couldn't fight. But then I didn't like fighting. The thing I didn't like about fighting was the consequence, and the consequence was pain. Me and pain have never got on.

When I was three, and my dad would come home and read his *Evening News*, I said to him, I want to read, because I saw my dad doing it. So he said, all right. He gave me two lessons. The first one I had to learn the alphabet, A to Z, all 26 letters in order. Took me a day. I came back and said to him. He said, right, C-A-T, cat. And my mum had Omo and Daz and Cornflakes, and I read the back of the boxes. We didn't have any books in our house. My dad brought home the *Evening Standard*, *Titbits* and *Reveille*, my mum got *Woman* and *Woman's Own*. So it was pretty low class literature that we had in our house. We didn't have a single book. My dad used to boast that he never read a book in his life. Well, that was never me. As soon as I could learn to read all I wanted to do is join the library, and then when I was five I did join the library. I got a book out called *Peter and the Crane*. My name's Peter, so I identified with that.

Then I went to school, and that was the end of my life. At school I was the only person who could read, so I used to have to sit there every day listening to people trying to read. This happened the whole of my school life. I remember having a book of poetry, and while the other kids were stuttering and stumbling and failing to make any sense of what they were saying I'd read the whole book. In fact I can still quote huge portions of Keats, Wordsworth, Coleridge, all those people I read back then in those books, *The English Treasury of English Verse*.

When I was about 11 I met a guy who loved rhythm and blues, and I loved rhythm and blues too, and all those people that I loved then — I think someone else said this yesterday — I still love. The people that I loved when I was 11 I love now that I'm 66. So that's six decades of loving the same music. I've never listened to a Clash record. I don't even know what U2 sounds like. No doubt I've heard them on the radio. My wife plays the radio all the time. But I can't tell what U2 or any of them sounds like, but I know what Ben E. King sounds like. Ben E. King dying the other week was a greater shame to me than B. B. King dying because Ben E. King was my hero as a child. The Drifters, I loved them. I bought every one of them singles. I had three LPs by him — *Songs for Soulful Lovers, Spanish Harlem*, and *Don't Play That Song*. That's what I bought, black, American rhythm and blues.

Charlie Gillett was a big influence. *The Sound of the City* was the best book on music I'd ever read. And Charlie mentioned a group called the Showmen, 'It Will Stand', and that was one of my favourite records. "*Rock and roll forever will stand/ Some folks don't understand it/ That's why they don't demand it/ They're always tryin' to ruin/ Forgive them for they know not what they're doin'*" And General Johnson was just a great singer. The *Sunday Times* brought out one of their magazine supplements, and it had a piece on reggae in it, and this guy that wrote it, I can't even remember his name, Simon probably knows, he met Rico in Ladbroke Grove, and various other people, Laurel Aitken. And I tried to write a piece similar to his, only I couldn't write, because all I'd been writing for the past ten years was poetry. I could write poetry that scanned, but I couldn't write prose. But I quickly learnt to write prose.

I took this along to *Let It Rock* of all places, because this was the magazine that to me had Bill Millar in it, and Simon Frith, and to me Simon Frith was a really good singles writer. He wrote about tunes, by people like Susan Cadogan, odd singles you just didn't read about anywhere in them horrible weeklies, them inkies, the *NME*, they'd never discuss it. I used to buy the *NME* as an 11-year-old for the American charts, and then I changed to the *Record Mirror* when they put a top 30 in rather than a top 20. So I just wrote this piece, took it along to *Let It Rock*. They rejected it, so I took it to *it* in Wardour Mews and they liked it.

And they'd heard of me. Felix Dennis had told them I was a good street seller — I used to sell the underground press in the street, *it*, *Oz*, *Gandalf's Garden*, *Time Out*. I remember Tony Elliott coming in the Roundhouse with a little printed mimeograph sheet that he gave away free. That was the first *Time Out*. I read all of those. I read *New Statesman* and *New Society* — and I also read books. As a kid I read Enid Blyton and Frank Richards and Richmal Crompton. My dream was getting out of hated school and getting some toast and tea made by my mum and sitting and reading my *Billy Bunter's Stolen Postal Order*.

And that's how I was. All my life I loved books. Words were just my thing. And I loved rhythm and blues music. And it got to the stage, around 1973, that I had to write this article, and that's what brought me into writing journalism. That's my story really. I didn't go to university. At school, I never bothered. The teacher would write something on the blackboard, I'd copy it, I'd never look at it again. I wasn't interested in school. The only thing I knew about school was I wanted to get out of it — I wanted to grow up and be a man so I didn't have to go to this boring place with these fucking teachers anymore. I really hated school.

So I worked for *it* and then I went to Nick Kimberley, this very similar experience — and he said, are you Penny Reel? Because I'd already written for *it* by then. I said yeah. He said, we're doing *Pressure Drop*, Chris Lane is writing an article — and Chris was the first white guy to write about reggae, and he was sympathetic. Now, he was a bit of a right-winger. He favoured the National Front. He said "All the niggers are fucking living on the dole." He was a bit ignorant. He was only 16 man. I mean, I can forgive him because he's not like that anymore. But that was the kind of attitude that was around in them days. There was a lot of racism.

Then I started writing for the *NME* and then *Echoes* and I met Saba, I met Imruh Caesar, all those people Paul's just mentioned. They were black intellectuals. They were influenced by Darcus Howe, Linton Kwesi Johnson and Frank Crichlow, who ran the Mangrove [*a Caribbean restaurant and community centre in Notting Hill — ed.*]. Anyway, I just wrote about reggae. Because people used to laugh at reggae. They used to say, "Well, it's made by Jamaicans who can't make music, and they can't even get the beat right, because it's an offbeat." Well, that was the joy of it. The joy of reggae and ska and all those Jamaican musics was the offbeat. The offbeat was fantastic to dance to. Now, I'm a big dancer. I used to go to four or five clubs every week and dance all night long to ska or even rock music. Creedence, and the Lemon Pipers, and all that kind of thing. That's me.

SF: One question I wanted to raise from what you've just said, Penny, to ask Paul, is that it's very striking to me the whole history of British popular music has been talked about in most of the sessions we've listened to that as if dancing wasn't central to it.

PR: Oh it was always central to my life. I've been doing the twist since I was ten.

SF: And clearly when rock came along one thing that happened, to put it very crudely, was that serious music moved into the concert hall and that unserious music —

PR: Stayed in the dance hall, yeah.

SF: Which means that you could dance if you wanted to, but nobody could write about it. It was both difficult to write about, and people didn't write about it. And something like Northern Soul, which seems to be a very significant part of the story, was written about in some magazines —

PR: Dave Godin —

SF: — but I don't remember *NME* writing a lot about it. And then somebody said this morning there hasn't been any interesting music since whatever date, since 1995 or whatever. I was thinking, well, you couldn't talk about the history of dance music in Britain for the last 25 years without thinking there's some amazingly creative and inventive and influential music. But it tends to be the area where people think oh well, that's black music.

PR: Well, black music's seen as lower class music, really. The Incredible String Band seen as more important than Delroy Wilson. That was the general thing. Everyone always used to write about the Rolling Stones and the Who. To me they were two horrible kind of sexually aberrant groups who just —

SF: — who you couldn't dance to.

CR: But Simon, that's a big difference right there. You're talking about whether people are part of a present-tense culture; that they're involved in some version of community, and that this is part of their everyday life, and music is part of that. I mean, I grew up in a neighbourhood where the radio was on, four or five radios sometimes in one house; it was a working-class, largely black, neighbourhood. And radio was central, music was central, dancing was certainly central, and it was only by the time I was at university that I realised that that there were plenty of people for whom all that kind of stuff was just a spectator thing. It was different. It was something that you consumed, albeit with as much joy and interest, but in a different way.

SF: I'm arguing that if you were to write a serious history of popular music in Britain for the last century, the history of dance would actually be central to it.

CR: Oh yeah. Well, I would agree.

SF: But if you read the academic and even journalistic stuff on the history of popular music, dance is *not* central to it. So it was interesting what Paul was saying. Davitt Sigerson was such an amazing writer because he wrote about dance seriously, and made you think about what he wrote about dance. Richard Williams is certainly one of the significant people here — I remember he commissioned me to write about disco for *Time Out*. And *Time Out* people thought it was really weird that he would ask somebody to actually write about discos in a sort of mock-serious way… And when Simon Reynolds comes along that's why he becomes an interesting critic.

CR: Yesterday I noticed that — I think, again, people were just interested in pursuing a certain line of thought and not particularly thinking of the context around it — but the fact is that there was a missing element all the way through which was going on at exactly the same time. So that, for instance, when people start talking about technology, the terrible crushing force of technology that now rules everybody… well, technology did make possible the whole warehouse party, rare groove thing, this burst of new record stores, this scene. That was technology, too, wiring record turntables into light posts and having a party.

SF: You could say the most significant do it yourself culture was not punk necessarily, but pirate radio.

CR: I would totally agree with that, because it involved more people. And while it became a media phenomenon in a way, it was actually via commodities and the people who made them got the money from them — and that was the difference with punk as well.

PG: I agree with the diagnosis, and I'm wondering how much that's because the body sort of disappears out of it. I don't think it's just dancing. How seriously do people write about intoxication? There are a number of other things like that, the corporeal or, I don't know, somatic aspects of life and being. There's something really oddly cerebral about the way this is supposed to be opened up to judgment. So I think that the loss of dance [from the story] and the loss of interest in that is actually to do with a bigger set of problems about where the body is in this. That's actually one reason why I feel so strongly about the history of Rock Against Racism — because I think that their founding commitment to black and white bands *sharing a space for performance* is absolutely critical to the way that things develop around them. So, yes, the body's a problem for people anyway, and sharing space is an issue which has a history, and you're absolutely right that the dance histories and dance spaces of that are fundamental.

At the same time I can remember thinking in maybe 1980, going round the back of Digbeth Civic Hall in Birmingham, Quaker City, and some sound system come up from London or whatever, and they're playing 'Bad to Worse' by Burning Spear, over and over. They'd let it play and then put it back on. It's like it's going from bad to worse, over and over again, and I'm beginning to think "What kind of a space is this, actually? It's doing my head in, and I hadn't smoked that much." How people dance in that. There's a bigger story to be told about what dancing was. It's not just dancing.

PR: Dancing was central to my love of music. There were two strands. There was working-class venues in which people stood around in mohair suits snarling at each other, and there were the middle-class venues, like Middle Earth and the Roundhouse, where people were very welcoming and very middle-class. And of course I was attracted to the middle class because, as I said, I didn't like fighting because it brought pain — and me and pain never got on. So I had the head thing — I'd go to Glastonbury and nod away to the Incredible String Band — and I had the dancing thing, where I'd dance all night to the twist and hoochy coochie coo, because that was really where I come from. But it wasn't a matter of where I'd come from, it was also a case of where I was going. I think that we're not born to be the same thing, we're born to grow and develop. So I've got interested in Mamie Smith, that you can't really dance to, and I got interested in Chubby Checker that you can, and Hank Ballard, and I got interested in the Incredible String Band that you can't dance to. So my taste in music is quite wide, although some people would say it's limited because it's virtually all black. That's it.

SF: When you first started writing who did you envision your readers to be.

PR: Whoever read it.

SF: But did you think of who it may be?

PR: No. I just thought whoever read it might get something out of this. I'm trying to tell people something. I'm trying to tell people that really you should be listening to Delroy Wilson, and not Pete Townshend or Paul Weller.

SF: And you didn't know who those people might be.

PR: I didn't care who they were. I didn't care if they were black, white, pink or green. I just didn't give a shit.

CR: I just didn't favour the personal approach myself. I didn't think about that stuff, because I was really uninterested in that whole cult of personality thing, to be honest. I was more interested in reporting, in journalism and what that was, and finding out about how to do it. That was what intrigued me.

PG: Paul Morley yesterday, I think, talked about writing the world that you wanted to be in. I suppose I think — I'm sure this is a horrible thing to say — but the conceit of that is dreadful. But I suppose that's what it is — you're *summoning* something aren't you? You don't know what it is. You can't see it, but you can sort of hear it somewhere in the distance.

PR: The other thing was racism. Racism was very important in that black people used to see themselves described on television as animals. I used to be round Fat Man's house or Robert Theron's or Matthew and Flaxy, and they'd always have the telly on, they'd always watch this racist shit that the BBC put out, just talking about blacks in a really patronising and demeaning way that disgusted me. That was what I wanted to counter. I wanted to say look, you don't have to listen to these fucking white boys. You can listen to Ben E. King, you can listen to Hank Ballard, and you can listen to Delroy Wilson. So that's the only idea I had. I wanted to appeal to people who were open-minded enough to appreciate what I was talking about.

PG: Also there was a layer of people like myself who hadn't migrated but who were born here. I'm thinking of people like David Hynes who I knew when I moved to Birmingham. A layer of us who hadn't had the experience that Linton and Dennis Bovell and others had had coming here as children. So after a while I began to realise that our formation was somewhat different, and that there was an audience, that there was something to build out of that particularity.

SF: That's an interesting aspect of being a freelancer. On the one hand you can try and call forth something, you don't really care who reads it — but then you've got to sell your story to somebody.

CR: You also have to keep yourself going. You have to have a lot of discipline.

SF: What I was meaning is that when you ask somebody to publish you and they say no — which certainly happened to Paul and Penny, from what he said, with *Let It Rock* — you start saying "Do I have to adjust what I write in order to find a space to publish it in?" I felt for some of the people talking yesterday that it was almost as if they adapted: "This is the only way we're writing and I can do it."

PR: Jonathon Green just walked up to Alan Marcuson and said, "I want to be a writer," and Marcuson gave him a job. Alan Marcuson hated me. He just saw me as some horrible little fucking working-class creep from Hackney he could insult. When I said to him I want to write he said, "Go out on the street and sell the newspaper."

SF: I found it interesting when I started writing for the *Village Voice,* because American editors are completely different from British ones. British editing I most noticed at the *Sunday Times* is essentially send in what you send in, and they're only interested in its length, and if an advert comes in they cut however many words from the bottom. So you have to make sure that your last paragraph is entirely irrelevant, and the one before it too. Whereas writing for the *Voice* I'd get these terrifying calls from Robert Christgau who'd spend like two and a half hours on the phone going through word by word: "What did you mean there and why did you put that?" It was interesting because it was a way of learning to write — but it meant that in the end you did feel your audience was Robert Christgau, which wasn't the ideal audience in a sense. But that kind of a relationship with an editor for a freelance, if you get a regular stint where you're always working with somebody, it does affect how you're writing.

PR: The way I wrote means I very rarely ever got cut. I knew it would get cut maybe if it was a bit too long. But I always got accepted. Once I started writing I was always accepted as a writer. Nobody ever questioned me. Except you did, when you said "What's a white man doing writing about reggae music?" But no one ever really asked me that question. And the black people loved it as well. That's the main thing. The black people loved what I wrote about. They loved me. To me, that's the bonus. Better than getting paid was getting the respect of black people, who I respected above the white people.

PG: I want to say actually that *Station Underground News,* your column in *Echoes,* is like Linton [Kwesi Johnson]. It emerges at the same time as Linton — and no one else was trying to do that with that language. It was just the two of you. No one else that I know of actually. *Station Underground News* was a very important experiment from a writing perspective.

PR: I used to sit on a bus watching some young black guy of 15 sitting reading my *Station Underground News* column. I was in my 30s. I felt so proud.

SF: What did you think of Carl Gayle's writing style?

PR: When he went to Jamaica, Carl Gayle developed really quickly as a really good writer, but he started out writing very basic ABCs for the whites, about the Pioneers and records like 'Penny Reel' and 'Pussy Price' by Laurel Aitken and Eric Morris. But I wanted to write for the blacks when I started. In fact when you asked who I was writing for, I was writing for black people really.

SF: I was thinking what Paul was saying about having to face up to the gatekeepers determining how people should write about what. I remember as an editor on *Let It Rock* dealing with Carl, and there was a tension without a doubt between what he wanted to write and what we thought was the correct way of writing.

PR: So you forced him to write about 'Pussy Price' and all that.

SF: No, no, we had nothing to do with content, it was to do with "This sentence doesn't make sense, what does that term mean?" Later on, I wouldn't have done that at all, but at the time there was a kind of tension that I wasn't really self-conscious about.

CR: When I was editing *City Limits*, I asked a guy from *The Voice*, David Upshal, who was doing freelance music stuff, to come in and take over because the news editor was in hospital. And it was like a revolt of the middle-class white guys and girls who were doing the news reporting. It was unbelievable. It's not like David was like a radical guy particularly, he was really good at what he did and he would have been good doing that. That [news] wasn't really what he wanted to do with his life — but nor did he want to spend it on community affairs at the BBC, I imagine, yet I think that was the next step he was offered. But their response was really surprising to me. Yet by the time I went to MTV Europe as a producer in the mid 90s, it was a relief to see that Brent Hanson actually hired black producers to produce shows about black music, and it was fun to work on. But: that is a whole thing that is really important — and it can apply to any group — if you're not going to be willing to work for these guys and listen to what they say about what you should do, then don't talk the talk.

PR: I was just going to say, Simon, are you saying that Carl Gayle couldn't write?

SF: No, I'm not saying that. I'm saying it's this thing — which is not very self-conscious but... You have a piece of copy in and it might have mistakes in, which anybody's copy would have, but it was more you'd have queries about a particular use of language.

PR: Because of his race.

SF: Because it was a different way of writing. Without really thinking about it, one had a set of conventions in one's head about how one should write about music, and he was writing about it in a different way, and in a sense it was a much steeper learning curve for me editing him than it should have been.

PR: And you think that's because he was a black man.

SF: It wasn't just to do with the fact that he was a black man, because that was kind of irrelevant. I just was reading the copy. It was because he was writing in a very different sensibility.

PR: OK, and writing about music that was quite strange to you.

SF: I'm putting it too crudely, but he was *within* a culture rather than *observing* a culture, which is what *Let It Rock* writing about reggae tended to be.

PR: He was coming from it. He talked about how he went to dances and his reactions to Maytals records.

CR: The same thing exists between America and the UK, because of this whole tradition of people going to journalism college, as opposed to a tradition of people doing indentures, joining a union, working on a regional paper or on Fleet Street, and then going into journalism — or just learning on the job. It's a completely different thing. The whole idea of fact-checking being done by an outside source rather than by yourself I've always found really offensive. It's hardly just a racial thing.

PG: I don't want to get hung up on Carl as a particular person on a journey as a writer, but I think what was being determined is how the black communities of this country were going to speak in print, and what kind of relationship they were going to have with themselves culturally, musically or whatever, was being determined. Obviously in my map of it *Station Underground News* is a really interesting marker. I can't remember what year it was that Linton published his BA thesis. I mean, there were other places — the *Black Liberator* or *The Hustler* or *Race Today* or whatever — but no one was interested in writing about music in any of those places.

PR: They never knew anything about it.

PG: I found when I first started to write about African American music, a lot of the African American academics and other people I ran into took it all entirely for granted, and I'm not talking about the Baraka people, I'm talking about Skip Gates, Cornel West, Nelson George, a very interesting example — they took it all entirely for granted. I think Nelson was one of the first who actually began looking over his shoulder at Greg Tate or whoever it was. Began to say, well, actually, there's a different way we can do this.

CR: But I think both of them had to depend on Robert Christgau to hire them. That's the deal. That's a thing that can't be overstated. Although now the possibility of doing things for yourself exists in a different way than it did then. Whether it's the same is a big debate, or how it's useful, that may be a separate conference. But I think people are still looking for the sense of community and involvement and participation in some form... whether it's as a spectator or as a semi-participant or whether you write a letter to the editor or make a comment and post it somewhere. Or you walk into Honest Jon's record shop and hang out there for four hours. It's the same. Or turn up at The Base on Saturday night and look for those people you need, to find out the information you want to find out.

Bohemians, Stamp Collectors, Revolutionaries and Critics

Paul Gilroy looks forward to a deeper understanding of the political sub-currents in the 70s music press, its problems and also its possibilities

It has been obvious for decades that Britain has been unable or reluctant to develop its own critical and historical understanding of the politics of race, racism and culture. Understanding this failure — or refusal — is as relevant to the writing of cultural history as it is to criminal justice and social policy. The reasons for it can't be fully enumerated here. It gets covered up routinely by slow, organic processes of acceptance and accommodation, as well as by the hard work accomplished by the movements against racism and injustice that appeared intermittently to challenge the worst excesses of violence and the most obvious instances of institutional misconduct.

In many settings, ongoing problems of exclusion, partiality and contempt have been concealed and mystified. Ameliorative strategies and racial rhetoric have been imported from the very different circumstances found in the USA. These off-the-shelf responses have been deployed repeatedly to absolve us from addressing inequality and its unforeseen consequences in their local manifestations.

Today, we can employ the notorious 1970 cover of *Oz* 28, the

Schoolkids issue, to suggest that the history of the underground press, like that of the British left, can provide plenty of cringe-inducing examples of how the cultural reach of black liberation, decolonisation and human rights struggles were misrecognised, dismissed and misunderstood. A host of naked black women, airbrushed in blue and heavily-stylised in a pseudo-Tom of Finland sub-photographic style, cavort before the reader in a fantastic orgy of exotic sexual play. Their wild transgressions are offset only by a small, green-tinted image of Jim Anderson in school uniform that has been super-imposed in the middle of the centrefolded panorama.

It provides a striking example of how London's attenuated hippiedom followed the scripts established by the emergent 50s youth cultures in the era portrayed in the novels of Colin MacInnes — which could accommodate the cool and hipness of hypersexual "spades" not only as exotic but, perversely, as prestigious also. However, that evident hospitality and occasional enthusiasm were usually remote from the lives of the country's post-imperial incomers as well as distant from their immediate priorities.

Memory tells me that those responses periodically spilled over into forms of racism that were considered innocent and routine. Everyday gestures of exclusion and contempt were often articulated as jokes; what is now called banter. It does not excuse the pain this generated when we recognise that it must have been hard to imagine how the world would look once it was emancipated from old, essentially colonial, habits of mind that still functioned during the 1960s and 70s as common sense. When it came to undoing racial hierarchy and injustice — the unholy residue of that departed empire — Hippiedom lacked imagination. The revolution would take care of it... or, as Eric Clapton said later, Uncle Enoch could be trusted to settle the matter.

Black Power altered the balance of cultural forces as well as the political mood. In its wake, the music imported and produced by black settlers acquired a new, wholly unanticipated value. Their intrusive presence had already begun to transform city life and leisure in the Ukay. Old class structures were amended, new styles and cultural possibilities created.

Today, the history of bohemianism's fateful, fearful intersections with racial hierarchy can still supply a useful perspective on the changing character of British culture during the vexed phase of decolonisation, civil rights and black liberation. Thrilling varieties of freedom seemed to be pending in jazz and its smoky penumbra. The existential challenges articulated through the blues proved especially resonant for the rising generation, which had been released from military service into the precincts of the art colleges, where their experimental re-making of self and community could safely be indulged. Rhythm and blues begat rock and, differently accented with regard to class and gender, creole Caribbean forms cross-pollinated with black America travelled back from the tropics into the imperial hub. Bluebeat, ska and reggae gradually entered the country's circulatory system. It was still easy to divorce appreciation of those intoxicating new pleasures from any welcoming response to the presence of their creators, brokers and enablers. Youth culture found black music exciting — but its adherents could still enjoy "Nigger Hunting" and "Paki Bashing", even as their noisy fun overlapped into the exotic spaces where blackness, by turns exciting and terrifying, was ambivalently lodged.

At school, we read *Rolling Stone* for its educative, clever music coverage and rich, alarming political commentary on the Nixon era. The black movement was a constant point of reference for a radical, antiwar culture that stretched from Phil Ochs to Peter Watkins via the Panthers' Californian cooperation with The Grateful Dead. By contrast, *it* and *Oz* showed scant interest in the music we craved. Those publications were valued above all for their transgressive charge — an impression confirmed as I witnessed the *Oz* obscenity trial of summer 1971 from the public gallery at the Old Bailey.

We began to prize the writing of Richard Williams and Val Wilmer in *Melody Maker* for its style and its seriousness. It took longer to appreciate that their contributions were part of working out a response to Baraka's new rules governing not only who could speak about black music, but how and in what solidary spirit. A. B. Spellman was another revelation — but, jumping a few years further on, I want to remember and celebrate the important work of Ben Sidran, a sometime fugitive from the Vietnam draft known for his keyboard duties with the Steve Miller Band. I sat in the library at Sussex University and read his D.Phil thesis before grilling its supervisor, Rupert Wilkinson. Davitt Sigerson is another, now forgotten pioneer analyst of what he called the 'Penthouse and Roadhouse' tendencies in the new, now danceable jazz being made after Donald Byrd's *Ethiopian Knights*, Archie Shepp's *Attica Blues*, Herbie Hancock's *Head Hunters*, and Donny Hathaway's *Live*. Sidran and Sigerson would not have written in this way if they had stayed away from Europe. They fused journalism and intellectualism to demonstrate what serious criticism of African American music would have to become. Behind them both, in contrasting ways, loomed the headmasterly figure of Ralph Ellison, whose writing combined extraordinary insight and palpable love for the music with repellent politics. Rebounding from Ellison's conservative agenda would generate new approaches to the theology and the rituals of the phenomenon that Hendrix eventually named "the electric church".

Thanks to *Rolling Stone* we had discovered Greil Marcus' *Mystery Train*, which included his enduringly brilliant essay on Sly, Curtis Mayfield and the politics of "Blaxploitation". It helped that most of these people seemed to want be recognised as writers rather than wannabe musicians or wannabe businesspeople. Those distinctions were important, because critical commentaries on the music issued closer to home were becoming increasingly intertwined with the growing commercial investments in it as an underground phenomenon, and as a useful resource for the reinvigoration of pop. Richard Williams worked for Chris Blackwell's Island Records for a spell during the early 1970s. Charlie Gillett, whose stamp collector's sociology of rhythm and blues, *The Sound of the City: The Rise of Rock and Roll*, had proved influential, also used his position as a DJ at Radio London to build up his own commercial operation in the form of Oval records.

Published late in 1975 *The Soul Book*, edited by Ian Hoare, included more serious and thoughtful commentaries on funk and soul from the likes of Simon Frith and Tony Cummings. Like Michael Haralambos' *Right On: from Blues to Soul in Black America* from the previous year, it was a benchmark intervention that extended the boundaries of music criticism.

The stamp collectors' approach to writing about jazz, R&B and soul did not, at this point, transfer into the very different critical world constituted around reggae — the dance music of the sufferers. Chris Lane had been enthusing about Jamaican sounds in *Blues and Soul* early in the 70s, and the arrival of *Black Music* in 1973 brought writing about all styles of the music together under one cover. That extraordinary publication promoted a clash of critical traditions that raised the standard of interpretative commentary just as Black Power was fading and the flames of Ethiopianism were being rekindled on the Caribbean frontiers of the Cold War by the obligation to think outside its deadly geopolitical categories.

Carl Gayle and Penny Reel responded to these developments by starting to write in the poetic registers of Jamaican speech that were being refined and polished by the Sound System Toasters, whose subculture was consolidated outernationally. They were followed by people like Sebastian Clarke and Imruh Caesar in the pages of *Echoes* and *Time Out*, and then by a host of others in important fanzine publications like *Pressure Drop*.

Though it may well be a welcome sign that the stamp collectors are now issuing and collecting stamps that bear their own likenesses, I am not very interested in approaching these important questions of history and criticism via informal ethnographies of the *NME* office circa 1977. Instead, may I suggest we attempt a thought experiment and put publications like *Black Echoes* (from 1976) and *Black Music* (from 1973) into the place that the *NME* occupied in the interesting discourse that characterised last year's conference at Birkbeck. That small act of reparation might contribute to the shadow history of England we still so urgently need.

My unsuccessful attempt at begging for work from Vivien Goldman at *Sounds* in the mid-70s taught me more than how to cope with being told, oh so very politely told, to go away and fuck myself. That memorable experience confirmed an early lesson in how easily many white self-appointed custodians of these musical archives could become threatened and defensive when faced even with polite requests to be minimally accountable for the way they used the music and its increasingly audible rebel ontologies.

The key issue here is a consistent distaste for the possibility that these musical cultures could encompass political and philosophical elements, and the related suggestion that black Atlantic music is always, openly or surreptitiously, addressed to and mediated by the social and historical predicament of its downpressed makers and users. As a result, for years I felt that I was having the same stupid argument repeatedly with a legion of notable watchdogs, guardians and taste-making critical commentators: David Toop, Brian Morton, David Widgery and Charlie Gillett, to name just a few. I'm very glad that unpleasant time is over. Today, we should accept that only deep, serious historical exploration of the politics and ethics of the critics' relationship to what was once black music will undo that blockage. Perhaps it may also salvage something worthwhile both for the itinerant history of the music and the contentious counter-history of this deluded, postcolonial country.

Paul Gilroy is Professor of American and English Literature at King's College London. He wrote for City Limits and The Wire in the 80s.

SELECT BIBLIOGRAPHY

General histories

Days in the Life: Voices from the English Underground 1961-1971
(Jonathon Green, Heinemann/Minerva, 1988)
*The History of the NME: High Times and Low Lives
at the World's Most Famous Music Magazine*
(Pat Long, Portico, 2012)
In Their Own Write: Adventures in the Music Press
(Paul Gorman, Sanctuary, 2001).
*Rock Criticism from the Beginnings: Amusers,
Bruisers, and Cool-Headed Cruisers*
(Ulf Lindberg et al., Peter Lang, 2005)
The Story of The Face: the Magazine that Changed Culture
(Paul Gorman, Thames & Hudson, 2017).
Underground: The London Alternative Press 1966-74
(Nigel Fountain, Routledge/Comedia, 1988)
Writing the Record. The Village Voice and the Birth of Rock Criticism
(Devon Powers, University of Massachusetts Press, 2013)

Collections

The Faber Book of Pop
(ed. Hanif Kureishi and Jon Savage, Faber & Faber, 1995)
Meaty Beaty Big & Bouncy:
Classic Rock & Pop Writing from Elvis to Oasis
(ed. Dylan Jones, Hodder & Stoughton, 1996)
Musics: A British Magazine of Improvised Music and Art 1975-79
(Ecstatic Peace Library, 2016)
The Beat Goes on: Rock File Reader
(ed. Charlie Gillett and Simon Frith, Pluto Press, 1996)
The New Journalism
(ed. Tom Wolfe and E. W. Johnson, Picador, 1975)
The Penguin Book of Rock & Roll Writing
(Clinton Heylin, Viking, 1992)
The Sound and the Fury:
40 Years of Classic Rock Journalism: A Rock's Backpages Reader
(ed. Barney Hoskyns, Bloomsbury, 2003)

Website archives:
www.rocksbackpages.com
rockcritics.com

Contributor publications

The Blue in the Air
(Marcello Carlin, Zero, 2011)
Art into Pop
(Simon Frith and Howard Horne, Methuen, 1987)
Music for Pleasure: Essays on the Sociology of Pop
(Simon Frith, CUP, 1988)
Performing Rites: On the Value of Popular Music
(Simon Frith, OUP, 1996)
The Sociology of Rock
(Simon Frith, Constable, 1978)

Sound Effects: Youth, Leisure and the Politics of Rock 'n' Roll
(Simon Frith, Pantheon, 1981)
After Empire: Multicultural or Postcolonial Melancholia
(Paul Gilroy, Routledge, 2004)
The Black Atlantic: Modernity and Double Consciousness
(Paul Gilroy, Verso, 1993)
There Ain't No Black in the Union Jack:
The Cultural Politics of Race and Nation
(Paul Gilroy, Hutchinson, 1987)
Small Acts: Thoughts on the Politics of Black Cultures
(Paul Gilroy, Serpent's Tail, 1993)
Spirit of '76: London Punk Eyewitness
(John Ingham, Anthology Editions, 2017)
Shots from the Hip
(Charles Shaar Murray, Penguin, 1991)
Ask: The Chatter of Pop
(Paul Morley, Faber & Faber, 1986)
±Nothing
(Paul Morley, Faber & Faber, 2000)
Words and Music: A History of Pop in the Shape of a City
(Paul Morley, Bloomsbury, London, 2003)
All You Need Is Love
(Tony Palmer, Futura, 1976)
Born Under a Bad Sign
(Tony Palmer, Kimber, 1970)
The Trials of Oz
(Tony Palmer, Blond and Briggs, 1971)
In Groves and Along Lanes: A Novel by Thomas Horace Whitmer
(Penny Reel/Pete Simons, Drake Bros publications, 2017)
Up the Dreary Slope: A Novel by Thomas Horace Whitmer
(Penny Reel/Pete Simons, Drake Bros publications, 2015)
Living in America: The Soul Saga of James Brown
(Cynthia Rose, Serpent's Tail, 1990)
Design After Dark: The Story of Dancefloor Style
(Cynthia Rose, Thames & Hudson, 1991)

1966: The Year the Decade Exploded
(Jon Savage, Faber & Faber, London, 2015)
England's Dreaming: Sex Pistols and Punk Rock
(Jon Savage, Faber & Faber, 1991)
*Time Travel: From the Sex Pistols to Nirvana
– Pop, Media and Sexuality 1977-96*
(Jon Savage, Chatto & Windus, 1996)
Yeah Yeah Yeah: The Story of Modern Pop
(Bob Stanley, Faber & Faber, 2014)
Cool Cats: 25 Years of Rock'N'Roll Style
(Tony Stewart, Eel Pie, 1981)
Exotica: Fabricated Soundscapes in a Real World
(David Toop, Serpent's Tail, 1999)
*Into the Maelstrom: Music, Improvisation and the Dream of Freedom,
Before 1970*
(David Toop, Bloomsbury, 2016)
Rap Attack 3 African Rap To Global Hip Hop
(David Toop, Serpent's Tail, 2000)
Text and Drugs and Rock'n'Roll: The Beats and Rock Culture
(Simon Warner, Bloomsbury, 2013)
Beating Time: Riot'n'Race'n'Rock'n'Roll
(David Widgery, Chatto & Windus, 1986)
The Chatto Book of Dissent
(Ed. David Widgery and Michael Rosen, Chatto & Windus, 1991)
Preserving Disorder (Essays on Society and Culture)
(David Widgery, Pluto Press, 1989)
Long Distance Call: Writings on Music
(Richard Williams, Aurum, 2000)
As Serious as Your Life: Story of the New Jazz
(Valerie Wilmer, Serpent's Tail, 1977)
Jazz People
(Valerie Wilmer, Da Capo, 1991)
Mama Said There'd Be Days Like This: My Life in the Jazz World
(Valerie Wilmer, The Women's Press, 1991)

Further reading

The Boy Looked at Johnny: The Obituary of Rock'n'Roll
(Julie Burchill and Tony Parsons, Pluto Press, 1978)
Rock Stars Stole My Life! A Big Bad Love Affair with Music
(Mark Ellen, Coronet, London)
Elvis Died for Somebody's Sins, but Not Mine
(Mick Farren, Headpress, 2013)
Give the Anarchist a Cigarette
(Mick Farren, Pimlico, 2002)
Shake It Up Baby! Notes from a Pop Music Reporter 1961-1972
(Norman Jopling, Rockhistory, 2015)
The Dark Stuff: Selected Writings on Rock Music 1972-1993
(Nick Kent, Penguin, 1994)
The People's Music: Selected Journalism
(Ian MacDonald, Pimlico, 2003)
Vital Signs: Music, Movies and Other Manias
(Ian Penman, Serpent's Tail, 1998)

ACKNOWLEDGEMENTS

Profound thanks are due...

To Savage Pencil for his illustrations
To Birkbeck Institute of the Humanities, who helped fund and host the conference (in particular Julia Eisner and Esther Leslie)
To Resonance FM, who recorded and broadcast the conference
To *Music & Letters* journal, who awarded £500 towards recording and transcription
To Barney Hoskyns and Mark Pringle at *Rock's Backpages*, the online library of pop writing and journalism, who gave me countless useful steers and contacts in the planning stages
To Val Wilmer, Penny Reel and Liz Naylor for letting us into their homes and workplaces to film them for the Kickstarter; to Cicely Nowell-Smith, Frank Kogan, Hazel Southwell, Joseph Brooker, Peter Baran, Psyche Thompson, Simon Frith, Steve Mannion, Tim Hopkins, Tom Ewing, Victoria De Rijke and Rebecca Sinker, for commentary and advice at various stages; to everyone who helped with or attended the conferences, to all at Groke, to the massed minds at ilxor dot com (without whom etc), and to all friends, relatives and colleagues for their input and support in recent months.

This anthology is dedicated with love and thanks to the late Richard Cook, who more than anyone got me started in this business, and cannot be held responsible for where I took it all. And it's also dedicated to contributor Peter Simons (Penny Reel), a remarkable, stubborn, lyrical voice, rich in self-taught knowledge and one of a kind. We're honoured he gave his time to this project.

The following pledged to the Kickstarter to enable this book to be published. Many thanks all, for your generosity and support.

Al Ewing, Alan Stephen, Alastair Dickson, Alex Macpherson, Alex Sarll, Alex Thomson, Alexandra Mitchell, Andrew Farrell, Andrea Feldman, Andrew Burke, Andrew Fenwick, Andrew Littlefield, Andy Kellman, Ann Holmes, Anna Fielding, Anthony Cohan-Miccio, Barney Hoskyns, Barum Ware, Ben, Ben Clancey, Benjamin Wilcox, Beverley Glick, Bill Walker, Brad Nelson, Brad Shoup, Brian MacDonald, Bruce Bowie, Cam Baddeley, caspar melville, Cass May, cee smith, Charlie Southwell, Charlotte Geater, Chr, Chris Bohn, Chris Charlesworth, Chris O'Leary, Christopher Alario, Cindy Stern, Colette Stevenson, Colin Overland, Colin Smith, Colman, croot, Dan Regan, Dani Neal, Daniel Barrow, Daniel Perry, Daniel Rendall, Danny Delgado Rosas, Dave Morris, Dave Rimmer, Dave Wakely, David Cooper Moore, david morris, David Quantick, david rule, Davin Kolderup, Des O'Loughlin, Dougald Hine, D S Reifferscheid, Elisha Sessions, Elizabeth Sandifer, Emma, Erik Highter, Erin MacLeod, Esben Svendsen, Ewan Munro, Frank Kogan, Gemma Cossins, Gershom Bazerman, Gervase de Wilde, Graham Parks, Graham Tomlinson, Greig Christie, Greil Marcus, hexenducted, Hind Mezaina, Humming Resonantly, Ian, Ian Fenton, Ian Pointer, Iain slack, J Smith, Jack Connell, James, Jeff Worrell, Jenn PB, jeremy leslie, Jessica Doyle, Jill Lee, Jim Derwent, Jo Coleman, Joe Banks, Johan Lif, John, John Darnielle, John Eley, John mcloughlin, John Muller, Jonah Wolf, Jonathan Bogart, Jonathan Melville, Jorge Lopes, Joseph Grafton Maggs, Joseph Tham, Josh Langhoff, Juliet Kemp, Kat Stevens, Katie Grocott, Keiko Yoshida, Keith Grosvenor, Keith Harris, Keith McIvor, Keith Watson, Kemuel, Kerr Amon Duul, Kieran Devaney, Laurent, Levi Stahl, Lim Cheng Tju, Luc Sante, Madeleine Furness, Magnus Anderson, Mark Banks, Mark Casarotto, Mark Grout, Mark Hibbett, Mark Morris, Mark O'Neill, Mark Richardson, Martin Gorsky, Martin Hand, Martin

James, Matt Black, Matt D'Cruz, Matthew Collin, Matthew Ingram, Maxwell, M E Gilligan, Michael Barthel, Michael Daddino, Michael Jones, Miguel Goncalves, Mike Atkinson, Mike Hardaker, Mike Harper, murray withers, Nick Dastoor, Nick Minichino, Nick Spicer, Nina Power, Nitsuh Abebe, Norman Fay, Nuno Robles, olivier treinen, Ophir Zemer Leibovici, Pam Berry, Pamela Hutchinson, Patrick St. Michel, Paul Kirk, Paul Scott, Paul Wilson, Peter Baran, Peter Miller, Peter Nuttall, Peter Quicke, Peter Slack, PhilD, Phil Dellio, Phil Edwards, Psyche Thompson, Rachel, rebecca meek, Rebecca Sinker, Rebecca Toennessen, Richard Boon, Richard Copping, Richard Gillanders, Richard Hopkins, Richard Tunnicliffe, Riley Fitzgerald, Rita Tushingham, rluckraft, Rob Brennan, Rob O'Brien, Rob Hale, Robert Carmichael, Roger Sabin, Ronan Fitzgerald, Sabina Yun Tang, Sarah Clarke, Sarah Morayati, Scott Woods, s.e., Sean Campbell, Sean Carruthers, Sean Walsh, shireen liane, Simon Price, Simon Reynolds, Spider Stacy, Stephen Smithson, Stephen Thomas Erlewine, Steve Burnett, Steve Hewitt, Steve Mannion, Steve Pittis, Steven Kerrison, Stuart Macpherson, Stuart McKinlay, Sue Terry, Sukhdev Sandhu, Tallita Dyllen, The Lilac Time, Tieg Zaharia, Tim Finney, Tim Hopkins, Timh Gabriele, Tim Riley, Toby Litt, Tom Ewing, Tom Rafferty, Tom Wootton, Tommy Mack, Tony (tones) Earley, Tony Stewart, Trish Byrne, Vick, Wes, will, William Shiel Dods, @xyzzzz__, Yancey Strickler, Zoe Dolce.

STRANGE ATTRACTOR PRESS 2018